PARENTING WHILE PHDING

PARENTING WHILE PHDING

Surviving and Improving the Working Conditions of Graduate Student Parents

EDITED BY

JACKIE HOERMANN-ELLIOTT AND
JENNA MORTON-AIKEN

FOREWORD BY

CAROLINE GRANT

RUTGERS UNIVERSITY PRESS
New Brunswick, Camden, and Newark, New Jersey
London and Oxford

Rutgers University Press is a department of Rutgers, The State University of New Jersey, one of the leading public research universities in the nation. By publishing worldwide, it furthers the University's mission of dedication to excellence in teaching, scholarship, research, and clinical care.

978-1-9788-4376-9 (cloth)
978-1-9788-4375-2 (paper)
978-1-9788-4377-6 (epub)

Cataloging-in-publication data is available from the Library of Congress.
LCCN 2025936420

A British Cataloging-in-Publication record for this book is available from the British Library.

♾ The paper used in this publication meets the requirements of the American National Standard for Information Sciences—Permanence of Paper for Printed Library Materials, ANSI Z39.48-1992.

rutgersuniversitypress.org

For Briggs. It's your turn, buddy.

—JHE

For my kiddos. I love you all the time, no matter what.

—JMA

For everyone who needs this book.

—JHE and JMA

CONTENTS

FOREWORD

When Jackie and Jenna first reached out to me about this project, my eldest was a junior at the University of California (UC) Santa Cruz, studying computer science and working as an undergraduate tutor. But they were also not working, as the union representing graduate student instructors and undergraduate tutors had gone on strike for cost-of-living adjustments. The university withheld their wages but the union provided strike pay to student employees who spent their teaching hours on the picket line.

It was a full-circle moment for me.

Thirty years earlier, I had been a graduate student instructor at UC Berkeley, walking the picket line when we struck for union recognition. While I needed the income from my teaching job to support myself, I was single and childless, so my stakes were pretty low. Still, I recognized the importance of contributing my voice to the strong collective effort that resulted, eventually, in union recognition, collective bargaining rights, and, decades later, my own child's strike pay.

I wasn't thrilled that the student employees had to go on strike last fall, but I was glad that the union was recognized by the administration (who negotiated with them) and that the strike was supported, both by their own union's strike fund and by other unions, like the Teamsters, who respected the picket lines. Although I'm not in the academic community anymore, I am still interested in improving the lives of educators—as we all should be. I want my and all our children's teachers to be well compensated and well supported with parental leave and other benefits, because if they are not, then how exactly can they teach?

In support of my own undergraduate student employee and all the people striking across the ten UC campuses, I walked up the hill from my house to UC San Francisco and joined the lively picket line. I made a routine of it, joining the strikers instead of going on my usual afternoon walk, talking to them about their research, comparing their experiences to mine decades ago. Ultimately, their action was successful—proof of the power of collective organizing, the impact of lifting voices in a chorus to demand change.

I tell this story because it seems analogous to how I feel about this vibrant new collection of essays: my slight discouragement about its need is completely outweighed by my interest in its compelling stories and my conviction that it can help move the needle for graduate student parents.

Parenting while PhDing is a wonderful response to and expansion of *Mama, PhD,* the collection I coedited because I wanted to read more personal accounts of combining motherhood and academic life. I didn't pull it off, myself. As I describe in my essay for that collection, I was hired to my dream job and discovered I was pregnant the same week. I taught until my child was born—ten days early and two weeks before the end of the term—advised my students via email, submitted their final grades during my "maternity leave," and, ambivalently, left the job. In the fifteen years since that collection came out, my involvement in education has been limited to serving lunch in the elementary school cafeteria and driving occasional field trips, cheering from the sidelines of cross-country meets and robotics competitions, and now, as both my kids are college students, reminding them to take full advantage of their instructors' office hours.

In the sixteen years since *Mama, PhD* came out, higher education has also changed, and this collection vividly reflects that. Graduate students are more diverse by every measure. More of them are represented by unions. The pandemic and new technologies, from Zoom to ChatGPT, affect both how they teach and how their students learn.

But higher education has not changed enough. As these essays detail, graduate students are expected to handle a heavy teaching load while still pursuing their own research in classrooms and labs. They are underpaid and underfunded, often needing part-time jobs outside the academy to support themselves. They often aren't eligible for parental leave, but if they are, they can be criticized for taking it.

This collection offers an essential look at the situation of graduate student parents today. The book is alive with the experiences of people of color, queer and nonbinary parents, parents in the sciences as well as the humanities, and students at different stages of their graduate work and parenting. It acknowledges that while the physical burdens of pregnancy and nursing fall most heavily on cis women, fathers, adoptive mothers, and all parents need to have their caretaking responsibilities valued and accommodated.

These writers describe their challenges, but they also detail their pragmatic solutions to those challenges, from careful spreadsheets to creative childcare arrangements, as in an essay written via conversation over Zoom:

BRITA: For me, daycare feels like we were expanding [my son's] village, in the sense of him knowing there are other people around him who will take care of him or who care about him.

CAMMY: I like that you've reframed childcare as part of your child's "village." It's easy to perceive childcare as an alternative to a village, but it's helpful to think of it as constituting part of that support.

BRITA: [Laughs] Yeah, even if I have to pay the villagers.

The contributors endure illnesses—their own, their partner's, their children's—emergency C-sections, and miscarriages (including one, harrowingly, during a campus visit). One writer describes her hesitation, when asked by a student how to make mashed potatoes, about offering advice that would cement her image as a parent, her simultaneous frustration that "parent" might be seen as "lesser," and her satisfaction, ultimately, when she feels able to successfully reconcile her identities and answer the question. All of these writers face not only the exhaustion of parenting while pursuing their graduate education but also this continual juggle of multiple identities—parent, student, teacher—and the varying external and internal responses to them. One of the writers refers movingly to the "everyday betrayals" of life as a graduate student parent, but her story and those of her co-contributors all work to warm up the prevailing "chilly climate" for parents in academia. As another reminds us, "Parenting has endowed me with superpowers I didn't have prior. I can make humans. I am a mother. I can sustain other humans beside myself. I turn this power over to my studies. I can and will meet deadlines because I do what I must to counteract forces that suggest otherwise."

While each of these writers tells their individual story, the collective effect is of a chorus whose voices ring out with their anecdotes, advice, and advocacy. They remind us that when graduate student parents struggle, we shouldn't judge, we should listen. It's time—past time—to improve the system they work in.

—Caroline M. Grant

PARENTING WHILE PHDING

CHANGE THE CONVERSATION

An Introduction

JACKIE HOERMANN-ELLIOTT AND
JENNA MORTON-AIKEN

"DINNER WAS AWKWARD!"

The anticipated text arrived as Jackie read her phone in one hand and reached for Watermelon Burst toothpaste with another.

Jackie had been scheduled to attend a local pre-conference networking dinner for women in higher education, but seeing her spouse already overextended after a long day, she had decided to stay home to help with bedtime protocols, remaining glued to her phone for live updates.

Friend, fellow faculty member, and mother of twins Ashley narrated in real time, especially after being seated at a table where the conversation had devolved into an episode of unsolicited advice for childless women, mostly grad students. Jackie's phone kept pinging as Ashley processed the most recent of many uncomfortable conversations about pregnancy and parenting in graduate school:

ASHLEY: One said have kids before your PhD and it's too hard.

ASHLEY: The other one agreed! She said you never know how your committee or mentor will feel about you having kids.

ASHLEY: I was hoping to offer more specific suggestions on how to navigate but then they started talking about infertility/IVF.

Meanwhile, between texts, Jackie wondered why on earth this is a conversation academic parents are still having in the twenty-first century.

Parenting and graduate school have a lot in common; not everyone understands what either experience entails or why some individuals embark on these arduous journeys in the first place. Graduate study, like parenting, has a seemingly inescapable impact on life: taking over how you speak, think, and make friends; controlling when and if you sleep; affecting your physical activity in odd and unexpected ways; and swallowing you whole if you let it. But graduate school and parenting also force us to grow, stretch, and adapt in ways we wouldn't have otherwise imagined, allowing insight from different orientations to the world than the ones we already inhabit, inspiring us to work hard, and motivating us to contribute meaningfully to something larger than ourselves. And while graduate school and parenting can feel incompatible at times, the narratives in this collection offer the experiences of the folks who have made both work harmoniously. They're not all happy stories. Some accounts brought us to tears while reviewing and editing, but we believe they are all important pieces that contribute to a larger conversation about what the academy represents today and what it could become tomorrow.

We, Jackie and Jenna, started on the journey of this book when we met on Zoom during a special-interest-group meeting for mothers in our field in April 2021. Like so many other parents struggling to work from home during the pandemic, Jackie attended from inside her car, parked far enough back in her driveway so her toddlers wouldn't catch a glimpse of her. Although the group had talked about the need for a book for some time, we were struck by the need for this book now, at the height of the pandemic and a time when we saw how mothers were shouldering more stress and experiencing increased marital conflict (Petersen 2020), particularly grad student mothers (Donnelly 2020).

We knew we were already overextended and exhausted, but we still felt called to hold space for a conversation in our professional discourse communities where others could share their stories about why parenting in academia—and graduate school in particular—feels so loaded and systemically prohibitive.

This collection builds on the voices in volumes that came before us, captured in the pages of *Mama, PhD* (Evans and Grant 2008), *Professor Mommy* (Connelly and Ghodsee 2011), and *Academic Motherhood* (Ward and Wolf-Wendel 2012), books that gave us raw insight into how parenting is made possible while rising up the professorial ranks. These books and others stand as founding foremother texts, the reigning authorities within a larger conversation surrounding gender equity in the academic workplace. *Parenting While PhDing* enters the conversation post-COVID, drawing out the stories and strategies that have proven to be pivotal—even life-altering, in some cases—for parent-authors navigating graduate school, offering a chorus of advice narratives that could uplift and support current and future graduate student parents as well as the faculty, advisors, supervisors, and administrators who serve them.

PARENTING WHILE PHDING IS HARD

We know that graduate students already constitute a relatively invisible class of students and workers within the academy that shoulders significant institutional labor despite receiving a fraction of the earnings offered to faculty or even the attention, support, and resources rolled out like a red carpet at the feet of undergraduate students (McCarthy 2019). Graduate students typically receive paltry stipends and are kept at part-time status to avoid offering them and their families health insurance, paid leave, and other essential benefits, such as the right to qualify for leave through the Family and Medical Leave Act (Cutler 2023).

All too often, a student's experience is contorted by a feeling of "habitual scarcity" in which "their bodies carry memories and markers of exploitative labor conditions, professional 'in-betweenness,' and injustice related to race, ethnicity, gender, dis/ability, age, and so on" (Walker et al. 2022). In *Do Babies Matter? Gender and Family in the Ivory Tower*, coauthors Mary Ann Mason, Nicholas Wolfinger, and Marc Goulden (2013) dedicate a full chapter to the graduate school years, noting that administrative infrastructures have not adapted to accommodate the most salient trends in higher education in the last sixty years: women are surpassing men in the attainment of doctorates, rising from 12 percent in 1966 to over 50 percent in 2008, and many students are matriculating into graduate programs of study later in life than their predecessors, which may pose challenges for students interested in conceiving biological children. Despite the significant shift in population, the machinery of graduate school has been slow to advance in many ways, and attitudes, practices, policies, and guidelines are still set up for the historically de facto white childless male.

At the same time, the pressure on parents has never been higher. In 2024, the US surgeon general released an advisory statement on the severity of stress and mental health issues American parents are now saddled with as they navigate the "complexity of managing social media, parents' concerns about the youth mental health crisis, and an epidemic of loneliness that disproportionately affects young people" (Murthy 2024, 3). Years earlier, when the pandemic shattered the illusion of perfect parenting in 2020, journalist Anne Helen Petersen reported that

> because of intensive work pressures and intensive parenting pressures, and because of a lack of adequate support from the government, their employers, or their partners, mothers who are working from home without childcare feel like failures—as both workers and mothers. They also blame themselves for those failures. Many are turning to food and alcohol as ways to cope—even hiding out eating Oreos in the bathroom to give themselves a break. Some mothers are also dropping out of the workforce to reduce the stress they face.

Although the description was published during the pandemic, it feels apt for how we felt as graduate and academic parents even before the pandemic. Exceptions are not given to pregnant or parenting graduate students, for whom the rhythms of the semester's instruction and grading don't end simply because a baby is on the way or daycare is suddenly closed. We still expect graduate students to undergo a rigorous program of study, to take on debt, and to navigate a ruthless job market as if they aren't parenting or interested in becoming a parent anytime soon. Meanwhile, outside the classroom, society expects those same graduate students to be fully present, engaged parents who must have oodles of time to spend with their children if they aren't employed full time. For those who are employed full time, graduate school may be written off as a "hobby" or a self-serving endeavor. The misconceptions are endless and chronically damaging.

To add insult to injury, the ugly truth is that parents face discrimination in the workplace and women and minoritized persons are disproportionately affected. The motherhood penalty manifests as significantly greater drops in employment for mothers compared to fathers or childless counterparts in the United States and in Scandinavian countries (Oster 2022). In one sociological study, mothers were 30 percent less likely to be called for a job interview than their male counterparts (González et al. 2019). Standing in stark contrast to the motherhood penalty is the fatherhood bonus, which sociologist Michelle Budig (2014) has researched extensively. Her statistical analyses found that fatherhood is generally considered to be a "valued characteristic of employers, signaling perhaps greater work commitment, stability, and deservingness." Budig does note that the motherhood penalty seems to disappear in the upper echelons of income distribution, but it is exacerbated at the lowest income levels, which is where graduate student parents reside. And although some decree the gender pay gap to be a phenomenon of the past, the 2023 *Annual Report on the Economic Status of the Profession* of the American Association of University Professors noted quite significantly that the average salaries of women serving in full-time faculty roles were 82 cents on the man's dollar (but failed to capture salary disparities for people who don't identify as male or female).

Beyond gender and salary discrimination, other intersectional aspects of graduate student parents' identities can be met with prejudice. Trendy ego psychology gurus in the 1940s and 1950s spread unsupported assumptions that pregnant women were susceptible to neuroses, projecting the harmful misconception that pregnant people are fragile and mentally unfit for rigorous intellectual work (Eisenberg 2010). Jackie vividly recalls her first pregnancy in graduate school, a time when numerous colleagues told her to slow down and not "work too hard on the dissertation," which offended her intellect and contradicted how she actually felt about writing and researching while pregnant. In fact, due to heightened hormone levels and an accompanying sensitivity to the smells, sights, and sounds of the world around her, she continued to write prolifically and creatively through all nine months of gestation.

These attitudes and practices are further complicated by the involuntary visibility of pregnancy. Jackie, for example, vividly remembers encountering a male faculty member in the hallway one afternoon not too long after she'd stopped wearing loose-fitting clothing. He asked rather bluntly if she was pregnant. She replied affirmatively, to which he retorted, "Oh, good! I thought you were just getting fat!" Such inappropriate remarks are commonplace, unfortunately, and graduate student parents rarely feel empowered enough to address these wrongdoings for fear of retribution and retaliation.

Discrimination is far more prevalent and harmful to historically underrepresented groups. People of color face brutal stereotyping (Moore 2017;

Hidalgo et al. 2022), particularly women in STEM fields whose voices and needs are too often set aside (Bender and Hoermann-Elliott 2021). As white, straight, cis-presenting women who have had the privilege of two or more healthy pregnancies, we recognize that individuals are often pushed into a growing number of contingent faculty positions that provide less pay and less access to resources or opportunities to continue research projects they started in graduate school (Sattar 2022) that could drive their careers forward. And while infertility challenges can impact all fields, the inflexible timetable for treatment can make it harder to retain women in STEM where fieldwork and other activities cannot be easily rescheduled to accommodate appointments.

To further advance practices supporting graduate student parents in a variety of fields and disciplines, we must ponder the dearth of systematic research on miscarriage and infant loss in the academy (Rogers et al. 2019). Likewise, LGBT parenting is understudied, as is single parenting (Jensen 2020) and stepparenting, despite the fact that the Pew Research Center indicates that an estimated 13 percent of Americans have stepchildren and fewer than half of kids today live in traditional, different-sex marital families (Pew Research Center 2011, 2014). Just as the institutional systems for supporting the childless male academic must evolve to accommodate changing demographics, so too must the focus of research intentionally and aggressively expand to support more inclusive and flexible research on pregnancy, parenting, and other understudied areas.

This book is one very small starting point for more conversation about parenting and diversity in parenting in academia. It doesn't suture together the gaps in these and other systemic issues we encounter every day on our way into the office and out to care for our children, but we hope it will empower and embolden graduate student parents today and prepare us all to leave a better foundation for the generations who follow.

JENNA'S STORY

In September 2012, Jenna walked into her PhD program orientation very visibly seven months pregnant. Nearly everyone in the room was surprised to see her condition. She felt like professors weren't quite sure what to do with her. Neither did the members of her cohort, as the facial expressions around her fluctuated among impressed, skeptical, and concerned. She was already an outlier in graduate school, coming in to do a PhD in English specializing in rhetoric and composition at thirty-one years old and after a career in business, but she had miscarried the previous year and was thrilled both to be pregnant and in that orientation. After all, how hard would it be to share her body with a tiny and very much wanted parasite?

Jenna gave birth by emergency C-section the day before Thanksgiving in her first year of coursework. She had been advised by multiple people, including her department's director of graduate studies, not to take the teaching assistantship she had been offered, so she paid fees for the first year where she (unnecessarily, it turned out) also took an extra class to ensure that she had full-time status. She finished that semester's coursework early for two classes and received an extension for the third class. She returned to coursework in the spring when her daughter was two months old, again taking three classes and now splitting childcare among herself, her spouse (who was often working in the next state), and her parents. She tracked the baby's schedule with an app for her own sanity and realized she could get in half an hour of work while the baby slept every two hours. That's how Jenna survived the first few months and how she thought she'd carry on.

At five months old, Jenna's daughter contracted RSV and developed significant respiratory health challenges. A year later, she was transported by emergency pediatric ambulance to Hasbro Children's Intensive Care Unit at 2 A.M. Doctors and nurses at the world-renowned hospital couldn't assure Jenna and her husband that their seventeen-month-old child would survive through the night.

Although their daughter is now a strong eleven-year-old who is taller than her mom, Jenna still remembers staring at her daughter's little diapered bum rising up in the air as she slept on her stomach, her torso using every muscle available to simply push air in and out of her lungs. Jenna also remembers asking her husband to bring her laptop to the hospital the next day once her condition had stabilized so she could complete a class presentation while her little girl finally slept peacefully.

Jenna intentionally got pregnant with her second daughter in time for her third year, completing the twenty-four-hour comprehensive exam at twenty-three weeks pregnant, a required full draft of an article at twenty-nine weeks pregnant, and an oral defense at thirty-one weeks pregnant, all while she taught two classes, took two classes, and strategized for the new baby via planned C-section. She went into labor the night after completing her on-campus responsibilities, and her second daughter was born early but healthy by a second emergency C-section.

In her fifth year, Jenna was awarded a fellowship that paid fees but no stipend. She successfully defended her dissertation five days before her younger daughter's second birthday. She graduated in May 2017, completing her program in five years with two healthy kids, marriage fully intact, and no job offer. She found local adjunct positions, kept applying, and landed a tenure-track job the following year. It meant a commute of more than seventy-five minutes each way, but Jenna and her spouse wouldn't have to uproot their family and Jenna wouldn't have to feel like she wasted five years of her family's life, her potential income, and/or five years of her family's finances.

By the time this book went to the publisher, Jenna had left the tenure track to become the senior associate director for writing and English language support at the Sheridan Center for Teaching and Learning at Brown University. She loves her work as a staff member and writing program administrator and continues to teach as a lecturer in the Department of English.

JACKIE'S STORY

Matresence, defined simply at first as the process of becoming a mother, is far more complex than its conceptual creator, anthropologist Dana Raphael, originally intended. Most scientists who study the neurocognitive effects of the transition into parenthood acknowledge that such effects can be studied "through preconception, pregnancy and birth, surrogacy, or adoption to the postnatal period and beyond" (Athan 2024), often manifesting in a variety of forms that benefit all parents, including "increased cognitive performance" and "younger patterns of brain activity" (Orchard et al. 2022). While having young children can significantly impact one's time, energy, and output of intellectual labor, the long-term benefits to overall productivity are worth noting. In 2014, a study of nearly 10,000 academic economists revealed that raising young children may temporarily decrease the productivity of academic mothers, but these women catch up later in life, often outpacing their childless male and female peers (Krapf et al. 2014). And yet despite these delayed benefits, the voyage into parenthood looks different for everyone and is unrecognized for many who parent in nontraditional ways.

As a mother of four, Jackie's matrescence was rooted not in caring for biological children but in caring for her stepchild. She met her "bonus baby" about three months after starting her doctoral program at Texas Christian University, where she met a handsome and newly separated alum of that university who had a three-year-old daughter. Everything about this situation—impending divorce, mothering but not mothering someone else's child, and acclimation to a rigorous program of study—was draped in glossy red warning flags, but over the course of the next three years came divorce papers, new family adventures, tears, rings, cake, comprehensive exams, more tears, and one eye-opening conversation with her dissertation director. "I think you should take a fifth year." Jackie's dissertation director told her. "Take your time working through the dissertation and navigating the job market."

But Jackie didn't want to. She didn't want to slow down because she felt ready to have kids—and soon. At that moment, she decided to start trying to conceive. A few months later, she was pregnant. Her first of three sons—often lovingly referred to as "the grad school baby"—was born via C-section in late August, which every academic knows is horrendous timing. Jackie went on the market that year and secured a job right up the road at Texas Woman's University, where she works to this day as associate professor of English and director of the First-Year Composition Program. Her second son arrived in October of her second year on the job, and her third son arrived (while we were preparing this book and with notably better timing than the first two) in early June 2022. Being visibly pregnant twice on the tenure track has resulted in many hushed conversations in her office with graduate students who want to talk so badly about family planning but don't know who they can turn to for advice that will support all of their ambitions, not just the ones related to the PhD.

THE STORIES AHEAD

Each chapter in this collection coheres around a central piece of advice associated with a tagline that appears in the chapter title. Many chapters evoke conventions of the "This I Believe" essay genre or function as evocative autoethnographies that "blur boundaries between nonfiction and fiction, research and reflection, memory and desire, poetry/literature/performance art and science" (Bochner 2017, 74). These advice narratives "engage in various forms of systematic reflection on experiences and memories to craft richly reflexive personal accounts that map onto or interrogate cultural attitudes, ideologies, practices, or times" (Jackson and McKinney 2021, 8). Our authors bring their lived experiences into the conversation and simultaneously empower readers to question the harsh realities graduate student parents face and to take action in their personal and professional lives.

Our review of seventy-six proposals confirmed much of what we already knew. For one, the overwhelming majority of submissions came from academics identifying as mothers, but we were heartened to see some fathers and nonbinary persons respond to our call for submissions. Second, the submission review process confirmed that many of the mothers were exceedingly hard on themselves or held themselves to unattainable standards, and we want to challenge rather than reify such thinking. Originally, we envisioned an organization strategy that would follow a linear path toward parenthood—moving from narratives about preconception to those about pregnancy, the postpartum period, and childrearing. Instead, we chose to organize the sections of this book in a way that resists the predisposition or expectation to always put babies first.

The collection opens with critical experiences and advice from our authors, intentionally situating parents' well-being first with the placement of the first section, Stay Alive. While we were tempted to lead with what became the second section, Your Body Has Other Plans, we felt it was critical in this post-*Roe* era to begin by addressing the health and wellness of parents. The third section, Juggle What Matters, examines the complex balancing act of parenting with graduate school, and the fourth, Push Back, spotlights the voices of parents who created alternate paths when they faced resistance and retaliation. The fifth and final section, Leave a Note, rounds out the collection with tried-and-true advice for any graduate student parent feeling uncertain about their future in academia.

AIMING TOWARD ACCESS

We designed this book around three aims to increase access for potential readers: brevity, diversity, and practicality. Unlike many academic texts, the chapters in this collection are short and narrative driven to make them approachable and easily digestible for the exhausted, busy graduate student parent or the thoroughly overworked graduate advisor or administrator. The book is designed to be picked up, put down, or revisited in difficult moments when readers feel isolated or like systemic change isn't possible. Parents, potential parents, and the folks who manage them: we wanted you all to be able to enter the conversation quickly, get what you needed, and get back to work.

Our next aim—a greater diversity of voices—is arguably a point of critique of the book, as it should be for any academic volume, especially one aiming to diversify perspectives on a particular experience in academia. The majority of chapters in the collection center one or more diverse perspectives in addition to academic parenthood. As much as we would have liked for every chapter in the collection to have explored more than one diverse perspective—above and beyond the diversity interests academic parenthood already represent—the reality is that even this level of representation cannot be taken for granted. Systemic inequities in academia have pushed many academic parents out of higher education altogether (a theme explored in several chapters), and publishing about one's experiences of parenting as a minoritized student, faculty, or staff comes with a heightened level of risk in our current political climate. With this collection, we have tried to create space for a multiplicity of voices without demanding identity disclosure, tokenization, additional uncompensated labor, or risk-taking that might place authors from historically underrepresented groups in more precarious positions than those they already occupy. That said, this work only begins to address what is a much larger, vulnerable, and necessary conversation about the diverse identities and lived experiences of graduate student parents. We hope the collection catalyzes additional research into supporting diverse graduate student populations.

With the third and final aim of practicality, we asked each contributor to emphasize a central takeaway for parenting graduate students and for faculty and administrators working with graduate student parents. While this book is meant for an audience of scholars, we invited our authors to explore their creative autoethnographic impulses, centering evocative individual experiences and relating challenges, identities, and complexity above all else. We believe that every chapter adds to a rich and colorful tapestry of autoethnographic perspectives on parenting in this unique context and does so in a way that elicits a strong emotional reaction from readers, offers critical insight, and suggests actions to improve or continue positive action. Our collective purpose is to speak to a new and rapidly changing academic landscape, and contributor chapters offer advice about how to navigate parenting while PhDing alongside fresh perspectives on managing both responsibilities in higher education.

ENTER THE CONVERSATION

From the outset, the goal for this book has been to help fill in gaps, answer questions, and make strides toward an inclusive, family-friendly landscape in academia. We encouraged all of our contributors to use their intensely personal narratives as a platform for telling stories that lift hearts, share burdens, and provide a way forward for the next generation of graduate student parents. Yes, parenting while PhDing is hard, but we believe that if we enter the conversation together, we can change the conversation together.

Graduate student parents, we hope this book speaks to you. We are with you as you grow, navigate, dodge, and balance. Advisors, administrators, and allies of graduate student parents, we hope this book speaks to you, too. We wrote it to give you a window into the wonderful, demanding experiences of parenting while PhDing.

Read our stories, then go write your own.

WORKS CITED

American Association of University Professors. 2023. "The Annual Report on the Economic Status of the Profession, 2022–23." AAUP. https://www.aaup.org/report/annual-report-economic-status-profession-2022-23.

Athan, Aurelie. 2024. "Matrescence: Education, Theory, & Practice." https://www.matrescence.com/.

Bender, Ashley, and Jackie Hoermann-Elliott. 2021. "Asking Big: Creating a Culture of Support for Academic Mothers' Advocating in Times of Crisis." *ADVANCE Journal* 2 (3). https://doi.org/10.5399/osu/ADVJRNL.2.3.10.

Bochner, Arthur. 2017. "Heart of the Matter: A Mini-Manifesto for Autoethnography." *International Review of Qualitative Research* 10 (1): 67–80. https//doi.org/10.1525/irqr.2017.10.1.67.

Budig, Michelle J. 2014. "The Fatherhood Bonus and The Motherhood Penalty: Parenthood and the Gender Gap in Pay." Third Way, September 2. https://www.thirdway.org/report/the-fatherhood-bonus-and-the-motherhood-penalty-parenthood-and-the-gender-gap-in-pay#:~:text=In%20a%20new%20and%20provocative,is%20increasing%2C%E2%80%9D%20says%20Budig..

Connelly, Rachel, and Kristen Ghodsee. 2011. *Professor Mommy: Finding Work-Family Balance in Academia*. Rowman & Littlefield.

Cutler, Dave. 2023. "What Higher Ed's Paid Parental-Leave Policies Look Like." *The Chronicle of Higher Education*, March 28. https://www.chronicle.com/article/what-higher-eds-paid-parental-leave-policies-look-like.

Donnelly, Katie. 2020. "Grad Student Mom: This Is Something I Can't Fix." *CNN*, June 29. https://www.cnn.com/2020/06/29/opinions/coronavirus-single-parenting-graduate-school-donnelly/index.html.

Eisenberg, Ziv. 2010. "Clear and Pregnant Danger: The Making of Prenatal Psychology in Mid-Twentieth-Century America." *Journal of Women's History* 22 (3): 112–135.

Evans, Elrena, and Caroline Grant, eds. 2008. *Mama, PhD: Women Write about Motherhood and Academic Life*. Rutgers University Press.

González, José M., Clara Cortina, and Jorge Rodriguez. 2019. "The Role of Gender Stereotypes in Hiring: A Field Experiment." *European Sociological Review* 35 (2): 187–204. https://doi.org/10.1093/esr/jcy055.

Hidalgo, Leigh-Anna, Christine Vega, Nora Alba Cisneros, and JoAnna Michelle Reyes. 2022. "Fierce Mothers: The Cords that Bind Us." *Feminist Formations* 34 (1): 122–146.

Jackson, Rebecca, and Jackie Grutsch McKinney. 2021. *Self+Culture+Writing: Autoethnography for/as Writing Studies*. University Press of Colorado.

Jensen, Erin B. 2020. "'We are not ok': Single Parenting during Covid." *Journal of Multimodal Rhetorics* 6 (2). http://journalofmultimodalrhetorics.com/6-2-jensen.

Krapf, Matthias, Heinrich W. Ursprung, and Christian Zimmerman. 2014. "Parenthood and Productivity of Highly Skilled Labor: Evidence from the Groves of Academe." Research Division Working Paper Series, Federal Reserve Bank of St. Louis.

Mason, Mary Ann, Nicholas Wolfinger, and Marc Goulden. 2013. *Do Babies Matter? Gender and Family in the Ivory Tower*. Families in Focus. Rutgers University Press.

McCarthy, Claudine. 2019. "Discover How to Effectively Advocate for Support Services Tailored to Grad Students." *Student Affairs Today* 22 (7): 1–3. https://onlinelibrary.wiley.com/doi/full/10.1002/say.30660.

Moore, Mignon R. 2017. "Women of Color in the Academy: Navigating Multiple Intersections and Multiple Hierarchies." *Social Problems* 64 (2): 200–205.

Murthy, Vivek H. 2024. "Parents under Pressure: The U.S. Surgeon General's Advisory on the Mental Health & Well-Being of Parents." U.S. Department of Health and Human Services. https://www.hhs.gov/sites/default/files/parents-under-pressure.pdf.

Orchard, Edwina, Helena J. V. Rutherford, Avram J. Holmes, and Shama D. Jamadar. 2022. "Matresence: lifetime Impact of Motherhood on Cognition and the Brain." *Trends in Cognitive Sciences* 27 (3): 302–316.

Oster, Emily. 2022. "How to Think about the 'Motherhood Penalty.'" ParentData, May 23. https://parentdata.org/how-to-think-about-the-motherhood-penalty/.

Petersen, Anne Helen. 2020. "Other Countries Have Social Safety Nets. The U.S. Has Women." Culture Study, November 11. https://annehelen.substack.com/p/other-countries-have-social-safety.

Pew Research Center. 2011. "A Portrait of Stepfamilies." Pew Research Center, January 13. https://www.pewresearch.org/social-trends/2011/01/13/a-portrait-of-stepfamilies/.

———. 2014. "Fewer than Half of U.S. Kids Today Live in a 'Traditional' Family." Pew Research Center, January 22. https://www.pewresearch.org/short-reads/2014/12/22/less-than-half-of-u-s-kids-today-live-in-a-traditional-family/.

Rogers, Jennifer L., Jamie E. Crocket, and Esther Suess. 2019. "Miscarriage: An Ecological Examination." *Professional Counselor* 9 (1): 51–66.

Sattar, Atia. 2022. "Academic Motherhood and the Unrecognized Labor of Non-Tenure-Track Faculty Women of Color." AAUP. https://www.aaup.org/article/academic-motherhood-and-unrecognized-labors-non-tenure-track-faculty-women-color#:~:text=It%20is%20easy%20to%20ignore,most%20visible%20only%20as%20numbers.

Walker, Kelsie, Morgan Gross, Paula Weinman, Hayat Bedaiwi, and Alyssa McGrath. 2022. "Graduate Student Bodies on the Periphery." In *Our Body of Work: Embodied Administration and Teaching*, edited by Melissa Nicholas and Anna Sicari. University Press of Colorado.

Ward, Kelly, and Lisa Wolf-Wendel. 2012. *Academic Motherhood: How Faculty Manage Work and Family*. Rutgers University Press.

PART 1 STAY ALIVE

1 ▸ EMBRACE THE MULTIPLICITIES

How Internarrative Identity Theory Transformed My PhD Journey

JUDITH CHRIQUI BENCHIMOL

YOU ARE LYING in bed, sick. Your bedroom door is locked. You are thirty-four weeks pregnant with your third child and you have just under five minutes to wash your face and comb your hair before your four-hour doctoral research course on Zoom. It's a lot; you know this. Your friends and family call you "hero" whenever they hear this. But you don't feel that way.

In fact, whenever you tell anyone about your plans to finish your doctoral program and earn your PhD within the next few years, the voice of your inner critic flips on the stage lights in your head and slicks their greasy comb-over as they prepare to roast you. You watch as the tired theater attendant (also in your head) yanks at the curtain pulley and tugs, tugs as the dusty, heavy red curtains pry open. Your inner critic takes the stage.

"Thank you, ladies and gentlemen. Please, no clapping" (no one is clapping). You are the sole audience member, sitting in a padded theater chair that folds if you stand up. But you don't get up and leave. You stay. You watch. You listen. Because in this moment of weakness you do not have the energy to walk away. You watch as they grab the microphone from the stand and tap on it. It screeches. "Is this thing on?" they joke. (They say that every time.) Then they look directly at you, and the inner monologue begins:

> Let me ask you a question: Why in the world would you undertake a PhD in English after having kids? You can't handle that. Maybe some other mothers can, like Jenny with the twins. She's already done with her proposal—incredible, right? But not you. You suck. And then—get this—you go and get knocked up in your third year. Are you some kind of idiot? You haven't even started your proposal yet. You're irresponsible. I bet Jenny feels sorry for you . . . and she has twins! You're not going to get this done now. Get it together or get out.

And then they bow and say, "Thank you, ladies and gentlemen. I'll be back in five minutes. And then again in an hour . . . and tomorrow."

This show has played in your head so many times that you've memorized the script. It's embedded in you. It's a part of you that you can't undo. Until one day your advisor assigns you a book that changes everything.

BEGINNING

When I decided to apply to a PhD program, I was pregnant with my second child. I had dreamed of pursuing a PhD for a long time, but I didn't think that I was a strong enough writer and thinker to exist in this academic space, so I kept delaying my entry into graduate school while teaching as an adjunct. I spent my time thinking my way out of pursuing this goal, but I started to feel inspired and motivated by parenthood. With limited pockets of time, I couldn't overthink the process and I couldn't afford to enter a spiral of thoughts and doubts. I didn't have the time to entertain the voice that told me that I can't write academic papers, who, unsurprisingly, is a close cousin of the inner critic who had taken up residence in my brain after I started my PhD.

Wanting to be a good example for my children, I posted an ad in an online women's writing group looking for someone who had recently completed their doctorate to help me navigate the application process. I also read Neil

Fiore's *The Now Habit,* which someone had suggested as helpful in overcoming perfectionism and allowing me to just take a single step in the direction of my goals. Fiore's words are what gave me the courage to stop delaying my dreams and face the blank page. By not trying to do everything on my own—and learning that most people around me were also getting help rather than accomplishing all of their goals independently—I felt more assured in my choices and my abilities. With these support systems in place, I was able to complete my application and gain acceptance to a graduate program I only once dreamed of attending.

During the first year of my PhD program, unsure of my professional direction, I took classes that related to my interests but covered a wide range of topics. I loved discovering unfamiliar literary theories, like Mikhail Bakhtin's carnival and Saidiya Hartman's critical fabulation. I was also interested in exploring how my Jewishness fit into my writing identity, and I simultaneously loved learning about John Daly and Michael Miller's writing apprehension scale. I didn't want to let go of those varied interests, but the classic message of graduate school is "Pick a lane; choose one thing," and I believed that I had to do that.

When I met with my advisor to ask her which lane I should choose, she told me "What if you didn't have to choose?" She explained that I needn't limit myself to one narrative and introduced me to Ajit Maan's internarrative identity theory. Reading Maan's theory provided a lens on the ways I had been limiting my PhD narrative. I'd been focused on forming a "coherent self," a unified identity that can tell only one narrative at a time. One that doesn't allow for my multiplicities, with their pasts, presents, and futures that existed in the same space. Finally, I saw that all of the parts of myself did belong in the same space. I could address my Jewish identity and its place in the composition classroom *and* write about my love of Bakhtin's theory of the carnivalesque; I could study Miller and Daly's writing apprehension, Frank Pajares's writing self-efficacy, *and* whisper stories in the dark with my children while lying next to them at bedtime. It was possible to be a scholar of more subjects than one and to recognize that being a mother is also a kind of scholarship. I learned that I didn't have to sacrifice one part of myself to privilege another and I didn't need to see those disparate parts as chaotic or disruptive. My identities are not, in fact, at odds with each other.

Internarrative identity theory provided a framework through which I could embrace rather than compartmentalize; I could combat the seemingly manic labels that student parents, particularly mothers, often face while navigating graduate school: caretaker, scholar, laborer, lover. My own nonfiction narrative of childrearing and childbirth while navigating a PhD program challenges the paradigm that these multiplicities do not belong in the same space. The fact that so many people believe in this paradigm explains why you don't see many student-parents in the first place.

BEGINNING AGAIN

Once I embraced the idea of not having to sacrifice the multiplicities of my identity, my scholarly work became a mirror for my life as a mom, wife, PhD student, and more. I began to recognize that I could do all of these things. They might not all get attention at the same time, but they could all coexist in the same space of my life. Acknowledging my kids even while I was in class and feeling—even spiritually and emotionally—that every part of my life is connected allowed me to write my papers in the body of a mother and have that body be present. I could actively draw from my experiences as a mother while doing the work of a scholar. Using the lens of internarrative identity helped me—and can help other student mothers—navigate the PhD without as much mental suffering or compartmentalization and can encourage prospective undecided student mothers to enroll in the PhD program that always felt out of reach. When mothers say they cannot be PhD students because they are already parents, they are denying their multiple identities. Joining those identities allows mothers to decompartmentalize by building a narrative that is not fractured but whole.

Internarrative identity theory emerged as a critique of Paul Ricœur's narrative identity theory. Ricoeur posits that identity is based on a sequenced narrative of temporally oriented events that change over time. In other words, the formation of our identity relies on a series of events that make sense in a particular order. Maan objected to Ricœur's theory because it insists on the focus of a single logical thread. It doesn't leave room for other parts of one's identity, so a path or moment or aspect of oneself that doesn't fit logically is omitted. Jumping among these multiple threads is thus viewed as chaotic, frenetic, and disorderly. While this ordered narrative theory has its benefits in extracting a particular kind of meaning, for me it feels limiting. The events that occurred before I was born to people who are not me but whose lives affected mine also shaped me. Those events do not fall into Ricœur's time-character paradigm but are still central to my existence.

As the daughter of an immigrant from a community that barely exists today, a mother who wants to be very present, and a PhD student, the separate threads of my life look disconnected or chaotic on the surface. Narrative identity theory asks me to choose one, saying that they don't all belong in the same place. But Maan's theory clarified that this messiness is acceptable and true and that I can and should talk about, write about, think about, and live all of them at once. She challenges Ricœur's approach and offers a new way to regard people who have multiple identities, especially people who are marginalized.

My writing blossomed when I found this theory because it gave me permission to explore these parts of my identity—as I am doing right now, in my academic work—in a space where they aren't usually discussed and where they might not seem to belong. My creative writing began to weave through, across, under and over my academic writing. I no longer had to separate these discourses. I no longer devalued my work as a storyteller in an academic environment that doesn't often let story stand alone as a kind of scholarship. At an earlier point in my career, I didn't think that these disparate parts of my identity mattered or carried any weight because they were so fractured. I didn't think I could talk about them in an academic space. While every writer might not want to bring their identities directly into their work, I felt that I couldn't separate them and had longed for them to be part of my work, which I now realize is possible. Even writers who don't draw on them explicitly can still acknowledge that they exist, which can itself be very powerful, giving weight to the entirety of oneself in all its messiness.

Caring for my kids is labor, just as writing an essay is, but the work of parenting is considered "less than" academic work. When parents recognize that both are equally important kinds of labor, their guilt can be assuaged. Because the labor of taking care of my children is part of completing my PhD and not separate from it, I feel less guilty about not having read everything, about not devoting 100 percent of myself to my scholarly work. I can be a mother who is present for her children and also get my PhD. While I once felt a lot of guilt around that fracturing, believing that I didn't deserve a PhD, I have come to realize that the knowledge I am cultivating is created from things outside the academy. My work as a mother is part of the knowledge I need to fulfill this academic goal. To any mother who is afraid to take the leap and can't picture themself as a scholar, know that you already are, because being a mother is being a scholar. Whether you are applying to graduate school or just need the reassurance to forge ahead, embrace your multiplicities. Don't be afraid to bring all of yourself into your work.

2 ▸ LEVERAGE YOUR ASSETS

How Parenting Shapes (and Benefits) Our Scholarly Identities

JENNIFER C. JUDD, WHITNEY ZAHAR RICH, AND ALICIA CHRISTINE BERETTA

During my first week of graduate school, I hurriedly dropped off kids to gymnastics, band practice, and therapy; tossed a mishmash of ingredients into a Crock-Pot; forgot to turn it on; then drove forty minutes to campus.

"She needs to learn the importance of finishing things." What was my supervisor talking about? I had spent years doggedly submerged in the task of wrapping up the lives of others.

In my roles as new mom, working mom, and student mom, I felt alone, isolated, overwhelmed, and overworked.

We offer these three glimpses into our lived experiences as mothers and PhD students to illustrate how our mother identities and academic identities often collide. We are students. We are teachers. We are parents. Ours is a multivocal narrative that acknowledges the challenges and roadblocks parents face as they struggle to build successful academic careers. Speaking from experience and from currently being in the trenches of our PhD programs, we know this is hard work. However, as mothers in varying stages of parenthood, we also recognize we've gained a meaningful foundation of empathy and resilience that has given us tools to thrive in our doctoral programs. In sharing our stories, we present an argument for the compatible nature of the work we do in parenting and graduate studies: we discovered that embracing our assets as parents allows us to engage more fully in our scholarship, teaching, and collegial relationships.

First and foremost, we wish to recognize our positionality as white, cisgender mothers whose experiences represent a narrow perspective in the richly diverse realm of parenthood. While two of us would be categorized as "nontraditional" students and one of us became a mother after becoming a doctoral student, we recognize that our experiences cannot speak for the myriad intersectional challenges PhD parents of diverse identities, genders, races, ethnicities, sexualities, and abilities encounter. However, we hope to highlight commonalities in our differing stories that have ultimately helped us become better doctoral students.

Few academic scholars would disagree that navigating the demands of parenting and the rigors of graduate school is a fraught endeavor. This is a well-explored narrative (see Mirick and Wladkowsi 2018 and Prikhidko and Haynes 2018, among others). For graduate student parents who navigate the complex frontier of emotional, logistical, and financial worries that accompany graduate school while shouldering a similar burden in child-rearing, the stigma may seem heightened, even if it is not directly articulated by faculty or mentors. Being a parent in graduate school is, without question, challenging and sometimes discouraging work. However, we offer an alternative perspective on what parenting can bring to our doctoral experiences. We posit that parenting experiences are assets we can leverage to navigate our graduate school experience with grace, empathy, and success.

LEVERAGE "BETWEENITY": THE ASSET OF NAVIGATING MULTIPLE IDENTITIES

Graduate student parents often experience the uncomfortable sensation of liminality—not sitting comfortably in either the world of parenting or the world of grad school. We affirm this from our own experiences: we've managed the overwhelming sense of imposter syndrome and the dizzying shift between two very labor-intensive worlds. For example, Jennifer, a doctoral candidate, describes feelings of "betweenity" and reflects on the challenge of merging these two seemingly disparate identities:

> I am a mother of five children ranging in age from middle school to college, including a disabled child who needs significant support. I easily meet the classification of "nontraditional student." While I've since grown in confidence as a student, teacher, and researcher, I felt wobbly-kneed as I transitioned to graduate school, anxious to find solid footing in a world so foreign to motherhood. During my first week of school, I hurriedly dropped off kids to gymnastics, band practice, and therapy; tossed a mishmash of ingredients into a crockpot; forgot to turn it on; then drove forty minutes to campus. As I slid into a chair in my first class, I felt my imposter syndrome and emotional angst permeating the atmosphere while I anxiously triple-checked to make sure I hadn't forgotten my laptop at home.

Most graduate students are highly familiar with imposter syndrome. However, betweenity is something more. Disability studies scholars and rhetoricians Brenda Jo Brueggemann and Allison Harper Hitt contextualize the rich complexity of betweenity from a disability standpoint, defining it as "a relational space between one's various identities" and "a rhetorical process of toggling between decisions and identities" (Brueggemann 2013; Hitt 2021, 21). Although betweenity can leave graduate students feeling discombobulated, rifling through the Rolodex of identities to remember which "hat" to put on is part of the parenting job. Whether running an infant to the pediatrician, sitting in a parent-teacher meeting, or taking a business call while turning down the *Bluey* theme blaring through minivan speakers, we become adept at toggling between worlds.

Rather than seeing this as an uncomfortable reality, we suggest that embracing our betweenity opens up space for greater understanding, relationality to our peers, and creativity. Jennifer leveraged her betweenity to connect with her cohort members, finding she was well positioned to support colleagues in their struggles with imposter syndrome. Ultimately, her observations and conversations led to inquiry and empirical research on graduate students' writing anxiety, a positive outcome she attributes to embracing her betweenity as a parent and graduate student.

LEVERAGE WISDOM: THE ASSET OF CREATING AND STRETCHING BOUNDARIES

Whitney, a third-year PhD student in counseling education and supervision, began graduate school when her children were in high school and college. The decision to begin graduate school was an awakening, as she noted that for most of her life,

> I paused personal dreams, ambitions, and drives: shrinking hopes for myself to a tiny flame cupped in my palm. I didn't think I could manage graduate school while raising little kids at the same time because I worried I'd have to explain too much to professors about why my life always felt sideways. "My kid is sick. Yes, still." I couldn't explain this to anyone, and I wasn't going to try. My plan was to raise my kids first and hope there would be time for me when they were older. Over the years, I worried that my original fiery excitement about further academic pursuit would exist when I finally returned to my graduate studies. So I guarded that tiny spark during the years I supported my husband through his dental school and residency, parented our children, and navigated intense hospital visits as my youngest toddler fought a two-year health battle.

Whitney recalls a memorable moment when she finally began a master's program in counseling. She received what she describes as "the most puzzling feedback from a site supervisor" during one of her clinical internships:

> "She needs to learn the importance of finishing things," she said. What was my supervisor talking about? I sat, stunned, listening to feedback from a site I reported for abusive working conditions. I had just spent years doggedly submerged in the task of wrapping up the lives of others—my family—before I dared to allow a bellows to breathe across the spark of my life's ambitions. I was so proficient at finishing things that I taught family lessons about it. While holding cleats at the edge of the sidelines, I had told my son, "We already signed the soccer contract for the entire year, so you're obligated to your team for the season." I once told my daughter, "You owe it to yourself not to quit" when she was standing on the pool deck of a swim league, vomiting. As I sat listening to a supervisor victim blame, I wondered if I had taught my children the wrong things. Instead, should I have taught them how to recognize their limits and how to ask other people to respect those limits? Should I have taught them how to assert their voices? Should I have spent these years teaching them what self-compassion looks like instead?

Whitney reflects on the irony of her experience as a sort of "a-ha" moment regarding what it means to honor oneself and one's limitations. As a parent, she knew she had the skill set to complete tasks, but as a counselor, she now understood how to recognize a problematic situation and advocate for boundaries that safeguarded an individual's well-being. Leaning into both of her identities helped Whitney negotiate the complex push-pull demands of maintaining wellness while managing the increasing responsibilities of graduate school.

LEVERAGE VULNERABILITY: THE ASSET OF SELF-ADVOCACY

Alicia, a PhD candidate who became a new mother to an infant daughter in the middle of her first year of coursework in her doctoral program, quickly learned the challenges and benefits of drawing on resources to successfully incorporate the new role of parenting into a hectic academic schedule. Her story emphasizes embracing the vulnerability of asking for help:

> I started my PhD program in the middle of the pandemic. Because my classes were online, I struggled to form essential support networks. When my daughter arrived, survival mode kicked in as I tried to nurse her during Zoom classes (struggling to turn off the camera or shove it at an awkward angle), complete assignments through sleepless nights, and support my students. In my roles as new mom, working mom, and student mom, I felt alone, isolated, overwhelmed, and overworked.

Alicia demonstrates how the scope of parenthood stressors mirrors what we may experience in our graduate work. Graduate students, like parents, also become completely overwhelmed, emotionally flooded, and confused about how to use resources.

> The end of the spring semester in my first year of grad school was also the end of my third trimester, and I was occupied with painting a nursery, trying to eat healthy, and counting baby kicks to make sure my daughter was still alive in my womb. However, I also faced a burgeoning pile of over seventy-five student essays and assignments to grade, an original multimodal pedagogy assignment to create, and a teaching portfolio to submit. And then my daughter was born

> two weeks ahead of my due date. Scared, elated, and stressed all at the same time, I realized I had to reach out for help.

Alicia's acute shift to parenting catapulted her to a vulnerable position but it also motivated her to seek support in academia, a skill that as graduate students, we sometimes neglect in an effort to do it all ourselves. Alicia ultimately discovered that help *was* available and that support systems within parenthood and graduate school don't have to be mutually exclusive.

> When I reached out, my colleagues and professors at school rallied to support me. Two wonderful colleagues offered to contribute to final grading and one professor allowed me to take an incomplete. As a new parent, I knew I needed help to care for my child effectively, so I reached out to colleagues and called on family members I might not have approached otherwise. My sudden shift to motherhood brought immediacy and humility, leading me to articulate my needs, seek support, and let go of the fear of judgment. I want my children and my students to learn these skills, too.

For parents, the quest for balance and wellness frequently means boldly shifting the chess pieces of our lives to accommodate our needs. The "you shoulds" typically originate as an external demand and agenda. Mantras such as "Be sure and take care of you," "Put that oxygen mask on yourself first," and "Hire a team of helpers" sound lovely. However, very few individuals offer practical suggestions for what self-advocacy might look like in real time, especially when competing with the time-consuming rigors of graduate school. We suggest that leveraging our vulnerability as parents can propel self-advocacy in graduate school, benefiting not only ourselves but also our students, clients, and colleagues. Articulating our needs and asking for support in our studies, classrooms, and workplaces encourages others to open up, leading to a more connected and supportive community for everyone.

LEVERAGE EMPATHY: THE ASSET OF CARE WORK

The empathy we develop in the refining crucible of parenthood is precisely what enables us to connect with students and colleagues in our graduate programs. Empathy in our homes is more than just feeling for or with our children; it's actively listening to them to understand their needs and how to meet them. We can use empathy in our classrooms by actively listening to our students and peers to understand their needs and how we can meet or help with those needs. For example, Jennifer recalls a moment early in her graduate career when a professor urged her to "get out in front of" her mother identity. While she understood her professor's genuine interest in supporting her growth as an instructor, Jennifer ultimately discovered how embracing her mother identity could yield valuable dividends:

> I remember how anxious I was to establish a "professional ethos" while teaching my first undergraduate class. I vividly recall a student approaching me after class one day to ask a question I thought concerned our writing assignment. Instead, he asked me how to make mashed potatoes. I was stunned; he was quite serious. A mix of emotional thoughts cascaded over me in seconds: "My students don't take me seriously. I have 'mom' tattooed all over my psyche. And of course I know how to make mashed potatoes!"

This millisecond-long micro-struggle to choose one identity over another exemplifies multiple struggles, both micro and macro, that graduate student parents experience regularly. However, Jennifer notes that this moment also provided an epiphany about the value her mother identity brought to the classroom:

> I saw this young man as a freshman away from home trying to navigate his new life and realized that his question wasn't a commentary on my lack of academic ethos. I blinked. I softened. Then I responded in a way that felt most natural: First, a quick, step-by-step tutorial on making mashed potatoes. Then, a reminder for him to turn in his journal entry by midnight on Friday. At that moment, my mother and graduate student/instructor identities didn't feel incongruous; they felt complementary.

This experience underscores perhaps the most important asset we can embrace from parenting and our doctoral programs: our relationship with and understanding of care work in multiple spheres of parenthood and academia. The ultimate goal of care work is to establish safety, trust, support, and collaboration so the resulting relationship facilitates the healthy growth of individuals (SAMHSA 2019). Ideally, growth-fostering interactions promote healthy development and mutual flourishing among all parties in a learning dynamic, whether in the home, at school, or in the work environments (Schwartz 2019). In essence, care work invites reciprocity: Both the givers and receivers of care benefit. We tap into the rich repository of knowledge we've gained from caring for complex individuals. We have the ability to recognize signs of struggle, check in, and invite conversations with our students and colleagues; we have learned these skills at home.

Whitney's mothering experience has provided a well of resources in her studies in clinical mental health and counselor education and supervision. She reflects, "When I sincerely ask clients how they are, many burst into tears. This is a simple and gentle check-in, but frequently the answer is 'I'm not okay.'" However, Whitney draws a powerful connection between these experiences in counseling and her years of experience as a parent. She notes the first time she sat in a quiet room and earnestly asked, "How are you?" and had someone quietly whisper, "I'm not okay." She was not with a client. She was with her child.

> It was the biggest truth that ever swelled within the belly of four walls. I did not care about commitments, money, other people, or finishing anything. I sat and listened to the weights sitting on my child, the "shoulds," and I saw so clearly that so much of what we worry about is filler. And just like my child, we are all born worthy of architecting a life that allows us to breathe in joy. Responsibly managing self-care can be an assertion of that worth.

This is how we leverage our assets as parents in academia—drawing on our caregiving instincts to amplify small moments of interaction that shape us into empathetic instructors, counselors, researchers, and writers.

LEVERAGE THE GIFT OF PARENTING WHILE PHDING

In parenting, experience is a powerful teacher. In graduate school, students, colleagues, and teachers respond positively to compassionate listening, empathy regarding their welfare, and encouragement. These qualities often mature in the act of caring for a family. The hope we have for ourselves and our students parallels the hope we hold for those we pack lunches for in our homes. In a world rattled by grief, uncertainty, conflict, and social justice concerns, our parenting experiences have tremendous real-world potency, particularly in academia. To this end, we offer encouragement to fellow parents and graduate students either deep in the trenches or perhaps standing on the periphery, uncertain whether they have the knowledge, skills, resources, confidence, and time to pursue a graduate degree while parenting. We can and should leverage the assets we've gained in parenting to navigate our identities as students in academia and, in turn, acknowledge that graduate education has made us better parents. We belong in both worlds.

WORKS CITED

Brueggemann, Brenda Jo. 2013."Articulating Betweenity: Literacy, Language, Identity and Technology in the Deaf/Hard-of-Hearing Collection." In *Stories that Speak to Us*, edited by Lewis H. Ulman, Scott Lloyd DeWitt, and Cynthia L. Selfe. Computers and Composition Digital Press/Utah State University Press. http://ccdigitalpress.org/stories.

Hitt, Allison Harper. 2021. *Rhetorics of Overcoming*. National Council of Teachers of English.

Mirick, Rebecca G., and Stephanie P. Wladkowski. 2018. "Pregnancy, Motherhood, and Academic Career Goals: Doctoral Students' Perspectives." *Affilia* 33 (2): 253–69. doi:10.1177/0886109917753835.

Prikhidko, Alena, and Cliff Haynes. 2018. "Balancing Graduate School and Mothering: Is There a Choice?" *International Journal of Doctoral Studies* 13 (January): 313–26.

SAMHSA. 2019. "SAMHSA's Concept of Trauma and Guidance for a Trauma-Informed Approach." https://www.samhsa.gov/resource/dbhis/samhsas-concept-trauma-guidance-trauma-informed-approach.

Schwartz, Harriet L. 2019. *Connected Teaching: Relationship, Power, and Mattering in Higher Education*. Stylus Publishing, 2019.

3 ▸ BE YOUR BEST ADVOCATE

Prioritizing Self as a Pregnant PhD Student

ELIZABETH M. WILLIAMS

Navigating the normal challenges associated with pregnancy and child-rearing is a difficult task in itself without the added pressures of graduate school. As Driscoll et al. note, "The challenges with self-care, burnout, and associated trauma in graduate school are largely borne out by national survey data on mental health and attrition for doctoral education" (2020, 454). Bearing and raising children while a graduate student undoubtedly exacerbates these concerns, as pregnant and parenting students must also often deal with discrimination and lack of proper accommodations. The academy's inhospitable nature toward mother-scholars is well documented; texts such as *Mama, PhD* describe its "oblivious[ness] to the struggles mothers face within its walls" (Evans and Grant 2008, xxi). And yet starting a family while completing my doctoral degree was exactly what my husband and I decided to do.

In what follows, I relate the story of my pregnancy and the obstacles that I encountered while simultaneously pursuing a PhD in English and working as a graduate teaching assistant. During that time, I also served two years as an assistant writing program administrator for my university's General Education English Program. It is my hope that by sharing my story with others (although it has been a painful reflection for me at times) I can offer some insight to graduate students who are dreaming of pursuing both motherhood and a PhD.

WORLDS COLLIDE

In the fall of 2021, I entered the fourth year of my PhD program pregnant with my first child but feeling ready to tackle the challenges of teaching, dissertating, and growing a human. Don't get me wrong—starting a family during my doctoral degree was certainly not the easiest choice I had ever had to make, but I was confident about my decision. Although many women in academia would agree that the ideal time to have a child is "before age thirty-five and ideally after tenure" (Rose 2020), this wasn't really an option for me, as I was an older returning student who had decided to switch from the accounting industry to study rhetoric and composition and I wasn't getting any younger.

Despite my initial optimism, I quickly learned that I would not be operating business as usual. As a self-described workaholic, I was disappointed to find that I was not able to power through the long hours of reading and researching as I had before. Luckily, I was not making my usual two-hour commute to campus because of pandemic-related accommodations, but I was still experiencing Zoom fatigue and just general exhaustion. The worst aspect, however, was the morning sickness that struck at all hours of the day. Looking back, I regret that I was more focused on my productivity than I was on my own health during this time. I was trying to keep up with the work ethic that had been ingrained in me since I first became a graduate student years before (which if I'm being honest with myself was not sustainable even before I became pregnant), but I regret the level of guilt and shame I felt as a result of tying my self-worth so closely to my productivity.[1]

While I did not want to disclose my pregnancy to the department yet, I felt I needed to be up front with my colleagues in the General Education

English Program as soon as possible because we were Zooming frequently to plan an upcoming graduate teaching assistant orientation and faculty curriculum meeting and I was worried that nausea would creep in and occasionally pull me away from the screen. These highly interactive meetings would also occur via Zoom, and I needed to prepare myself for long days spent sitting in front of my laptop and actively engaging with my peers. In addition to the sickness that affected my productivity I was also worried about my immunocompromised state in light of the ongoing COVID-19 pandemic. This resulted in added stress over how I would manage working and attending on-campus events. Studies indicate that contracting the virus while pregnant increases one's risks of serious illness and pregnancy-related complications, and those weren't risks I wanted to take (National Institutes of Health 2022). Thus, I made the difficult decision to disclose my condition to my superiors in General Education English—something I would not advise graduate students to do unless they feel secure enough in their relationship with their supervisors to do so safely.[2]

I wasn't actually sure how to approach the topic of my pregnancy with my team. I knew that those with children would be understanding, but I was more concerned about the reactions of the others. It felt strange to expose my personal life to my professional one, as I had always worked to keep them neatly delineated from one another. This was a new level of vulnerability that I wasn't completely prepared for, but I decided to send my supervisors in General Education English a brief email explaining my predicament and then waited on pins and needles for their response.[3] Babies and the responsibilities that come with them make some folks uncomfortable—I used to be one of them—and I hoped this decision to disclose during my first trimester would not backfire on me.

Luckily for me, my disclosure was immediately met with heartfelt congratulations by all. Having small children herself, my mentor (who was also serving as one of my supervisors at the time) is the exemplar of what it means to be a badass mother-scholar. In fact, she is part of the reason why I had the courage to take on motherhood at this stage in my career. Having her as a role model reassured me that I could have it all—a career, a family, and an identity outside of both. Undoubtedly, having someone who understood the challenges associated with bearing and raising children in academia was paramount to my success. I was able to negotiate the accommodations I needed with someone who knew how difficult the journey ahead would be and was committed to helping me succeed in both finishing my degree and thriving in my new role. She arranged for me to continue working remotely, which thankfully quashed any worries I had about exposing myself to sickness or spending long hours commuting.

TAKING THE INITIATIVE

Around this same time I began to research my options for maternity leave, as I wasn't sure if there were any rights or accommodations for part-time graduate teaching assistants. Although my supervisors were understanding and flexible, I wasn't sure how I would manage the loss of income or the stall in progress toward completing my degree. No one in the department had ever mentioned anything about a maternity leave policy, so I wanted to find out what my legal options were before broaching the subject of accommodations with administration.[4]

One night as I sat in front of my laptop and exhaustedly Googled the bleak information about maternity leave in the United States, I found a policy for pregnant and parenting students at my university.[5] I couldn't believe my bloodshot eyes. Under the policy, I was permitted up to 180 days of medical leave. As a graduate teaching assistant, I was also excused from my work duties while on leave but still allowed to receive my monthly stipend. The affordances were more than I could have ever hoped for. I fully expected to have about eight weeks of unpaid time off and then a small amount of time left to furiously try to finish my degree while caring for a newborn. Armed with this newfound information, I felt that I had made the right decision to add to my family and thankful that I had taken the time to do my own research into leave policies and accommodations.

When I brought this policy to the attention of the department, surprisingly, no one had heard of it. I thought to myself, *I can't have been the first pregnant student to come through this program.* In fact, I remembered that during my first year as a PhD student one of my classmates had been pregnant. Thinking about how difficult her situation must have been without having knowledge of the leave policy was disheartening. I understood the difficulty in deciding whether or not to disclose the pregnancy, when, and to whom. I couldn't imagine doing so without having the leverage of the leave policy to rely on. If I had not had such a solid relationship with my supervisors, however, perhaps I would have been hesitant to petition for the necessary accommodations, too. Undoubtedly, there had been other women in this same position who felt unable to ask for help, and I felt even more grateful that I had stumbled upon the policy.

Luckily, the graduate advisors in my department were more than accommodating to my needs, and after dotting some *I*'s and crossing some *T*'s with the university, I worked out a plan to complete the current semester and then work up until the point of going into labor the following spring. Thus, I continued to teach, dissertate, and work for the General Education English Program that fall. I kept pushing myself to the limit, always torn between the need to rest and the need to stay ahead of the game.

REALITY CHECK

Unfortunately, things can change unexpectedly when you're expecting. In January 2022, a few weeks before the start of the spring semester, I started to experience increasing pain in my left leg, but I thought that perhaps I had injured myself while working out. I was entering my third trimester and I wasn't exactly what one would describe as limber. One night, as I was drawing myself a lukewarm (not hot, mind you) bath to ease my muscles, I noticed that my leg appeared to be discolored and slightly swollen. My family has a history of blood clotting disorders, so I was immediately alarmed and called my OB-GYN's office. I was sent to the obstetrical emergency room, and after several hours of waiting around and a very brief ultrasound of my leg, I was sent home with the diagnosis of a torn muscle.

I knew my body however, and something wasn't right. Over the next week and a half, I visited my family physician and a chiropractor, in addition to repeatedly calling my OB-GYN's office about the excruciating pain I was experiencing. Eventually, I was unable to stand—let alone walk—because of the pain and swelling in my leg. Through gritted teeth and tears, I remember speaking to a nurse on the phone about my quickly deteriorating state. I told her I was in so much pain that I was no longer able to get around on my own to which she responded, "Bless your heart." I was dumbfounded by her callous response and hung up the phone feeling even more defeated than before. As I can personally attest, dismissal of pain and unconscious gender bias are unfortunately still prevalent aspects of women's healthcare (Katz Institute for Women's Health 2022).

Even though no medical professionals took my pleas for help seriously, I continued to voice my concerns to anyone who would listen. Finally at my own request and almost two weeks after my original trip to the emergency room, I was recommended to a physical therapist for help with my pain. At this point, I had to use a walker to get around, but I was determined to find some sort of relief. After spending just a few minutes assessing me, the physical therapist knew something was extremely wrong. After I hobbled out of her office, she immediately called my OB-GYN. I was again sent to the emergency room where I was diagnosed with an "expansive" blood clot in my leg that had been accumulating over the past weeks. After spending a few days in the hospital, I was sent home with a little box of Lovenox injections and orders to rest and recover.

What had previously been a normal, healthy pregnancy was now deemed high risk for both myself and my unborn daughter. Thus, I found myself unable to work and desperately needing a break from the demands of teaching and dissertating. Thankfully, I remembered that the university policy allotted 180 days of medical leave, and it dawned on me that I could start my leave now and still have plenty of time off to spend with my baby once she arrived before returning to work in the fall. While it was a difficult decision for me to leave work and my responsibilities earlier than I had planned, it was clearly the right choice. And it was also a choice I would not have made as easily—even with my health scare—if I had not known about the parental leave policy.

REFLECTIONS FROM A MOTHER-SCHOLAR

Looking back, I regret those initial feelings of hesitation and disappointment regarding my choice to start my leave early, as my life literally depended on it. I was too concerned about the impact my absence would have on my colleagues in General Education English and my standing in the program when I should have been more concerned about my own health. Looking now at my daughter's sweet face, I would make the same decision to leave a thousand times over—this time without any hesitation at all. She has changed my perspective on having a healthier work-life balance and I am a happier version of myself because of her.

I completed my degree in the spring of 2023, but if I had not taken the initiative to find out what my leave options were as a pregnant student, I'm not sure that I would have ever made it back to the academy. I am forever grateful for having secured my medical leave and the approval and understanding of my department early in my pregnancy; otherwise, I would have been left floundering in the middle of a serious health crisis, trying to make difficult decisions I was in no condition to make. I hope that by reflecting on my experiences over the past two years I can help other graduate students feel better prepared to traverse the intersections of childbearing and working toward a doctoral degree. For those who are considering becoming pregnant while PhD-ing, I have boiled down the knowledge gleaned from my experiences into the following pieces of advice. I hope my reflections provide a little more confidence to those contemplating motherhood in addition to professorhood:

- Take the initiative to research your university's parental leave policy before becoming pregnant (if possible).
  - If you can't locate a policy, reach out to your Title IX coordinator as soon as possible for help.
- Advocate for the accommodations you need to manage your workload while pregnant.
  - Along with your Title IX office, the website The Pregnant Scholar is a great place for pregnant and parenting students to learn about their rights to accommodations.
- Cultivate relationships with mentors who have experience raising children while working in academia.
  - These are your people. Find them early during your program and lean on them for support and guidance.
- Prioritize your health and your child's health over your productivity.
  - It's the norm in graduate school for students to "shrug away their own self-care because of the 'always-on-mindset,'" but it's more important now than ever to prioritize your physical and mental well-being (Driscoll et al. 2020, 460).
- Make informed decisions about when and to whom to disclose your pregnancy.
  - Disclosure is an extremely personal choice and dependent upon your own circumstances, but there are online resources to help guide your decision.

NOTES

1. As many graduate students and other contingent faculty can attest, this prioritization of productivity over well-being often results in burnout. Scholars in rhetoric and writing studies have "long taken note of the burnout that happens surrounding the everyday labor of our field, particularly in writing instruction and writing program administration" (Driscoll et al. 2020, 455).
2. I encourage discretion because although employers are not legally allowed to discriminate based on pregnancy, it still happens. In "Scholar, Negated," Jessica Smartt Gullion (2008) presents a common workplace scenario in which pregnant women's ability to produce quality work is unfairly questioned.

3. Since I had been working remotely and had a strong relationship with my team, an email felt like the appropriate mode of communication. However, other circumstances may warrant an in-person meeting to deliver the news (although I typically prefer to let others have time to digest weighty information before requiring a response).
4. I did not discover this resource until after my pregnancy, but the website The Pregnant Scholar contains helpful information for students, faculty, and administrators regarding Title IX and support for pregnant and parenting students.
5. See MTSU Policy 321 Educational Adjustment for Pregnant and Parenting Students.

WORKS CITED

Driscoll, Dana Lynn, S. Rebecca Leigh, and Nadia Francine Zamin. 2020. "Self-Care as Professionalization: A Case for Ethical Doctoral Education in Composition Studies." *College Composition and Communication* 71, no. 3: 453–80.

Evans, Elrena, and Caroline Grant. 2008. Introduction. In *Mama, PhD: Women Write about Motherhood and Academic Life,* edited by Elrena Evans and Caroline Grant, xvii–xxv. Rutgers University Press.Gullion, Jessica Smartt. 2008. "Scholar, Negated." In *Mama, PhD: Women Write about Motherhood and Academic Life,* edited by Elrena Evans and Caroline Grant, 16–19. Rutgers University Press.

Katz Institute for Women's Health. 2022. "Gaslighting in Women's Health: No, It's Not Just in Your Head." Northwell Health. www.northwell.edu/katz-institute-for-womens-health/articles/gaslighting-in-womens-health.

National Institutes of Health. 2022. "NIH-Funded Study Suggests COVID-19 Increases Risk of Pregnancy Complications." National Institutes of Health, February 7. www.nih.gov/news-events/news-releases/nih-funded-study-suggests-covid-19-increases-risk-pregnancy-complications.

Rose, Jeanne Marie. 2020. "Mother-Scholars Doing Their Homework: The Limits of Domestic Enargeia." *Peitho* 22, no. 2. cfshrc.org/article/mother-scholars-doing-their-homework-the-limits-of-domestic-enargeia/.

RESOURCES

MTSU Policy 321: Educational Adjustment for Pregnant and Parenting Students. Middle Tennessee State University, Reviewed December 2024, www.mtsu.edu/policies/p321/

The Pregnant Scholar. thepregnantscholar.org/.

4 ▸ THIS TOO SHALL PASS

Strategies for Mothering While Studying as a Distance-Learning Graduate Student

ELISE A. GREEN

Disclaimer: This chapter discusses pregnancy loss.

I WAS TWENTY-EIGHT YEARS OLD and at my annual gynecology exam. My doctor of five years knew I was teaching full time and applying to doctoral programs in English and she knew my ambition to be a mother. As I sat up from the stirrups, she remarked, "Elise, I know you're really focused on your career, but if you want to have children, you shouldn't wait too much longer to start." Her comment lingered as she left the room, and the physical helplessness I had experienced during the exam was replaced with an emotional helplessness.

The doctor wasn't wrong, but she also didn't tell me anything I didn't already know. When my husband and I married four years earlier, we chose not to have children right away. I was still in college and he was working hard to advance in his field. So we mapped out our future: get married, finish school, get a promotion, buy a house, and then grow our family. In our youth and naiveté, we assumed that everything would happen according to our plan. And everything eventually did. But not in that order and not without many unanticipated trials and heartaches.

I approached school and life as though it would all happen on my time and on my terms. I didn't know it would take me three years to get into a PhD program. I didn't expect the trial of a miscarriage while in the middle of coursework. I didn't foresee that mothering and wife-ing and PhDing all at the same time would fracture me as a person and limit the mental, emotional, and physical investments I could make—that I wanted to make—in each area. Each relationship. And yet, through the challenges of young motherhood, emotional grieving and physical healing from pregnancy loss, and complex graduate coursework, I endured. With much resilience and grit, I earned my PhD.

In this chapter, I will describe the strategies I used to ensure my productivity and sanity while pursuing a doctoral degree during some unanticipated, life-changing events. Your story might intersect with mine in few or in many ways. I recognize that my experiences are not the same as those of others, but it is my hope that in sharing some small lessons I learned, someone else might enjoy great benefits.

STRATEGY #1: I WORKED WHEN I COULD AND I NAPPED WHEN I COULD

After three years of trying, I was finally accepted into my graduate program in March 2016, right around the time my husband and I planned to get pregnant. We were fortunate—and shocked—to conceive right away. As a new student, I chose not to share this news with any of my professors because I was afraid of being dismissed as not serious about my studies and my career. I completed summer and fall classes without too much trouble while also teaching full time as a non-tenure-track lecturer. Of course, I told my department chair that I was expecting in December, and because of a generous maternity leave policy, I enjoyed the spring semester off from teaching. This affordance allowed me to continue coursework while staying home with my baby.

My daughter was four weeks old when the spring 2017 semester began, and her sleep schedule was completely backward. Though I tried to keep her up during the day, she would inevitably fall asleep and then be awake all night. Well-meaning mothers and friends would encourage me to keep working toward getting her to sleep at night. This advice was not helpful in my world as a graduate student and a new mom. I was losing valuable time during the day to try to keep the baby awake when I could be sleeping. As a result, I abandoned a traditional sleep schedule and decided to use the midnight hours to be productive. I napped during the day when she slept.

I also want to note that when my beloved daughter was between two and twelve weeks old, she cried nonstop whenever she was awake and not being held. I'm not exaggerating—every time I put her down, she screamed. So in order for me to get work done while she was awake, I typed my papers with one hand while holding her in my other arm. I suppose this skill came from the inexplicable patience mothers have for their little ones; my friends without children thought I was nuts and my husband thought I was spoiling our daughter. I didn't entirely disagree. But if holding her kept her hushed so I could work, then that's what I had to do. Looking back, I don't regret this time. Though I was greatly challenged, the memory of holding my first newborn while researching and writing is, I think, more precious than any alternative.

All that said, sleeping while the baby is sleeping is easier to do when you only have one child and don't have to be in the office. When I returned to full-time teaching in August 2017, I packed a travel pillow and a blanket and would take a fifteen- to twenty-minute nap in my office each day before I left, setting the alarm on my phone to ensure that I woke up. By then, the baby was sleeping longer stretches at night but still not all the way through. A brief rest gave me just enough energy to get through the evening hours of classes and studying until I had the opportunity to take another nap.

STRATEGY #2: I ACCEPTED THAT B'S MAKE DEGREES

While I kept up with my assignments by working at night, my participation in class was severely lacking—somewhat on purpose. The coursework for my doctoral program was mostly conducted via online synchronous meetings through WebEx on weeknights between 4:00 and 10:00 P.M. Although our classes were not face to face, we were expected to participate orally in class discussions. I understood this expectation and as an educator myself I appreciated it. But I was also very conflicted about it. I had always been a high-achieving student, but an A-level standard for participation was not entirely achievable for me during this season of my life. I wanted to be engaged in discussion and earn the respect of my instructors and peers, but I struggled to function separately from my baby.

In addition to the mental and emotional consequences I was navigating in my new role as a mother-scholar, I often experienced physical, logistical challenges in juggling my daughter and the unmute option on the WebEx interface. At any given time, I might have been nursing or pumping or changing a dirty diaper below the frame of the camera. Volunteering thoughtful responses to assigned readings felt somewhat inconsequential, given the other obligations I was negotiating. I would try to add comments in the chat as a means to supplement my lack of vocal engagement, but I was slower in responding than everyone else and I never felt my contributions were as substantial or as meaningful as those made by my colleagues.

Ultimately, my grade at the end of the semester reflected my lack of participation. I attended class regularly and I submitted my work on time. I asked the professor questions when needed and was an equal contributor on collaborative projects. Yet I could only do so much, and for my own well-being, I made the choice to be okay with the consequences of not engaging with class discussions. Given my circumstances, I decided that a couple of B's would not disqualify me from earning my PhD nor would they define my long-term professional success.

STRATEGY #3: I CHOSE TO PRESS FORWARD

December 2017 came quickly, and in addition to dealing with the typical end-of-semester demands, we were preparing for my daughter's first birthday celebration. Between that and the approaching holiday season, I wasn't paying attention to my menstrual cycle. It occurred to me one day that I was over a week late. With an anxious feeling in my gut, I took an expired pregnancy test that I had dug out from under the bathroom sink. The result was positive. In a bit of a panic, I rushed to the drugstore to purchase an unexpired test. The result was positive again.

I was immediately nervous. Another pregnancy this soon was entirely unplanned. I was barely keeping myself afloat as a full-time student, lecturer, wife, and mommy. My husband, however, was immediately excited. His response was encouraging to me, yet in addition to my uncertainty about how I would navigate this next chapter of my life, I felt unsettled about the pregnancy in general. I can't name why. I just sincerely felt as though something was off. Wanting to see my OB-GYN right away, I called and learned that I couldn't get an appointment until I was at least twelve weeks along.

At ten weeks pregnant, I began to see an occasional light pink discharge. Over the next few days, it became heavier and darker, and eventually, extremely painful. It was a Sunday evening, but I was able to reach my OB-GYN through an emergency line. In between phone calls, I was changing maxi pads every ten to twenty minutes and rocking back and forth on the floor as I experienced unrelenting contractions. After about eight hours, the pain subsided. A visit to the doctor the next day confirmed that I had had a miscarriage. I'll never forget seeing my empty womb on the monitor during the exam. As the nurse left the room, she said, "I'm so sorry for your loss." I didn't have a response for her. I struggled to reconcile the fact that I wasn't overjoyed about the pregnancy in the first place and now I had lost it.

Although I was no longer pregnant, I bled for several weeks. In the meantime, spring 2018 courses started and assignments resumed. I tried to participate in class conversation and continue working on projects, but at this point, my contributions and research just felt forced and disingenuous. Every visit to the bathroom reminded me of the loss of a child. I was sad, and I was falling behind in my courses very early in the semester.

I felt alone during this time. In all my planning, I never planned for a miscarriage. I didn't know who to turn to for personal help and felt certain that a distance-learning professor would be able to offer only limited help. I looked for late policies in the course syllabi, which felt ridiculous. I had never submitted past-due work before, and an empty pit grew in my stomach as I considered doing it now. *I can't ask for an extension or share this with a professor. They expect professionalism. I'll draw negative attention,* I said to myself. I assumed that graduate faculty would not take me seriously if I asked for additional time. *I need to just tough this out,* I thought.

And that's what I quietly did for another two weeks, when I finally confided in one professor—also a mother—I was taking a course with that spring. Her response was kind and understanding and she encouraged me to press forward. Her positive remarks were what I needed, and I wished I had communicated with her sooner than I had. The bleeding finally stopped, and one assignment at a time, I caught up on my work. Emotionally, though, I was far from being healed.

STRATEGY #4: I WAS PERSISTENT EVEN WHEN I FELT LIKE AN IMPOSTER

Two months passed and I became pregnant—unexpectedly, again—in late March 2018. I continued my practice of napping at all hours of the day and night, both at home and at work while my one-year-old daughter napped, and my participation in class still wasn't stellar. In contrast, many of my peers seemed well rested and able to cite any scholar at will. Through this time, I began questioning whether or not I belonged in a graduate program. I was the only person in my cohort who was in a child-bearing season, and frankly I felt quite inadequate in most of my classes. My head was filled with worries of pumping and nursing and napping schedules. I was consumed by constant questions about cradle cap, colic, baby acne, diaper rashes, and was I drinking enough water?! But aside from all my motherly concerns, as a student—the first one in my family to graduate high school, let alone attend college—I have always felt I had to work harder than my peers to understand and apply course content. I have continuously worked hard in my process, and while my products have consistently been good quality, they have rarely been acknowledged as exceptional. Now, at the doctoral level, I felt ignorant as I listened to my classmates' astute interpretations of the assigned readings, how they intersected with other scholars and fields of study, and how those conclusions informed current research. My peers were amazing, and I was intimidated.

I always thought I would feel empowered through earning a PhD, but as I navigated it alongside motherhood, I instead questioned why I wanted to pursue advanced study in the first place. *Is teaching college English what I really want to do?* I asked myself. My academic life and personal life felt so separate as I realized that the research conversation would advance with or without me. I felt more like an imposter than ever and was battling the ugly beast of comparison.

Although I felt supremely ignorant, I was bullheaded and wanted to prove that I could finish the degree. I pushed forward and mapped out all my deadlines through the end of the year on a calendar and decided that instead of looking at the entire mountain of work ahead of me, I would take just one project at a time. Focusing only on a given week's to-do list kept me from panicking.

In October 2018, I was nearly eight months pregnant while also parenting a twenty-two-month-old toddler when I took my candidacy exams. To say I was relieved when I completed them is an understatement, not only because it was a massive burden off my shoulders but also because that marked the end of my coursework. I carried the baby to term, delivering him in December 2018, and I wrote and defended my prospectus the following June. Later, I would become the second person in my cohort to successfully defend the dissertation—second to another working mom. We had previously met on campus during a summer residency that was a required element of our program. After her dissertation defense, I was so excited for her accomplishment, I emailed to say congratulations, and asked, "How did you do it?"

She shared, "I had to just get it done. My family needed me back. We could not sustain the way we were going."

I knew exactly what she meant. Her words captured so many of the struggles I had endured through my doctoral journey to that point, and seeing her resolve was a great source of encouragement to me. Although I did not enter a PhD program for the sole purpose of completing the degree, the allure of having graduate school out of my and my family's life became the motivation for finishing.

FINAL THOUGHTS

Today, people sometimes ask if I have children. "I do!" I reply enthusiastically. "I have two." I then proceed by bragging about "my babies," as I call them. Non-academic friends ooh and aah at how I persisted through a doctoral program while growing a family. What they don't know, and what I don't talk about, is the physical and emotional turmoil I experienced through the process.

In my more critical moments, I do not find my stubborn nature to persist impressive at all. Although my PhD is finished, I fumbled my way through much of the program, feeling as though it took me away from my family, and in return, my family took me away from it. Cobos, Hocutt, and McKittrick, fellow contributors to this collection, conclude their chapter by naming the ways in which they are remarkable parents. As I read their accounts and others, I realize how so many of us former PhD students were deeply, personally challenged during our programs. So instead of focusing on my struggles and regrets, I too end on a note that celebrates my strengths and accomplishments:

> I am resilient. Although the intersection of life and school was at times nearly unbearable, I not only finished the degree, I also experienced three pregnancies and birthed two children while journeying through coursework, candidacy exams, writing and defending a prospectus, and writing and defending a dissertation.

> I am not alone. The completion of my PhD was a milestone achievement, and as much as I felt the process took me away from my family, in the end, I learned to appreciate them much more. I realized their sacrifice on my behalf because of their love for me, and now we enjoy the privilege of growing together without the burden of school hanging over our heads.
>
> I am an awesome mom. Now a tenure-track English professor, I have set an example for my children that shows they can do anything they put their mind to.

I still have a stack of diapers from a baby shower that friends had written words of advice on. The intent was that during midnight diaper changes, I would be encouraged with their words of wisdom. One reads, "This too shall pass." When I had a miscarriage, my professor's guidance reminded me that trials are temporary and that although I was experiencing a devastating life event, I could choose the path forward that I would take. This perspective is applicable for the student as well: PhD school is not permanent, although it sometimes feels as if it will never end. And while the wisdom might be uncomfortable, it is true that everything always gets done.

5 ▸ JUST BE OKAY

A Reflection on Pandemic Parenting, Burnout, and Healing

EMILY GRESBRINK

TUESDAY, FEBRUARY 22, 2022, 8:30 P.M. You're parenting alone for the night. While your partner works his second job, you're sitting on the couch, hoping to get some semblance of work done. For whatever reason, your house-trained dog decides to pee on the floor. The TV is too loud. Your kids are bickering over personal space, forgetting that you asked them to feed the pets or rinse off sticky pasta dishes, even though they clearly rolled eyes and exhaled sharply at a simple request. *Can one of you take out the trash, please? I could use the help.*

An hour later, the cat still screams for food, the pasta dishes are unrinsed, and the trash hasn't moved. You asked for help because you've been parenting all day and haven't finished your grad school to-do list in days.

The stack of projects from an advanced writing course needs grading. *Sorry, students.*

Your dissertation? *Sorry, committee.*

Oh, and the scholarship app and call for papers? Next week, maybe. Did you respond to comments for your advocacy team report? Whoops, do that quickly . . . but not too quickly since it affects thousands of students. *Focus, focus . . .*

Nope, someone's down here asking about what's for lunch next week. *Focus, focus . . .*

The pets need food. The trash needs to go. *Could I get some help, please? I asked an hour ago.*

Oh, god, your work project is coming up soon too. Gotta finish those revisions to your writing, too. Did that dog pee get cleaned up? Gotta clean that up. *Where is that enzyme spray?*

While hunched over the rug, thoughts float in and out of your head. Dissertation, project, grading, keeping kids alive, laundry, dishes, taking kids to Scouts, did you even submit that draft to your advisor? *Oops.*

Then there's the perpetual elephant in the room: There was a COVID-19 exposure in your kid's class. Right. We're vaccinated. Anyone could still die from *that.* You constantly hear people calling it "the flu" and saying, "Masks in our restaurant? No, we're good." *Gotta swab everyone . . .*

But being overwhelmed needs to take a back seat. That dog pee needs cleaning up. That trash never got taken out. The cat is still screaming for pâté. There's work to do.

If you're lucky, you'll get to bed before midnight, only to start at 6:30 A.M. tomorrow.

PANDEMIC-ING, PHDING, AND PARENTING

That scenario is a typical weeknight for me. Most evenings are a hectic, stressful time. Anyone parenting, doing school, and living through the pandemic would experience some degree of stress. I'd be remiss if I didn't acknowledge that that was a standard scenario for many parents.

I'll start by saying that my partner and I co-parent his two kids, who, as of this writing, are thirteen and ten. Wholeheartedly, I consider them my kids. I've been co-parenting since April 2018, when we had them every other weekend. To me, having the kids around, even for a few days a month, still counts as being a whole parent. I loved them (and still do). We always had a fun time together. We learned and explored together. We fought and cried. We did holidays, birthdays, and vacations—all of it. We were a family, even if we weren't physically together all the time. And yes, I wanted kids. My partner and I had talked about and anticipated the day when the kids might come to us full time and what that could look like: we'd be ready to go, with lots of planning involved. And both of us knew well before their arrival that full-time physical custody is a different level of parenting and involvement. When I relocated to Minneapolis to finish work on my master's degree, my partner came along. The weekend schedule stayed the same: we had them every other weekend, but now in a different city, a few hours away from the kids. Everything was in a good holding pattern. Then it switched: the kids moved in with us full time in March 2020.

That hypothetical moment of becoming a full-time parent became a reality when the coronavirus arrived at the beginning of my PhD program. The kids moved in with us full time the same week my institution closed in March 2020. The kids' move-in was in response to their school closing and their mom's work schedule. In retrospect, I did not think that becoming a full-time parent would be a decision I would make in twenty-four hours or fewer. But to me, it wasn't a decision. It was the only thing to do; no questions asked.

But parenting during a new-onset pandemic, quarantined in the same space together, was an immense change. It was a chaotic blur. Every day for me lasted twelve to fourteen hours, during which I switched between the roles of parent, student, and pandemic threat monitor at a moment's notice. My partner was an essential worker and the kids' mom was ninety miles away, so I immediately took on the responsibilities of co-parent, tutor, homemaker, distance learner, and student-teacher in hours.

Living in three concurrent, stressful realities is a lot, and that's putting it lightly. As a doctoral candidate, I am asked to do so much. We all are tasked with professional development, research, coursework, teaching, examinations, dissertations, conferences, and so on. And that also doesn't include the unwitnessed, frequently unpaid labor we perform: the emotional parts, the social parts, and working through those red-tape scenarios.

The same could be said for parenting and living through a pandemic. I was asked to do so much: adapting, changing, surviving, from minute to hour to day. There was unpaid and unwitnessed work across these realities. But the thing about living in multiple realities is that it's possible. Three realities separately require immeasurable mental, physical, and emotional labor, but in tandem these realities ask so much of parent-scholars, putting us at risk of burnout and mental health struggles. And for me, burnout was a perceptible threat and an eventual reality. I know I was not alone in this feeling.

THE PRIMAL SCREAM AND PARENTAL BURNOUT

As I worked through this complex lived reality, I turned to reading stories and hearing other parents' experiences. During the early phases of COVID-19, "The Primal Scream" (Grose et al. 2021), an interactive project at the *New York Times,* powerfully demonstrated the emotional turmoil and burnout experienced by parents. Part of the project is a phone line meant for parents to call in and "scream" about parenting during the pandemic. It encouraged parents to call the number and complain, unload their feelings, cry, yell, or just talk. One caller into The Primal Scream line, labeled as Mom 11, spoke through tears on the recorded line: "This pandemic has made me realize that maybe I'm not cut out to be a mother. I love my kids, but I don't like being a mom. And I don't like being a mom in America, because it's just so much more clear that America hates women and hates families. We don't have support. Moms are not heroes. And this is just so hard, so hard." Mom 2 gave an equally direct if not slightly funny, candid call-in: "Hello, *New York Times.* I'm calling you from the toilet. Because I literally just had to say to my kids, "I'm going to pee. Leave me alone!" (Barbaro 2021).

In a series of interviews collected over time, mom Elizabeth Halfhill was featured in a piece by Michael Barbaro for "The Daily," in conjunction with "The Primal Scream" project. Halfhill's experience, like others, echoed themes of frustration, discomfort, and a lack of preparedness for filling the roles of parent, teacher, and at-home caregiver all at once: "I would like to let it be known for the record that I am not a homeschooler. I never wanted to homeschool. I always put my kid in school. This isn't me. It ain't me. I'm doing my best, but this is not my frickin' talent. This is not my talent space, OK? Not me. I'm a great mom and I'm good at momming, but I'm not good at educating" (Barbaro 2021).

I listened to this project when it was first published in the *New York Times.* Honestly, I still think about this project years after its conclusion. The calls into the line were deeply visceral and honest. In many ways, those calls spoke into existence feelings that I couldn't share myself but that others figured out how to do in an act of cathartic release. Halfhill and the parents who called in were expressing vulnerable emotions. You can hear it in their voices. While sometimes humorous and honest in content, those calls unveiled feelings of real pain and stress. While hiding in the bathroom from your kids is sort of funny, the feeling of hiding in the bathroom is different. I know why that mom was hiding in the bathroom; she needed a break and that's the most private place in the house. That shower was a respite and her phone was a lifeline.

I felt those calls from "The Primal Scream" project: it was the feeling of anger over having to homeschool with minimal tools or support. It was the feeling of frustration over a rapid-onset pandemic and having to juggle all the balls in the world to keep everything together. I knew that feeling, and hearing others put the feeling into words was a punch in the gut. I still feel it, albeit not as hard, in this upcoming change of my life: as I finish my PhD, as the pandemic's quarantine phase becomes a memory as I walk past bedrooms where the kids once learned online for over a year. I remember the diffuse boundaries and how precious silence became and remains to me. I remember how much I took on in 2020 and how much I took on every day as a co-parent. Everything has changed, yet nothing has changed in many ways. I want to forget it, I want to move on from the stress. But the ghosts of 2020 linger. They probably always will.

Listening to the parents who called into "The Primal Scream" project makes me think about how parents, particularly women, felt stress during the COVID-19 pandemic so intensely. This seems unsurprising, given the fact that the uneven distribution of gendered work-life roles is not new. Amanda Barroso and Juliana Menasce Horowitz (2021) have explained that before the pandemic, working mothers surveyed by the Pew Research Center were more likely than fathers to claim that being a working parent made it harder for them to advance in their career; over 25 percent of mothers said they were treated as if work wasn't a priority or as if they were uncommitted.

Besides the anecdotal evidence, a survey of 3,000 Canadian parents conducted in 2021 found 44.3 percent of parents with children eighteen or younger at home reported worse mental health as a result of the pandemic. The research team, led by mental health researchers Anne Gadermann and her colleagues (2021), reported that "among parents with children at home, deteriorated mental health was significantly more prevalent among women, parents under age 35, parents with a pre-existing mental health condition, parents with a disability, parents of younger children (≤ 4 years) and parents reporting financial stress" (5).

It is worth noting that the pandemic affected those in multiply marginalized groups financially, socially, and mentally, and those doing academic work are in this category. Bender and colleagues published an article in *Family Relations* about academic moms (that is, faculty and students) navigating parenting, higher education, and their experience during the pandemic as it related to their scholarly work. The study found that many survey participants had to shift to at-home childcare and address all of their children's needs (Bender et al. 2022, 55), which led to a diminished engagement in academic work and an increase in negative emotions. Research participants described "feelings of anxiety, exhaustion, frustration, depression, guilt, and resentment" relate to attending to familial needs and academic needs simultaneously (58). In March 2022, the journal *Women's Studies in Communication* released a special issue titled "Collective Rage: Unpacking the Constraints, Privilege, and Roles of Academic Mothers During a Global Pandemic." Sarah Jane Blithe's introduction to the issue she spoke of both motherhood and academia as greedy institutions whose demands often leave academia moms feeling overwhelmed and scrambling for time (Blithe 2022, 4; see also Ward and Wolf-Wendel 2012). The concept of a greedy institution reminded me of what another caller from "The Primal Scream Project" said: "So, I'm a single mom in the pandemic. And I'm a teacher, so I feel like single mothers and teachers—and mothers in general—all take on more than they can. And so, I have like three strikes against me, and it's just impossible" (Barbaro 2021). I remember hearing this caller and thinking, "Wow, they're onto something. Impossible is right." I was constantly keyed up and extraordinarily on edge during the early phases of COVID-19. I was always surveilling areas for appropriately masked folks, keeping hands clean, and testing regularly—for myself and my family. I was thrust into the role of a teacher of two kids but I am not a K-12 educator (and seriously, to those who are, thank you/bless you). Sometimes I felt like no one was having a fun time. Sometimes, I felt like a garbage co-parent and guardian.

I still think about all the parents out there who felt (or still feel) this way and wonder how many more primal screams went unheard. Even today, I still have deep, gut-punchy feelings about the greedy institutions Sarah Jane Blithe described: parenthood, academia, and COVID-19 anxiety take and take but leave nothing left for me. I still occupy this body, this mind, this being: and this body is tired. I know my kids are tired. I know we're all just . . . tired

At this point, a primal scream sounds excellent.

A TIME FOR HEALING

As I write, it's 2023, and I think it's fair to say that parents are still shaken up. I've got a bad case of burnout that I'm working through with the co-care of my partner, a therapist, and a few supportive colleagues. I eventually concluded that I needed to speak with someone to help sort out the complex thoughts that were bogging me down. I felt stuck and frustrated by my new role as a parent, the stressors of being a student, and the consistent doom of the pandemic. I could only do so much on my own before I needed to talk to someone else who was trained to help. I encourage others to do the same if things start to feel too heavy and too much; there are folks out there to help you heal and recover from those feelings of nothingness.

Life seems to be moving into endemic phases in most senses of the word: COVID-19 is part of the woodwork (albeit still scary and a real threat), I've obtained candidacy in my program, and we're figuring out what it means to be a family of four. The kids are back in school in person and doing better. Chaotic Tuesdays, like those described earlier, are still a thing. Our routines are still shaken up now and again, but mostly we are a typical family brought together by a strange, wild exigence.

I am better.

But getting better took work, so I want to pass along two things that helped me immensely in my healing. They were pivotal to my journey in addressing burnout and I still lean into them a lot when I'm feeling sour or upset. First, I looked for moments of happiness. Amid all the stress, piles of work, and everything that stacks up during a global pandemic, sometimes we forget to soak in the moments or things that make us feel good. I found that taking a nap or sitting in the car by myself for a few extra minutes really did make a difference. I went out for sushi or coffee with a friend. Sometimes, I took the day (or days) off from writing. For me, the smallest joys were a necessary catharsis and a remedy for burnout.

Second, I found a way to express tough emotions so they wouldn't push my burnout, stress, or anxiety farther into the danger zone. In other words, I found a way to speak about big feelings that was refreshing and genuine. The goal for me was—and remains—to restore, not deplete. So often, we hear, "Just talk about it over brunch." Not to hate on brunch, but sometimes that doesn't work. Sometimes therapy is the right move. Sometimes disconnecting from people is right. Sometimes movement feels good. Sometimes combinations of these things feel right. Sometimes a parent group chat needs to hear you out or you take time to hear them out. But the critical part that I've found is that it doesn't work if it makes you feel worse. If you're unable to do your daily tasks or you're irritable to the point where others are calling you on it or you feel very down for more than a week or two, it might be time to call in the pros. And that's okay. Taking care of yourself is vital. You deserve the best, and so does your family.

MAY 26, 2023, 11:50 P.M.

You're lying in a tent in the middle of the woods. You hear the sound of crickets, frogs, and a gentle early summer breeze that brushes the nylon walls around you. You hear the fire crackle nearby as your family roasts s'mores and giggles about the coming weekend. You're just a little too tired to eat; the moment alone in the tent is well warranted and needed.

As the sounds of the Minnesota Northwoods fill the tent, your breathing steadies. It's the first time in a long time you've been able to tune into your breathing consciously and mindfully You realize that you've finally caught your breath. And as you lay there, you begin to wax poetic—as one does—about the past:

We've been through it, huh?

We sure have. But this moment, this stillness, this moment of joy is needed. It's what makes the grind and burnout start to feel like a distant memory.

You are happy.

You know that working to recover from burnout is an ongoing project of recovery and healing. You may not know what you're doing when it comes to being a parent, being a student, and living in a pandemic, but it'll be mostly okay. And you're okay with being okay, and okay is what it must be for the sake of your projects, health, and—of course—your family.

There is no need to scream into the void for now.

It's okay just to be okay.

WORKS CITED

Barbaro, Michael. 2021. "The Agony of Pandemic Parenting." *New York Times*, April 6. https://www.nytimes.com/2021/04/16/podcasts/the-daily/parenting-covid-pandemic.html?showTranscript=1.

Barroso, Amanda, and Juliana Menasce Horowitz. 2021. "The Pandemic Has Highlighted Many Challenges for Mothers, but They Aren't Necessarily New." Pew Research Center, March 17. https://www.pewresearch.org/fact-tank/2021/03/17

/the-pandemic-has-highlighted-many-challenges-for-mothers-but-they-arent-necessarily-new/.

Bender, Sara, Kristina S. Brown, Deanna L. Hensley Kasitz, and Olga Vega. 2022. "Academic Women and Their Children: Parenting during COVID-19 and the Impact on Scholarly Productivity." *Family Relations* 71 (1): 46–67.

Blithe, Sarah Jane. 2022. "Collective Rage: Unpacking the Constraints, Privilege, and Roles of Academic Mothers During a Global Pandemic." *Women's Studies in Communication* 45 (1): 1–9.

Gadermann, Anne C., Kimberly C. Thomson, Chris G. Richardson, Monique Gagné, Corey McAuliffe, Saima Hirani, and Emily Jenkins. 2021. "Examining the Impacts of the COVID-19 Pandemic on Family Mental Health in Canada: Findings from a National Cross-Sectional Study." *BMJ Open* 11 (1). https://bmjopen.bmj.com/content/11/1/e042871.

Grose, Jessica, Jessica Bennett, Melonyce McAfee, Farah Miller, Sharon Attia, and Dani Blum. 2021. "The Primal Scream: America's Mothers Are in Crisis." *New York Times*, February 4. https://www.nytimes.com/interactive/2021/02/04/parenting/working-moms-coronavirus.html.

Ward, Kelly, and Lisa Wolf-Wendel. 2012. *Academic Motherhood: How Faculty Manage Work and Family*. Rutgers University Press.

6 ▸ KEEP A LABOR LOG

Analyzing Master Narratives about Time and Toxic Work Culture

KEITH JACKSON

I AM A FATHER of three children, aged nine, seven, and two. One son and two daughters. Being a father is one of the best things to ever happen to me. It's also one of the most challenging. But fathering isn't the only role that makes up my identity. I'm also a first-generation college student and I'll be completing my PhD in my mid-thirties. If you are reading this book, you are likely in a similar situation, traversing the tumultuous and exclusionary waters of academia. If you're reading this book, you likely have children or are expecting to soon. This chapter has a dual purpose: to help parenting graduate students avoid the same pitfalls I encountered throughout my graduate career and provide a frank discussion of the exploitation you'll encounter, especially how that exploitation looks to parenting graduate workers. In sharing my experiences and advice, I hope to illuminate the often nuanced and complicated relationship between our academic work and our private lives.

Whether you are a seasoned or a lively new graduate student, it's a safe bet that much of your time is spent managing labor and doing "all the things." More specifically, you're managing how to balance your academic labor with the other types of labor in your life. I found it important to name and critically examine the roles and identities I embody that vie for my time and effort. For example, the roles I often balance and navigate are that of father, teacher, husband, friend, researcher, assistant director, and committee member, just to name a few. And these roles all act like gravitational poles, tugging me in various directions. Each pole tugs and drags, but occasionally a specific role is more taxing than the rest, particularly parenting or caretaking. For example, if my children are sick, my role as father demands that I spend much more time, energy, and labor caring for them. Eventually, you will have to reckon with the weight, priority, and required resiliency of each of the roles you embody, or you will risk burning out.

Parenting while attaining a graduate degree has been a battle of balancing roles, relationships, and my mental health capacities. It's also been isolating, since so much of parenting, and care work is behind the scenes, invisible, and undervalued. We can't control what or who demands our attention. There will always be something or someone that needs our attention. This labor builds and builds if we let it. For those of us who are juggling roles as caretakers, teachers, students, and workers, it is important to try to build healthy boundaries within our work. Despite what some advisors expect, our work in academia is a job and it can't be more important than our children or personal lives. You're tempting burnout in that scenario since we are meant to experience life, not work through every waking minute of it. This mindset can be quite hard to shake and in fact very difficult to avoid in a work environment that emphasizes individual excellence and rigor.

The first section in this chapter is a discussion of the hardest aspect of parenting while earning a graduate degree: the art of balancing the many, many roles you will adapt to, foster, and embody. I'll walk through how to balance your work and what I recommend for tracking the labor and time you spend working. I think that once there is an honest understanding about your work, you can better speak out about your experiences. Doing so will help shine light on the toxic work culture that neoliberal academia has happily adopted over the past several decades. Although I have experienced some mentors and professors that believe in the all-or-nothing academic lifestyle, I believe most can sympathize with the difficulty of raising children while pursuing a graduate degree and the exploitation that all too often happens in that context. That is why we must share and speak out about our experiences, even when we feel like those who control the spaces we inhabit in the academy prefer that we keep our heads down and work.

TRACKING LABOR TO FIND BALANCE

I look across the haphazard, tornado-like destruction that my kids worked on throughout the day. I see crumbs from chips smattering the rug, baby toys sprayed in all directions, and a sink full of encrusted plates and silverware. I consider running hot water and letting the dishes soak to buy me a little more time with this chapter. As with all things parenting, children add heightened urgency to our daily responsibilities and the roles we inhabit. Everything needs to be done all the time. Laundry needs to be started because the kids don't have clean school clothes or the pans need cleaning because dinner needs to be prepared. Or this rug needs to be swept before my two-year-old eats who knows what clinging to the carpet fibers. I don't need to explain the balancing of roles to parenting graduate students—you know what this is like, you're living it right now—but to those who work around us, this kind of stuff, the invisible labor of the role of a parenting graduate student, isn't explicit. As graduate workers building confidence and academic identities, we might even opt out of sharing our parenting experience and its intersections with our academic work.

I've come face to face with traditional, exclusionary attitudes about what was expected from graduate students. For instance, I've been told that graduate students are expected to attend every single class. There are also expectations to attend things like conferences and service committees that we (as graduate workers) are not paid for. I've been told that I'm simply not keeping up with the rigor that is expected of academic work and should consider dropping the class (or even dropping out). Any graduate student who is serious about becoming a professor must show that through their work and commitment to that work, which includes attendance. This toxic perspective about academic work made moments when my wife or my kids needed me feel like I was breaking some ancient academic law. Taking a sick day for myself or to care for someone else used to make me feel extremely guilty and stressed. I felt like I was letting everyone down. In these small moments of crisis, we can get a sense of how our roles as graduate students and parents create friction. This friction is omnipresent.

What caretaking and academic work have in common is their intense demand for time, specifically time that is spent helping another person.

Although my family deserves more of my time than academia does, I have found a few tools that have helped me balance these two dominating roles. You might be familiar with some of these already, but they have helped keep my projects and work organized and on track. One tool I want to share is simple: reflection. Take time to reflect on how you are spending your time and the quality or quantity of your work. For me, this meant keeping a detailed labor journal or labor log (see Appendix C). I keep track of quite a few factors, like number of interruptions, my mood, my engagement, where work occurred, what the work is, whether I completed it or not, and any notes I might have about that work session.

You can track your labor and the factors that go into it any way you like, but I recommend tracking most of the factors I've listed above. Tracking the number of interruptions, like getting distracted by your cellphone or interruptions by family (like an impatient child that wants to watch *Bluey* again and not the commercial) is important because it allows you to see how efficiently you're using your time and whether some communication about boundaries is necessary with the people in your life. Keeping a labor journal or using a digital time tracker enabled me to better communicate my work demands with my wife, my advisors, and my committee and to see how often I'm wasting time or getting distracted. Tracking interruptions gives you a sobering look at how often you are engaged with your work. This engagement, often called a flow state, is when you lose track of time because you are fully engrossed in work. Reaching a flow state means you are working at your best and in your most focused state. If you're constantly interrupted, you aren't hitting your flow state. You can generally find a correlation between the number of interruptions and whether you achieved a flow state or not, which is important for understanding unique, individual work habits and boundaries.

Additionally, tracking labor allows you to understand what time of the day you work most efficiently. For me, I find I'm most efficient once I've gotten the kids off to school (around 8 A.M.). I slow down around lunch time, which is likely more a consequence of what I eat or how much sleep I got the night before. I get a second wind at night once the kids are off to bed. I have figured out that there is a window of time in which I'm completely and utterly swamped with my duties as a parent. This window begins at 3 P.M. throughout the week and ends at around 8 P.M. At these times, I'm doing homework with the kids, preparing dinner, cleaning, wrapping up any housework I didn't get to throughout the day, and attending to any number of extracurricular activities the kids are involved in. Perhaps the most important discovery for me is understanding which parts of the day I'm most effective and efficient at my work.

Even though you can find a billion reasons why a labor log isn't going to help with everything, especially when children are thrown into the mix, keeping one will help you take stock of your labor in specific ways and help you engage fully with your work. Additionally, you can begin to see all the things that demand increasing amounts of time. At the very least, your labor journal can serve as a document to help you communicate your work-life boundaries with your family, friends, and mentors; it can help you set up expectations for all the people involved in your life and your journey. It will still be messy, but messes are unavoidable for parents.

The labor journal can help parenting graduate students see all their roles in one space, interacting and communicating with each other in a medium that isn't as abstract and random as life is. Placing your roles and responsibilities, capturing them in a permanent record, can make balancing those roles more manageable. Lastly, you can see where and when you have bitten off more than you can chew. I'll never forget what one of my mentors told me once: "The academy will happily take whatever you give it while giving very little in return." That is a dangerous situation for yes-people, overachievers, and perfectionists. I might have shrugged off this advice at first. I began taking on more work, more roles, and more responsibilities, saying yes to everything because I wanted to remain competitive for a job market that is shriveling up. Very quickly, this became an out-of-control spiral. When you've taken on too much work, the labor journal cannot create more time for you. As neat as that would be to create time out of thin air, labor tracking can help you recognize where, perhaps, you spend too much or too little time.

To illustrate how tracking time helped me through a tough spot, and hopefully help you avoid potential burn out, there was a moment during the summer of 2020 when I was convinced I needed to drop out and stop pursuing a PhD. COVID-19 was raging around the globe and times were uncertain for everyone. Reflecting on that moment now, I realize I had a lot more time to be home with my kids, where I grew to understand I was throwing time to academic work that belonged to my family. As a young academic, I was burned out, and I felt guilty about not spending more time being a part of my family members' lives. Several factors that were outside my control and several that were in my control were snuffing out any love I had left for my work. After talking with a few mentors and my wife, I was able to pinpoint what specific factors were oppressively taking over my time and forcing me to constantly feel behind in my work.

These conversations were productive because I had kept a labor journal that tracked how I was specifically spending my time while doing academic work. It helped me contain my academic work within boundaries and pinpoint exactly where I was giving in too excessively, such as during dinner time or on weekends. I wasn't treating academia as a job but as a lifestyle. As academics, we tend to equate unfinished work or even saying no to work as a failure, but being a workaholic and not sharing our laboring realities is toxic to ourselves, our loved ones, and our coworkers. We will never get that time back if we let it consume us. Graduate contracts differ greatly from one school to another, but I'd be willing to bet that most of us are paid for twenty hours of work each week, or part time. In a labor census survey of graduate workers in writing studies by Cornell University, 62.8 percent of respondents worked more than their contract hours each week (Labor Census Task Force 2019). It's not uncommon for graduate workers to work far more than their contracted hours, whether in response to their new roles as teachers, academia's toxic work culture, or both. Recognizing when we're freely giving ourselves up to exploitation is a good first step. Second, then, is speaking truthfully (even aggressively) about our experiences.

DISMANTLING MASTER NARRATIVES BY SPEAKING OUT

In graduate school, you will do so many things alongside forming your academic identity and carving out your academic niche. Graduate school is a time of rapid growth and maturity. It's a time to explore who you are as an academic, what your discipline will be, and what you really care about and want to spend your academic life doing. Some of us will do all of this while raising children. In a work environment that exploits contingent labor, parenting graduate students carry additional responsibilities and thus feel exploitation more keenly. Admittedly, graduate work isn't conducive to raising a family. It's an environment that privileges those without children and one in which people wrongly assume that parenting graduate students are uncommon.

Our academic working conditions are fueled by this metanarrative, or master narrative, and the assumptions it encourages. Master narratives are overarching narratives, or theories, that provide more comprehensive explanations of various historical events, experiences, and social phenomena. They appeal to universal truths or values. Master narratives are used to legitimate who has or is allowed to have power, authority, and control over social customs. In terms of graduate student exploitation, the overarching master narrative controls how the public, the university, and politicians view and treat graduate students through various channels. It even influences how graduate students think of themselves and encourages blind gratitude for the opportunity to work in academia, even though it isn't guaranteed that graduate students will have a space in academia post-graduation. Most importantly, the master narrative surrounding graduate school assumes a graduate student's identity, making other identities invisible and silenced. It assumes that we are childless and have nearly unlimited access to time, money, and resources (Morse 2022, para. 2). Upper administrators, the public, and sadly, some professors have accepted this master narrative as general fact, and anyone that doesn't fit the mold simply doesn't have what it takes.

These master narratives are immediately felt, and because of this, we might keep to ourselves the fact that we are parents, either for fear that we'll alienate ourselves or that our peers might view us differently. Those of us who are mothering graduate students have far more challenges to navigate, such as locating safe spaces to breastfeed or pump, finding affordable childcare, acquiring parental leave and healthcare, and coping with the sexist and misogynistic views that a person's role as a mother will interfere with the rigor of their academic work (Swanson and Johnston 2003; Guendouzi 2006; Kulp 2016; Winters 2019; Cho et al. 2021). These views remain prevalent because systemic injustices within the academy work to determine who is allowed, or not allowed, access to higher education.

It may come as little surprise that parenting graduate students choose to keep their identity as a parent to themselves, particularly mothering graduate students. Mothering students often hide pregnancies or their identity as a mother so they can appear to be committed students (Isaac 2023, 242–243). Mothering and fathering students also experience "time poverty," or a severe lack of time, and, consequently, struggle more with their work than their nonparenting peers do, which they'll also keep to themselves. Lack of childcare is the number one reason for time poverty (Wladis et al. 2018, 822). Parenting graduate workers keep the most intimate and important parts of themselves hidden from others, often to their own detriment. They're hiding their identities as parents and they're hiding the struggle they face in balancing two dominant roles.

Of course, universities perform many injustices on the bodies of its contingent faculty, but one of them is certainly this idea of making academic work the sole reason for living. The university will exploit contingent labor, spending and tossing workers away like depleted batteries. As graduate workers, we are treated like a waste product (Isaac 249). That academic lifestyle assumes a childless and fully dedicated machine. That is why it is so important to understand our labor; contain it in a concrete, tangible space, like a labor journal; and communicate labor expectations with the people in our lives. We can lean on our cohort and our mentors for help, guidance, and acceptance. Through an open dialog about our labor, we can create spaces of hope within our departments. We can also use these realities to paint a sobering picture for those who need to see, like upper administrators who stonewall and engage in patronizing discourses about increasing our wages and giving health insurance to graduate workers.

CONCLUSION

It took me a long time to realize that I have an unhealthy relationship with my professional work and the labor that work demands. We all have our vices, and one of mine is the work I let control my life. I used to work every single weekend. I used to work at dinner time. I even worked on family vacations and answered emails of distressed students at all hours of the day and night. I let my work control me. I've gotten better about this unhealthy relationship at work, particularly with tortuous emailing habits. Academia will gladly consume the time your children need from you, even bullying you at times to make these sorts of sacrifices. If you are someone that inhabits and embodies multiple identities, particularly ones in which you are responsible for the well-being of another human being (what is referred to as care work), the demands of academic labor can feel, at times, constricting and oppressive—even incompatible. Although I know this isn't an uncommon feeling among graduate students generally, the oppressions of graduate school are felt more keenly by students from marginalized and nontraditional backgrounds, such as parenting graduate students.

Learning how to better balance, and soberly reflect on, the roles and identities I embody has been a key professional development in my academic career. Although I'm constantly reflecting on and reevaluating this balancing act, I know how to communicate my labor needs and concerns better with those who also need time commitments from me. Academic work can and will take all that you give it. It's toxic and parasitic. It can also be a highly rewarding profession with set boundaries. So we must remember that academic work will take and take. It will sap and consume you entirely in your pursuit of prestige, happiness, and success. It hides behind the prestige of knowledge and the promised lifestyle we're seeking, but it is fundamentally like any job. Academic work must be placed within boundaries. Now, as I work on finishing up my degree, I set healthy boundaries between my personal time and the time needed to complete my work. With a visual depiction of tracked labor I'm able to see where I can begin building those boundaries, and that has done wonders for my mental health. I've noticed a considerable uptick in the topic of work realities showing up in serious discussions. Working realities are hot topics right now, and for good reasons, but we must listen to ourselves, our peers, and work to build better material working conditions. Speak out, organize, and take action.

WORKS CITED

Cho, Soo H., Roudi N. Roy, and Nancy Dayne. 2021. "Student–Parents' Mental Health: Factors Affecting Anxiety and Depression." *Family and Consumer Sciences Research Journal* 49 (3): 254–269.

Guendouzi, Jackie. 2006. "'The Guilt Thing': Balancing Domestic and Professional Roles." *Journal of Marriage and Family* 68 (4): 901–909.

Isaac, Jonathan. 2023. "'Fees Are Wage Theft': Graduate Labor Unions Confronting the Neoliberal University." In *Graduate Students at Work: Exploited Scholars of Neoliberal Higher Ed,* edited by Tessa Brown, 241–263. University Press of Kansas.

Kulp, Amanda M. 2016. "The Effects of Parenthood During Graduate School on PhD Recipients' Paths to the Professoriate: A Focus on Motherhood." *New Directors for Higher Education* 176 (Winter): 81–95.

Labor Census Task Force. 2019. "Labor Census Survey Data on Graduate Student Instructors in Writing Studies." Writing Program Administration–Graduate Organization, March. sites.google.com/cornell.edu/gsi-laborcensus-writingstudies/home. Accessed June 14, 2023.

Morse, Anne. 2022. "Stable Fertility Rates 1990–2019 Mask Distinct Variations by Age." Census.Gov, April 12. www.census.gov/library/stories/2022/04/fertility-rates-declined-for-younger-women-increased-for-older-women.html?utm_campaign=20220406msacos1ccstors&utm_medium=email&utm_source=govdelivery. Accessed July 26, 2023.

Swanson, Debra H. and Deirdre D. Johnston. 2003. "Mothering in the Ivy Tower: Interviews with Academic Mothers." *Journal of the Association for Research on Mothering* 5 (2): 63–75. https://jarm.journals.yorku.ca/index.php/jarm/article/view/2003.

Winters, Catherine A. 2019. "How Has (White Middle Class) Feminism Affected Graduate Student Labor?" *Journal of Feminist Scholarship* 16 (16): 67–69.

Wladis, Claire, Alyse C. Hachey, and Katherine Conway. 2018. "No Time for College? An Investigation of Time Poverty and Parenthood." *Journal of Higher Education* 89 (6): 807–831.

7 ▸ SEND AWAY THE CUCUY

One Mom's Journey through Graduate School While Battling False Expectations

KAREN TELLEZ-TRUJILLO

I'VE OFTEN FELT lucky that I grew up in the Southwest. Summer nights, with clear skies and temperatures that are far more tolerable once the sun goes down, are usually the most beautiful time of year. Dark becomes an exciting time for the inhabitants of the Southwest. Nocturnal animals emerge to hunt and play. The wind whips through the salt cedars along the banks of the Rio Grande, producing cries that belong to either the wind or to La Llorona.

At the base of the Organ Mountains, where I grew up, we learned to enjoy the desert landscape but to also respect the dangers that abounded. One can imagine that this soulful, enchanting, yet mysterious land is the perfect setting for the creation of many cautionary tales. These stories have a range of audiences, from children that need to be aware of their behavior to adults who have forgotten to mind themselves. The cautionary tales of the Southwest are told for those who might forget to follow the rules or who have become comfortable behaving outside societal and religious expectations. Unfaithful men, mischievous teens, independent mothers, and unruly children are often the targets of these tales, who remind recipients that breaking rules means there are consequences to pay.

One of the earliest stories of caution I remember is that of the cucuy, whom others might know as the boogeyman. Threats associated with the cucuy are that he will come and get you or take you away from the people you love. The cucuy has to watch out for bad children. Adults most often call to the cucuy, their guilt calls him in their sleep or in their most vulnerable moments. He doesn't even have to look for adults; they do the work for the cucuy. At least, that is what happened to me in the busiest, highest-stakes months of PhDing. My guilt, fear, false expectations, and worry beckoned the cucuy. At first, he only showed toes around the edge of a wall, then a furrowed brow behind a curtain, until he became strong and brave enough to look me in the eye.

During the months when I worked on my dissertation, I carried the present and future weight of my imminent move to accept a faculty position, numerous drafts of chapters still to be written and revised, online interviews, campus visits, a dissertation defense, packing a household filled with items and memories from my and my sons' lives, and the final transition of my two youngest sons from my home to their dad's home. Rationally, I understood that my sons didn't want to move to my new university with me because their lives were in New Mexico. Emotionally, I wished I could force them to come with me. Physically, my body was suffering. Beneath all of my obligations was the cry of the cucuy, saying that I was a selfish woman who was entertaining the idea of moving away from my hometown and family and more than that, a neglectful mother for dedicating years to education and double time to the PhD process. What follows is a bedtime story that tells of a long journey for a PhDing mother who in one afternoon takes back some control from the cucuy and got the strength to take the steps needed to begin quieting all of her greatest fears regarding her children.

A MONSTER AND A MYTH: A BEDTIME STORY

"How old are your kids?" the pony-tailed nursing assistant asked, as she took the woman's blood pressure at a nonroutine doctor's appointment. The nurse squeezed the ball at the end of the blood pressure cuff, watching the dial on the gauge drop, never making eye contact with the woman, whose eyes moved quickly from the dial to the nurse's face and back again. "Erm, the oldest is twenty-nine, the others are twenty and eighteen," the woman responded while wrapping her ankles around the cold legs of a hard plastic chair. The icy shock from the metal legs reminded the woman abruptly that she had forgotten to put on socks. It was winter: prime cucuy weather. She was becoming more and more forgetful. "Well, they're not babies anymore. Stop worrying, girl! You've got this!" the youthful nurse responded to the woman in response to the answers the woman had given to a number of qualifying triage questions. The woman had just admitted to the nurse that she was worried about the way her sons, Jon, Nick, and Jack, would be affected by the next steps coming in their lives. She told of the reasons why she was worried that she was spending too much time on her PhD and her dissertation.

The woman was anxious and tried everything she knew to manage daily bouts of nausea. She felt her that body had reached a breaking point where she was struggling to function. She had to finally accept that she was not invincible. What the nurse didn't know was that the woman had developed patterns of negative self-talk during sleepless nights, thinking that she could bully herself into conjuring more strength and into making more of her waking hours. "Stop being afraid of what's ahead and get to work," the woman would say to herself. By the time she made an appointment with her doctor, she had gone three months on fewer than four hours of sleep per night. The hours she spent awake were busy hours, so busy that she often forgot to eat.

As the nursing assistant prodded the woman for more information, the woman looked at the calendar and photos on the wall of the assistant's station and said between full sobs, "Look, I need to find balance. A lot of other women have done all of this stuff that I'm doing—harder stuff—and they weren't falling apart. I don't want to worry. Really. I don't." The woman felt incredibly weak and ashamed in that moment. She was sick of thinking ridiculous thoughts, like, "It's never been this bad" and "I just need to be better" while refusing to acknowledge that she'd felt poorly before, in fact throughout the PhD process. She felt guilty and was certain that she was neglecting her family for her studies, and she knew that with these feelings came the cucuy, who would visit and get stronger. She'd seen him in the past when she started her real estate business and when she'd taken a month in the summer to go abroad for research. He had the power to derail her health when she needed her health most.

Just before her visit to the doctor, the woman had seen that the cucuy had gotten bolder than before. He would stand next to her and over her bed, a constant reminder that she was doing things she was not supposed to do, like flying across the country for interviews. She wasn't supposed to leave her sons, no matter how old they were. She wasn't supposed to spend so much time on herself, writing, interviewing, preparing when there was so much to be done at home. The woman believed that there were consequences to not behaving as a mother was expected to behave. She should be selfless and eternally dedicated to the needs of her children, even if she knew that the reason she was doing what she was was to give herself and her sons a better life. She often heard the voices of women in her life saying, "I always put my children first." It didn't surprise her to see that the cucuy had come to remind her that there were consequences to her behavior. He kept her in constant fear, awaiting the punishment that she believed was inevitable. The punishment came in the way of flare-ups of her autoimmune disease, which in turn would stop her academic progress in its tracks.

"There's no such thing as balance, honey," the nurse said to the woman, breaking her sob. "It's a myth. It's like all of the other make-believe ideas we have. We just have to do our best every day. Get that monster out of your head." And with that thought, the cucuy took two steps back and the woman felt herself able to breathe for a moment.

THE BACKSTORY

When I enrolled at my local university as a nontraditional, full-time student in 2009, my youngest son, Jack, was seven years old. By the time I defended my dissertation, my family had been on the education path with me for eleven years. Jack started his senior year just as I started my career at a southern California university, seven hundred miles from Las Cruces, the town I had called home for forty years. This was not the first milestone of his I would miss. Although we texted and talked on the phone throughout his online, COVID-upturned senior year, I knew that I was far from him and far from the daily responsibilities of motherhood.

To give you an idea of who I am, I am a forty-something, middle-class cisgendered Chicana with a chronic autoimmune disease who completed all three degrees at the same southwestern university located forty-five miles from the US-Mexico border. I'm what we might call a university "homegirl," having never left the same institution to complete higher degrees. Now, in my fifth year as an assistant professor at a Hispanic-serving institution in Southern California, I am several years removed from that day in the doctor's office. I am better able to reflect on my experiences and on what worked well for me to pacify the cucuy that still occasionally pokes a fingernail through the bedroom curtain to let me know I am not 100 percent in control. I won't live under the delusion that I've slayed the monster that keeps me feeling guilty, tired, and sick to my stomach. I work hard to keep him quiet. What follows is some of the strategies I have developed to deal with him.

NIGHTLY SCHEDULING OF THE DAY AHEAD

Many years ago, I read Brian Tracy's *Eat That Frog!* Although I don't remember every detail of the book, I remember that the goal was to help procrastinators finish their work. The big idea was to do the thing you dread most first thing in the morning to get it out of the way and to create space for other important tasks. What I also learned from the book was that I could prioritize what needed doing and create separate sections on my to-do list for tasks that could wait or that I could delegate. By creating this list at night, in my bed, I found that I slept better and that this routine reduced the number of times I would spring up in bed, panicking that I'd forgotten a task. This occurred most often when I was faced with things I dreaded doing. If I "ate the frog" when I got to work each morning, it truly helped me get other tasks on my list done.

Although my oldest son, Jon, did not need me to consider him in the day-to-day operations of our home, I still had Nick and Jack at home while I was in graduate school and they were in college and in high school, respectively. Admittedly, I was able to delegate some tasks to them, but I was still responsible for reminding them of dentist and doctor appointments, school-related needs, or for providing meals, groceries, or money for meals. Keeping a written list of what needed doing also served as a reminder to me at the end of the week, when I was sure I hadn't been productive, that I, in fact, had done plenty.

PROTECTING TIME IN MY CALENDAR

Sectioning off time in my calendar for myself has been one of the easiest strategies to begin and the most difficult to honor. Using Google Calendar, I learned to keep my life mapped out months in advance. Using the ability to select an event in red, I made sure to write, in bold letters, "PROTECT" on Sundays to make time for writing and revisions. Whether it was time for rest, exercise, yoga, watching *Bob's Burgers*, family, the kids, friends, showering, nourishment that wasn't out of a box or a bag, or even a date, I made sure to section off time in red. I do not mean to suggest that I was able to do all the activities on my list each week. Not even close. But I was able to get to a yoga workshop at least once a month, allow myself time to sleep in until 8:00 A.M. on Saturdays, and take my mom to church once or twice a month. Above all, the most important detail I learned about this strategy is that if I didn't protect time for myself on the calendar, I didn't get it. Period.

SETTING LIMITATIONS

If I feel that I am overpromising, that someone is asking too much of me, or if I am simply uncomfortable in a situation or with a request, I set a boundary. Boundaries have come in the way of asking for more time to think before I decide to say no without an explanation and immediately asking myself if future Karen will have the energy to keep promises. If someone brings chaos to my life, I limit my time with them or stay away altogether. If a person has continuously hurt me, I privately thank them for the lesson and move on. These are some of the most important strategies I've learned in the last five years. It has given me the space, clarity, and time to introduce and maintain habits that serve my mind, body, spirit, and home. The greatest surprise that has come to me from setting limitations is that it gets easy quickly and the freedom that follows has given me control over myself, my time, and a sense of pride because I am showing myself the same love I would give to others.

ADVICE FOR QUIETING THE CUCUY THAT STEALS PEACE

Lean on Your Support System

Support systems look different for everyone. I had family close by that could help with the responsibilities of the house when my children were younger. As my sons grew, they became my support system. I learned to delegate tasks to my sons, such as do your own laundry, clean your own bathroom, wash your bedding regularly, gas up your own car, clean up after yourself, throw out the trash, make sure you eat when you are out of the house (they had money to do so), and don't have me remind you of these tasks regularly because it can be as stressful as having to do them myself. If you have friends or family nearby, you might think of how you can ask them for help or ask how you can exchange help. The major takeaway here is that we need people and getting through a PhD with children without help is not impossible but incredibly difficult.

Journaling

Ten minutes. Whether you type for ten minutes on your laptop or write on paper, take time each day, very early or late at night, to journal. I solved most of my own problems by listening to myself while journaling, and this extended from stuck points in my research to personal concerns. By taking ten minutes a day to write for myself, beliefs were dispelled, feelings were hashed out, thoughts were organized, and I was less prone to rambling to my loved ones as a way of organizing my thoughts and feelings. When I stopped relying on the people I love to be containers for my random thoughts, I started feeling less guilty about potentially taxing my support system. I was then able to use my support system more productively for different kinds of help.

Move and Don't Move

Because I can't know readers' physical limitations and abilities, I ask that you find a way to move your body. I am not a fan of exercise. I like going for walks if the weather is just right and I enjoy yoga. Most recently I have added Pilates, but this wasn't my practice during the time I was PhDing. That sums it up. Attending yoga at a studio gets costly, so I have mostly watched YouTube videos and practiced yoga at home. If taking classes at a studio fits in your budget nicely, I would recommend working it into your schedule because of its value. I am one of the least consistent people I know when it comes to exercise, but what little I did during graduate school made a world of difference for keeping my mind clear and my body agile. With as much passion, I ask that you take time to meditate, even if it's for ten minutes a day. You can do this in bed. You can do this at work. Find quiet and stillness, rest your eyes parked outside the grocery store, gather your thoughts, and breathe. Nothing fancy.

Both parenting and graduate school were taxing in similar ways. There were financial constraints, constant draws on my time, and issues that needed my attention on someone else's timeline. In the same way that I didn't get to choose when I was going to teach, or when students were going to need a meeting to discuss the class I taught as a TA, my sons needed rides, meals, and attention to the issues going on in their world. I caught myself repeating in the shower, under my breath once, "I just need a minute." Both exercise and meditation were actions I could control and use to take care of myself, but they were for me because they didn't benefit anyone but me. Meditation helped me to quiet the to-do lists and comments on drafts of my dissertation. Exercise helped me work out the anxiety tied to the obligations, revisions, and stress that I either denied I was under or could no longer recognize because it had become a way of life.

Making Assumptions about What Others Need

During graduate school, I could quickly and easily come up with a list of all the ways I was failing my sons. On a Sunday afternoon soon after visiting my doctor's office with a desperate cry for help, I asked all three of my kids what they needed from me and how I could be a better mom to them. This is how the interaction went:

JON: I really don't need anything from you, Mom. You call, I call. I visit, we spend time. It's all good.
MOM: Really. That's it?
JON: Mom.

NICOLAS: I like to take drives with you.
MOM: So, maybe we can schedule to take a drive every Sunday?
NICOLAS: We'll see. That's a lot of together time. I think we're good.

JACK: I hate driving. Take me to and pick me up from school. Take me to my friend's houses.
MOM: But I already do that. I haven't baked and we eat out all the time; the house is messy.
JACK: Mom. I am gluten intolerant. We have food we make. You also buy healthy food and have it delivered. We have it delivered. We don't care. We're fine.

I know this seems scripted or like it is a problem that was solved in moments like mysteries on *Murder, She Wrote,* but this is what went down. If I could only get back the hours I spent awake at night, crying or planning because I was sure I wasn't meeting my family's needs. So much negative self-talk was erased with three short and simple conversations. I trusted my sons to tell me what they needed, and they did.

Making Assumptions about How Others Feel

I will spare you the back-and-forth between me and my sons on this one. The interactions were like the conversations I shared above. Also similar is the number of hours of sleep I'd lost or spent worrying that my kids resented me for being in school most of their lives, that I spent most of my time writing, and that they felt abandoned by my need to take a faculty job out of state. They not only met my worries with reassurance that they did not feel the ways I was certain they felt, they also presented solutions to the distance we would experience in the future. I suggest that you take time to ask your children, if they are old enough, what they need and feel. Listen to their requests and ideas. I learned that my sons were aware of what I was going through and that I was not protecting them by pretending I was okay. I also learned that my sons had more strategies for coping than I'd ever imagined. I've traded fretting for pausing, assuming for asking, and ignoring for acting.

These are simple suggestions, but they are not always easy to implement. Everything I have recommended took time to practice and still take time to work into my life. However, all that I hold in my small basket of hope and advice I can give to anyone who is certain they aren't doing enough for the family or believe they have lost track of their priorities. If I could spare anyone the experience of watching the cucuy, that huge monster of uncertainty, doubt, fear, and shame, slowly creep into their life and punish them in the ways that are most harmful, I would give my all. I want the cucuy in my life to stay asleep—or at least to play quietly while I am busy enjoying a life well lived. I want that for you, too.

8 ▸ *ÓRALE*! APPLY AND EARN *TU* DEGREE

Parenting While a (Chicana!) Doctoral Student

DALEL SERDA

THE WEEK BEFORE I finished my master of fine arts degree, my thesis chair asked me if I had considered a doctoral program. She had never mentioned that possibility to me before. I said I had not. At the time, I remember feeling I was getting close to a fantasy I had imagined for myself when I first learned what a graduate student was. *Doctoral degrees are what my professors have,* I remember thinking. It was not what I could imagine attaining.

I told her I hadn't. She said, "You'd be a shoo-in." I remember that was the first time that phrase presented itself to me. *You'd be a shoo-in. Me. I'd be the one shooed in.*

When I told my husband, who was ever ready with support, he suggested that I move to the East Coast, where the schools she said would want me were. He'd stay in Houston, where he had just landed a job. I remembered my mother, the traditional ever-present homemaker of my childhood. "Be a good wife." she said. "Be a good wife." While my feminist tendencies resisted the subservient nature of that phrase, my Lebanese and Mexican sides relented, reminding me that I was the one who had decided to get married. My husband was a good husband. I thus would be a good wife, and a good wife lives in the same city as her new husband. Thus, I didn't apply to doctoral programs because of my husband, but also, I had no clue how to go about applying to them.

Months before my thesis chair asked me about doctoral programs and my life as a married partner prevented that exploration, one of my committee members ensured that I second-guess marriage before I was even married.

"Your writing life is over," he said to me when I told him of my pending marriage. It was then my first year as a master's student. A graduate student. My fantasy come true.

"Be a good wife."

"You're a shoo-in."
"Your writing life is over."
¿ Pues que me ves, carnal?

I thought about these memories when my first daughter Phoenix would fall asleep right after feeding. I would hold her close to me, her face up to mine. I would feel her pink skin's silkiness against the back of my fingers. Her milky baby scent intoxicated me. I thought only one thing: *I will be a good mother.*

I hail from the Rio Grande Valley. I am the daughter of a father who was born into a family of migrant workers *piscando algodon* from south and central Texas all the way west to Califas. He is, as I have often said, a *macho Chicano* from Lozano, Texas. Born and raised, *vato.* And although it took me into my twenties to realize it, I too am a Chicana—born, raised, and self-identified.

My fair-skinned mother is an ethnic Lebanese woman born in Mexico City. When I was growing up, my family spent school years in south Texas in our hometown of Harlingen and summers in Mexico City, where my extended family members had housekeepers, gardeners, and chauffeurs. The streets of Mexico City, where *muchachitos* sold *raspas* and *aguas frescas,* stuck fire down their throats, or quick-washed windshields to violent waves of dismissal from drivers, also made clear what it meant to hustle for daily survival.

All of this made me realize much that mattered about how people live in my home country to the north and the difference for a vast majority living to the south. Much of that difference was due to socioeconomic circumstances that too often mapped neatly to the color of their skin.

When I was an undergraduate student at the University of Texas at Austin (UT), my father would tell my brother and my sisters that he was happy if we passed classes at UT because it was UT and he couldn't ask more of us than that. It struck me as a low expectation even then because I knew I could do more than pass, and so I did. I more than passed. My mother had begun working at her mother's store in Mexico City at the age of sixteen. She too was pleased we were at university, but her aspirations were for us to be happy, maybe get married, and always stay close to family. My father never attended university because he wasn't mentored or guided toward that decision, although he was awarded a full ride to a university on a football scholarship. That was a big deal in the late 1960s, when minoritized young people were not yet pipelining into colleges and universities. Instead, in macho Chicano style, he forewent his scholarship for the army pipeline because he fantasized about becoming an airborne ranger and a *real American hero*.

When I was an undergraduate student, I realized that this fantasy is one that many minoritized young people felt and likely still feel. The idea of the military as a pathway to feeling validated on our American soil is a worn one. My father's fantasies were not unique.

My fantasies aren't either.

When he came back from the military, where he had trained as a medic, he attended community college and became a licensed vocational nurse. When I was in junior high, he earned his registered nursing license, an associate's degree. That was the highest credential he attained. I remember his long hours at the dining table highlighting stacks of nursing school textbooks—his furrowed brows and single-minded focus. I would stand next to him for minutes waiting to ask him a question. In his concentration, he hadn't noticed me.

I remember thinking that I looked like he did when he was an undergraduate student. I highlighted the pages of my books as I hid away in the corners of university buildings all those years later.

I remember also when I noticed the graduate students for the first time. They walked with purpose as they made their way to the front of some of my classes. They were lecturers and instructors of record. I fantasized about being one of them one day also. I fantasized about a life devoted to study, research, books, reading, writing, and teaching.

Like I think my father did, I also sought validation on our American soil. While the military and nursing school provided that for my father, I believed that my validation would come from a big American university. If I could be a graduate student earning credentials no one in my family had considered, I could be a *real* American.

I know what I felt then and likely what I still feel now in some version of that: it's a pursuit of validation that yields some kind of separation from the dark-skinned *niños de la calle*, for whom food, safety, and shelter is not a constant. Our skin tones don't separate us. Maybe American training, credentials, and pursuits of validation would act as an armor against the cruel inequities in living poor and living brown. It was an attempt to prove something to someone about myself. I know now, decades later, that proving anything to anyone other than my daughters is wrong-minded.

It cannot be *¿Pues que de que, vato? ¿Que me ves? ¿Que te traes?* I hear my father raising these questions on the streets of Lozano. This is how he tells it. His former military service and school experiences acted like metaphorical fists, metaphorical armor to protect himself from victimization of all kinds.

I didn't have to raise my fists to anyone growing up, but I think in my mind I did. *¿Que me ves, ese? ¿Que me ves?*

Despite what the committee member said to me, I landed a tenure-track position at a community college two years before Phoenix was born. I thought then that I could not do better. It was my dream job and where I was meant to be. I had the energy for the heavy teaching load and the demands of students coming to us from such varied paths. But Phoenix changed what I thought was already the affection I had for my students. Phoenix's birth helped me see her in every student I had after her birth. Regardless of their age, sex, gender, race, and ethnicity, every student became Phoenix. And for me, Phoenix was every *Chicanita de Texas y el southwest* and *las niñas or niños de la calle de la cuidad de Mexico* who never had much of a chance to get off those streets.

The year Phoenix was born, I read that Latin@s were the fastest growing ethnicity in the United States. That year, we were also not faring well in college; we were not yet attending at the rate we were growing. We were also not graduating at the rate we were attending. It was that year that I realized that to face my own daughter and to face my students, whom I was making read and consider this and other similar statistics, I had to add fully and positively to them.

Pero . . .

¿Que me ves, vato? ¿Que me ves, ese?

Not everyone was supportive of my decision to apply to a doctoral program while parenting Phoenix and her little sister. "You'll neglect them. You will be a bad mother. How will you do it? Why are you doing it? Your job doesn't require it," they said.

My husband said, "Move forward." He is a good husband. I am a good wife. I did.

I do not know whether I was a shoo-in for the doctoral program where I am embarking on the second year of coursework. I do know that my writing life has suffered because I have other responsibilities, but my writing life is not over.

I am a full-time instructor of English at my community college. I have over eleven years of experience there and consider myself an established part of my department and college community. I am also a part-time doctoral student taking two graduate courses, compared to my fellow classmates, who are taking three. I am a full-time mother and wife. Life is not easy, but it is worthwhile.

Here is why: I do this because I know how to do it. Parenting has endowed me with superpowers I didn't have before. I can make humans. I am a mother. I can sustain other humans beside myself. I turn this power over to my studies. I can and will meet deadlines because I do what I must to counteract forces that suggest otherwise.

Here is why: I have to return to what allows me to do the best work I can. Spending time systematically researching as a doctoral student reestablishes the habits of mind that yield deeper thought in me. Doctoral studies help me sustain attention, force deep thought, require commitment, and demand that I love what I do.

I love what I do because the work pays off in making me a better teacher.

I love what I do because the work pays off in making me a better mother.

Here is *como lo hago*. Here is how I do it: I have told myself that I will see this work as a labor of love. Parenting requires as much love as PhDing. Both roles require around-the-clock commitment. But children sleep, and I'm adult, so I can sleep less. When they sleep, I study. On weekends, I study. My husband has become weekend parent supreme, taking on all roles on Saturdays and Sundays while I am at home studying. My daughters, who are now six and nine, see me like I saw my father: I read around the clock and am reading and writing at my desk, modeling commitment, modeling work ethic, and raising my face to kiss them when I finish a chapter and am ready to turn a page. When I finish a paper or am in the middle of research, I can search for their face and kiss their cheeks. These kisses feed my motivation, for they are the ones who motivate the work. My students motivate it too.

I study on Saturday and Sunday. All day. Both days. I teach and work during the daytime hours during the week and in the afternoons and evenings. I read while waiting for my children to get out of after-school extracurricular activities. I never do not have a book with me. I never do not have my laptop with me. But I do not teach or do coursework in the summer. The summer is for revitalizing and reconciling my identity as mother. It is in the summer when I am the best wife and the best mother. I invest myself in my family heavily in the summer months and let the investment pay dividends during the academic year, when I ask my daughters and husband to help us each thrive as team members with the same goal of improving our lot. We validate each other.

My expectations for what I can do are high. My expectations for what my daughters can do are high too. I may or may not be seeking validation from my country or from my family's complex histories, but I know that my daughters, my husband, and I validate each other's efforts. I recommend that if you are a mother, move forward. Whether you are inching along or running, move forward. Earn your PhD because you can. Because you must. Your children are watching, and they will be the ones whose legacy will forever change in the wake of your labors.

If you are a mother of color or a father of color, move forward. Whether you are inching along or running, move forward. Earn your PhD because you can. Because you must. We do not need to be validated by forces that do not recognize our value, but we can validate ourselves. It is self-recognition that opens doors to others' recognition. Perhaps.

If you are an administrator in a position to facilitate a parent's journey through a doctoral program, do so. A parent already knows how to achieve success against odds. A parent knows how to labor for love. A parent has a clear understanding of how to problem-solve, how to lead and manage, how to commit and see paths forward when they seem obscure to others.

Move forward, *amig@s. El mundo* needs your perspective and a doctorate affords you an opportunity that deepens and strengthens your humanity, for as you well know, intellectual interrogation yields a more human(e) human. *Y* parenting yields a more human(e) human. *Adelante. Órale, ese. El mundo lo merece. El mundo te merece. Y tu, te mereces el mundo.*

My initiation into parenthood was fraught with unforeseen health challenges that helped me reconsider my position as a community college instructor with a master's degree teaching composition and survey literature courses to people who were also looking to improve their positions.

I see though that it was not motherhood alone that instigated my intellectual turn inward. What began that move was the preceding decade of travel and teaching. It was travel and teaching that caused the latent recognition that to the world at large I was not a woman but rather a brown woman. What was less obvious, to me at least, was the recognition that I was also a Chicana, or rather that I was a brown American Chicana. This recognition led me down a path of knowing too much about what I did not know and did not have and about what I was and am and what I was not and am not.

9 ▸ STAY ALIVE

A Black Mother's Responsibility to Ride Grief's Hills and Live

LISA E. WRIGHT

Disclaimer: This chapter discusses suicidal ideation and murder.

IN THE FALL of 2017, the week leading up to the orientation of my first year, I was a mess. As excited as I was to begin my journey as a PhD student sixteen years after completing my master's degree, I couldn't figure out how I would get our children to school and arrive on time in Stillwater, Oklahoma. My husband, Ibrafall, a middle school special education teacher at the time, could only alter his schedule by so much, and usually the hours after school were better times for him to help with parenting responsibilities. Plus, for four years, I'd driven our children to their Islamic private school because I was a seventh-grade English and social studies teacher there. Our mornings operated like clockwork. The children learned to slip into their uniforms after morning prayers and pack their book bags. My husband churned out bacon-and-egg sandwiches for breakfast and cookies, fruit, juice boxes, and halal pepperoni pizza pockets for their lunches. I rushed behind the children with lotion, socks, brushes, hair grease, barrettes, and hijabs. Now, since I had quit my job to become a full-time student, in order to arrive at orientation on time, I needed to be on the road an hour before they had to be to school.

My first inclination was to seek permission to arrive a little late. I sent an email to my first-year composition administrator to explain my situation. She noted that missing or being late to orientation wasn't an option. It was my responsibility to be there and to be there on time. This was before COVID. Zoom was not an option. Her response got me thinking more broadly about how my schedule would change since I had committed to this graduate program. There might be several days where I wouldn't be able to drop our children off at school, and on some evenings I would still be in class when they finished.

I would soon find out that I was the only woman in my PhD cohort who had children, and often my peers would say, "I don't know how you do it with four kids!" I've never fully explained to anyone that the support I had from my Muslim community and my mother's fortitude emboldened me. In my late teens, I knew I would attend undergraduate school because my mother had graduated from Coppin State College. I watched my mother, a single parent, leave before my brother and I left for school in the morning; she'd work until five. We had specific afternoon snacks that we could prepare: ramen noodles, cheesesteak subs, Vienna sausages. Some evenings, she'd come home to pick up her latchkey kids, order us pizza, and sit us down on her office floor while she worked extra hours to pay bills. My brother and I were expected to be quiet, do our homework, do puzzles, or watch ants march across the office floor. Her tenacity taught me that I could work full time while completing my undergraduate degree, and so I did. Yet it felt different to be a mother and wife who would be required to teach writing courses and tutor writers while completing my required course assignments and personal research. To successfully navigate this journey, my husband and I would need assistance from our community.

In my last semester, hours after I submitted my dissertation in preparation for defense, my mother and I discussed her decision to start a career as a loan processor in real estate as opposed to continuing her education and pursuing her aspirations to work in a STEM field. In 2014, my mother completed her master's in social work when my youngest child was three years old. She told me that she had thought about continuing her education right after she graduated with her bachelor's degree in May of 1980. When I asked her why she hadn't kept going she replied, "I thought about it, but I didn't think I could leave you with your father." Around the time I was born, my mother was learning that my father was an alcoholic who struggled to keep jobs. My mother is a Black woman who always excelled in math and science. She is who other family members called on when they needed math tutoring. She tutored me in algebra I and II while I was in high school.

After completing her bachelor's in science at Coppin State University (formally Coppin State College) and becoming the first woman in our family to graduate with a college degree, she aspired to obtain a degree in nursing or forensic science or to start a career as a radiologist. I was born at the start of what should have been her last semester of college. It would take her another two years to graduate. Maybe I didn't want to think of myself as the barrier that stopped my mother from obtaining her goals, so I tried to retroactively solve her dilemma. I offered, "You could have left me with grandma while you attended class. I'm sure she would have kept me." I'd always had a special relationship with my grandmother. I don't remember a time when she wasn't there for me. Therefore, I couldn't imagine that she wouldn't have changed my diapers, fed me, and snuggled with me while my mother attended night classes. From a place of peace, my mother spoke confidently, "Maybe, but she worked too, and I felt like you were *my responsibility.*"

In my mother's language, *my responsibility* equated to her saying "Mama's baby, daddy's maybe." When I was a teen, she would repeat that phrase to me every so often. It was one of our mother-daughter mottos. My mother wholeheartedly believed that once a woman became pregnant, no matter what the relationship status was between the mother and father, it would be the mother who ultimately was responsible for the children. I imagine this line of thinking may have begun with my great-grandmother, who became a widow with four children by the age of twenty, or maybe my mother's upbringing by her mother, who chose to raise three daughters on her own with little to no help from their fathers. Neither completed school past eighth grade. The type of independence my great-grandmother and grandmother exhibited left an impression of maternal independence on my mother. As I see it, my mother's independence fostered a sort of isolation from a community of caregivers who could have supported her had she decided to further her education after I was born.

On day one of my orientation as an Oklahoma State University writing center tutor, I asked Laura "What's my schedule going to be?" To me, Laura's name was the most important name in our English department. Laura, the glue of our writing center, replied something like, "Just tell me your availability and we'll make it work." That was music to my ears. I thought I needed my schedule to work in alignment with my family obligations. I thought I needed to know exactly when I had to jump in my car and head to Stillwater and what time I would be able to leave and head home. Would those times allow me to pick up my kids from school? Could I take them to tutoring sessions in math and reading after school? Could I stop with them for an after-school snack of French fries or tacos?

No, the nature of my PhD program caused me to lean on women in my community before I knew the act had a name. To be transparent, in my first semester I wasn't familiar with Patricia Hill Collins' *Black Feminist Thought* (2000), which centers on the importance of othermothers in Black communities. Essentially, othermothers are women who are not biologically related who assist each other with completing tasks that lead to the survival of families. During the first semester of my PhD program, I found that the othermothers in my circle were Muslim women I'd worked with at my children's school. One sister, a mother of four whom I had co-taught kindergarten with, allowed me to drop my kids off at her house around seven o'clock in the mornings so that I could make it to orientation on time during my first week. After school, another sister stuffed our children into her seven-seat SUV with her three children. She filled their bellies with Lebanese meat or spinach pies, reviewed their homework with them, and let them nap on her sofa until my husband or I could pick them up.

On the days that we could not pick up our children after school, and there were many, we relied on Shakurah, an art major in her second year of college. Shakurah is the daughter of a Muslim family in our community. Our children attended her art shows and she tutored them in math at her university library on the weekends. During the week, she would pick up the kids from school, drive them home, and eat halal marshmallows with them as they started their homework. This schedule worked for us until we became unhappy with the teacher-child relationship at our children's school. We were done with their school when the fifth-grade teacher of our terribly shy daughter told her, "You won't succeed in life if you don't start talking." We knew we had to remove her from that toxic environment. This same teacher catered her lessons to the advanced students and left the minority students and students who didn't learn as fast with little to no support. Our eldest daughter, who had struggled in math, left her class more aware of her race, her economic status, and her class than how to solve math problems. As a result, we pulled our children from their brick-and-mortar school and enrolled them into a virtual school. While I no longer had to worry about before- and after-school care or teachers whose educational philosophies did not mesh with ours, this meant that my children's education was now mostly *my responsibility.*

Depending on the day, I'd teach math and English lessons to the children or ensure that they were on task before I left for Stillwater between ten and eleven A.M. Several mornings during the week I drove around sixty-six miles from Oklahoma City to Stillwater. On some rides to campus, I hadn't had time to finish listening to an article for my own class. On most rides, I would be on the phone going over unfinished lessons with one of our four kids, who were in third, fifth, seventh, and ninth grades. On many rides home, I dictated or thought about an essay I was in the process of writing. This nonstop schedule left me feeling pressed between two stone slabs. I felt pressured to keep going but drawn to join the hills. When I drove past the horses and cows in the pastures, they seemed to stand back off the road, leaving me just enough space to drive my car in a ditch. Yet dying was never on my immediate to-do list. I couldn't even pencil it in, because I felt overwhelmed with my work and my children's work. I still had work to do. I had responsibilities.

"Sometimes I really feel like ending it," I told my husband on a rare coffee date at Starbucks. Despite an urge to float away, the coolness from the cushioned seat grounded me. I never wanted my husband to be shocked if I penciled death in on my calendar. He looked out the window, agitated. Speckled white and brown horses pulled couples with thick knitted scarves and fuzzy boots in their carriages. Ibrafall could never wrap his head around why people would want to kill themselves, so our conversations were not productive. I accepted that it was not his place to be my therapist. When my mother and I talked about stress management, she encouraged me to stop talking about getting help and just walk in.

Around the third year of my PhD, I started planning the suicide. Small hills consumed my eyes. I wanted to stop, sit still, and become one with them. My tentative plan was to run our family van, a burgundy Toyota Sienna, off a cliff, become one with a hill, and grow grass. In between listening to some assigned articles that I needed to be ready to discuss as an emerging scholar once I arrived at class, I considered that space right in front of the hills, the emptiness between what appeared to be the end of the highway and the sky. The emptiness invited me to fill it. From my place in the car, that space felt far away until I drove right up to it. Then each time I got close, I would have a split second to decide if today were the day or if I would continue to class or a tutoring session or a meeting. I kept showing up because of my responsibilities, because I never felt like I had done enough to be ready to die.

When I finally found myself on the sofa of an OSU campus therapist, he remarked, "I don't know what I would do if I had all your responsibilities on my plate. How do you manage your calendar? Let's talk about what you can remove from your calendar." Ibrafall and I had committed to our children attending virtual school. We'd missed the application process for charter schools and didn't trust the schools in our residential zone. So putting our children in a public school wasn't an option. One behavior my therapist and I discussed in a session was that I could spend car rides talking to adult family members so that I wouldn't feel so isolated as a mother and a student. One conversation was pivotal in my decision to live.

I had just finished a night class and was headed back to Oklahoma City from Stillwater. My husband called and said that his baby sister had phoned him to say that something had happened to Chad, his oldest sister's husband, and that Chad wasn't doing well. I felt enclosed in the middle lanes, unsure of Chad's future, and held into a life of uncertainty. I called my father-in-law after my mother-in-law hadn't picked up. He explained that Chad had gone to talk to a couple who had moved into his father's house, the home he and his family had grown up in. We knew that Chad had not been happy that his family home had been sold and that he'd hoped to get the land back. Later we learned from the police that there had been an altercation. We'll never know the truth because Tennessee is a stand your ground state. Maybe there was an argument. Maybe the wife shot Chad because she saw a big Black man talking or arguing with her husband. I took my exit past the Oklahoma state capital as the last of the sun huddled under the night sky. I'd left the cows in their pastures. The hills long behind me. "What do you mean, Daddy?"

"He's dead." My father-in-law said flatly.

I'm sure I continued to accelerate the car. It felt weird knowing my life was moving forward and sometime in the last hour Chad's heart had ceased to beat. "What did you say, Daddy?

In Daddy's voice I heard a sorrow I never wanted to cause. "They shot him. He's dead."

At Chad's funeral, our youngest daughter sat closest to me. It was her sobs that first encouraged me to cling to life. Her breathing grew heavy as the preacher, another one of her uncles, reminded us of Chad's inviting smile, his generosity, and his love of family gatherings. Her shoulders hiked up and down grief's hills. Her siblings and cousins echoed her grief. Chad's oldest son, who had never had his hair cut by anyone other than his father, spoke of his mother having to find a barber to cut his hair for his father's funeral. I thought of the chocolates that Chad hid from his family but always shared with me. My own tears reminded me that my family's life would go on if I ended my life. Laundry, hairstyles, a proofreader for their essays for school assignments, these were the things that my children would have to replace. I folded tissue after tissue into their warm wet hands and thought of the void I'd leave my family with.

One evening, about a year after Chad was killed, I fell asleep with my laptop on my chest after a long night of drafting a chapter for my dissertation. Each word came slowly and I had spent the night chiding myself because I felt like I should have been farther along. That night, I dreamed of Chad. He and I sat on his back porch. His vibrant plants soaked up the smoke from his cigarettes. We chatted about traveling. We wanted to take our children to see The Gambia, West Africa. Chad stood facing his garden. His blueberry bushes were heavy. Each berry decorated the small hills that draped his backyard. Chad pulled from his cigarette and glanced over his shoulder at me, "I'm proud of you. Don't let these people drive you crazy. You've got this."

I thought back to Chad's funeral. There I had rubbed my kiddos' backs and wished I could soothe the grueling hurt that rose up from their cores. Their bodies heaved for their uncle. If I ended my life, their bodies would heave for their mother. I would not take my own life to escape my anxieties, stress, and feelings of uncertainty. I could not shift those feelings onto them and leave them in despair. I knew then that it was my responsibility to live. Their grief saved us.

WORKS CITED

Collins, Patricia Hill. 2000. *Black Feminist Thought: Knowledge, Consciousness, and the Politics of Empowerment*. Routledge.

PART 2 YOUR BODY HAS OTHER PLANS

10 ▸ "A LOT OF US CAN SWIM"

One Queer Student's Advice for Mentoring Pregnant and Parenting Graduate Students

RACHAEL JORDAN

> I asked my friends: "A woman writing: what do you see?" . . . "She's sitting at the kitchen table, and the kids are yelling."
>
> —URSULA K. LE GUIN, "The Fisherwoman's Daughter"

Disclaimer: This chapter briefly mentions suicidal ideation.

I DIDN'T EXPECT to get pregnant and have my older child during the middle of my master's program, just like I didn't plan to be starting my PhD with two kids under the age of ten during a pandemic.

I completed my MA because my thesis advisor was herself a mother. In one session in her office as I sat slumped over, my hand twitching across my swelling belly, she slid papers across her desk toward me.

"You need to read this," she said, her eyes seeming kind behind her glasses. I scanned the black-and-white page, my sluggish brain taking a moment for the words to register. "The Fisherwoman's Daughter," I read aloud, a 1989 essay by Ursula K. Le Guin about writing, motherhood, and collaboration. My advisor and that essay may have saved my life.

The next year I sat in her office, my son tied to my chest, as we discussed revisions to my thesis. She looked from my baby to me and simply said, "Don't blink."

He was nine months old when I graduated. I adjuncted across three different universities for a while and then, in 2012, I got a full-time lecturer position. Between an amicable divorce in 2013, a new marriage in 2015, and another kid in 2016, further graduate study felt far away. However, in 2019, when my older kid was nine and my second child was three, I applied for admission to a PhD program. The following April, as COVID-19 raged across the country, I got my acceptance letter.

DECEMBER 2009

The pregnancy test was positive, so the next day I made my way to our local Planned Parenthood. I drove up the grade, the morning fog rolling down the hills as I creeped up the freeway in the Jeep I had borrowed from my ex. I hadn't told him about the test.

Luckily, it was a morning on a weekday, so I didn't have to push past any of the protesters I had seen before that usually stood outside this particular Planned Parenthood with homemade signs. The parking lot felt calm, and the building was an unassuming brown. When I went inside, I didn't look at the other women in the waiting room and I checked in for my appointment. For the first time in my life, I felt nothing. Felt nothing as they called my name. Felt nothing as I peed into a cup.

I could feel the warmth radiating off the nurse who came into the exam room. "We're going to confirm your pregnancy test, and then I'll be right back, okay?" she said. What felt like moments later, she returned. "Rachael," she said. "You're not pregnant."

I immediately smoked a cigarette in the parking lot.

JANUARY 2010

I still hadn't started my period, so I took a pregnancy test inside a dirty stall in a Vons grocery store bathroom, my Converse sneakers planted on either side of the toilet as I hovered over the seat.

Positive.

I drove across the street to a diagnostic facility because I decided I needed blood proof. At twenty-four, I was still on my dad's insurance and knew they would cover the test. I explained what was going on to the man there, and he handed me a small, circular plastic calendar. He showed me how to twist one side to my last period start date and how the other sign would show me the baby's due date.

"I'm pretty confident you're pregnant," he said. I didn't feel the pinch of the needle in my arm.

He called me hours later as I sat in the borrowed Jeep in a parking lot, uncharacteristic rain pummeling the roof.

"Congratulations," he said. "The due date is September third."

Everything I thought I knew about myself disappeared in that moment. I leaned my forehead against the steering wheel and cried.

As the product of a teenaged, unplanned pregnancy myself, my first thought was *I've become my mother.*

My second thought: *What a straight girl thing to do*.

MARCH 2010

My ex and I decided we'd try to "make it work," and I wondered how long I could hide my stomach from my classmates in our graduate queer studies course. For some reason, my pregnancy felt like a betrayal of my queerness and at twenty-four, I didn't know where to put those feelings.

My heart fluttered in panic every time I thought about telling my thesis advisor. I knew I would have to take the following semester off, since the baby was due the second week of school.

Even then, I knew that telling people about my pregnancy could break me.

I sat in my queer studies professor's office, pulling my long sleeves down over the Sea-Bands on my wrist, my attempt at trying anything to ease the morning sickness that had plagued me for over sixteen weeks still failing. My professor sat back in her chair, hands folded in front of her, and smiled. In class earlier that day, I had asked our guest speakers a question about pregnancy. "You're going to be okay," she said to me without prompting.

My throat tightened, and I continued to look at my chipped black nail polish. "I just," I started, feeling my voice constrict around my throat, "don't know what this means. For me. About me." My professor laughed a warm laugh, her curls shaking around her face. "Rachael, you are not the first queer woman to have a baby."

Somehow, hearing that from her, my queer professor, began to break apart something I had kept coiled tight. I could feel the pressure begin to ease.

Later that week, I sat at the burger joint across the street, picking at my fries and holding a limp veggie burger in my hand. My best friend in the program, Rae, sat across from me. We had bonded in a creative writing class where I wrote a "fiction" story based on my ex-girlfriend and she wrote a surreal story that included overt queer themes. Instant friendship.

When I set my unappealing burger back down on the grease stains in the lined red basket, she reached across the table and took my hand.

I wish I could remember our conversation that day. There's so much about the early months of my pregnancy that I don't remember, that only comes in flickers: calling my dad in the Jeep in the rain to tell him, telling a friend on the phone, a voice crackling from Oakland asking why I changed my mind about having an abortion and not knowing how to answer, climbing the hill on the forty-minute drive to campus wondering what would happen if I just let the wheel go and flew off the edge into the fog. I hadn't told anyone about that. Rae seemed to know, though.

I walked out of that burger spot feeling less alone.

When I returned to school after my older son was born, it was Rae who had watched him while I taught my classes. He'd sit in the back of the car, looking in the small mirror I attached to his rear-facing car seat, and we'd drive those same hills up and then down into Northridge.

Rae would meet me on the grass or in the Freudian Sip, and I'd pass her my cherry diaper bag and his soft little body.

"Auntie Rae's got you," I'd say and kiss his soft forehead and rush up the stairs to teach.

Three years later, he'd be the ring bearer in Rae and her wife's wedding, and I'd look around at all the love in their backyard, and it would hit me like lightning to my core that queer women saved my life.

AUGUST 2010

A month away from my due date, I was still scouring the internet for anything I could find about being a mom. I had taken the semester off, so didn't have classes to teach or attend, and I had made it through *Pushing Daisies, Dead Like Me,* and more Del Taco chicken soft tacos than I could count. My boyfriend brought pies home on a regular basis. We had moved in together at that point and I'd eat them in one sitting. Down an internet rabbit hole, I found a site called Offbeat Mama. Across the site were stories and features from women of all identities and backgrounds. I found an early post by the site's creator and read through her story. Even though her pregnancy had been planned, I was comforted to read that she initially had all the same fears as I had about losing herself or who she was. I don't remember the content of the post, but I do remember the ending: "Being a mom isn't even the most interesting thing about me."

AUGUST 2020

"Please introduce yourself, your research interests, and any of your hobbies or other interests."

This simple prompt had me bolted to my seat. My MA baby was now in third grade, and, at that moment he was sitting in his room in Zoom school. My three-year-old toddler sat behind me as an iPad read him a book, so I figured I had time to write a basic introduction.

Instead, I stared at the blinking cursor. Nine years since I had completed my master's, six months into a global pandemic, eight years of full-time teaching, and I couldn't find the words. Do I write about my queerness? That I'm a mother in my late thirties? That I'm the first person in my family to pursue a PhD? Will any of these things make my professor and classmates automatically assume something about me?

Not knowing where else to go, I sent an email to our graduate student advisor. Heart pounding, I started and restarted the email:

> "~~I have a question . . .~~",
> "~~I was wondering . . .~~"
> "~~This may be weird, but . . .~~"
> "~~Forgive my anxiety, but I don't know who else to ask . . .~~"

Eventually, I just asked for an advising meeting. During that meeting, in a pause while discussing my degree plan, I blurted out, "Can I talk about my kids?" I stared at my computer screen, the Zoom link holding steady, as my graduate advisor smiled and considered.

At that moment, I couldn't help but think back to the way some of my professors and fellow students had reacted to my pregnancy nine years before. Walking down the hallway after a meeting for first-year composition graduate student instructors and lecturers, belly protruding too far to hide, and sensing a woman's eyes on my body.

"Well, that's going to interrupt things," she said before continuing to talk to her friend.

I wanted to snap back that I was going to finish. That one semester off wasn't going to derail me, but my throat closed and my cheeks grew hot.

Or sitting at a table on the second floor of a dining area as I slurped down my vegetable pho. An older student, a mother herself, sat across from me. She was a doctor who came back to school after retiring from her practice. "I told you that you should have gotten an abortion," she said, shaking her head. "Don't get yourself stuck."

I suddenly wasn't hungry anymore.

These moments flashed through my head as well as less specific ones. Subconscious murmurings reminding me that academics who became mothers were often hurt in their trajectory for tenure while fathers who had children before tenure were praised. For a moment I worried that I had done everything wrong.

I blinked back into my Zoom meeting. I don't remember my graduate advisor's exact words, but as an alumni of the program she offered her own perspective and advice. I thought back to this conversation as I drafted that first introductory post and included a sentence about my children. Luckily, my professor, Dr. Rebecca Rickly, was a mother herself and had raised two kids, just like I was doing. I didn't know it at the time, but one mentoring relationship had begun where another had ended.

SEPTEMBER 2022

I'm drafting this chapter as I sit on the floor, my laptop over my crossed legs. My almost-six-year-old child works on a LEGO set he bought with some early birthday money that came in the mail. I would much rather be on the couch—I can already feel stiffness creeping up my lower back—but he wants me here because the LEGO set "is a 5+, but I might need help with the little pieces." I look up and see him hold the tip of his tongue against his bottom lip, his sign of utmost concentration, as he works two LEGO pieces together. My older son, twelve now, sits in a chair by the window listening to music on his headphones, working on his math homework. My spouse is in the kitchen prepping dinner and looking over an article I sent about being a stepparent.

This is how much of my work gets done for school. I do homework when my kids do homework. Or I do homework as I sit on the couch with them and drown out the voices of two Australian cartoon dogs talking and playing as my kids' laughter filters through. I sometimes do homework as the kids sword fight in the next room over, occasionally calling out "Is anyone bleeding?"

I wake up at five A.M., while the house is still quiet, and walk down the hall, over the pink-and-blue LED lights that filter from each kid's room and start the coffee my spouse prepped the night before, then I go for a run. I drink my coffee and eat my peanut butter on an English muffin. I'll write or answer emails or leave quick feedback for my students until I hear the patter of feet across the floor.

I sit in Zoom meetings where the younger one's hand creeps up onto my shoulder as he crouches below the webcam's purview or where my older guy pops onto the screen to wave, loving the attention as my advisor or classmates or research partners yell out, "Oh, hi, Liam!" My spouse takes the kids out skateboarding, to the movies, or to the park to give me an hour or two when big deadlines are looming. Liam's dad will take him for an extra night or on a special trip. This life is truly a team effort.

My favorite thing about my PhD program is that it's *mine*. Neither my spouse nor my co-parent are academics, no one in my family has a PhD, and my research has nothing to do with my kids or being a mother. My program is something that I'm doing that is outside my role as a parent, yet it is completely affected by the fact that I'm a parent.

I'm realizing, though, that I had only two semesters of graduate school where I wasn't pregnant or had a child. Doing graduate school as a parent is really the only way I know how to do it.

Just one supportive mentor can make all the difference. What I needed most were examples—other people writing about being writers and parents—and someone there to just listen as I went through it. Early on, listening meant having an advisor who would let me bring my six-month-old baby to our meetings, and now it means having an advisor who will create standing meetings with me so I can fit our dissertation discussions into my routine. Having advisors that didn't make me feel like having kids was a detriment was pivotal. I was already, am already, so hard on myself. I needed the reminder, the examples, that there is not one right way to do academics. It turned out that having my first kid during my master's program was wonderful timing—I didn't have a heavy teaching load, I had a supportive community of other queer graduate students, and I had the flexibility to be with him. I actually got to stay home with my firstborn much longer than I did with my second son, who was born when I already had a three-year contract as a full-time lecturer.

However, academia is not set up to support parents, especially graduate student parents. I applied to one PhD program in 2019. One. The only one I applied to was a fully online program with a two-week May seminar because two weeks away is manageable. Whole summers away aren't doable. Quitting my full-time job with benefits to become a teaching assistant is not an option. The weight of that—that academia excludes mothers, nonbinary, and gender-queer parents—infiltrated my thoughts even after I got into my program. What I needed from my mentors was someone who was willing to work within my schedule and remind me when I was doing well, advisors and professors who

- Don't assume we are "too busy" with our children to want to collaborate or work with us.
- Adjust their ideas about "professional" Zoom meetings—hearing kids in the background or seeing kids in the background shouldn't be cause for disdain.
- Connect us with any resources available—funding, student-parent groups, mental health services—that we could use, if needed.
- Understand when and if our family means that our prospective job market locations are geographically bound.
- If they have children, talk about them in academic contexts to help normalize that we are all human beings with full lives outside our work.

Mentorship isn't just from advisors. I wouldn't have finished my master's without my friend and fellow graduate student Rae, another queer woman, who watched my baby while I taught classes. So many graduate students, both then and now, talked to me about their own kids once they found out I was pregnant. Just this month, graduate students from the Council for Programs in Technical and Scientific Communications Graduate Student Committee created a separate channel on the Discord server specifically for graduate student parents. This type of mentorship and connection between graduate students is also of paramount importance to our success.

When I first got pregnant during graduate school, it felt like one of those moments from childhood, swimming at the beach, when the waves become relentless and pound over your head, only giving you enough time to catch a quick breath of air before being tumbled over again, and you're never sure whether you'll actually make it out of the water. However, Le Guin reminds me that "it does not always follow that one drowns. A lot of us can swim."

WORKS CITED

Le Guin, Ursula K. 1989. "The Fisherwoman's Daughter." In *Dancing at the Edge of the World: Thoughts on Words, Women, Places*. Grove Press.

11 ▸ EXPECT THE UNEXPECTED

Navigating the Early Dilemmas of Becoming a Graduate Student Parent

LAURA FITZWATER GONZALES

Disclaimer: This chapter discusses pregnancy loss.

On the day of my dissertation proposal defense, I was thirty-eight weeks pregnant with my second child. My defense was supposed to be completed the week before—at thirty-seven weeks—but an ice storm hit the city, shutting down the university, and the defense was pushed back one week. I bargained with my baby to stay put just a little longer. The last thing I wanted was to defend my dissertation proposal in the postpartum brain fog of exhaustion. I woke up that morning, rolled my very pregnant self out of bed, and as I showered, I slowly looked up at the skylight in the bathroom, only to find it covered with snow. *Snow*! Once again, on the rescheduled day of my proposal defense, our city was covered in snow, and it was completely unexpected.

While my stories of pregnancy, miscarriage, and childrearing during graduate school are likely not unique, they did take up more than half of my graduate school experience. In this chapter, I highlight key moments in my journey of graduate school parenting life. My aim is for you to be encouraged by my experiences, to laugh a little, and to take away some practical advice that might help you during the beginning stages of parenting and pursuing your PhD.

DISCLOSING PREGNANCY AND LOSS

After my third year of grad school, my husband and I started talking about having kids. I had finished my master's degree and was teaching, taking one class per semester, and working on passing my preliminary exams. My husband had just finished his PhD and was transitioning into a full-time job, and we were both approaching thirty, so it seemed like a good time to have a baby.

Let me just pause right there: Is there ever a "good time" to have kids? I think if you're truly waiting for a perfect time, you just might never get there. Having kids changes everything. You've got a tiny human who is 100 percent dependent on you for survival. There is no way that things won't change. So there might never be a good time to have kids, but for me, having babies in graduate school worked out well. I didn't feel pressure in terms of my time to degree and my department was full of faculty and graduate students with young kids. But this wasn't something I realized initially.

My first pregnancy happened much faster than I anticipated. As someone who went to the doctor only in the direst of circumstances, I didn't have an obstetrician. I just put it off. (I wouldn't recommend that.) I was about ten weeks pregnant, and one morning I woke up spotting and cramping. The internet told me this was a bad sign, so I emailed my professor to say that I wouldn't make it to class that day. I canceled my own class, and my husband took me to an urgent care. I still remember their sad faces when they read my intake paperwork and said they couldn't help me. I'd have to go to the emergency room. In retrospect, I wish I'd never gone. But the shock of getting pregnant and having a miscarriage helped me see how truly unprepared I was. As I recovered, I realized I needed to do some research.

Not knowing where to start, I talked with a fellow grad student who I knew had a toddler. She introduced me to the local birthing center, which was staffed with midwives and nurses who were all women. The environment was welcoming and warm. Being seen at the birthing center was a game changer for me. My advice to you: don't procrastinate about finding your doctor or midwife or a practice that makes you feel safe, seen, and heard. Take time to do your research on local options and attend any events or open houses a practice you're considering offers or take a tour of their facility. And ideally do this before you get pregnant or really soon after conception. I procrastinated again about calling the birthing center when I became pregnant with my second child and we almost did not secure a spot.

But back to my miscarriage. My adviser was also a woman who had children, although she didn't talk about her personal life very much. I decided to tell her about the pregnancy and miscarriage, even though our conversations typically focused on academics rather than personal life. I didn't know what she would say or how she would react. I was especially worried that by having this conversation that disclosed my desire to have kids, she would be focused on my time to degree and might not want to work with me anymore. I based my fears on horror stories I'd heard from others about having to choose between family and career. But I was wrong. We met in her office and I told her that I had been pregnant but had had a miscarriage. And I cried. She handed me a box of tissues and let me cry while being kind, gentle, and encouraging. She affirmed my desires to be a parent and a PhD student. I never felt marginalized because I was pregnant or had kids; instead, I felt embraced and supported. Again, this was something unexpected. Over the years, my professors made it clear that I could bring my babies to meetings or classes if I needed to. Faculty members hosted events where everyone was encouraged to bring their families. My identity as a PhD student included my identity as a parent. And now, as a professor, I always tell my student-parents that their children are welcome in class and I try to support them with the gentleness and care with which my professors supported me.

FIRST-PREGNANCY LESSONS

Exams

My first pregnancy coincided with the timing of my second preliminary exam. I had taken and passed my first exam before pregnancy, and at the time, each exam was scheduled for one twenty-four-hour window. Most students expected to start the exam early in the morning and work feverishly for the entire time. I was about seven months pregnant and I knew my body could not handle staying awake for twenty-four hours. I also knew I would need many bathroom and snack breaks. I had a good relationship with our graduate program director, and with encouragement from some fellow students I decided to ask for accommodations. I emailed him, explained my situation (although he already knew I was pregnant), and asked if there was anything that could be done differently. I left it open to his suggestions. He immediately responded, suggesting that we have a 12-12-12 schedule, for which I would work for 12 hours, take a 12-hour break, and then work again for 12 hours. I was relieved and thankful for the accommodations and the fact that they came with unexpected ease. I passed the exam, thank goodness, because I knew I would not be successful if I had a baby at home while I was trying to take this kind of exam because of the sleep deprivation, feedings, and the distractions that come with parenting. My lesson here is twofold. First, if you need to take an exam, try to do so before having a baby. And second, if you need accommodations, you should ask for them. Talk with your institution's Title IX coordinator. If you have colleagues who have had children, seek out their support and advice, especially if you fear that disclosing your pregnancy could have social ramifications in your department.

Maternity Wear

A practical thing I wish I'd known about during my first pregnancy was where to buy maternity clothes on a budget. If you're teaching and working with others, you probably want to present yourself in a way that you feel positive about. It's also important to keep in mind that you'll need these clothes for weeks or months after giving birth. Your friends might have clothes to lend or give. You should also look for local consignment sales or stores (which are also great for any baby clothes or equipment, except the car seat) or the second-hand online market. If you have time and energy, garage sales offer the cheapest deals, and people in online groups often give away baby or maternity stuff.

When you're done with those clothes, pass them on to another mom in need. Trust me, as cute as you think that dress or top is now, you may never want to see it again after wearing it for nine (or more) months.

Health Insurance

Another lesson I learned during my first pregnancy was about health insurance. During my time as a grad student, I had one of the best offices in the building, and I shared it with six other people. I had a great desk in the corner and plenty of privacy, except when it came to phone calls. That is how some of my colleagues found out I was pregnant, because I had to call my insurance company while my office mates were present. Before you get pregnant, it is important to know what your health insurance covers, what medical expenses will need to be paid, and if the baby can be added to your health insurance . I'd been working part-time before graduate school and I'd never had my own health insurance. And since I had successfully avoided doctors, I really had no idea what I was getting myself into financially. And let me tell you, if you're going to plan to have a baby at a certain time, try planning to have one during one insurance year so that you don't pay your deductible twice, especially if it's a high deductible.

Health insurance is great, but specific plans or rules about the insurance can also change. With my first child, the way our graduate student insurance worked was that because I was taking a "time out" from school, I was able to go on Consolidated Omnibus Budget Reconciliation Act (COBRA). I put the baby on my insurance rather than my husband's insurance because, at the time, it was a more affordable option for us. However, our graduate student insurance had changed unexpectedly by the time I had my second baby. When I called customer support for the insurance carrier for round two, they let me know that COBRA was no longer an option due to a change in how graduate students were classified at our university. As long as I was still paying my tuition and fees, I was still able to have insurance, whereas in my first pregnancy I was able to take a financial time out. I'm sure the rules have changed since then and differ by university. The take-home point for you, however, is to make sure you call your insurance company and find out what you're covered for if you have a baby, and especially if you have to take time out of school. Whether you're a full- or part-time student, a lecturer, a teaching assistant, or a research assistant, you need to find out what taking a break means for your insurance and what would happen if you extended that break.

I had finished my fourth year of graduate school, I had passed both of my preliminary exams, and I was ready to start figuring out my research topic for my dissertation. My first child was born in September, and I'd already decided that I would take off that fall semester. I thought that three full months at home with my baby would be plenty of time, and then for the spring semester, after the holidays, I'd be ready to jump right back into teaching and research.

Wrong. During that time, my spouse was employed full time at a well-paying job, we owned a house, I had my COBRA insurance, and we had supportive friends, but I couldn't leave my baby just yet. So once again I contacted my adviser, afraid of what she might say or that she might tell me I had to come back or else I could not continue in the program. But she didn't. I wish I'd kept the email she sent because her words lifted every burden of fear from my shoulders and gave me the freedom to stay home with my baby and not think about school for a few more months. She gave me the space to keep figuring out how to be a parent instead of starting to plan my syllabus.

I know this isn't everyone's path. One of my friends left the hospital after having a baby to conduct participant observations and collect a few interviews. She didn't have the time or the space to take a break. But that's a problem with the system, folks. And it becomes personal because we are the ones left to manage the lack of support. We cannot rest and recover, we cannot heal, we cannot be with our babies. If you had that time ripped away from you, I am so sorry. Let's try to fix the system.

FULL-TIME PARENT, FULL-TIME GRADUATE STUDENT

I hate the phrase "part-time mom." I heard someone say that once in reference to going back to work after having a baby. She said she didn't want to be a "part-time mom," so she quit her job to stay home with her baby. But the truth is, if you have kids, you're always a full-time parent, no matter what. It doesn't matter who is with that child; you are the parent who is responsible for everything. You're responsible for arranging childcare. You're responsible for making sure that child is fed and cared for. You're responsible when they cry in the middle of the night or get sick in the middle of the day. It's on you. And if you have a partner, luckily (hopefully) it's on both of you.

Yet despite that responsibility, we also need the support of others when we become parents. When my first child was around eight months old, I was (mostly) ready to go back. A good friend had had a baby around the same time as me and we decided to share a nanny. This turned out to be an unexpectedly excellent decision. The savings of splitting the childcare costs were a huge help to both of our families. Finding good childcare can be challenging, but if you're able to pay well and offer a full-time job, it will be easier. Our girls had the best time growing up with each other. They spent about two years together until our situations changed, and they still remember each other as their childhood best friends. Use your networks, mom Facebook groups, or even Care.com (we found some good nannies there) to meet these folks. Meet up at a public park or playground to test the waters. Figure out whose house would be best for the kids. Find a nanny who wants to spend time with them, who wants to play with them, and who comes highly recommended. I know the cost of childcare is a burden, but I'd recommend paying well. It's the best way to hire and keep someone who is good. Try to get home on time, and when you can't, give a good tip. These folks are taking care of your baby. Don't you wish someone had paid you?

Speaking of time, your time changes unexpectedly and dramatically when you have a baby. Time is no longer your own. If you don't have kids yet, soak it up while you have it. You won't realize what an amazing gift it is until it's gone. When I was working on my independent research or reading for my classes, I could work when and where I wanted. I could come home and lay on the couch and read. I could stay in my office on campus until late at night. Having a baby at home who demanded my time and attention forced me to change my rhythm. My schooling took on a very structured schedule. I left home in the morning when the nanny arrived, I dressed for work, I worked on campus in my office all day, and I came home in the evening, even when I wasn't teaching or meeting with others. It forced me to fit my work into the day, instead of letting it bleed into my nights and weekends. Some people are better at creating this structure than others and some people don't enjoy the structure, but for me, it was productive. I knew when to focus at work and I knew when I could take a break from work. Finally, my days were becoming more predictable and less unexpected.

EPILOGUE

I started this essay sharing about the crazy snowstorm that arrived during my dissertation defense. Luckily for me, the snow was so unexpected that the university remained open long enough for me to pass my proposal defense. We all rushed home, and then I waited almost two more weeks for my baby to be born. I guess I had nothing to worry about after all.

Expecting the unexpected was a motto I lived by during my pregnancies. From the interviews I conducted for my dissertation research about the breastfeeding experiences of new parents and the anecdotes I heard from friends, it seemed like no one had the experiences touted in the birthing classes or videos. For each stage of parenting, there are so many experiences that are totally normal. It's normal if your baby doesn't latch right away with breastfeeding. It's normal to be confused or scared about making the right decision when it comes to pediatricians or formula brand or sleep training. It's normal to have your baby sleep next to you. It's normal to have your baby sleep down the hall from you. Parenting probably won't come naturally. It takes time and practice, and it will probably cause you some pain. But through it all, know that you are not alone. There are so many parents—and parents with PhDs—who have gone through this before you, and they want to help you and support you and give you lots of unsolicited advice. Lean on your people: your family, neighbors, friends, community, and fellow graduate students. Keep practicing parenting and you'll get better over time, even when you encounter the unexpected.

12 ▸ DO HAVE KIDS IN GRADUATE SCHOOL

Resisting Chilly Advice to and Treatment of Prospective Parents in Graduate School

NATASHA TRACE ROBINSON

Disclaimer: This piece includes discussion of pregnancy loss, high-risk pregnancy, and mental health.

Author's Note: Some of my descriptions/timelines about graduate program leaders are vague because they would be otherwise identifiable.

WARM POSSIBILITIES: GRADUATE SCHOOL BEFORE PREGNANCY AND BEFORE MOTHERHOOD

In late August 2014, I sat listening and taking notes in my graduate school orientation. The presentation took a jarring turn when the graduate program leader told us that 50 percent of our marriages would end during graduate school. Additionally, he advised us not to have kids while in graduate school. Neither warning had an explanation, although it is true that graduate school and higher education can be difficult on marriages and personal relationships. According to an article in the *Chronicle of Higher Education,* "Marital hardships are easily traced to academe's toxic work culture" (Wedemeyer-Strombel 2018). Although the graduate English program faculty leader did not create the system that harms many marriages, he wasn't doing anything to disrupt it—and this became a clear theme from some faculty at my graduate institution. Even though multiple graduate faculty members saw that once I was pregnant I experienced unfair treatment, little changed. For example, when I became pregnant, I was passed over for assistantships I was well qualified for and would have benefited from. In another instance, I did not even get a notification that I was not chosen for summer funding. I had to reach out to a graduate program leader to find out I had been rejected. The faculty expressed that they cared for me; however, their best advice was often to just let go of my frustrations about being passed over or left out for the sake of getting along.

I had zero interest in children when I began my doctorate degree. Children were never on my mind except for knowing that I did not want them. After I earned my doctorate degree, I planned to return to a leadership role for my former employer, where I had been employed full time as a professor and department chair. My decision to enter a doctoral program is a common choice that many women make, according to an article in the *New York Times*: "Over the past decade, as more women of all social classes have prioritized education and career, delaying childbearing has become a broad pattern among American women almost everywhere" (Tavernise et al. 2021). It was clear to me when the male graduate program leader advised us not to have kids that my choices were either to have a child in my late twenties or early thirties or to further my education. Luckily for me, I did not want kids, so I did not think much of his warning at the time.

About halfway through my first year of graduate school, baby fever hit me hard. After the conclusion of my first year in the doctoral program, my husband, Craig, and I decided to try to get pregnant. I did some digging to see if my private university had a maternity policy for graduate students, and it did not. The only mention about taking leave was that it would be unpaid for either an entire semester or the entire academic year. I was determined to avoid losing my income. I had left my reliable, compensated, full-time teaching career to go to graduate school. Our household budget had been split in half; we were losing about $40,000 in yearly income and we knew a baby would increase our expenses exponentially.

I planned to give birth over the earlier part of summer, thinking it would be easy and I would not miss any school and teaching. Once I was off birth control, I got pregnant after a couple of months, only to quickly lose the pregnancy. Months later, I got pregnant again and lost the pregnancy further on. Those losses were emotionally draining and physically excruciating. We decided to try to get pregnant one more time, knowing it meant a late August birth. We reasoned that if I got pregnant it would end in a loss and we would just take a break until the timing was right again. Fate had other plans. Right after my thirtieth birthday I found out I was pregnant with Orion. We were elated. I stayed pregnant thanks to progesterone and careful monitoring.

THE BEGINNING OF A "CHILLY CLIMATE": LIFE IN GRADUATE SCHOOL AFTER BECOMING PREGNANT

I had no choice but to inform the school of my pregnancy when I was six weeks along because I had terrible morning sickness. Unfortunately, the moment I told a graduate program leader (who was female) that I was pregnant, I felt like an outsider within my graduate program. She gave me lukewarm congratulations and informed me that there was no policy about maternity leave for graduate students. Having previously researched this, I explained my plan to return to classes a couple of weeks into the semester and that I hoped we could work something out. She said I would have to get permission from the first-year writing director, and the conversation ended with a chill in the room. According to Dana M. Britton, "The prevailing metaphor for understanding the persistence of gender inequalities in universities is the 'chilly climate'" (2017, 5). It would make sense if the chilliness came from other graduate students because most of my cohort were a few years younger than I was and no one else had children. Instead, it came from the higher ranks within the department, many of whom had children themselves.

It did not matter that I was thirty years old, formerly a successful department chair and an accomplished college professor, and that I had completed a year of intense coursework. I was suddenly excluded from the names that were suggested for service committees and funding opportunities offered to graduate students. I was confused because my choice to try to become a mother at age thirty was no longer considered a rarity. The median age of women who give birth in the United States rose from age twenty-seven in

1990 to age thirty in 2019 (Morse 2022). About 60 percent of women who earned a doctorate degree in the humanities and arts in 2020 were between the ages of thirty-one and forty (National Science Foundation 2021). I was angry that faculty leaders in my graduate program were choosing to ignore what I could contribute to the department and what I would benefit from most because I was pregnant.

My pregnancy was also complicated outside the university, and I often felt like a burden to those around me. During much of my pregnancy I coped with high stress as I taught seven classes among several institutions, struggled with gestational hypertension, and experienced typical first-child parental nervousness. Many faculty in the department were quietly kind and considerate during my pregnancy. They understood when I sometimes needed to leave early or arrive late due to a high-risk appointment. Most faculty in the department genuinely cared about me and would inquire about how I was doing. Unfortunately, some fellow graduate students made disrespectful comments to me in front of graduate faculty. One graduate student remarked repeatedly about how "big" I was becoming. I don't believe she had any idea about how offensive her comments were. My developing pregnancy measured very small (my son's femur measured in the 3rd percentile), and we were concerned about uterine growth restriction, in addition to complications related to gestational hypertension.

While no faculty member said anything negative to me about my decision to become pregnant, it was clear that no one wanted to make waves in the department by speaking out. Britton notes that Roberta Hall and Bernice Sandler, who formed the concept of a chilly climate toward women in 1982, define it as "patterns of inequitable treatment that, as they accumulate, inhibit women's confidence, self-esteem, and accomplishment" (2017, 7). In her study, for which she interviewed female academics, Britton found that "overall, these interviews indicate that the resistance among many women faculty to seeing their workplaces as 'chilly' is grounded in the fact that this metaphor, with its implications that gender is both systemic and pervasive, does not fit their understandings of how gender matters at work" (2017, 23). I recognized this chilliness and became angry because I continued to be ignored or denied opportunities I was qualified for. No one said that my pregnancy was the cause of these issues, but others around me were not ignored or forgotten and I was the only one pregnant. When I raised the issue of being passed over for a funded research assistantship (which would have afforded me more flexibility) and for summer funding, no one could give me an answer as to why. Professors and leadership blamed each other, and one excuse I was given by that second department leader (a woman) was that other graduate students who received the funding were more senior than I (which was untrue). When I was advised by a supportive female graduate faculty member to let it go, I did. Her advice was that I needed to focus on myself, my health, and my future baby instead of trying to fight the entire system, and I recognized that she was probably correct.

Orion, my son, was born healthy three weeks early, after medical induction for gestational hypertension. Shortly after birth, Orion developed jaundice, struggled to breastfeed, and was tiny (3rd percentile body but 98th percentile head), yet perfect. I had little time to heal—at two weeks postpartum I virtually attended a weeklong teaching orientation with Orion next to me in his bassinet. Despite my teaching and leadership experience, even the virtual arrangement was an exception. The female first-year writing director had to get the approval of graduate department leadership for my physical absence. She went out of her way to allow it, friends of mine in the graduate program made sure Zoom worked, and another graduate student friend, Annette, sat with me at home to care for my dogs so I could focus. An AAUP statement about families and academic work discusses the need for flexible and responsible treatment of faculty who have given birth. Although it does not discuss graduate students, much of the research it discusses still applies: "Physicians routinely certify six to eight weeks as the physical disability period for a normal pregnancy and birth.... The AAUP recommends that all educational institutions offer paid disability leaves for pregnancy" (2016, 341). Four weeks later, at six weeks old (two weeks earlier than the Centers for Disease Control and Prevention recommends), Orion received vaccines so he could begin daycare. To keep my funding, I had to attend when classes began. My choice was to lose pay for an entire semester or sacrifice time with my newborn to continue graduate school. I chose the latter, believing wholeheartedly that was my only choice.

Looking back, I realize that I made the wrong choice for myself and my family by going back so soon. However, and this might not make a lot of sense to readers so far, I do not regret my choice. Some of the negative consequences of going back too fast included that I did not heal properly—not physically, not emotionally, and not mentally. On weekends I slept extensively to make up for my inability to recover from giving birth. I ended up on antibiotics because I developed an infection, and my white blood cell count went sky high. During this time, I was supported by multiple professors, most of whom were mothers or caretakers themselves. A female future dissertation committee member and my graduate writing group went out of their way to accommodate me. Additionally, there were a couple of new students who had small children. We often chatted and they gave me advice about pumping, milestones, and teething. Fellow graduate students made us food and visited us on weekends to keep us company. Regardless of the difficulty of that time, I look back on it positively because I realize how many people cared for us despite their own busy lives.

Outside of a few close friends, few knew the struggles I experienced internally and outside school as postpartum anxiety set in. My close friends knew how little I bonded with my son. At times, my husband took care of Orion at night alone because I physically and mentally could not bring myself to do it. Well-meaning graduate students exclaimed, "Wow! You're Superwoman!" and "I want to be like you someday! You've got it all figured out!" while having no idea that in reality I was not taking care of myself. I did not have much figured out, much less everything, and I was not Superwoman as I hid my declining physical and mental health behind the scenes. Karishma Kaushik (n.d.), a former graduate student, described her experience as a new mom: "After my child was born . . . I continued being discreet about my 'non-work' life, avoiding topics related to health concerns, child-care conflicts, or personal upheavals. This came from both self-imposed and institutional pressure to operate within a system that did not account for a 'non-conventional' graduate student. "I became an expert at toxic positivity, hiding reality behind dry shampoo, makeup, and a smile. I sacrificed my own wellbeing in what I thought I had to do, returning to classes, not quite realizing what I was giving up."

My experience was different. I do not regret my choice to return to school because I kept my mind busy and could often ignore my postpartum depression and anxiety while my medication kicked in. My funding allowed us to pay for daycare and I saw that I could accomplish a great deal of work on the days Orion had daycare. Thanks to daycare and careful planning, I did not fall behind in my graduate studies.

THE SPRING THAW: CHANGE IN LEADERSHIP LEADS TO LESS CHILLINESS

Progress was made within my department as more of us had babies and the department became more aware that they needed to support new parents, even though it could not change the university's lack of parental leave. After Orion was born, a wave of other graduate students in my program had babies. This wave included my own second child, Celeste, born 19.5 months after Orion and following another devastating loss of my own. Celeste was also tiny and experienced even worse jaundice than Orion had. She needed home care and lights to expel the excess bilirubin. Yet my experience with her was different from my experience with Orion. Supportive graduate faculty leaders had replaced the chillier leaders, and many of the new leaders later became members of my dissertation committee. Thanks to this leadership change, I was lucky enough to be allowed to teach two classes in the fall before I gave birth to Celeste (meeting the requirements of my graduate instructorship) and I could take my spring semester to be with her after I gave birth. Because of the support I received, I bonded with Celeste in the ways I was unable to with Orion, including successfully breastfeeding her for over a year. The second time around, I was able to care for Celeste alone most nights, and I enjoyed our bonding time.

Along with others, I set a path of some positive change by encouraging more inclusivity toward graduate student parents. I was already close with several women in my program, but we became even closer as we navigated pregnancy, childbirth, recovery, and raising babies together. As a person who prides herself on both her cynical nature and her rose-colored glasses, I refuse to look back and see only how my well-funded private university let me down (it could have had a maternity leave policy that offered partial funding) and how some of the former leaders within my department let me down. Instead, I pay attention to the network of new mothers who came after me, including Jackie, one of the editors of this collection. I also think about the professors who nurtured me when I needed it.

I know I am a better mom because I granted myself fulfillment in my doctorate program while I had children, even though much of that three-year period was difficult and hard on my body and my mind. I had the privilege of choosing to break through assumptions that graduate students should not have children. I also had the privilege of personal fulfillment by becoming more educated and by having children. I am keenly aware that not all have that privilege. My instinctual disposition is closest to that of a bull in a china shop—I will knock it all down if I must—and not everyone can or wants to do the same. I managed to be the first person on my father's side of the family to earn a college degree. Then I went on to earn a master's degree and finally a doctorate degree. Similarly, I broke molds designed to prevent graduate students like me from becoming parents. I share my experience so that others might be able to do the same, should they want to. I also share my story to encourage graduate program leaders to be more mindful of graduate student parents and to advocate for change both at the departmental level and the institutional level.

I do not think that the graduate program leader who advised my cohort not to have children meant harm or that the other two leaders who became chilly toward me had bad intentions. Yet, passing over graduate student parents for opportunities that could benefit them is ill advised. I am no longer hurt or angered by the treatment I experienced while I was pregnant; instead, I have paid careful attention to the things I would do differently.

ADVICE AND FINAL THOUGHTS ABOUT CHILLINESS TOWARD GRADUATE SCHOOL PARENTS

Parenthood and the decision to become a parent has never been easy. Neither is the choice to go to graduate school. When we combine graduate school and becoming a parent, it becomes a mind-bending exercise in will and tenacity that re-forms and changes throughout the journey. Redefining expectations for pregnancy and parenthood in graduate school is a tall order. As many know, higher education is full of problems that are counter to what we teach our own students. I argue that we should continue to break the molds of higher education to be more inclusive of all, including those who are pregnant and new parents.

In my role as an administrator, I work to build a culture that supports the choices people make and the realities that follow those choices. I work to support my faculty in as many ways as I can. This advocacy includes asking hard questions of other leaders at my college to improve the working conditions for all, including adjunct faculty, who are overall, generally left out of many conversations about those conditions. I am careful in conversations with newly pregnant employees who feel safe enough to disclose their plans to me. I reach out to human resources often to make sure faculty who are going to be gone more than three days know about the Family and Medical Leave Act. I stress to my faculty that their health and the health of their family is important. I do not want any of my faculty to put themselves through turmoil, physical and mental pain, and so on, for the sake of putting their job above all else. As a result of these views and practices, faculty confide in me and I keep their confidence. I am determined to listen and to care for my faculty. My advice to leadership in higher education is to recognize that while leaders are often limited in the changes we can make, we must revise our institutional practices to be more inclusive. We need to ask tough questions and advocate for those who need advocacy, like expecting and new parents.

Reflecting on these experiences has enabled me to become a better colleague and administrator.

I hope that readers will gain perspective from my experiences. Having children in graduate school is hard and it might not be supported by your institution. Even so, there are ways to find your own path to parenthood in graduate school. My advice to future parents in graduate school is this: create a cohort of support. Find people who will care for you and about you, who will help you to be successful in finishing your graduate degree. Having children in graduate school was difficult, but having a small group of faculty and other graduate students I could trust made it more manageable, even at the hardest moments.

WORKS CITED

AAUP. 2016. "Statement of Principles on Family Responsibilities and Academic Work." American Association of University Professors, February 5. https://www.aaup.org/report/statement-principles-family-responsibilities-and-academic-work. Accessed September 19, 2022.

Britton, Dana M. 2017. "Beyond the Chilly Climate: The Salience of Gender in Women's Academic Careers." *Gender and Society* 31 (1): 5–27. Accessed August 25, 2022.

Kaushik, Karishma S. N.d. "'Letting Go of Guilt and Enjoying What We Have Is Certainly a Good Choice.'" Mothers in Science. https://www.mothersinscience.com/journeys/karishma-s-kaushik. Accessed August 18, 2022.

Morse, Anne. 2022. "Fertility Rates: Declined for Younger Women, Increased for Older Women: Stable Fertility Rates 1990–2019 Mask Distinct Variations by Age." Census.gov, April 12. https://www.census.gov/library/stories/2022/04/fertility-rates-declined-for-younger-women-increased-for-older-women.html#:~:text=Fertility%20rates%20in%20the%20United,women%20in%20that%20age%20group.

National Science Foundation. 2021. "2020 Doctorate Recipients from U.S. Universities." In *Doctorate Recipients from U.S. Universities: 2020*. NSF 22-300. https://ncses.nsf.gov/pubs/nsf22300/report/path-to-the-doctorate. Accessed September 19, 2022.

Tavernise, Sabrina, Claire Cain Miller, Quoctrung Bui, and Robert Gebeloff. 2021. "Why American Women Everywhere Are Delaying Motherhood." *New York Times*, September 30. https://www.nytimes.com/2021/06/16/us/declining-birthrate-motherhood.html. Accessed October 20, 2022.

Wedemeyer-Strombel, Kathryn R. 2018. "Why Does Graduate School Kill So Many Marriages?" *Chronicle of Higher Education*, October 17. https://www.chronicle.com/article/why-does-graduate-school-kill-so-many-marriages/. Accessed October 5, 2022.

13 ▸ SEND THOSE DAMNED EMAILS

Experiences and Advice from My Premature Delivery

TIFFANI K. TIJERINA

Disclaimer: This chapter discusses pregnancy complications, preeclampsia, and premature birth.

When my husband and I learned we were expecting our first child, due in January 2022, I was enrolled in online coursework for a PhD in technical communication and rhetoric with only one course left to take in the following semester. I already worked full time for my home state's university system, and I was also teaching online undergraduate courses part time at the same institution. I had a full plate, but I am a big planner. About three months into my pregnancy, I started making my plans by communicating with my supervisor and human resources. Then I notified the director for the PhD program that I wouldn't be teaching in the spring so that I could focus on bonding with my newborn and recovering. I only had one class left to take, so I enrolled in it, but I notified the instructor of my pregnancy and due date because it would likely impact the first few weeks of the semester. I even planned for the unlikely chance that our daughter would make her appearance early enough to impact the fall semester—I notified those instructors, just in case. My due date was January 5, 2022, and my perfectly laid plans left room for up to about three weeks early or late, covering mid-December to late January.

Sophia was born on November 24, 2021. Best laid plans, am I right?

THE BITTERSWEET BIRTH STORY

But let's start at the beginning. My husband (Josh) and I got married in April 2021, and we decided to start trying to conceive a couple months before our wedding. Starting us off on a high note (catch my sarcasm), my doctor told me not to be surprised if it took us up to a year to conceive "at my age," as if twenty-nine is somehow an abnormally old age for having a baby. Joke's on them—I had exactly one menstrual cycle before becoming pregnant, a happy bit of news we learned of on the last day of our honeymoon in Cancún. Most of the pregnancy went swimmingly, with only minor pains and sickness.

Then, six weeks before my due date, at a routine obstetric appointment, the midwife took my blood pressure and asked me if I was feeling stressed out. I had just come home from a particularly stressful week of family wedding festivities, but I felt fine when we returned home—so that's what I told her. After about an hour of blood pressure monitoring, she told me that I was showing signs that could indicate preeclampsia. Because Thanksgiving was the next day, the midwife sent me to the hospital to have bloodwork done so we wouldn't have to wait until the following week for results. As I was walking out the door, she said to me: "Don't worry, you're not having a baby today."

Spoiler alert: I had a baby that day.

I wasn't worried, but I knew my husband would be, so I went home to pick him up first so we could go to the hospital together. At the time, the situation didn't feel dire yet. I didn't have any symptoms, so I thought it had to be a fluke. But the on-call midwife confirmed that I did indeed have preeclampsia. For the next couple of hours, my blood pressure rose steadily and rapidly even though I had no other symptoms. Eventually, after my blood pressure had reached something like 160/120 (yikes), I was diagnosed with "preeclampsia with severe features" and I was hooked up to magnesium to prevent seizures while we got a plan in place. Let me just say: magnesium is not pleasant. I felt like my body had been heated up to a boiling point, and I was sweating through my clothes and the bed sheets. Then a whirlwind of midwives, doctors, nurses, anesthesiologists, and probably a few other white coats that slip my memory arrived, and I was told that I would not be leaving the hospital without having a baby—that birth was the only "treatment" for preeclampsia this severe.

After telling us that we were, in fact, having a baby today, the doctors gave us a choice: I could be induced and we could try for a vaginal delivery or I could be scheduled for an emergency C-section that day.

Let me start by saying that before that conversation, I had done *a lot* of research (I'm a planner, remember?) on vaginal versus surgical delivery, the pros and cons of epidurals, and the importance of "the golden hour" of breastfeeding. You name it; I had researched it all, and I had a birth plan in place, more or less. I wanted to deliver at the hospital but with a midwife instead of a doctor. I wanted to try to go without the epidural. I wanted to exclusively breastfeed. In retrospect, I think I probably did a little too much research on my ideal, perfect birth scenario—which ultimately set me up for more disappointment with the birth experience I had than I probably would have had if I had been a little more flexible in my expectations. After some discussion and a lot of crying with my husband, we made the decision to schedule the surgery for that day in order to avoid causing any unnecessary stress on our infant, who we already knew would have to stay in the Neonatal Intensive Care Unit (NICU) for an unknown amount of time just because she would be born so early—even before knowing if she'd have complications or not.

My surgery was scheduled for 5:00 P.M. and Sophia was born at 5:37 P.M., weighing 3 pounds, 9 ounces. I'm told that the surgery was textbook, with no real complications. Part of me feels like the shock of everything was a blessing in disguise because despite my extreme fear of needles, I don't remember anything about the spinal anesthesia and there are very few things I remember from the surgery. I remember my husband sitting next to me, holding my hand, and talking to me through the surgery, although I don't remember much of what he said. I remember getting very nauseous at one point and having just enough cognitive thought to turn my head toward him before puking. (Yeah, you read that right; I puked on my husband during surgery.) I remember hearing my daughter's first cry and I remember physically convulsing with relief and crying myself. I don't know how long I had been holding my breath, but I know I took a big one. The surgical team allowed my husband to take photos of the delivery (with my approval) and then of our daughter while the nurses cleaned her up. They called for me to turn and see her tiny face wrapped in a bundle of blankets from across the room, and then she was gone.

I didn't get to see, touch, or hold my daughter until the following day. I didn't fully process that until later that night, but it felt like I was missing a part of me—like the doctors removed a vital organ and then told me I was somehow still supposed to function without it. My husband was able to go take more photos of her in the NICU that night, though, and I was glad for that.

Instead of holding and nursing my baby that night, I laid in my hospital room feeling miserable from the magnesium and itchy from the anesthesia, not sleeping a wink. My husband, who had just spent the day in a whole different kind of stress (he later told me that he was afraid that he was going to lose us both, a thought that surprisingly hadn't even occurred to me), had genuinely earned the little bit of sleep he was able to get on the hospital couch, so I didn't want to wake him. So, not knowing what else to do with my time, I pulled out my phone and started sending emails—the first time I was thinking about grad school and work since my appointment that morning. (Not what you'd expect, right? I'll come back to this.)

On Thanksgiving Day, the day after my daughter was born, I was instructed to eat breakfast (really, I wanted to just skip that), and then I was pushed in a wheelchair to the NICU so that I could finally meet my daughter for the first time. If you've never seen a 3.5-pound baby before, it is a bit of a shock. But when it's your baby, the shock doesn't last long. Just by seeing her and touching her little hand, I felt whole again. They let me hold her later that day, finally having the skin-to-skin bonding time that we should have had immediately after birth, and suddenly it didn't matter that it was a day late. Holding her tiny body against mine was every bit as special and perfect as it should have been.

I spent five days in the hospital while the doctors worked on finding the right dose of medication to keep my blood pressure under control until the preeclampsia subsided, which took about two months. During those five days, my husband and I spent most of our time in the NICU, returning to my room only when my nurses made me—and feeling slightly annoyed that I had to be a patient instead of just being a mom. I was allowed to breastfeed her one to two times a day, and I spent a lot of time chained to a breast pump. The night I was discharged and had to go home without her was the hardest thing I've ever had to do. I cried when we said goodnight to her, and I cried the whole way home.

Earlier that day, my husband had gone home for a bit to check on our pets. He pulled out all our Christmas decorations (we have a lot) as a surprise to cheer me up, and I'll admit that it did bring a much-needed smile to my face. After that, we spent a few hours every night at the hospital with her. The nurses originally told us not to expect her home until her due date, and one nurse—who really needs to work on her bedside manner—ridiculed us for having hope that she would come home earlier. Our strong girl beat those odds by a mile, though, and she came home after only thirteen days—a full month before they expected her to. She was still so tiny the day we brought her home, barely four pounds.

Something I came to realize over the early months of our daughter's life was how traumatic her birth and the first two postpartum weeks were for me. I was also feeling a little ungrateful—I mean, what's important is that she was healthy, right? Even though I knew that in the abstract, I really struggled to come to terms with my daughter's birth story. I felt robbed of the "natural" birth I had planned and of the early days that should have been spent holding and nursing her that were instead spent at the mercy of the NICU nurses. I felt that my body had betrayed me and was continuing to betray me by how fast it was healing. I healed remarkably quickly from my C-section. I was up and moving and felt almost completely back to normal by the time we brought her home. That fast healing, though helpful in some ways, also made me feel that dwelling on my emotional trauma meant I was just being stubborn. If my body can heal quickly, why shouldn't my heart? And because of that, I didn't feel like I could talk to anyone except my husband about how I was feeling. Sometimes I didn't even talk to him about it.

I tried professional therapy a few years ago for grief and clinical depression, and it just wasn't for me, so I opted to process this experience informally. In many ways, just spending every day watching my daughter grow into a healthy (albeit extremely petite) toddler is my therapy. It's taken a lot of self-reflection over the last year to get to a point where I can talk about our birth experience positively, but I now feel pride in my emotional and physical strength. My C-section scar is now my favorite part of my body, and I hope it never fades.

THE ODDLY COMFORTING TRANSACTIONS OF GRAD SCHOOL

I was surprised by how easy I found it to work with the grad school through all of this. The night of my daughter's birth, I sent a lot of emails—because what else was I going to do, sitting awake and miserable in my hospital bed? I emailed my instructors to let them know and to ask them what I needed to do to request incomplete grades so that I could focus on recovery and return to finish my classes in the spring. One said I didn't need an incomplete because I was going to get an A in the class either way. The other didn't reply, but he did later grant me an incomplete, and I finished it a few months later after I'd had settled into life with a premature newborn. I also emailed my dissertation advisor, just to keep him in the loop.

Then I emailed the program director and the coordinator for the course I was teaching that semester, and that is where I really needed support. Despite the plan, unrelated circumstances meant that I had, unfortunately, already fallen well behind on grading for the class I was currently teaching, leaving my students with quite a lot of ungraded work. The program leadership essentially told me to focus on my family and that they'd be in touch if they needed me. I learned a couple weeks later that another faculty member in the department offered to finish all my grading for me. I still have yet to adequately thank this person, and I don't even know if she was compensated for all that extra work, but I truly hope she knows how meaningful that help was to me.

THE LESSONS I'M STILL LEARNING

My story is far from over. There is a lot more to tell and a lot more to come, but the small narrative I've shared with you is loaded with lessons I learned along the way and advice that needs to be called out and emphasized.

Advice on Priorities

People will tell you to ignore your phone, not check or answer emails, or focus only on you and your child. That is good advice that comes from a good place. But it doesn't work for everyone or every situation, so you do you. If sending emails in the middle of the night after a major abdominal surgery and the trauma of being separated from your child gives you some semblance of control, as it did me, send those damned emails.

Advice on Classes

The best first step to take in preparation for childbirth is to keep the lines of communication open with your instructors and to know what your options are at the program level. In my program, we are required to be enrolled in at least three credit hours every semester, so I didn't have the option to take a semester off completely, but I was lucky that my early delivery still fell at the end of the semester, when taking an incomplete grade was an option. (Although I realize now that I never did any research about other options, and I probably should have.)

Advice on Advice

Take it or leave it. You'll get all kinds of advice from all kinds of people. Some of it will be great advice, some of it will be terrible. Don't be afraid to just not take the advice if you don't think it's right for you. But also, don't be afraid to take the advice if it might help. I tend to be someone who shrugs off advice in order to do my own thing, but I was pleasantly surprised at how useful I found some of the advice to be.

Advice on Getting Help

Accept it. If you find yourself in an impossible position and you have people offering to help you get through it, accept that help. It's okay to need help, it's okay to ask for help, and it's absolutely okay to accept help. Had I not had help from the department that semester, my grading very simply would not have gotten done. I don't know what the protocol would be in the department for an instructor just not grading a class, but I'm certain that it would not have been a good experience for anyone involved.

Advice on Healing

Sit with your birth experience. Your feelings, positive or negative, are valid. Do what you need to do to heal emotionally as well as physically. Although professional therapy wasn't for me, I know that many do well with it in the postpartum period. It's worth considering whether therapy is right for you. I did and continue to do a few other things to heal myself:

- I read *My Caesarean: Twenty-One Mothers on the C-Section Experience and After* (Fields and Moritz 2019), which validated my feelings about my unwanted C-section delivery.
- After returning from maternity leave and working remotely for a while, I quit my full-time job so that I could continue to stay home and care for my daughter myself. Then I found a fully remote teaching job that worked for me because our family still needed two incomes. I continued in my PhD program and continued to teach online there as well.
- I focused on establishing an exclusive breastfeeding relationship with my daughter. Something you don't really understand until you actually have a

tiny human, who you are now responsible for feeding, is that breastfeeding is hard. It's like a full-time job even if you aren't having to pump, but when you're in a situation like mine where you have to pump in order to establish an adequate milk supply, it's even more exhausting. I could write a whole other chapter on my breastfeeding journey, but I found solace in focusing all my efforts on being successful at nursing.

- I joined a local and free mom-and-baby playgroup, where I found a village of like-minded moms in my area. These wonderful women quickly became my closest friends, as did their kids with my daughter.
- Most recently, I joined a local nonprofit dedicated to maternal mental health as a "theraparent," a role in which I am able to offer new parents in my area peer support as they work through the challenges of the early years. At the time I wrote this chapter, I had been able to offer my story and support to two other moms with premature infants who spent time in the same NICU as my daughter.

I still like to plan things out, but I've learned through these experiences that things just don't always go to plan (another aptly titled chapter in this collection); it's important to be open and prepared for deviations in our plans. Having a premature and unwanted C-section, not meeting my daughter until the day after her birth, temporarily losing control of both my and my daughter's well-being, and after regaining that control, balancing the emotional work of caring for my daughter while also caring for myself: this is labor that can't be quantified in plans and to-do lists. But I had no choice except to just roll with it. I made a new plan, and it changes every day to meet our needs. So send those damned emails or do what helps you get through the tough moments of the postpartum period.

WORKS CITED

Fields, Amanda, and Rachel Moritz, eds. 2019. *My Caesarian: Twenty-One Mothers on the C-Section Experience and After*. The Experiment Publishing.

14 ▸ DON'T DIVIDE YOURSELF

Building Hybrid Work Practices to Reconcile the Competing Identities of Graduate Student Parents

JENNIFER BURKE REIFMAN

Disclaimer: Infertility is explored in this chapter.

After several years of struggling with infertility, I became pregnant with my first child one month into my PhD program. My husband and I had nearly given up on the idea of having a child in the immediate future, but after medical intervention, the pregnancy test was positive and our lives began to change. Needless to say, the pregnancy was very planned and extremely wanted. As a financially independent, adult woman with a supportive partner, I was prepared for and elated about this new stage in my life. I was nearing thirty-three years old, and it felt like a wonderful time to become a parent in almost every aspect of my life—with the exception of my new academic endeavor as a PhD student. So began my journey into a hybrid identity and, ultimately, a hybrid work world.

As an older first-generation graduate student thousands of miles away from my family of origin, I was already out on a precarious limb as a recently admitted PhD student. I was unlike many of my peers who were typically much younger and more traditionally prepared for graduate studies, and I felt it in each classroom interaction when they described the research they had already conducted, the publications they had already begun working on, and the dissertation plans they had already formed. I already felt like a fraud in a foreign world. Then, one crisp October morning, I walked into class as a pregnant graduate student and felt more like an outsider than ever.

It was immediately clear that my pregnancy would be a novelty in this experience and another reason for me to stand out as different from my peers. My immediate reaction to learning I was pregnant was to hide my news from those around me. At the time, I didn't fully understand this instinctive need to hide my pregnancy, thereby dividing myself as a student in one space and a parent in another, but eventually the news became too big to hide. My fears were realized when I noticed I was getting cut from research projects, left out of cohort conversations, and treated as less capable or attentive in my classes.

My son was born the summer before my second year on a hot July day. He was long and skinny and had the most serious face. His dark eyes looked so intently into mine. It felt so good to have him there with us, finally, after all that waiting.

As a new parent, I continued to separate my student self from my parent self. There was no paid parental leave that I knew of through the university, and while the state of California offered its own maternity leave, I could not access it because although I was an employee of the university, I was classified as a student. I returned to work and school less than two months after giving birth. We chose to hire an at-home nanny for two days a week while I was teaching or taking my own class. The nanny earned $5 more per hour than I did, but having her help was the best option for our family. Even then, faculty and peers would send me links to the "affordable" group childcare centers near my campus without prompting. Or they would ask me: "Why not just stay home?" as if choosing that option was so simple. The baby didn't sleep well for those first five to six months and it showed on my face in those early morning classes. If I ever mentioned my exhaustion, young cohort members would comment: "No one told you to have a baby in a PhD program." When I took an evening class, which I needed to complete my coursework, I had to negotiate with the custodial staff to still be able to use the designated lactation room—a cold, dark closet-like space off the bathroom—to pump milk. In each conversation with staff, I was reminded that the room had standard 9–5 operating hours, suggesting that if I had needs past that window of time, I simply shouldn't be there.

As a new parent and a new graduate student, I was consistently made to feel like I could not be both; somehow my attempts to manage both in ways that suited me were always in conflict. As I reflect on it now, I was made to feel like all my personal and professional choices were not my own and were at odds with one another. Even though I made a clear choice to have a child, adapted my life to be both a mother and a student, and was succeeding, passing my preliminary exams and excelling in all my classes, it never felt like enough for some of the people around me.

Graduate programs have long been concerned with the retention of students from diverse backgrounds, especially in terms of recruiting and sustaining linguistically diverse students, undocumented students, and first-generation students. Research has found that parenthood greatly contributes to attrition, particularly for mothers (AAUP 2004), largely because the societal expectations for mothers directly contradict the expectations for being a successful graduate student (Alsop 2008; Lynch 2008). Being a good mother means sacrifice and total devotion to your child, while being a good student means the same, albeit for your career. As a graduate student parent and a mother, in particular, you are meant to make impossible choices and navigate a myriad of structural difficulties.

It is in this negotiation of identity that I repeatedly felt split in two throughout my graduate experiences. Karen Danna Lynch notes that because of these competing roles, "graduate student mothers further employ a strategy of 'maternal invisibility' to hide their motherhood role from their academic institutions and maintain their status as 'good students'" (2008, 603). The experiences I had sharing my life as a parent did make me want to hide, even before I experienced them. I did not need to be lectured about affordable childcare options or coming back to work too soon; I needed the financial support to make decisions for myself. I did not need to be chastised for being tired or taking up more space as a breastfeeding mother; I needed to simply exist within the complexity and multifaceted nature of simultaneously experiencing motherhood and graduate school. I needed and wanted to be both a mother and a student in the ways that worked for me, empowered to make decisions for myself and without judgment. By the end of that second year, I think I might have quit the whole program if it weren't for the pandemic.

My son was eight months old when we all went into lockdown. The first weeks sometimes felt fun and lighthearted, but then the isolation persisted and the fear grew and my husband and I were alone with full-time careers and our small child. The childcare was gone, our family was far away, and no one could help us. What saved us was the inherent flexibility of that time, when my husband could work remotely from home and I could both teach and attend class remotely. Of course, this was the experience of nearly all parents at this time, but the lessons I learned were invaluable in terms of my needs as a parent and PhD-seeking person. While my on-campus experiences were fulfilling and engaging, I felt a lot of difficulty handling the synchronous demands of graduate school during the early years of parenting. My multiple identities of mother, student, and emerging scholar, which pushed and pulled against one another, were calmed by a hybrid work and school life.

The heavy days of the COVID-19 pandemic stand as some of the most difficult moments of my life; the solitude and pressure of those moments were truly detrimental to my mental health, and I know I am not alone in that experience. However, as my family reemerged in the world nearly two years later, the paradigm that had originally favored in-person, on-site interactions had shifted in my favor, and it became clear that it was impossible to go back to a time before this flexibility. In this new world, any classes I wanted to take were accessible no matter what time of day it was. In online learning, I could also turn off my camera and attend to my child if I needed to. In this new world, I was no longer breastfeeding, but I could have pumped easily in the comfort of my home instead of in a cold, difficult-to-reach room. I saved money on commuting, my meetings were more flexible than ever because we could hold them over Zoom on my own schedule, my teaching was on my time because classes were remote and asynchronous, and so on. A hybrid work life met the demands of my dueling, hybrid identity.

To this day, I am still advocating for myself to maintain a hybrid teaching role, so that I can spend less time commuting and on campus and I have gone through credential programs to retain hybrid teaching assignments. I have pushed to make research meetings online to maintain flexibility. I have pressed my home department to keep offering Zoom options for attending job talks, meetings with guest speakers, and so on. I work with fellow graduate students to consider remote professional development opportunities and I help peers to advocate for their own hybridity.

Nonetheless, I understand that many graduate student parents won't have access to a hybrid work life in the same ways and that my advice on this issue is, in some ways, more of an argument about how systems need to make space for student parents instead of physically pushing us out. However, I would invoke the work of accessibility scholars who study online instruction; they push us to consider how time is differently experienced across contexts and how asynchronicity and hybridity are strategies for allowing for a variety of experiences (Anglesey and Ubbesen 2024; Wood 2014).

In the summer of 2022, an email thread began in the Rhet/Comp Mothers Listserv that illustrates this need. In this thread, mothers and parents from all stages of their careers began the necessary conversation around the need for flexibility in attending the upcoming Conference on College Communication and Composition. "Why can't we have both in-person and online options?" the group asked. As a result of this and the commitments of other groups, the 2023 conference provided opportunities for virtual presentations, an essential element of maintaining access to professional development and key experiences for those who are parents. This type of action, in which we advocate for continued flexibility, will continue to be a deeply important act of advocacy for graduate student parents as time goes on.

As I revisit these experiences, our family has just celebrated the first birthday of my second child—another miracle of medical intervention—who joined us in the midst of finishing my dissertation and navigating the job market. I am thankful for the Zoom meetings with my supportive and kind committee and even more so for the Zoom interviews with potential employers who never even knew I was days away from giving birth. However, hybridity did not save me from in-person campus visits, where I had to carefully navigate asking for rooms to pump in and space in the interview schedule to do so. Nor did it save me from leaving my six-week-old to interview for a job I had spent years working for.

Inevitably, I ended my graduate studies with less of a split identity than I started with, finding people who saw all parts of me as valuable and welcome and who knew the importance of flexibility. As I end my first-semester on the tenure track, I maintain that the flexibility I fell into during the global pandemic enabled me to be both a doctorate holder and a mom. As we roll back on pandemic era practices, forcing and instituting more in-person meetings, professional development, and interaction, I wonder who we exclude and who we deny multiplicity to by not embracing both hybridity of identity and presence.

WORKS CITED

AAUP. 2004. "Inequities Persist for Women and Non-Tenure-Track Faculty." American Association of University Professors. https://www.aaup.org/2004-05-report-economic-status-profession.

Alsop, Rachel, Stella Gonzalez Arnal, and Majella Kilkey. 2008. "The Widening Participation Agenda: The Marginal Place of Care." *Gender and Education* 20 (6): 623–637.

Anglesey, Leslie, and Molly E. Ubbesen. 2024. "Accessible Affordance of Asynchronicity: 'Cripping' Online Instruction." Research in Online Literacy Education (ROLE) 4 (1): 36-50.

Lynch, Karen Danna. 2008. "Gender Roles and the American Academe: A Case Study of Graduate Student Mothers." *Gender and Education* 20 (6): 585–605.

Wood, Tara, Jay Dolmage, Margaret Price, and Cynthia Lewiecki-Wilson. 2014. "Moving beyond Disability 2.0 in Composition Studies." *Composition Studies* 42 (2): 147–150.

15 ▸ YOUR BODY HAS OTHER PLANS

Finding Support and Forgiveness for Morning Sickness

KATE LAFFERTY-DANNER

When I saw the blue line pop up on the at-home test, I thought it was too good to be true.

My spouse, Patrick, and I had decided that it was a good time to try and get pregnant. We had recently bought a house in Scranton, Pennsylvania, and felt settled, finally, after years of graduate school and uncertainty. I had a full-time job as a writing center coordinator and he worked as an assistant professor at a local university.

In 2015, before we settled in Scranton, I had been accepted into the comparative humanities PhD program at the University of Louisville and I had quickly decided to add an additional master's degree in bioethics and medical humanities. It took three years of full-time graduate study to get through my coursework with the additional classes I needed, and I worked as an adjunct for the first half of the coursework before accepting a graduate teaching assistantship for the remaining time I had in the program. In November 2018, I completed my qualifying exams and my prospectus was accepted, so I would start the spring 2019 semester focusing on my dissertation while working.

When we moved to Scranton from Louisville, Kentucky, in the summer of 2019, I had a chapter completed and was looking for full-time employment. I started working as a writing center coordinator at Penn State Scranton in January 2020 with one chapter completed but not much progress otherwise. I was struggling through my dissertation while working full time, so after years of being stuck in the dissertation drift, I applied and received a dissertation completion grant for the spring 2022 semester. I quit my full-time job with two chapters written and an outline of the other three chapters, knowing that if I dedicated an entire semester to focusing solely on my dissertation, I would finally be able to finish my PhD. However, my body had other plans.

About seven weeks into pregnancy, at the end of February, I stared at my computer, tears streaming down my face, a peppermint tea at my side. Trying to catch my breath, I read through feedback from my dissertation chair and highlighted the main takeaways for the tenth time as I attempted to make sense of them. I opened a new Word document and pasted the feedback into it, hoping a change in scenery would make me understand the feedback, but nothing seemed to make sense to me anymore. I stood up and wiped away the tears as I fought back a wave of nausea, attempting to settle my stomach by taking deep breaths in and out as I focused on a static object in the room.

I was once the type of person who could balance teaching, writing, graduate coursework, and everything in between perfectly. I could write fifteen pages in one night if I needed to, I never missed deadlines, and I kept up with my course readings, even if I sometimes resorted to a quick skim. Why was it so difficult for me to understand feedback on writing that I had been working on for years? At that point, I felt like I barely remembered how to write or read anything at all.

Thankfully, I was working on my dissertation from the comfort of my home, in sweatpants and my own office. I could not imagine working full time in any other setting while trying to wrestle with the onslaught of first-trimester symptoms, one of which, nausea, seemed to be the most severe in the first few months. I was constantly running to the bathroom thinking I would get sick or gagging at any unusual smell. I kept ginger chews in my pocket at all times, but they never worked. Peppermint tea made my office smell nice and that was about all. The doctor prescribed medication that just made me drowsy and did very little to assuage the urge to vomit. I wore Sea Bands on my wrists all day and all night; they claimed to apply pressure to a certain spot on the wrists to calm any nausea. I ate saltines before I even got out of bed in the morning, hoping the dry cracker would help. I tried every old wives' tale to conquer the consistent nausea that overcame me, but nothing ever worked. Although nausea is a common symptom that impacts many pregnant people, it seemed there was little anyone could actually do about it. And my case of morning sickness was nothing compared to those who experience hyperemesis gravidarum, which is so debilitating it can result in severe dehydration or hospitalization.

From weeks seven to thirteen of my pregnancy, I felt like a completely different person. I felt weak and incompetent. I felt hazy and unable to concentrate, and any task—even checking emails—felt too overwhelming for me. During week seven, I caved and did what many tell pregnant people not to do: I told those I was working with that I was pregnant and having a hard time. Usually, pregnant people are told not to say anything before the second trimester to avoid any awkward conversations in case of a miscarriage, but I was on a tight deadline to finish my dissertation and I knew would not be able to complete it without the full support and understanding of my program and committee members.

As I trudged through those first few months of morning sickness, I constantly felt inferior. I had always suffered somewhat from imposter syndrome, feeling like nothing I did counted as "real" academic work. However, this was imposter syndrome at another level. Not only did I feel incapable of living up to ideals of academic rigor, but I also felt as though my brain and my body were actively working against me. Working on a dissertation was difficult enough, but tacking on my out-of-control hormones and the fact that I was growing a human made finishing the dissertation feel even more impossible. Each day was a different embodied experiment in what would make me nauseous or what would make my stomach churn so hard I thought I would throw up at any moment. Sitting at a computer would make me feel sick, knowing I would have to exert my very limited brain power to even read an email. I would try to get comfortable at my desk with no luck, then I would use that as an excuse to move to the couch and cozy up for a nap. The temperature of my office just never felt right and I would find myself sweating even when it was cold outside. My anxiety, which had usually been well under control, was at its maximum during those first few months, and there was very little I felt I could do about it.

Another layer that added to my morning sickness was the fact that my dissertation was on abortion in American culture and how we need to work on destigmatizing the procedure to have nuanced conversations about the issue. Not only had I dedicated years to researching and writing about abortion, I had also spent countless hours as a volunteer abortion access hotliner, helping others in Kentucky get funding for abortions or transportation to their appointments or just assisting them with whatever knowledge I could pass along. The spring of 2022 was the time when *Roe v. Wade* looked like it would be overturned, and my inbox was flooded with updates about states prepared to overturn abortion access if *Roe* fell. As I sat at my computer, battling morning sickness, I couldn't help but think about the countless numbers of people who will have to suffer through working with morning sickness while carrying a pregnancy they do not want. The combination of my attempts to keep up with the constantly changing abortion developments and my anxiety about perpetually falling behind made writing the dissertation even more difficult than before.

I often thought about how we rarely talk about how debilitating morning sickness can be, as though it was a social taboo instead of a very common (yet awful) result of being pregnant. In popular culture, we see women running to the bathroom just in time to throw up a little. Or if we do not know a character is pregnant, usually getting sick is a sign that they are pregnant. Women typically do not throw up on screen for any other reason. For instance, in the 2007 movie *Knocked Up*, the female lead Alison Scott realizes she is pregnant when she throws up twice while at work. What these depictions leave out is the consistent nature of morning sickness, the everyday, around-the-clock, many months of nausea that accompany pregnant people wherever they go. We do not get depictions of trying to find something in the fridge that will not make us gag or the countless slices of toast some people make because they cannot stomach anything else. We do not get to visualize what it's like to be unable to think because the nausea is so all consuming.

Telling my committee I was pregnant during week seven was difficult. I felt like I was making excuses to put off the dissertation. I told myself I was overexaggerating the constant nausea and brain fog, that I could work on my research but I must not really want to. I've always been my biggest critic, and throughout those early stages of pregnancy, my inner critic often took over, leaving me with self-doubt and insecurity about my ability to finish my dissertation.

After telling my committee, I stopped being so hard on myself. I gave myself permission to reenvision how my dissertation progress would unfold from there on. I allowed myself to extend the completion of my dissertation for one more semester, because *what's one more semester if I'm able to finish?* Aside from the out-of-pocket candidacy fees I really couldn't afford, there was no other reason to not extend my deadline into the summer. I was due in October and it was now already the middle of March and I had barely three of the five chapters written. I knew there was no way I would be able to power through and finish the last two chapters in less than a month while giving my committee time to read them all. For me, a few months would not make much of a difference, so I worked on telling myself that I wasn't necessarily failing by delaying completion.

Throughout pregnancy, I tried hard to accept my missed deadlines, going two days without checking my email, not touching my dissertation in a week, and so many other times when I felt completely guilty about my lack of work ethic. Even though I could not help the fact that I was experiencing a difficult first few months of pregnancy, I still felt as though there were things I could be doing better, a result of my own inner critic telling me I needed to always do more. It was hard to let myself go in that way, difficult to ask for extension after extension, difficult to be patient about with late replies, but I had to.

And it made all the difference.

If I didn't constantly "forgive" myself throughout pregnancy and give myself permission to not always strive to do more, I would never have a completed dissertation, a new job as an assistant professor, a healthy baby, and a stable mental state.

By week thirteen, I slowly started to feel more like myself, and as my nausea subsided I gained back my energy and the confidence I needed to finish my PhD. It was the beginning of May, and at that point, I had to finish a draft of my dissertation by early July so I could defend three weeks later. I put everything I had into working on my chapters and revisions, attempting to make up for the nearly two months I had been barely able to function. My committee members were impressed with my drive and the quick work I made in response to their feedback. I was finally able to see the end after so many long years of struggling through the dissertation stage. I successfully defended my dissertation at the end of July and gave birth to a healthy baby girl in October.

Throughout those first few months of pregnancy, I relied heavily on my dissertation committee to steer me in the right direction. As I worked through drafts, my chair consistently provided excellent support. He was the most patient, understanding, and quick-to-respond professor I ever worked with during graduate school. Even when I felt like my writing was going badly or that I was not making sufficient progress, he encouraged me to keep going. There were days when I emailed him a draft and he would immediately respond with: "Great work, Kate! Keep it up!" And while that may seem simple, it meant so much to me during those vulnerable moments that left me feeling insecure. It gave me the motivation to continue writing, even if I felt that inner critic sneaking up in my head, trying to get me to give in and quit.

There is so much talk in academia about mentorship and the importance of having someone guide you through graduate school to make it manageable. For me, the acknowledgment from my committee that it is hard to finish a dissertation while you're pregnant was enough for me to keep going. I didn't need constant reassurance or someone to take hours out of their schedule to talk to me about my research and how I'm feeling; I just needed some simple emails saying, "You got this! Keep it up!" These messages, along with my newfound forgiveness to myself, was enough for me to set aside the inner critic and finally finish.

There are countless systemic barriers in place for pregnant people in academia and so many aspects of the system that could lower these barriers, but many of the changes we need are more localized and personal. It doesn't take much to send an encouraging email to a graduate student who is struggling. That one simple act could determine whether that person stays in graduate school or not. Acknowledging that pregnant bodies sometimes have other plans could allow the student to give themselves permission to ask for more time or to take a mental break and refocus, which is sometimes all that is needed.

PART 3 JUGGLE WHAT MATTERS

16 ▸ "GO TO F–CKING DISNEY WORLD"

Establishing a Work-Life Balance and Learning When to Say No

JAMES B. HARR III

On June 22, 2022, a Twitter thread created by Tobi Emonts-Holley (@PeakTobi) went viral. He posted, "Over the past 10 years, I have earned a PhD & got promoted to CEO while having 6 kids. The secret to keeping it all under control?" never mentioning his wife (or external support, such as his advisor or his committee). The warranted backlash from Twitter users was palpable. Some examples included:

> You don't have 6 kids, your wife does. You have a paying job & your wife does not. Your secret is having a wife to manage your home & family for you, leaving you enough free time to work a full-time job & earn a degree. I did it as a single mom with 3 kids. You're not special.—Mindy Bee (@MindyBeeArt)

> Now add a full time paid job, subtract up to 40 hours of childcare (if you're so lucky) and remind me why women's wages are still lagging behind men's?—Ilana Ettinger (@ilanaettinger)
>
> As I understand it, she draws fulfillment from knowing her unpaid, thankless work provides him time and space to write lists. Then tweet about writing lists. This man has no idea how clean clothes appear in his closet or how food gets on the table—Stunt Double (@pillar_of_salt)

As for his "secret," he posted that "[t]he key idea is you sit down once a week and check everything under your control: ToDos, projects, calendars, physical inbox, goal and vision alignment. Then plan out the next week."

Yes. Really.

Emonts-Holley later posted an apology and deleted the thread, but the lack of self-awareness in the original post provided an opportunity for me to stop and reflect on the reasons I was able to work, research, write, and complete my PhD. To begin, I would be completely remiss if I were not transparent in saying that I had an unbelievable support system through my family while I was working on my PhD. Both my parents and my wife's parents lived about ten minutes away from our house, so we never had to worry about daycare, and, while my wife and I did work, we were always encouraged to take our children to our parents' homes so that we could focus on our work. Additionally, I was fortunate enough to have committee members—particularly an advisor—who also had children and understood the challenges of raising a family while working and being enrolled in a graduate program. While full access to extended family is not something every graduate student is afforded, in many ways, a carefully selected dissertation committee can help fill emotional voids that graduate students too often feel.

Balancing parenting and doctoral work is one of the most difficult challenges one might face as a professional in academia. While it doesn't end after the dissertation defense, setting boundaries early in an academic career is absolutely important if one is to survive. Having the support of an excellent mentor who pushed me to learn when to say no, particularly when saying yes meant sacrificing mental health and time with family, helped me succeed in my doctoral program and encouraged me to prioritize my children. I also understood that while I was the one who was in the graduate program writing a dissertation, the degree itself was a collaborative effort among myself, my family, and my advisor.

This chapter focuses on my ongoing struggle to say no, even when saying yes would affect my mental health. The goal is to encourage others to reflect on their needs in balancing a personal and professional life and perhaps evaluate what advice they might be receiving from advisors. Too many of my colleagues have quit or extended their research as a result of poor advice or because a "work comes first" philosophy too often prevails in academia.

Being a PhD parent was not easy. It was challenging and, at times, inexplicably lonely. Essentially, I was not fully prepared to be a parent and a full-time doctoral student (while also working full time as an assistant professor of English at Wake Technical Community College), but I knew I wanted both to be a father and earn a PhD. Through my doctoral journey, I learned that speaking openly about and embracing the reality of becoming a parent in the face of fertility challenges was therapeutic for me and helpful for others. While my wife and I were concerned, we never gave up hope. We often joked that if intrauterine insemination (IUI) worked, it would be great if our doctor could produce boy-girl twins and then we could call it a day. Unbeknownst to us, that joke would become reality. We were ecstatic to become parents for the first time, but we never expected to become new parents of twins around the same time I was applying to doctoral programs.

By the time my son and daughter turned one, I was a month into my doctoral studies at North Carolina State University. In addition to my full-time studies, as an assistant professor of English at a local community college, I was working a full-time teaching job that carried a 5-5 load (primarily because my graduate stipend was far below a living wage) and my wife was working full time and completing her bachelor's degree at Western Carolina University. While we had the full emotional support of our family and considerable childcare thanks to my parents and in-laws, it was the mentorship of my advisor that helped me keep the work-life balance in perspective.

Those who know me frequently remark that I take on too much. I have always been this way, but I doubt I am unique in this respect. Anyone courageous and masochistic enough to endure doctoral studies surely has struggled at one point or another with taking on too many roles and responsibilities. My ongoing struggle is that I constantly feel like I am never doing enough. My wife and my advisor warned me about the possibility of burning out. I realized that my constant need to be busy primarily stemmed from two sources: my personal definition of success in higher education and my obsession/borderline addiction with staying academically active. Although in many respects, I continue to evaluate myself through a lens of "inactivity equates to laziness and academic apathy," thanks largely to my often-misguided perception of a what a productive academic looks like, a turning point in my idea of a "good" PhD student came halfway through my program.

It was just before fall break and during the time that I was preparing for my oral and written comprehensive exams. My wife's parents wanted to go on vacation for the week and asked us to go with them. Without giving it any real consideration, I immediately said no. Keeping in mind this was October, I told them that I had to prepare for my exams that were coming up in February. My wife and my children were obviously disappointed, but I convinced them that I would not be successful in my pursuits as a graduate student if I did not devote every free moment I had to working on my degree. And at that point, the conversation ended.

At the next meeting with my advisor, I sat down and said that I wanted to ask him a question but that I already knew how he was going to respond. I told him I just needed professional reinforcement that I was doing the right thing. He asked me what the situation was and I explained to him why I told my family I could obviously not go with my children to Disney World over fall break. He stared at me for a moment and then asked me to tell him why I thought I could not go; he said that he would then tell me why I was wrong. I told him that my exams were coming up in the spring, the holidays were right around the corner, and I would lose preparation time then, and, most important, I don't think a good PhD student should take vacations when there is so much work to do for exams.

My advisor knew my background: the challenges my wife and I had had getting pregnant, how important being an involved father was to me, and the fact that I had approached that stage of exams preparation when you become an emotional powder keg ready to ignite at any moment. In no uncertain terms, he told me that I was wrong and that he had all the faith in the world that I would be prepared for the exams. To put everything in perspective, he reminded me that after the exams, very little of this would matter because I would move on to the dissertation; the exams would be behind me. The time I committed to preparation would be meaningless in the long run. These words made such an impact that in the acknowledgment section of my dissertation, I wrote,

> To [my] advisor, mentor, and—if I may be so bold—friend, I owe so much, and I look forward to our continued collaboration. Over the past four years, when I wanted to take on more and more, you subtly helped me prioritize my research and health, whether I heeded your advice or not. I will always recall your response to my push back on taking a family vacation while I was studying for qualifying exams: "In eighteen years, when the twins are getting ready to go to

college, will you sit back and fondly remember the two extra weeks you spent studying for your exams? Don't be an idiot; Go to f–king Disney World."

Needless to say, when I told my wife about our conversation and his response, she started crying and said, "Thank God for your advisor." From that conversation on, before I committed to work over family, I tried to stop and evaluate whether it was truly an opportunity I could not pass up or just something to fill time.

As mentioned, I had a support system that was unparalleled. Many of the opportunities that have been afforded existed only because I was able to stand on the shoulders of so many people. But as a first-generation college graduate and someone in the throes of academia, in my mind, no one in my family could tell me exactly what I needed to hear except for my advisor and my committee. At all costs, avoid this habit. Often my wife would provide the exact same advice (just worded differently), but it was my advisor's advice that I heeded. Was my wife upset about this? Definitely, but because his advice was still accomplishing the same goals for our family and supported a balance between work and family, she came to value my advisor's input as much as I did.

As I speak to other individuals who are in PhD programs and as I think about some of the reasons why they sometimes struggle, the root cause of the problem is often related to relationships or misperceptions of advisors. So, in the spirit of this book and of this chapter, the best advice I can give to parents who are considering entering a doctoral program or are currently getting their PhD is to find an advisor (and committee) who respect that life exists outside academia and that graduate students are people who require attention to their own mental health and personal lives. An advisor who understands that although the PhD may be important for one's future professional life, it does not replace family and personal life.

To rework PeakTobi's cringeworthy tweet from my new perspective, "Over the past 6 years, I have earned a PhD; received an amazing postdoc; taught at several major universities including University of California, Berkeley; eventually landed a tenure-track professorship; and had 2 kids. The secret to keeping it all under control? Unpaid time and labor from my wife, my parents, and my in-laws; support from my friends and colleagues; and advice from my advisor. Everything I accomplished in graduate school was possible only because of my circle of support. As I get older—for the sake of my own mental health—I have learned to stop looking to the past for affirmation and accolades; instead, I have shifted my focus to the future. Each day, I ask myself, "Are my children proud of me?" I hope they are and that they always will be, but I also hope they recognize that any cause for pride stems from the fact that I was never alone.

Parents, we will never be perfect, and as much as we try to resist, academia—simultaneously soul-sucking and rewarding as it is—will always demand our attention. Choose your advisor very carefully. And while they may not be academics, listen to your family, be honest about your priorities, remember that your work and the seemingly important opportunities outside your immediate research will always be there, and understand it is okay and healthy to say no, to take a break, and to go to f-cking Disney World.

17 ▸ COBBLE TOGETHER THE VILLAGE

Securing Childcare as Graduate Student Parents

CALVIN OLSEN

WHEN MY DAUGHTER was born in the summer of 2017, her mother (HB) and I were both graduate students. HB had finished her master's in public health six weeks before the birth and was set to start her PhD six weeks after, and I was halfway through a two-year master's program. The pregnancy had been planned and we were thrilled to be parents to a kid with such impeccable timing, but we were also in need of suitable and flexible childcare. Finding suitable and flexible childcare is a tall order for everyone, but it feels like a venti order when you're living off graduate student stipends.

For us, the adage rang (and rings) true: It takes a village to raise a child. Many of you have been, are currently, or will be in graduate school far away from your support system(s), and like us, you will have to build the village that raises your child. In this chapter, I will describe how we managed to build a village in the hope that our experience will help you as you build yours. I am very aware that what worked for us may not work for everyone, but there were enough different types of people in our village that I hope this chapter helps you think through places you may find some villagers. (I'm now 100 percent committed to this metaphor.)

I will start by offering a little more detail about our situation. As I said, we became parents between semesters and we were both attending the same university. We lived about a mile from campus in a 500-square-foot two-bedroom duplex—it was so small—and our respective buildings on campus were about half a mile apart. There was a bus stop a few minutes from our house. We were extremely lucky to live in a city where it was free to ride the bus, which was amazing at the time and seems even more incredible now that we are without this free service. Free bus transportation allowed us to get to campus a little more easily and made it easier for people near campus to get to our house. This also made it easier for us to ask them to do so since transportation wouldn't cost them or us anything other than time.

Having established a little more context regarding our situation, allow me to offer three steps for cobbling together your village:

1. Prepare everyone (as much as possible). One nice thing about pregnancy is that it allows a little bit of time to plan. Once you're settled in the area where you're going to grad school, start preparing other people for your new parenting role. Doing so will make the experience less jarring for everyone.
2. Tap into your network(s). If nothing else, graduate school is a series of small and ever-changing networks. Think of everyone as a possibility, including your advisor, your cohort, your professors, and your classmates. If you have extracurricular networks, tap into them as well.
3. Plan to pay (and try not to worry). As much as you work to cobble together your village, chances are you'll still need to pay for at least some of your childcare. Preparing others and tapping into your network(s) can sometimes lower the financial burden, but don't be too hard on yourself if it doesn't.

I will organize the rest of the chapter around these steps, but please note that they need not be taken in the order I have presented them. Instead, please enjoy the hodgepodge nature of our first years of childcare and consider ways you might cobble together your own village.

PREPARE EVERYONE

There will inevitably be times you need to prioritize parenting over school, so it's important that the people you interact with know you'll be making that call once in a while. It's not groundbreaking to say that a little preparation goes a long way, but the best piece of advice I would give to graduate students is to make a list of everyone you interact with in grad school and find ways to incept your baby into their minds. (I know the movie *Inception* won't have the lasting cultural significance I want it to, but it's still relevant enough.)

Our list of inception candidates included advisors, cohort members, classmates, professors, and even students. Informing our advisors was the most straightforward interaction. Ideally, your advisor will already be clued into your extracurricular life enough to know that parenting is one of your responsibilities. If they're not, I suggest telling them as soon as you're comfortable doing so (and are fully matriculated). If your advisor or your environment doesn't feel safe or welcoming enough to disclose this type of information, seeking advice at your school's diversity or accessibility office might be the right step. It's always been interesting to me that being a parent was a commonality I shared more with professors than peers, which sometimes (though not always) made things easier. There were two other student-parents in HB's PhD cohort, but I was the only student-parent in my entire department. Incepting members of your cohort is a relatively seamless process since you're a group by default. The easiest way to keep them informed is to attend—or, better yet, organize—a cohort event where everyone is invited to bring along significant others of all types. Just show up and the baby bump does the rest.

If you're in the early years of your graduate school, your coursework will put you into close contact with professors and peers who are less familiar to you and with whom you will interact for only a limited time. This can make the stakes seem higher, so try to prepare the people in these situations as soon as possible. Start with the professor. Before each semester started, I emailed all of my professors individually to introduce myself and to inform them that I was a student-parent (and a new one at that). I let them know that I had coordinated my calendar to minimize any interruptions, and then I very directly asked the following question: If something unexpected does come up, may I attend class with baby in tow or would you prefer that I miss class that day? I didn't make any promises about how much notice they would receive or that baby would be quiet—I simply gave them two options and left it at that.

Many factors will influence a professor's decision, so before asking I made the decision to honor whatever decision I was given and to thank them for ensuring we were on the same page. Most of my professors understood that life happens and were willing to have the baby in class on occasion. I thought this might have had something to do with my gender (too many bars are on the floor for men), but HB ended up with an even better track record of yes responses; two professors told her the baby was welcome before she even asked. Classmates will generally roll with whatever the professor approves, so it may be less important to let them know that you may bring your baby to class until you need to. I generally found that emailing the whole class an hour or two before class started was enough. You won't be able to control how they react (although most don't seem to mind), but if you've done your work with the professor beforehand, then there's no need to worry.

TAP INTO YOUR NETWORK(S)

After you've incepted your baby into the minds of the people who will be immediately around you in your program—your grad school network, if you will—it's time to tap into that network. Many people won't really know what to do with a baby or a young child, but as they interact with you over time a few of them will grow more comfortable. Over the course of our first few weeks, a handful of grad school people asked how they might help us, and we simply asked if they'd be willing to watch our kiddo for the occasional short period of time. One of HB's cohort members spent a lot of time studying in the common area outside their classroom, so one day HB asked if she could leave the sleeping baby next to them for a few minutes while she went to a meeting. It was an easy assignment, and afterward they told HB that she could leave the baby with them any time, even if kiddo was awake.

The next semester, we asked that same person if they would watch the baby for an hour every Wednesday, when we were both in class, and promised to pay them for their time. They took us up on it and graciously did so free of charge. I would walk to HB's building any time I got out of class early and take over, and although it ended up being just a few hours of care spread over the semester, it was extremely helpful for us. We made sure to take them out to dinner once or twice to thank them. On another occasion, my advisor told me I could bring the baby—stroller and all—to a weekly committee meeting. We had a tight-knit group of PhD and master's level students in our workspace, and since I had already been there a year, I had a read on the overall vibe. (Don't worry if the warm-up period takes a little time, though.) After everyone got used to seeing the baby, I asked one or two of them to watch her while I ran meetings or bounced around the building for a while taking care of other business. I found it helpful to remind everyone that they could call or text me to bail on their caretaking (especially if the baby was fussy), and most people who knew me and had met the baby felt fine with taking short and low-stakes turns making sure the baby stayed asleep.

Once you've tapped into your grad school network, it's a good idea to look outward to see how the university system might help you cobble together your childcare village. One of the unfortunate truths about university systems is that most of them offer little to no assistance for student-parents, which is a institutional failure in diversity, equity, and inclusion efforts. Student-parents confront a wide range of extracurricular factors that affect their ability to participate in university offerings, and spearheading accommodations is the least an institution can do to improve retention of student parents. (Get on it, administrators!)

Because of this unnecessary uphill battle, it is daunting to ask for what you need, but we learned that specific requests can go a long way. When HB started her PhD program (and the baby was six weeks old), she found out quickly that she would have to advocate for herself to obtain any assistance from the school. Making a specific request—asking a simple question, in fact—got things moving for her. She asked one of the administrative personnel where the nearest lactation room could be found. The answer was that one did technically exist in the building but it hadn't been used in a long time and was very small—two chairs and a dirty sink, essentially. After getting a glimpse of the space, the admin started asking around and found that there were seven or eight mothers who would use an available lactation room. Then she advocated for more space, and after a few follow-ups, the school set up a multipurpose room and outfitted it to work as a lactation room. The admin went the extra mile and took the time to paint it, mount a shelf, order a fridge for storing milk, and add a microwave for sanitizing equipment. HB was less successful in the other building she most often frequented, but voicing her concerns and asking the program to meet a specific parenting need led to a small but much more comfort-creating win.

PLAN TO PAY (AND TRY NOT TO WORRY)

I wish I could say that it's possible for everyone to build a village that allows them to find childcare without having to pay much out of pocket, but that most likely won't be the case. It wasn't the case for us. Even with our extreme luck of being established in the city where our universities are located and living close enough to campus that we could pass the baby back and forth as we took turns going to class and studying, we ended up paying for childcare, and our daughter did a lot of traveling over the course of a semester. We were both in the coursework portion of our respective degrees and we couldn't really plan for the childcare we would need until schedules were released, so we simply did our best to react as circumstances changed every four months or so.

Preparing everyone around us and tapping into our networks did ease the financial burden some. For example, a woman at church, Jamie, heard we were cobbling together a village and offered to watch our daughter one day a week. We asked if she would let us pay her and she told us she would accept $10 per hour, which was so much cheaper than anything else we could find in the area. On top of that, Jamie graciously made us a second great deal. She wanted one of her preteen daughters to gain some babysitting experience, so the preteen would watch the baby (and Jamie would watch the preteen) for an hour or two at half price. It was the first win-win-win I had ever experienced and we will sing Jamie's praises forever because of it (and we volunteered to watch her kids and get them to school any time she traveled).

I also talked to a few of the guys from my pick-up basketball group who had teenagers attending the local high school to see if any of them wanted to earn a few easy bucks on occasion. It turned out that one of them had a son who had ninety minutes to kill after school while he waited for his stepmom to pick him up on her way home from work. It ended up being perfect timing for us that semester. Every other Wednesday, HB would pick him up from school, put the baby down for an afternoon nap, and head to class. His only job was to make sure nobody that wasn't me came through the front door. He would do homework on our couch for the 30–45 minutes it took me to get home from my last class, and then we'd play video games until his mom came to get him. We tried to stock the kitchen with food he liked and I always paid him for a full hour, so it was easy cash for him and peace of mind for us. (And I was never sad about playing video games.)

I finished my master's in 2018 and started a PhD program at a different university in 2019. While a PhD for me was always in our plan, I was surprised to be accepted so quickly (having applied off and on for a decade). Between our programs picking up in intensity and our daughter being a little older, we decided to enroll her in a local daycare. Not only did it take a lot of time and energy to find a place that both had space and felt right, it also took a toll on our finances. It's not news to say that childcare is expensive, and since every daycare in a drivable distance cost more than our graduate student stipends could afford, we ended up with a three-part approach: (1) I stayed part time at my job rather than quitting outright, (2) we took out student loans, and (3) HB found a scholarship that helped defray some childcare costs.

I would have preferred to dedicate all my time to school and family time, but my job was a necessity with a new commute and daycare bills (plus the occasional takeout order when we were too tired to muster up dinner). We became amazing budgeters and decided to stagger the student loans, taking one out in HB's name the first year and another in my name the next year. It was more debt than we wanted to take on, but this well-calculated cost made all our lives a touch easier: I could complete my degree in four years, HB could allocate more time to dissertation research and writing, and our daughter could have access to enriching care from trained professionals alongside kids her age. So we took out the loans and reminded ourselves (over and over) that it was an investment in ourselves and that graduate school would improve our chances of securing long-term employment. (Spoiler alert: I successfully defended my dissertation and now we both have job offers in our respective fields.) HB found the childcare scholarship by hearing about it offhand from another PhD student (tap into those networks!), who told her to visit the student services office in person to ask about a childcare scholarship. It wasn't easy to procure—we had to reapply every semester, the application required a ton of documentation, notifications often went out after the semester had started, and the amount we received fluctuated—but it was money. It certainly would have improved our financial situation and mental health if we'd known about it the entire time, but instead of worrying too much about that we decided to be grateful that we got a little help, and we advertised that scholarship to every student parent we could find.

ENJOY THE VILLAGE

It takes quite a bit of time to build your childcare village, especially when you're cobbling it together. Preparing everyone you know, tapping your networks, and figuring out finances are massive undertakings individually, let alone collectively. But if you distill them down, a lot of the village-building takes the form of asking—actively, bravely, and constantly—for what you need. And once you have a little village, enjoy it. Thank those who help, forget those who don't, and pay it forward every chance you get. (To our future students, you're welcome to bring your child[ren] with you any time.) It's not easy, but keep cobbling.

18 ▸ THE WORLD WON'T PAUSE

What to Expect When Co-Navigating the Academic and Professional Job Market with a Newborn

DANIEL HENKE AND ERIN HENKE

As our daughter Raegan lay in a neonatal intensive care unit, Daniel was negotiating an academic job offer in the hospital bathroom and Erin was being told to delay her graduation due to the pregnancy. Our story, like so many of the stories surrounding Raegan's birth and the first few years of her life, taught us that the world won't pause when life-shifting moments happen because life simply does not slow down.

Erin graduated with a master's degree in applied behavior analysis in 2021 and currently oversees a center for children with autism as a board-certified behavior analyst. And Daniel is a nonbinary parent who navigated the academic job market with more than a few difficulties but is now the director of writing programs and the associate director of the Writing Center at Lake Forest College. We chose to write separate narratives instead of creating one narrative to highlight the different experiences of two academic parents and the roles and responsibilities that are expected of them. We crafted these stories independently for authenticity, then we worked collaboratively to finalize the piece. We begin with Erin's narrative of completing graduate school with a baby on the way and eagerly awaiting a significant income increase, and then we transition to Daniel's narrative of navigating paternity leave while negotiating the academic job market. We end with reflections and our overall takeaway for prospective graduate parents.

ERIN'S NARRATIVE

I found out I was pregnant in July 2020. We were both over the moon to find out we were becoming parents, but being pregnant in the early days of the COVID-19 pandemic came with its own set of obstacles. At that time, so little was known about the spread of COVID-19 and a vaccine was far from available. People were scared. Masks and social distancing were mandatory and only essential stores were open. It was rumored that only essential workers would be allowed to leave their residences. Grocery stores were silent as you shopped, and people were afraid to cough or sneeze in public. I remember being embarrassed when I stepped out of the house while obviously pregnant. There was a huge stigma attached to going out in public while pregnant or with kids because of the potential health risks. People were expected to limit the time they spent out in public places, and people were discouraged from going out together. Many doctors were not allowing partners to come to appointments, not even for pregnant patients. We felt lucky to find an OB-GYN who would see us both.

At that time, I was enrolled in an online-only, asynchronous master's program. I was working days in a clinic setting and evenings as a waitress. Any extra money we had went to preparing for our soon-to-be newborn, but it wasn't much. When I found out I was pregnant with Raegan, we were both in our second-to-last semesters of graduate school and incredibly eager to graduate, having been in higher education for most of our adult lives. Between outside work and grad school work, we felt like we were moving nonstop. For both of us, graduation signaled a huge decrease in workload (or so we thought) and a significant increase in income, which was necessary for expanding our family and beginning our next chapter.

Raegan was due in March 2021, when I was enrolled in my last two classes. One was a graduate-level course with a huge group project that was assigned early and was not due until the end of the semester. My group members and professor were all helpful and easy to work with and I was able to finish everything I needed weeks before the baby came. My other class was an undergraduate elective class and was significantly less accommodating to the pregnancy. I reached out to the professor early in the semester to let them know that I was having a baby in mid-March and to ask what I could do in advance to make up for the time that would be lost during my first few weeks as a mother. Specifically, I requested access to one assignment about two weeks early so that I wouldn't have to do it the week I was planning to give birth. I also did not want the lateness of the submission to negatively impact my grade. I offered to provide documentation for the pregnancy and asked them if there was anything they could do to help accommodate me.

The answer was no. The professor wasn't going to provide me with the assignments early and they would not give me an extension. My alternative option was to reach out for an official disability accommodation, but the professor noted that for most pregnant students this meant taking a semester off. Now this was an undergraduate-level course and this professor didn't know me at all, so I don't blame them for their short and scripted response. But after all of the planning, all of the coursework, all of the unpaid time collecting my fieldwork hours, and all of the graduate-level classes that I had completed to get to this point, taking my final semester off was the worst solution for me. To give some background, there are two requirements to becoming a board-certified behavior analyst: complete graduate school coursework and accumulate the required number of largely unpaid fieldwork hours. Beginning with my first semester of graduate school, I carefully planned my courses and my fieldwork. Taking a semester off would mean postponing my graduation and my entry into my career by least six months. After quickly realizing that the time off would be a much bigger hit to my future than succumbing to this professor's demands, I gave up on the conversation. This class wasn't going to pause for me.

The need for accommodations only started there. After Raegan was born we had a few wonderful days at home before our two-day checkup. We had no idea there was something wrong, so we were caught off guard when we were readmitted to the hospital. The doctors told us she needed to stay for at least two more days to monitor her blood oxygen and body temperature.

Once her condition improved, we rushed to get our laptops to the hospital. The work didn't stop; it didn't even slow down. On our second day in the NICU, Daniel accepted a job offer and we knew that we were moving to the greater Chicago area. Raegan's levels had all returned to normal, so we were hoping that that would be our last day in the hospital. That is when my job search began. I was breastfeeding through a phone call with a potential employer. Because of COVID-19 and since we were relocating, my interviews were all conducted virtually. I received an offer, and the employer asked if I could come see the facility. I politely declined because at this time I really couldn't. The academy, the job market, and the world wouldn't wait for me, even if I couldn't keep up.

DANIEL'S NARRATIVE

I want to briefly mention that I am nonbinary and we did not want to call me father as we felt the language was too gendered. We ended up deciding on mod or modder (a combination of mom and dad), as it sounds more inclusive as a moderating figure rather than a patriarchal figure.

Unlike my partner, my graduate school experience with our pregnancy was pretty productive. I was teaching two sections of composition and communication for my college while assisting with a course in another department. Money was very tight and my partner was taking unpaid leave, as her job did not offer paid leave. At the college where I worked, we were guaranteed two teaching courses and we could request a third, which wasn't granted often. I had worked hard to get to the position to teach three courses a semester, and I had deep worry that this third class would be canceled. I was also worried that the college would pay for only two of the courses for my paternity leave, as a three-course appointment was beyond the norm. I applied for paternity leave six months before Raegan was born, and it was initially denied because I applied too early. I waited until winter break (not a break for me, as I was teaching a winter session course) to redo the process. Erin was already working so much..

Because of COVID-19, all classes were being taught virtually. The spring semester began at the end of January and Raegan was due in late March. I was worried about balancing a teaching load and then having to hand off my classes to someone else a few weeks into the semester. I expressed my concerns to the department chair, who told me that due to COVID-19, there was really no need for substitutes so I could have the entire semester for leave. I was ecstatic. However, I wish my school had been more transparent about that information, or perhaps had provided more department-specific information given that I worked at a large R1 institution.

The college that housed my primary department still wanted me to assist with the course up until the due date, which was obviously fine. However, this department was a small one, and I was their only TA. I felt they were somewhat unhappy that I had to take leave and that they needed to find someone else and pay them to replace me. I primarily did grading for the department, and of course there was an exam scheduled right before Raegan's due date. I let them know when the baby was born, but the faculty wanted me to finish the grading. The class didn't stop for me. I didn't want to complain because they had always been good to me, so I sat in the hospital room grading exams with a single light on while Erin and Raegan rested. It was an oddly serene experience, and although I was clicking away on my computer in near darkness as I scrambled to get my work done, I was happy.

While my experience with leave was favorable, having a very pregnant partner and soon-to-be newborn while being on the job market was beyond taxing. I was graduating in May and I had been applying to jobs on the academic market since December. I had a few interviews lined up and I made it past the preliminary rounds for some of them. I kept telling prospective employers that the baby was going to come any day now. I was concerned that I was going to be scheduled for an interview on the due date or that I would miss a scheduled interview due to the arrival of Raegan. Raegan was due on March 17 and arrived on March 11. I had completed final interviews with two colleges by then and I was waiting to hear back from both of them. I was full of so many different emotions. I was elated that our baby had been born, but I was dreading an uncertain future without a job. How well would I interview with a newborn? The job market refused to pause for me.

We ended up staying in the hospital for four days because Raegan had severe hypothermia. Nothing was medically abnormal with her—she just "wasn't ready," the doctors said. She lay in an incubator for two days like a chick as her body climbed back to normal levels. During this time, a college in Texas called me for a final interview. They were prepared to offer me the job, but they wanted me to meet the college president first. I was super excited until they told me that I had to meet them in person for the final interview, even though I had just had a baby, it was peak COVID-19, and I lived in central Iowa. I asked them if there was any chance that I could do the interview remotely and they told me no. I told them I needed some time to think about it as the baby had just been born and was diagnosed with severe hypothermia.

After that phone call, I pocket dialed another prospective employer in Illinois. "Hello? Hello? Hello?" I heard from my pocket. "Daniel?" I was so confused and pulled the phone out of my pocket. Embarrassingly, I told them that I had called by accident. Since I had them on the phone, I asked about the status of my application, as I had already completed a final interview. They told me that they had made the recommendation to the dean and that I was going to receive an offer the next day. Erin and I jumped up and down in the hospital room as the nursing staff peeked in to see what was causing us to squeal with excitement. The next day I received the call, and I negotiated the offer in the hospital bathroom as five nurses came into the room to check on our daughter. I had to close the bathroom door and frequently apologize to my prospective employer, sharing that I had been in a neonatal intensive care unit and had had little sleep in the past week. I accepted the offer. After the call ended, I called Texas to let them know I was declining their offer and we celebrated by ordering a faux buffalo chicken pizza (Erin's favorite, which had given her horrible heartburn during the pregnancy). We hungrily ate as Raegan cooed loudly. We were excited for this next chapter of our life.

REFLECTIONS

Erin's experience with requesting leave was much more difficult, whereas Daniel's process to paternity leave was more easily received. As Daniel is male appearing, we believe that this was due to patriarchal constructs. We both felt that the professors and administrators we spoke to viewed having a child in graduate school as a choice we should have planned better, even though we were both graduating and on the job market.

Of course, the experiences that we shared through this process are unique to us. Completing graduate school is already a daunting task. Completing graduate school while pregnant is even more complex. While we were in graduate school, we were already living paycheck to paycheck, and the pregnancy basically left us out of paychecks. Erin's employer was accommodating, but because she was a part-time worker, there was little income coming in. We put all of our energy into not falling behind in either of our intended graduations, which meant that days were spent working and nights were spent doing graduate school work, both before the baby came and after. The world did not stop for Raegan. The world didn't pause for us as new parents. We recommend finding out early how your graduate school can help you through the process of pregnancy and parenting and what accommodations (if any) are offered. Although we had different experiences through our final semesters of graduate school, our departments and the job market did not adapt to our situation. The world continues to go on. And because of that, many of us fall behind. Try not to let that worry get in the way of everything that matters to you.

19 ▸ REFRAME THE NARRATIVE

A Conversation on Navigating Childcare in a PhD Program

CAMILA RING, BRITA M. THIELEN, AND HAYLEY E. VERDI

AT THE TIME of this conversation, we are:

CAMMY RING: Two children (a two-year-old son and a four-month-old daughter). Fifth-year PhD.

BRITA THIELEN: One son. Graduated with a PhD in May 2022, when son was fifteen months old.

HAYLEY VERDI: Two daughters ages four and one and pregnant with a son. Fifth-year PhD.

All three of us attend(ed) the same English doctoral program at Case Western Reserve University (CWRU) and became parents while in the program.

We each identify as cis/hetero and are married. We feel lucky to have had four years of friendship and support for each other as accountability partners and grad student mothers before coauthoring this chapter.

The following conversation about our experiences as grad student parents was held via Zoom on September 7, 2022, and has been edited for clarity. Using a cluster of questions to cover three discussion topics, we begin by discussing the topic of childcare because our university does not have a childcare center on campus. This has required each of us to find our own unique childcare solution.[1] We then move on to parental leave and end with advice for managing the academic work-life-parent balancing act.

QUESTION CLUSTER 1: CHILDCARE

How have you navigated childcare?
What have been the benefits of this approach, and what are the challenges?

BRITA: Before we begin this conversation, I think it's worth mentioning where our kids are. My son is at daycare, which he attends full time Monday through Friday. Cammy, I can see that you are holding your sleeping newborn and bouncing on a birth ball during this conversation.

CAMMY: Yes, and my two-year-old is napping right now. My aunt is here to watch him when he wakes up.

HAYLEY: My oldest daughter is in school. I'm actually having this conversation in my car while I wait for pickup to start. My other daughter is at our babysitter's house.

CAMMY: As far as how we've navigated childcare, we've been fortunate to have some family help in combination with a sitter, who we pay to come eight hours a week. But I don't think even this part-time paid care would be affordable on my stipend alone. Thankfully, my husband and I can make it work with our combined income.

A lot has worked well with this arrangement. It's convenient being able to keep my son at home (my mom, my aunt, and a sitter all come to our house), especially if I'm working from home. And my being more present and accessible works well for me and my son personality wise. It's important to me that we spend more of our waking hours together than apart, so I've wanted this more cobbled-together, part-time setup for childcare.

But it's also had its challenges. One is that it often feels like I never have enough time to do the bare minimum in terms of work, which right now is teaching and dissertating. Altogether we have about sixteen hours of childcare a week, although it is often less due to schedule conflicts, illness, and so on. So I usually end up working most evenings a week after the kids go to bed, which can be exhausting. My ideal setup would be more like twenty hours a week, but that isn't possible right now due to schedule limitations of those providing care. So it feels a bit like I have to choose between full-time childcare or never-enough childcare.

The other challenge is that this setup is informed by a parenting approach that for me often feels out of the ordinary in graduate school culture. I'm interested in responsive and attachment parenting, or basically trying to maximize my physical and emotional proximity/accessibility to my infant and my toddler. In my mind, trying to find out-of-the-box ways to parent in accordance with these values shouldn't be at odds with graduate school culture, particularly in the humanities, a field that (in theory) encourages open-mindedness to different ways of being, thinking, and living. I'm an idealist, so I want to take the ideals of both higher education and the humanities at face value. But I think even academic culture still has a ways to go in challenging typical perceptions of graduate students and parents, particularly the compartmentalization of these roles. For example, when I went to an out-of-state academic conference a few months ago, I wasn't comfortable leaving my two-year-old overnight without me, so he and my husband tagged along. My husband was the primary caregiver, but I was at least able to see my toddler between commitments and at night. I was also seven months pregnant at the time. I remember that when I walked up to the person at the conference registration desk, pregnant and with my toddler in a stroller, they asked me if I was at the right place! I also remember some colleagues responding with polite surprise when I shared that my spouse and my child would be in tow at the conference. There's just not really a cultural infrastructure in place that would make this kind of approach normal or expected or supportable in practical ways.

HAYLEY: Since the birth of my first child, we have relied on a combination of a babysitter and help from family members for childcare. The babysitter watches my children in her home, which is located on my way to campus. She has been flexible and, depending on the semester, she has watched my children anywhere between ten and twenty hours a week. My mother-in-law also regularly watches my children one day a week. We also took advantage of our local school district's pre-K program, so my oldest daughter went to school in the mornings four days a week. Now she is in school full time, which has helped alleviate some of our childcare needs.

One of the main benefits of this arrangement for me as a graduate student is the amount of flexibility it gives me. During weeks when my workload is lighter, I am able to keep my children home more. Then, when things get busier, I can easily schedule more time with our babysitter. But while this flexibility is a benefit, it can also be a big challenge. Every semester I have to reevaluate what our childcare needs are, depending on my teaching schedule and other commitments. Another challenge has been learning how to maintain the amount of childcare I need to get my work done. I'm tempted to take on the duties of a stay-at-home parent because my husband's work schedule is very regimented. As a graduate student working on a long-term project, I have had to get past seeing increasing the amount of childcare I schedule as an indulgence or worrying that others will see it as such.

CAMMY: I can relate to that feeling of constantly having to justify that you're actually doing work. Even though my spouse works from home most of the time so he can watch the kids when I'm in a pinch with my work, he still has to clock in forty hours at the end of the week. I technically don't have that obligation or accountability as a grad student.

BRITA: And then there's still that societal expectation that childcare should be something you (as the woman in the relationship) do, right?

My situation is a bit of an outlier here in a couple of ways. First, because we relocated to Ohio from Minnesota when I started the program at CWRU. My husband and I don't have any family here and our support networks are mostly tied to the English department. Second, because of my husband's job, we are able to afford full-time daycare for our son. The big benefit here has been reliability, as the childcare center is rarely closed. Having my son in childcare all the time during the week gave me a lot of freedom to organize my time how I wanted to in terms of writing my dissertation, teaching, prepping for teaching, grading, and other responsibilities within the department. I don't know that I would have been able to complete the program if I had not had this childcare arrangement—or at least I would have been much more stressed, especially in the final stretch.

However, because he's in daycare, he gets sick much more often than I think he would otherwise. Fortunately, my husband has worked remotely during the pandemic, so he's been able to trade off childcare responsibilities on days when our son is home sick from daycare so that we could both get work done.

I do really like that at daycare, my son gets social interaction—not just with other little kids but with adults, too. For me, daycare feels like we are expanding his village, in the sense of him knowing there are other people around him who will take care of him or who care about him.

CAMMY: I like that you've reframed childcare as part of your child's "village." It's easy to perceive childcare as an alternative to a village, but it's helpful to think of it as constituting part of that support.

BRITA: [Laughs.] Yeah, even if I have to pay the villagers.

HAYLEY: The socialization opportunity has also been a benefit of our arrangement. Our babysitter has children who are a few years older than my oldest daughter, so it's been good for my daughters to form friendships with these girls. In addition, both my daughters get the chance to spend time with another adult who truly loves them and is invested in caring for them. At first, when my oldest daughter was only four months old and I was thinking of leaving her with anyone else, I felt very anxious. I thought of hiring a babysitter as a necessity but I did not think of the benefits of the arrangement. I think that reframing my thinking to see childcare as an opportunity for my daughter to form a positive relationship with another caregiver helped me a lot with this transition.

QUESTION CLUSTER 2: PARENTAL LEAVE

What was it like to go back to work for the first time after having a child or beginning childcare for the first time?

Did parental leave feel long enough?

CAMMY: My first child was born in May, so I had the whole summer off plus six weeks of paid parental leave. Altogether, that did not feel like nearly enough leave. We had a rough time with me going back to work when my son was four months old. I was constantly sleep deprived, nursing and pumping around the clock, and my son and I were both slowly adapting to being separated even for a couple of hours at a time. At that time, I was working from home because it was during the peak COVID months. While this had the benefit of being a kind of slow "on ramp" to separating from my child, it also made it hard to focus. I'd be on Zoom working with a student and I could hear my son wailing downstairs because he wanted me. I'd sometimes run downstairs in between writing center appointments to nurse him. It was all kind of disorienting, to have one foot in mom mode and the other in school mode at the same time. Really, I was just in constant survival mode.

Even as I say all this, I feel a kind of mild embarrassment. As a feminist, I imagine other feminist scholars being like, "You should have boundaries with your body and not give your baby access to your body 24–7" or "You should make your baby adapt to your lifestyle and career." So on top of the exhaustion, there were the projected judgments—a combination of what I assumed to be others' perceptions as well as my own internalized judgment of myself—that I wasn't doing this right, that the exhaustion was preventable, and that I shouldn't prioritize my baby so much. It took a lot of time for me to own how I wanted to parent, even if it felt antithetical to my internalized expectations of what ambition for a "career woman" should look like. This informed my decision to take a leave of absence with my second baby, who was born in July 2022. I feel so much peace and relief about this decision. But I know a lot of folks aren't in a place to forgo a semester of pay without major financial repercussions.

BRITA: When I had my son in February 2021, we were still under the six-week parental leave policy. However, in academic year 2020–21, I took on an additional role as a writing program assistant, which came with a teaching release for the spring semester. But that was on the condition that I did all my administrative hours. In order to get in all of my admin hours, I had to double up on my hours in the fall. So I was working twice whatever the hourly appointment was in the fall plus dissertating and teaching, and I was also in a collegewide dissertation seminar. It was a really stressful semester on top of being pregnant!

But it was great having the spring off; I didn't work on my dissertation again until June. We started my son in daycare in June, when he was four months old, because I wanted to be able to ease back into my dissertation without the added pressure of teaching. I felt guilty about this choice even though it was deliberate. I felt like since I was home, I could also be taking care of my son—even though I knew that if he was at home I wouldn't get anything done. After a while, though, I really enjoyed being able to shift out of parent mode for a while each day and control my time and how I want to get things done.

So while initially my parental leave didn't feel long enough, I think in some ways I was ready, but I definitely would not have been ready after six weeks. As I think about my own experience alongside Cammy's, it's clear that flexibility needs to be part of this larger parental leave conversation, as there is no one "right" amount of leave for everybody.

HAYLEY: I had my first daughter in April 2018. I believe I was the first graduate student within most faculty members' memories to be pregnant and give birth during the program. It worked out that I was able to take my six-week leave at the end of the semester, and then I had the summer off before beginning work again in the fall.

My daughter started with our babysitter at the start of my fall semester, when she was about four months old. That was a very challenging semester for me as I was still in coursework, I had a lot of evening classes, and I was trying to continue breastfeeding. A few of the lecturers in the department who also had young children were very encouraging. They told me about resources available to university members as well as about basic practical things, like where there were decent pumping rooms on campus that weren't bathrooms. I also often felt like I didn't want people to know or to remember that I had a baby because I believed it would make them think I wasn't working as hard as other people or that I couldn't possibly be producing as high a quality of work as others were. Acknowledging that I was a parent seemed like it would undercut any sort of professional identity I had.

Thankfully, I received a lot more support than I expected. My advisor was encouraging and helped me continue to meet my professional goals. Other professors in the department were similarly positive and continued to support me as a developing scholar. I had my second daughter when I was in the dissertation phase of the program, and by that time I felt as though the policies and people had already been tested. I knew how my advisor and the department would handle my situation. I also felt a lot more confident as a parent and knew how much childcare I would need. As a result, going back after the birth of my second child felt much easier.

ADVICE SECTION

As we conclude our conversation, here is the advice we wish to send out to future PhD parents (and their institutions):

CAMMY: Remember that it's possible—and empowering—to get creative about working around academic cultural norms if they are not conducive to your parenting approach or values. But since that might sometimes mean a "swimming upstream" kind of effort, be very intentional about seeking help and support.

BRITA: Utilizing daycare or other outside childcare so that you can make progress in your program does not make you less of a parent. It can help to reconceptualize outside childcare as an expansion of your child's village.

HAYLEY: As a grad student, remember it's okay to accept that there are seasons in your PhD program. [Being in] coursework is not the same as writing your dissertation. Semesters will vary in intensity and in productivity. If your work style or your childcare arrangements vary from semester to semester, that's okay. If you have a semester where your childcare arrangements aren't working, it doesn't mean that every semester will be the same. It's okay to try different options and give yourself time to adjust. Figuring out childcare is more than just logistics: It's a process of figuring out what your personal values and goals are and how they tie in with your family's values and goals.

You are allowed to want things other than your dissertation and you are allowed to pursue childcare options that will help you balance your life as a graduate student with your role as a parent. Don't be afraid to make people aware of your situation and to ask for what you need. It's not an excuse; it's a reality.

BRITA: To institutions, whatever your current parental leave policy is for your grad students, it's probably not enough. Make it longer or classify students as employees so they can qualify for leave under the Family and Medical Leave Act.

Finally and from all of us, our last piece of advice is this: Our children need a village, but we parents need a village too. For every day that our children need reliable, attentive caretakers, we ourselves need emotional, physical, and professional support to manage the delicate and demanding balance of parenting and grad school. You deserve care too.

NOTE

1. Settling on each of our unique childcare solutions was a complex process that required various forms of support, perspective, and trial and error. For some of us, recruiting the help of a therapist was a critical component of this and other aspects of graduate student parenting.

20 ▸ KNOW WHEN TO MOVE

Intentionally Choosing When to Share News of Fostering with Your Committee

ALEASHIA WALTON VALENTIN

WHEN I FIRST arrived at the English Department at the University of Cincinnati, the quintessential collegiate surroundings coupled with my lifelong impressions of "what PhD programs are meant to be" provided me with an antiquated sense of what being a doctoral candidate was all about. Although I failed to realize it at the beginning of my PhD journey, change is a welcome and expected companion in my department. The experience of watching my mentors embrace student life changes as a fluid, positive part of graduate studies has reinforced this. It's unrealistic for our professors to expect graduate student lives to remain perfectly static during such an intellectually evolutionary period in our lives. It's also not realistic for students to believe their lives will remain on hold.

CHANGE AND TRANSITION

During my first year at the University of Cincinnati, I experienced a nine-month-long migraine that stopped me in my tracks. While recovering from this and adjusting to a new regime of more than twenty migraine days per month, I was given a double diagnosis of occipital neuralgia (damaged nerves in my neck and head that lead to debilitating pain and headaches, possibly stemming from a car accident I had been in two years earlier) and vestibular migraines (a nervous system vertigo-meets-migraine nightmare that is genetic). Why did my health problems become literally disabling? Graduate-level stress and a complete misunderstanding of my body's signals were certainly a part of it. Although my mentors remained encouraging, grappling to find a foothold in the program felt impossible. Moving through graduate work with invisible disabilities has been a rollercoaster of finding compassion for myself, developing as a scholar, and maintaining any semblance of a social life outside academia.

Then I embarked on my greatest role to date—becoming the foster mother (and later adoptive mother) of a wonderful ten-year-old little girl named Lizzie, who suffers from her own set of invisible disabilities that stem from neglect and abuse. As I transitioned into this new role, I carved out space for our new family during a time when I wasn't ready to share the happy news with my dissertation committee due to what turned out to be unnecessary fears about committee member fallout. In the end, cloaking my life nearly brought about failing my comprehensive exams due to my lack of openness about fostering Lizzie during the time and not allowing my committee to provide me with the support I needed.

I felt a sense of connection with Lizzie the first time I saw her in a photo. In person, the adorable tilted tip of her nose and sparkling hazel eyes melted my heart tenfold. Although the timing was off because of the intensity of my schoolwork and health struggles, my husband Edwin and I decided to foster, and later adopt, the little girl who tugged at our heartstrings. She came to our home unexpectedly, although she was much wanted. Lizzie transitioned to us from another foster family facing an unexpected emergency. Her situation had been heartbreaking, but we loved her from the start. The tiny girl with the fierce personality bowled us over. As new parents, we rushed to catch up and catch on to all of the important things: *Which dentist? Which school? Do I pack your lunch? What do you mean you only like chicken nuggets? How are you alive, kid?!* Indeed. With everything she had been through with her birth parents, all of the abuse and neglect she had suffered, how was she alive? It was her fierce spirit that persevered.

In all its glory, becoming a new parent in addition to being a PhD student landed me in anxious territory. Overwhelmed with my new family scenario on top of my health issues and the demands of my upcoming comprehensive exams, which had already been delayed due to my health issues and the pandemic, I held off on telling my committee about the new little girl in my life. *How would this add to their perception of me as a student? Would they encourage me to postpone the exams again?* My lizard-brain began to contemplate whether or not the committee might even ask me to leave the program (part of my evolving imposter syndrome). It became a revolving part of my new fearscape as a frequently failing perfectionist. Particularly since becoming disabled, I couldn't shake the feeling that I didn't belong in academia. PhD programs weren't really built for misfit toys such as myself. I'm always battling the need to stretch myself out or shrink myself down to fit the academic mold. *Just... hold my breath... a little... and squeeze in.*

FRICTION AND FEAR

I was reluctant to share my happy news even though I had seen firsthand how other graduate students in the program had been supported with encouragement to bring children to class if babysitters canceled at the last minute and so forth. I was afraid that my committee would view fostering a child at such an important juncture in my academic career as meaning that I wasn't serious about my academic career, particularly when they were fully aware of my newfound struggles with disability. I had seen other students navigating parenthood successfully in grad school, but not disability and parenthood. The cozy comfy walls of my home life filled this new, bustling world of Lizzie with happiness and struggles, but it also created even more friction related to what I already expected of myself at school, where the looming questions were getting more powerful: *Are you well enough to do this? Can you complete the comps exams now? How quickly can you complete this and move through your dissertation?* Between the novel joys of shopping for dresses and park visits, my grad school fearscape montages increased their frequency in my mental rotation.

"Are you going to tell them?" My husband hissed at me between Zoom calls, bobbing his head into my home office door long enough to hear that I hadn't announced the news of becoming a mom yet.

"When it's time," I said. "I'm not ready."

The timing for this announcement did not feel right. I've always been stubborn, but apparently when I became a foster mother, my first move as a PhD student was to *not* move. I realize now that I think I wanted to guard my new relationship a bit, to give it protected space away from the pressures of school. I kept this exciting information quietly percolating in my private space, careful not to leave any crumbs trailing across the border area between my private life and the more public graduate student persona that I attempted to keep tidy from personal messes. I imagined each of my committee members' faces wincing as they realized I was fostering a child at such a tenuous moment. Although none of them had ever discouraged me—or anyone else in the program—from having children, it seemed a silently understood mantra throughout all graduate programs as far as *I* could see that one should finish the PhD and get a job before having a baby or adopting or fostering. I couldn't shake the feeling that I had already made things messy by becoming disabled after my first semester, which was followed by me sitting out for a semester, then moving to a part-time schedule in order to complete coursework in concert with my body. It seemed I was always moving the needle in the wrong direction, at least by my account.

SOUNDS, OBJECTS, AND CHICKEN NUGGETS

Learning how to be a mother as a graduate student was a tumultuous transition. I had to learn to simultaneously be a parent and be a graduate student in concert with my disabled body. This was unforged territory for me. Physically, I was still learning how to lace together loose threads of words on the corners of my lips, a condition caused by the side effects of the eight migraine medications I take. Cognitively, I had to work even harder in coursework to access analytical thoughts about stifled feminist voices at the university. And now, weighed down by piles of pills, invasive injections, and sweaty, pain-filled nights, I was asking still more of my body and myself in addition to understanding and meeting the needs of another wonderful human.

As I tried to reconcile my identity as a parent and my identity as a grad student, life carried on. Preteen pop star Jojo Siwa rocked through my Jeep on the way to therapy sessions for Lizzie, while my husband Edwin worked on his laptop in the parking lot and I clicked and clacked away at papers that needed grading in the waiting room of the therapist's office. Preparing for my comprehensive exams consisted of rereading what my medicine-fogged brain had forgotten over the summer, compiling notes, and learning after trial and error that Lizzie really did only eat chicken nuggets. Although she was still scrawny for her age due to years of malnutrition, we complied.

In my field of college composition, we discuss the implications of sounds, objects, and writing instruments that might bring a writer closer to (or farther from) their work, drawing them deeper into a discourse as elements of a piece emerge. Sketching out a dissertation chapter with a child present requires a unique approach to adjustment. Lizzie has a severe anxiety disorder that often translates into her needing more one-on-one time at home. As I and my husband work in our offices, Lizzie is a frequent coworker to one of us. To complicate things further, Lizzie also has attention-deficit/hyperactivity disorder, and her expression of ADHD means that the person attempting to do work next to her must adjust to the constant sound of the pop-it or fidget she uses as a method to focus her scattered thoughts. Unfortunately, these noises tend to diffuse my coherent thoughts, already seemingly few and far between, into scattered ones. The lo-fi YouTube videos I watch to reverse course once this has happened have the opposite impact on Lizzie, disrupting her already shaky emotional and mental self-regulation. We are the worst writing partners, like many parent-children combos who first start out, or so I tell myself (because I don't dare to ask). Eventually, we'll find our rhythm. And while Lizzie functioned well as a writing-break buddy and pencil-admiring companion, those moments weren't going to be enough to see me through my comprehensive exams.

COMPREHENSIVE EXAMS AND TRAUMA

I worked with my husband to wrap Lizzie in love and comfort, helping her adjust to her new home as I moved toward the deadline for taking the comprehensive exams. I decided to check into a hotel room for five days and focus solely on the exams—free of the new child noises sung through the house (and darted into my home office). We were still in the adjustment phase of Lizzie's homecoming and I was getting used to simple changes, such as the sound of a ten-year-old chasing my Yorkie through the hallway and the not-so-subtle noise of the daily after-school meltdowns. Although I would miss being there to soothe her as fifth grade math homework became too difficult, the comps exams would go more smoothly without these still new-to-me types of distractions, I thought.

I had four glorious days to work on the comprehensive exams (with extensions granted based on disability-related needs). I responded to two sets of exam questions: One from my primary field of research and the other from my secondary field of interest. I chose two questions from each set of exams to respond to. Each response was ten to twelve pages long and pulled from relevant readings on my reading lists. During the first day of my exams, my health held up and the work went by smoothly. Ideas flowed and I felt connections between the exam questions and my previous coursework. I was given extra time from the start due to my disabilities, which gave me the ability to get extra sleep and take breaks so that I could "write with my body," as Sondra Perl (2004) says, during the exams. This was a blessing.

The next day, I woke up with a vestibular migraine and had difficulty moving. I knew I wasn't going to be writing much and reached out to my committee. They kindly extended my response time out by a day to compensate for the migraine, which was a somewhat expected passenger on my comprehensive exams journey. My husband called that afternoon to inform me that "Lizzie missed [me] and kept asking if [I] was coming back." I wasn't used to a little person missing me and decided to invite Edwin, Lizzie, and my Yorkie, Archer, to the hotel room for dinner.

After pizza and nuggets, Lizzie made it a point to ask for ice cream so that Edwin would have to go to the hotel lobby and she could steal a few minutes away with me alone. Of course, I was flattered. She sat with me sweetly on the couch in the hotel room, recounting her day at school and rhythmically petting Archer to sleep. It was in this moment that she decided to reveal two trauma moments from her past, one that I was already aware of and another that I wasn't. I was fairly that certain no one else was aware of the second trauma either. As a person who cared directly for her, it was my responsibility to take action in a scenario I never dreamed I would be in for another individual, much less a child. Because we were foster parents, the state had was a process in place that we could follow, but nothing or no one told me how to go about mending the damage inflicted upon Lizzie. This was our first glimpse into the trauma she had experienced before coming to our home and it gave us a greater understanding of what it means to parent a child who is actively unpacking abuse while experiencing complex mental health issues.

The next morning, Edwin took off work to stay home with Lizzie, making sure she was emotionally and psychologically stable before returning her to school. She was distraught and increasingly anxious, so we decided to "divide and conquer" the necessary phone calls out of her earshot. Day three of my exams began with phone calls and emails back and forth with Lizzie's case worker and state-appointed therapist, appointments made in haste with my own therapist, and mind-numbing medications intended to block out the migraine throttling the back of my skull. My perfectionist self couldn't consider coming clean to my committee during such a high-stakes, sensitive moment in my academic career. I knew I was struggling and not fully focused on my exams, but I shakily attempted to push through rather than ask for additional time. The deadline quickly approached, and my responses were too brief in areas or flat-out missing in others. My mind was elsewhere as my body was wracked with pain, and it showed. *No one's comprehensive exams go exactly as planned,* I repeatedly told myself.

Eventually, the committee asked to meet with me, knowing I wasn't well, and graciously agreed to give me even more time to fill in the gaps within my exams. I couldn't help but cry. They gave me the additional time I needed not only for my body to recover—my disability truly wasn't holding up well to the physical schedule/time allotment of the exams process—and unknowingly to accommodate my daughter's trauma too.

PASSAGES

I passed the written and oral comprehensive exams with extra time, but it wasn't with the fanfare I had dreamed of. In retrospect, taking my own space and keeping my family's new development from my committee might have granted me more personal freedom, but it hurt my performance and muted my ability to ask for help. When I look back over the situation as a whole and embrace the complexity of it all, I realize that there's nothing wrong with adjusting a dissertation timeline—or any timeline—for parenthood. Priorities shift, and I hadn't yet processed what it would mean to prioritize Lizzie. I might have been uncomfortable pushing out my timeline for my degree because of the perceived optics of it within my department and the desire to complete the hurdle before me, but there was much more at stake than the exams. Despite the risk of academic failure, I knew I wanted to keep my focus on Lizzie and how she was processing a complex trauma. If I could, I would go back and reassure myself that that moment and the ones that followed played out as they well should have.

For a time I found comfort in the stability of my secrecy, separating the worlds of my family life and university life. The roaring pandemic left me cut off even more than usual from graduate school, and that made my unusual circumstances feel temporarily sustainable. After working through difficult moments during my comprehensive exams, I realized that not keeping my committee in the loop of my private life prevented them from understanding the difficulties I was experiencing at the time. I was allowing my fears to take over. Ultimately, I had projected my deeply embedded fears about the perfectionist, ableist, and sexist expectations of the larger university community onto my committee, holding them at a distance instead of giving myself compassion and asking for what I needed as my life changed.

Instead of attempting to play a perfect game of statues throughout grad school as I complete my work, I've come to realize that there is room for fluid life events to take place, even when academia itself seems immovable as an institution. As I've moved into teaching undergraduate students, I've learned new lessons every semester about the swiftness with which life can unexpectedly change within my students' lives. My own experiences have given me the compassion needed to accommodate and adjust for life changes in both the curriculum and socially.

RISKS, REAL AND IMAGINED

I cautiously waited to share my happy news with the people in the rhetoric and composition program. Eventually, I chose the random, awkward email route along with a cute photo over the higher-stakes social gatherings in departments that bridge school and social worlds. Photos of small children seem to smooth out a lot of rough edges. They support me as I continue working on my dissertation and raising my newly adopted daughter. This experience has led me to consider the roles of public and private space within graduate school and how such spaces can feel brokered as graduate students balance the emotional labor of becoming new parents. How do we begin to convey such information to our mentors when we exist in prickly boundaries? How much information should parents share without scrutiny? How can we engage in discussions about what nontraditional graduate life might look like while also considering shifting priorities throughout student careers?

Compartmentalizing personal life during graduate school can be useful depending on the situation at hand and timing, but I would encourage folks to consider the risks, both real and imagined, against the potential payoff. In retrospect, I wish I could tell myself that such compartmentalization meant that I nearly failed my exams because I didn't communicate with my committee about important milestones in my life. If this is you, I encourage you to give yourself space to breathe and consider your next move based on what you want from your whole life and self, no matter how dramatic, strange, or messy it feels in the moment. And when you are ready, give your mentors and committee members a chance to be supportive of you in all the ways available to them, including inviting them to your celebrations.

WORKS CITED

Perl, Sondra. 2004. *Felt Sense: Writing with the Body*. Boynton/Cook Heinemann.

21 ▸ FIND WAYS TO SHIFT

Reimagining Labor in the Postpartum Period amid the PhD

COURTNEY LUND O'NEIL

AT HOME IN our apartment east of Los Angeles, my newborn asleep in my arms, my husband in graduate school, and my savings account dwindling, I realized I needed a different kind of future in academia. When I gave birth to this child, my first son, I was an adjunct instructor with an MFA teaching composition courses at a private school in California. I loved this job—chatting with students before the start of class, seeing their eyes light up during the magical experience that follows an effective peer-review session, and exuding optimism as newly minted undergraduates. However, the joy I received from teaching was not enough now that I had a newborn at home. Happiness does not pay the bills, and given that I was the primary wage earner, the pay wasn't enough to support my family. The university I taught at offered neither paid maternity leave nor health benefits for contingent faculty. At the time, I was on government-funded Medi-Cal, which left me with little to no options for a future. So I quit, knowing I could not return to a job that was a dead end.

When my son was eleven months old, I applied to one PhD program. The future I imagined included a stable teaching job that had benefits for my whole family. In one of those many sleepless nights from that first year, I emailed a faculty member at a university for which I thought would be a good fit. I was interested in a PhD in English with a focus in both creative nonfiction and rhetoric and writing studies. Not all English PhDs are quite so interdisciplinary. Typically, many English PhDs with a focus in creative writing have another genre as their secondary focus or a specific area of literature. But there was something about the composition classroom that I had fallen in love with, and I wanted to conduct research as part of my experience in the PhD. I applied, I was offered a spot, and I went. My husband, who had just completed graduate school, and I packed a U-Haul and we drove east to Stillwater, Oklahoma, home to Oklahoma State University, with our toddler.

I enjoyed my work in the program and could now picture myself in the future I imagined when my first child was a newborn. I conducted qualitative research on the power of vulnerability in the first-year writing classroom and how vulnerability can enact positive social and cultural change (hooks 1994; Mathieu 2015–2016; Brown 2012). I taught various writing courses as a graduate teaching associate. Eventually, I became an assistant director for the university writing center and then later also for the first-year writing program. The workload as a parent was manageable. I could afford daycare for my son and my husband was working.

Life began to change when our school shut down halfway through the spring of 2020. I was in my second year when the COVID-19 closures occurred. At the start of my third year in my PhD program, we were about six months into the pandemic. Life seemed fleeting. On the news, thousands of people were dying from a terrible illness. It was frightening. My husband and I had dreamed of growing our family, but we wanted to wait until I was mostly out of coursework. A week after my 33rd birthday and during the start of my third year in the doctoral program, with three courses left to go, I took a pregnancy test. It was positive.

Being pregnant while being a student wasn't an issue for me. I completed my coursework while sitting at my desk for Zoom meetings and seminars. I completed my work on time, needed no extensions, and enjoyed reading books upon books with my growing belly. Although the days were reasonable, I knew that soon enough the days would become more difficult. The postpartum period brimmed with days and nights and months that bled into each other. The labor of caring for a newborn is some of the most strenuous, important labor I have ever done. The newborn phase requires adaptability. And I was about to do it again, with a second child who was then a four-year-old.

My second son was born the June after I completed coursework. In a way, this was serendipitous. I imagine that for a PhD student, having a baby that is due midsemester offers its own host of challenges. But the most significant issue I had the first time around remained: no funded maternity leave. The university offered no funding for birthing graduate students and I could not afford not to work, even with my husband's income. I had daycare to pay for along with other bills.

I thought about my options. I didn't want to quit. I didn't want to take a medical leave. I didn't want to fall behind. I needed the money. Even though the TA salary was meager, it had helped. Birthing parents, especially graduate students, rely on monthly paychecks, and taking the payments away for maternity leave is often not an option. It was not for me. I needed to work that summer, as I had worked every summer before.

As the summer session approached, I reached out to a mentor in the English Department that I trusted. She was the writing center director, and I was one of her assistant directors. Together we brainstormed a way for me to keep my paycheck and delay some of my work during the summer term when my baby would be born. I would still collect my pay but I would hit pause on my labor. This turned out to work efficiently, as I was able to bond with my baby for six weeks and then begin to work on a project from home.

Our summer sessions are about eight weeks long. I knew I had that amount of time to complete my work. I knew I that probably would not be able do much in the early weeks of the summer session. I moved all the work I had to complete to the end of the summer term instead of doing some each day. The workload did not decrease; it just shifted. For me, the first six weeks with a new baby are so special, so fast, and so incredibly challenging. There are feeding issues, sleepless nights, a new routine. The flexibility with my graduate work helped significantly in both my home life and my academic life.

In my administrative position, one of my roles was to help train writing center tutors for asynchronous tutoring sessions. That summer, in between feeds and naps, I built a two-hour workshop for tutors who were interested in engaging in meaningful asynchronous sessions with writers. In the fall, while my baby napped in the swing next to me, I delivered that presentation with my director to new and old tutors via Zoom. I felt proud. I needed help and had asked for it. I did not stop collecting a paycheck. I did not take a leave. I pushed the labor back, but the work still got done.

Looking back, I can see how not all PhD students have the same flexibility that comes with working in an administrative role. Not all PhD students are privileged to have such a caring, flexible, and kind director, who also served as a mentor. And I have been thinking about what another PhD in a similar situation as I was but with different tasks might do.

The first thing I recommend for birthing PhD students is to figure out what you need. It takes time to heal physically, mentally, and emotionally in the postpartum period. It takes space. It takes energy to bond with a newborn, too. These are nonnegotiable needs. However, think about what other needs you have in your program. Are you a student delivering your baby midsemester, while in coursework? Then it may be wise to take a semester off. If you cannot afford to do that, which many cannot, who can you speak with to push back your work? See if you can set flexible deadlines. If you are a candidate and in your dissertation hours, see if you can push back a chapter you are working on. If you are teaching, see how you can shift the class to Zoom or to an asynchronous model. Or see if you can receive a course release for other administrative or departmental work. Often departments need something. Maybe it's being the webmaster of a department's website. Maybe it's planning a conference to bring in visiting scholars. Maybe it's building a workshop on a topic that can serve the department in a meaningful way. You know your department's needs. But it's also important to know who to speak with about these needs.

It was clear to me when I began my PhD that I was a nontraditional student because I was a mother. Mothers were rare in my program. There were just a handful of academic mothers that I can remember, but we had each other to discuss ways we were managing and succeeding as doctoral students and mothers and to discuss ways to pivot in our many roles, both in the university and at home.

When I began my PhD, I was concerned about failing as both a mother and scholar. But in my heart, failure was not an option. I would do whatever it took to excel in both roles. To begin shifting my mindset to thinking about how I would succeed rather than how I would fail, I reached out to other parents who had been in the program longer than I had. I saw what they did, what they recommended, what they didn't recommend. I found faculty who respected my choice to grow my family during my graduate education. I ignored faculty who did not value my choice. Life does not stop just because you are a graduate student. Looking back, I am so grateful for my efforts to not give up on being a successful academic and mother to my two children, the one in preschool and the newborn.

The postpartum period is a raw state. It should be approached with tenderness, care, and support. Or as Paulo Freire (1974/2011) suggests: a pedagogy of love. How can we better love PhD students who are also parents? There is power in opening to those around you, to asking for what you need. There is power in reimaging what labor looks like for a parent in a PhD program.

ACKNOWLEDGMENTS

I want to acknowledge bell hooks, Paula Mathieu, and Brené Brown, who have inspired me in my teaching, my leadership, and my ways of connecting with others. I want to thank my Writing Center director, Dr. Anna Sicari, who helped guide me as I reimagined my labor in the postpartum period. Anna, this narrative has a happy, hopeful ending because of your work and your reimagined notion of what labor means for birthing PhD students. All of these women have influenced my leadership and passion for social change. May we all rethink how we can help graduate student parents succeed as both parents and scholars.

WORKS CITED

Brown, Brené. 2012. *Daring Greatly: How the Courage to Be Vulnerable Transforms the Way We Live, Love, Parent, and Lead.* Gotham Books.

Freire, Paulo. 1974/2011. *Education for Critical Consciousness.* Seabury.

hooks, bell. 1994. *Teaching to Transgress: Education as the Practice of Freedom.* New York: Routledge.

Mathieu, Paula. 2015–2016. "Being There: Mindfulness as Ethical Classroom Practice." *Journal of the Assembly for Expanded Perspectives on Learning,* no. 21, 14–20.

22 ▸ GIVE YOURSELF A BREAK

Juggling Rugrats, Experiencing Regrets, and Cultivating Compassionate Community

APRIL COBOS, DANIEL L. HOCUTT, AND MEGAN L. MCKITTRICK

WE ARE THREE recent graduates of the same hybrid English PhD program at a large East Coast public research university. As married parent colleagues of children who ranged in age from sixteen to one at the time we defended our dissertations, we reflect here on common struggles that defined our experience. Doctoral work is a distinct source of pressure from other education and/or professional labor, particularly when it competes with parental, marital, and professional responsibilities. We each experienced strains as competing priorities clashed, often struggling to balance marriage, parenting, and scholarship, all of which had implications for our health and our families. We share our narratives to prepare parents who are current and prospective graduate students for the unique challenges that are to come.

INTRODUCTIONS

April Cobos: My circumstances were unique—far from the traditional academic journey. After receiving my MA in 2005, I taught at several universities and community colleges throughout the country because I moved often with my husband's military service. He deployed frequently during the Global War on Terrorism, so I was the primary, and sometimes the sole, care provider to our two children, which required work and school flexibility. This PhD program was the only viable one for me and my family and the only one I applied to because it was a hybrid program that offered course options for both on-campus and distance students. Given the high likelihood that we would need to move before I completed the program, such flexibility was critical while I was working through my dissertation..

I started the program in person in the fall of 2012, completed my coursework in 2014, and defended my prospectus in 2015. I struggled after this to balance the needs of writing a dissertation and taking care of my family, especially because my children were school aged at the time and were very busy and my husband was often gone. In 2017, I found out we were moving to Spain while I also got the news that my first chair was retiring. My new chair became Dr. Dan Richards. Our working style and vision for the project fit well together, but I had to scrap the more than three chapters I had already written and start again in order to make that vision work. However, strangely enough, the move allowed my husband to be home more and gave me more focused time to write, so the final product was much stronger as a result of this and the experiences with my new chair. I was able to finish writing in the winter of 2018, defend in March 2019 via Zoom, and graduate in May 2019. It was four years from prospectus defense to dissertation defense.

Daniel Hocutt: In the fall of 2013, I started online doctoral coursework, fifteen years after completing my master's degree. I worked on staff at a different higher education institution and taught English undergraduate courses regularly as an adjunct. As undergraduate enrollments declined and graduate enrollments increased, the program chair encouraged me to pursue my PhD in English to be eligible to teach at the master's level. Even before beginning the PhD, I was already working full time, teaching each semester as an adjunct, and co-parenting our two children, ages 10 and 8.

Since I'd been teaching undergraduate composition courses for over a decade, focusing on composition and rhetoric in my PhD seemed appropriate. I entered coursework with the goal of earning the degree to be able to teach graduate students without investing much energy in the program, as I had little energy to spare. My full-time position was our family's primary source of income, our two children were heavily involved in school activities, and my partner's sometimes-challenging health conditions required flexibility.

Once I got started, however, I found myself immersed in a world of English studies that I didn't know existed. Not only was technical communication a subfield of English studies, but it turned out I was a technical communicator and I could center my studies on my professional role. I invested more energy than I had planned to spare in my doctoral studies, but that didn't change the circumstances of my professional and personal life: I was still working full time in a twelve-month position, still teaching a class every term, and still co-parenting two preteens. Juggling competing priorities became the main priority: learning to be productive in short spurts, agreeing to share responsibilities for attending special events, and using every moment to accomplish something. I was able to keep up this schedule for the six years it took to complete my PhD, but it certainly would not have been sustainable for much longer than that.

MEGAN L. MCKITTRICK: In 2012, I was a full-time instructor and part-time PhD student in the Department of English at the same institution where the three of us were enrolled. Both my job and my studies were temporally flexible. On paper, it appeared that I could balance the responsibilities of motherhood and family with those of my career. In theory, I could be the mother I wanted to be and the scholar-teacher I wanted to be. In reality, I never felt adequate in either role. When I was working, I worried about the time I spent away from my young children; when I was parenting, I worried about my performance as a researcher or my lack of participation in conferences or student organizations. I should be reading; I should be writing; I should be finger painting; I should be playing hide-and-seek. The balance mostly tipped in favor of parenting, and I learned to adjust my expectations as reality unfolded.

In 2016, I defended my prospectus a month before my first child was born. It was a healthy pregnancy and delivery, and I intended to complete substantial work on my dissertation while I was on paid maternity leave for sixteen weeks. Once into my leave, though, I discovered that people go on leave for a reason: sleep deprivation. The physical and emotional labor of motherhood left little time and energy for intellectual labor, and before I knew it, I was back in the classroom full time.

I struggled through full-time work, full-time parenting, and part-time dissertating for three years, feeling simultaneously proud of and guilty about my performance in all three, and I managed to complete a full draft of my dissertation in 2019. By then, I was pregnant with my second child and my mother had been diagnosed with cancer. I wanted to finish the program to focus on my family, but my committee found reasonable gaps in my dissertation draft. I'd need to revise and defend another semester.

My daughter arrived a month later, and my mother started ineffectual rounds of chemotherapy. The pandemic arrived a few months after that. It was the fall of 2020 before I could defend my dissertation, with four years from prospectus defense to dissertation defense and eight years to complete my PhD. My mother succumbed to cancer a year later.

PARENTING WHILE PHDING TAKEAWAYS

While undertaking a PhD program in traditional circumstances is grueling and stressful, undertaking such an endeavor while parenting adds stresses that none of us were adequately prepared to encounter when we enthusiastically began the program. As we advanced in our studies, our time and labor commitments increased, our children grew, and our family responsibilities became more complicated, requiring ongoing flexibility to meet the changing needs of parenting and schooling. Some of the shared experiences we found unique to being caregivers of our children while trying to focus on such a rigorous program included time and scheduling issues, work and writing expectations, socializing and networking expectations, and financial and marital stresses.

The remainder of this piece will focus on our takeaways and advice for those who plan to undertake this challenging but fulfilling professional endeavor while parenting. We focused on three main areas: time and stress management, emotional support from the student PhD community, and finding the right committee chair.

TIME AND STRESS MANAGEMENT

Classes were always in the evening, which was well suited for graduate students who had assistantships or jobs during the day but not well suited for parents, as this is the time when activities occur for older children or when small children have bedtime. This required lots of scheduling and planning just to make it to class. Megan and Daniel relied heavily on their spouses to take over the childcare responsibilities while juggling both a full-time job and part-time graduate school. This created additional stress for their spouses and thus for their marriages. In April's case, night classes required her to consistently find reliable evening childcare while her husband was deployed, causing constant worries about being able to get to class or whether her children were getting their needs met without either parent home in the evening. Classes in our hybrid program could not be rearranged to suit our specific demographic because they required classroom scheduling. Being prepared for these schedule clashes, having adequate childcare structures in place, and having open conversations with your professor and spouse or other caregivers can help mitigate this stress.

Finding time to work and write was also an issue shared all of us shared. As April's first chair often suggested, she should be making writing a priority at the beginning of the day, but when kids wake up at 6–7 A.M. and need help getting ready for the schoolday and the workday starts soon after, April, Daniel, and Megan all found it challenging to implement this suggestion. Both April and Megan tried, for a period of time, to wake up at 5:00–5:30 A.M. to get thirty to sixty minutes of writing done before the day started, but that schedule was exhausting to sustain. Daniel wrote in coffee shops after dropping his girls off at school and church activities, carving out an hour several nights a week. We all felt squeezed for time. While there is no perfect solution, all of us agree that finding a way to integrate writing into our unique daily schedules and making sure we did not expect perfect circumstances in order to accomplish good writing were necessities.

Time and life stresses also inhibited our ability to network and professionalize. This ranged from participating in graduate organizations, activities local to the campus, and networking opportunities that occurred at conferences. Taking part in these opportunities required a lot more planning when children were involved. For instance, for April to attend a conference, she would have to schedule her parents to fly down from Ohio to watch the kids for a few days if her husband was deployed. Megan and Daniel both attested to shortening conference time so as not to take advantage of the other spouse or parents, friends, and neighbors who were helping fill those parenting gaps. Megan chose to skip a number of conferences to care for their baby and felt somewhat behind on the latest research trends and sidelined in academic circles. While we could have just skipped these kinds of professionalizing events altogether, they are particularly essential for networking as an academic, so prioritizing the most important ones and attending for a limited time helped us navigate these challenges.

EMOTIONAL SUPPORT FROM THE PHD STUDENT COMMUNITY

While immersing ourselves in our graduate program presented challenges, it also provided much-needed support in the form of a community of like-minded learners. We were fortunate that our peers were seeking to support rather than compete, and we are grateful for the feminist ethos of empathy and care inherent in our cohorts. The mix of full- and part-time, remote and on-campus students and the hybrid nature of the program meant that nearly everyone enrolled was also grappling with unique sets of pressures and stresses (balancing parenting and/or full-time employment with coursework, conferences, publications and other professional development efforts, all while navigating hybrid learning expectations). This dynamic meant that we understood one another and could empathize and help manage these pressures as well.

The three of us met regularly online to share experiences and advice and hold each other accountable as we worked. Each of us also did this with other students in our program. Megan found support from the other mothers in the program, like April, as she navigated pregnancy and early parenthood, and she took solace in the stories they shared. She felt understood by her peers, and that understanding helped assuage her feelings of guilt and pressure. While Daniel didn't find a father-focused cohort, connecting with April, Megan, and other parents provided an inspiring model for what could be achieved by someone who was working through doctoral studies as a parent.

SELECTING THE RIGHT CHAIR AND COMMITTEE

We also recommend spending time assessing which chair (and committee) would be the right fit for their circumstances, not simply the chair who has the right expertise in their field of interest. We all shared the same chair, Dr. Dan Richards, who was a parent like us, and he demonstrated a sense of empathy that enriched our dissertation experience. While we don't believe peer or faculty mentors must have children of their own to be empathetic toward the challenges of parenting while PhDing, we certainly believe it helps to have that experience, and we recommend seeking out both faculty and students in the field and within your programs who might share your experiences. This can help you create a strong support network of caring students and faculty.

As a mother with two active school-aged children whose husband was deployed to a war zone, April struggled to balance her children's social and academic lives with her own professional and academic responsibilities. With two small children of his own, Dr. Richards could relate. In fact, he was preparing to read through April's final dissertation project, getting her ready to defend, at a point when his wife was about to give birth to their second child. Megan defended her prospectus while she was pregnant with her first child, navigated the unique newness of motherhood while writing, and was preparing to defend her dissertation the month before she was due to deliver her second child. Dr. Richards propelled her as far along as he could, understanding that she wanted to finish the program before her second child arrived, and she was grateful for his effort. Likewise, Daniel had two school-aged children, balancing fatherhood with his profession and his studies. Dr. Richards knew firsthand the pressures we felt and could spur us all toward success.

The three of us, as well as Dr. Richards's other ABD students, met regularly online to provide a status update as an accountability measure, but these meetings also provided a valuable forum where we could vent and receive emotional support and encouragement. While these meetings began with discussions about writing roadblocks or research-related questions for the chair and the group, they often transitioned to confessions about work-life balance. Dr. Richards treated these topics as equally productive, joining in with perspectives about his own experience navigating parenthood and tenure-track work and giving room for the other students in the meeting to do the same. It created an environment that welcomed the messiness of this process, covering everything from data analysis to effective bedtime strategies. We encourage students to consider whether they can rely on their prospective chair for such support, and we encourage faculty to adopt this model by establishing accountability meetings with ABD students that welcome topics about whatever their present needs might be, whether they're related more to the work or life side of the work-life balance we all struggle to achieve.

CONCLUSION: YOU WILL DROP THE BALLS YOU'RE JUGGLING. RESOLVE TO GIVE YOURSELF A BREAK

Parenting while PhDing is a juggling act. At the very least, you're juggling parenting and student responsibilities. You're probably also juggling professional responsibilities to support your family during your program of study. You're certainly juggling interpersonal relationships, perhaps as a component of co-parenting and likely as a member of multiple social groups. Hard choices will need to be made. You will miss some of your children's activities. If you're co-parenting with a partner, you will likely neglect them sometimes and rely on them to cover your absence more than once. You will manage yourself and your time poorly sometimes. You will make mistakes and drop all the juggling balls. Some of these mistakes may be costly—to you and/or your children, your partner(s), your coworkers, your friends, and your colleagues in the program. You will feel inadequate in your studies, you will feel guilty about treating others poorly, and you will probably believe yourself to be a terrible parent.

That's one way to look at it. Here's another way, and this is how the three of us see each other,

April is a remarkable parent who has seemingly infinite patience with her incredibly active children and her often-deployed husband. She handles being the wife of a commander and the expectations of that role in the armed services with aplomb and rhetorical sensitivity. She developed a remarkable line of study in her dissertation, one that was extraordinarily hard to complete, and the field is better for her contributions and perseverance.

Megan is a remarkable parent who somehow managed to defend her prospectus while teaching full time and pregnant with her first child; to complete her dissertation while still teaching full time, parenting a newborn, and giving birth to a second child; and to defend her dissertation successfully in the midst of a global pandemic while navigating the grief of her mother's terminal illness. She performed meaningful multidisciplinary work in her community while developing her dissertation study and she contributed to the important task of preparing several different publics for climate change.

Daniel is a remarkable parent with the ability to get things done when too many things are due. While working a full-time, 9–5 job, he started collaborating and publishing research projects outside required coursework, added more adjunct teaching responsibilities as he became more proficient in online writing instruction, and cared for his wife who regularly struggled with serious, sometimes life-threatening ongoing health issues. While doing that, he developed novel theoretical and methodological approaches for tracing rhetorical agency.

The point is that we have accepted (and we continue working hard to keep accepting) our limitations, we remember and highlight our strengths, and we draw healthy boundaries regarding our capabilities and capacities. Whether this acceptance requires time and task management, finding colleagues who share our experiences, or the mental fortitude needed to break through the negativity that sometimes weighs us down, the skill of accepting our mistakes and moving on from them is a quality we commend to anyone planning to parent while PhDing. Although difficult, these concurrent roles are possible, and we each found our way in the end.

We are remarkable. We are inadequate. We are simultaneously both and neither. We are humans PhDing while parenting, and we, too, have significant contributions to make to the academy.

23 ▸ CREATE A TOOLKIT

How We Developed Practices of Care to Survive as First-Gen GTA Parents

DANIELLE MARIE KOEPKE AND
GITTE FRANDSEN

THIS IS A STORY about two moms trying to survive a system that wasn't made for them. We write this chapter in dialogue to invite you into conversation with us. By doing so, we embody the feminist act of storying our lived experiences (hooks 2020). To us, story is central to how individuals see the world and make sense of it (King 2003; Powell 2014). We offer our interwoven stories about being graduate teaching assistants (GTAs), moms, and dissertators to other parents and GTAs who are striving to survive the dissertation process. Throughout, we find that care can take many complicated forms. Care is not "a warm pleasant affection or a moralistic feel-good attitude" (Puig de la Bellacasa 2017, 2). It is "manifested in practice—action, labor, work—it is integral to our ways of doing" (Malatino 2020, 41). We see care as maintenance work done for collective survival. Following Sara Ahmed in her book *Living a Feminist Life* (2017), we share what we include in our toolkit for parenting while PhDing and invite readers to build their own feminist survival toolkit.

GITTE: Do you remember our summer writing sessions?

DANIELLE: Yes! I remember one time well. We were sitting at City Market, coffee getting cold, power scones half eaten, trying to work on our dissertations. Not ten minutes into writing, you were interrupted by family members calling, I had to reschedule appointments for my children, emails were coming through for our multiple roles in and out of academia that needed responses—all these labors gnawed at our attention as we tried to focus on *one thing*: writing the dissertation.

These labors, or care work, are necessary to keep our households running. We make sure the kids make it to activities, everyone gets fed, and we all have what we need each day. These often-invisible labors do not stop when the workday ends, and they are not paid for or validated. As we juggled these layered labors that vied for our time and energy on a daily basis, we sometimes wondered if we would make it through the PhD.

As first-generation PhD students, GTAs, and moms, we found that our identities placed us on the periphery of the graduate community at our university. Our program in the English Department at the University of Wisconsin-Milwaukee is called Public Rhetorics and Community Engagement. The program draws graduate students interested in technical and professional communication, teaching and writing program administration, activist rhetoric, and more. While each incoming cohort is not overwhelmingly large, there are twenty or so new graduate students each year at the MA and PhD levels, including those with GTA contracts. Our department hires GTAs as instructors of record. This means that we were the teachers; we were not assistants to a professor. We created lesson plans and assignments, curated materials and activities, and completed all the grading and feedback. While it is suggested that GTAs spend about twenty hours per week teaching, holding office hours, grading, and prepping, anecdotally we know that number to be much higher. Even before the global pandemic, we were already in a precarious and underpaid position.

The two of us met in a seminar before Gitte transitioned into the program and when Danielle was completing her MA, but we got to know each other better as we both embarked on the PhD in the same year. Because we were both extremely busy, it took time for our relationship to grow. Through small conversations before and after classes (comments like "How can they expect us to do this much reading?!" and "This paper will just have to be what it is" come to mind) we built a small community of parents within our program.

DANIELLE: My experiences in academia have always been interwoven with my experiences of being a parent. I became a mother at seventeen years old; then, I finished high school, earned an undergraduate degree, and worked as a freelance writer. In the back of my mind was a goal I'd had since I was young: to earn a PhD. I didn't know if it was possible anymore as a working mom and wife, but with support from my spouse I decided to embark on the seven-year journey. My lack of knowledge of graduate school was clear in that first year of the MA—it ranged from not knowing what a literature review was to teaching concepts I was still learning about to students. I'm not sure how I survived that first semester. I learned as a first-generation college student that I had to ask a lot of questions that made me feel dumb and that I had to figure out a lot of things on my own. I wasn't aware of rhetorical scholarship or even the names of any academic journals. I remember poring over sources that I apparently should have been familiar with ahead of seminars that already had hundreds of pages assigned each week. No one else in my cohort had children, so I was often isolated in my experience of running from campus to pick up my kids from school, making dinner, helping them with homework, and spending time with them before starting my own homework or grading. Even those peers I did get advice from were not quite understanding about what it meant to be the main caregiver (i.e., I couldn't just work all day on campus and go home when I was "done with work"). I was working over thirty-five hours per week across three jobs while taking a full PhD courseload and caring for two kids. I always remained committed to finishing, but when COVID-19 hit, there were times when I wondered why I was putting so much energy into this and if it would just be better to quit and work one salary-paying job instead of struggling along this way.

GITTE: I graduated with my MA degree from the University of Copenhagen in my mid-twenties and started teaching, first as a high school teacher in Denmark and later as a lecturer at the University of Wisconsin-Milwaukee. I had children in my mid-thirties and came back to graduate school in my early forties. As a first-generation student whose entire educational background had previously unfolded in a non-US context, I felt completely out of place coming into the doctoral program. Although I had worked in higher education, as a student I lacked the navigational understanding of how graduate school worked. Almost everything about graduate school in Denmark seemed significantly different, and my fifteen-year hiatus from being a student did not help matters.

Being a nonnative speaker of English added to the stress and my perception that I was on the margins. My prior educational experiences as a student were in a deficit-based learning environment where language difference—that is, any divergence from *standard* English—were seen as a flaw that had to be fixed (Delpit 1995). While I perceived my English proficiency as high, I came back to graduate school with a long history of *fixing errors* and feeling like a failure every time. Although I was a PhD student, a teacher of English, and an adult, I still had a deep-seated, embodied fear of sounding different. If being older than everyone else in the program, a first-generation student, and a nonnative speaker were not enough outlier traits, I was also a mom. When I started in the program, my son was eight and my daughter was five. My children were absolutely my first priority, but I also consistently felt like I was never doing enough as a parent or as a student. COVID-19, of course, aggravated that feeling.

DANIELLE: It definitely did!

GITTE: Remember that last Friday before the lockdowns?

DANIELLE: Yeah, I remember walking out of Curtin Hall together, each of us wondering about the severity of COVID-19. There had been one positive case on campus, and the plan at that time was an extended spring break. Wisconsin went into lockdown, our kids came home from their schools, and we began transitioning our classes to be online for the rest of the semester. That is when it became very clear to me that our institution expected much out of us as GTAs without supporting us as students. University messaging was geared toward being caring and understanding to undergraduate students. What was not made visible was the laborious care work this required of GTAs, and what was never addressed was the needs of parenting students. That was when we realized the need for our own survival toolkits.

I think back to one of the early COVID-19 days. I was working on transferring in-person course materials to online course materials (something I'd never done before) when my younger daughter needed my help because the computer she was using was not connecting to Google Meet. I gave her mine and helped her get set up. As I was walking out of her room, my older daughter was having an issue with accessing materials linked through Google Classroom, and so I did troubleshooting with her for a while. During this time, my husband was in a meeting in our main living-room space and our dog was calmly sleeping in the corner (at least for the moment). Since I didn't have my computer, I used my phone to tutor because I couldn't not show up for students who were stressed out of their minds and just trying to survive the semester. The COVID-19 lockdown flattened all these layers of care responsibilities, and I was drowning in them. How could I care for my kids? For my kids' teachers, who were overwhelmingly stressed out? For my own students? For those I was tutoring, who had professors who weren't making allowances for COVID-19? For my own studies and deadlines? And where in there was caring for my own self?

GITTE: In early August 2020, I made the impulsive decision to relocate temporarily to Denmark with my children but without my husband. Denmark was handling the pandemic much better than the United States, but the pandemic isolation was hard for my elderly mother, so I figured I might as well make lemonade from all the pandemic lemons by having my children connect with their Danish family and culture, learn the language, and attend school in person. All of that sounded great until the reality of the seven-hour time difference set in, and I understood that I had to teach my own classes around dinner time and take graduate classes in the middle of the night. In other words, I needed to be present in two time zones while single parenting. It felt like nonstop emotional, intellectual, and household labor: helping my children adjust to a new life and navigate in a partially familiar language, supporting my mother, co-parenting via FaceTime, doing chores, studying and trying hard to engage with complex ideas, teaching and providing an unprecedented type of radical care for my students. I took up running during this time, and running felt like the only time I was doing something to care for myself. More than exercise, it was a space for breathing.

Gitte and Danielle: At this time, our institution sent multiple emails entreating teachers to increase their care for students. These institutional calls for care felt like BS because they weren't followed up by actions that alleviated our material conditions as we took on the multilayered and embodied work of care (Ahmed 2017). While laboring to provide support for our own students to fill that gap of care left by our institution, we found ourselves lacking support as both graduate students and teachers. Since the university did not manifest care in their actions (Puig de la Bellacasa 2017), we learned that we needed to build relationships that we could depend on.

GITTE: When I started dissertating in the fall of 2021, most activities were back in person, with masks required. I was entirely unfamiliar with the genre of a proposal or a dissertation. As a first-generation student, I lacked a familial network to help me navigate these new genres and my program did not provide too much support either. My advisor tried to help me fill these gaps, but I was longing for more support on the dissertation genre and strategies for getting started. Without this support, I had to deconstruct the genre based on samples, which I know how to do but which is time consuming and taxing because I always found myself questioning my understanding of things. Having programmatic or institutional support would have provided me with more clarity about the dissertation or it could have helped me create a community of writers to be accountable to that, in turn, would have made the writing process less lonely.

In charting this unknown territory by myself, I felt increasingly stressed and overwhelmed, which was challenging for me as a student and a parent. It also meant that I often decided to tackle more concrete tasks such as lesson planning, grading, or nonacademic chores because I knew what these tasks asked of me. Eventually, I joined a fourteen-day writing challenge organized by the National Center for Faculty Development & Diversity in the early summer—right when my children's summer vacation had started—that pushed me to write for at least thirty minutes every day. This was incredibly helpful because it helped me get started and appreciate getting at least some writing done between drop-offs at camp, get-togethers, and outings.

DANIELLE: My dissertation proposal was approved in May 2022. I was trying to finish a year early because while I have a spouse contributing to our family income, my contribution (even across four part-time jobs) was not enough. The stress of the PhD was spreading to the rest of my family. Choosing to finish the PhD meant that I had literally one year to go from a blank Word doc titled "DISS" to a full dissertation. So I was motivated to get writing.

Writing, however, has not been a simple task. Because of the nature of my dissertation project, I've had to make concessions, change goals, and alter plans to get the thing written. I remember starting out in June thinking, *I'll have drafts of three chapters by the end of August*. That did not happen. What did happen? I took my kids to Six Flags; I took them to the beach, to rollerskate, to visit family, to play with friends; I practiced their math facts with them; and went on bike rides to the library. I did what I could. Gitte and I took a couple of trips to a small water park with two of our kids so they could swim while we wrote. It wasn't the ideal writing situation, but we got words written. Didn't we?

GITTE: Yes! Words were written. Meanwhile, we also had multiple other school-related responsibilities to take care of. Throughout graduate school, we have both signed up for numerous service-oriented roles: I have been a graduate student representative for the Graduate Policy Committee for two years, a team manager on two research teams, a co-chair for two years in our Rhetoric Society of America student chapter, and a mentor for incoming GTAs for two years.

These roles added to the layers of care work I was already engaged in. Part of the reason I took on these responsibilities was my inclination to provide support for others and help create opportunities to fill some of the gaps I talked about earlier. I have no doubt that for me, the desire to provide this type of service and care and the resources I was able to offer are related to my experience as a parent. I also have no doubt that some of the resources I have been able to offer come from parenting two children. Another motive for taking on these roles was more strategic. Knowing the competitiveness of the academic job market, I also knew I had to work on my CV. The stress of being on the job market was compounded by the fact that my husband and children had no desire to leave Milwaukee and I was unable to go on a national search. I was contemplating how far I was willing to commute or if I would be willing to split up our family to gain employment. Even contemplating these ideas felt like emotional labor because I didn't want to be apart from my family and I didn't want my children to be forced to move because of me. But I needed a job.

DANIELLE: I, too, needed a job! I had to be realistic about what jobs were possible given my limited ability to move; I have had to account for the lack of resources within our department for nonacademic job searches. This suggests assumptions about people being able to figure it out on their own or already being in networks with contacts who can offer resources or job leads, and it makes visible the preference for the academic job market over nonacademic job placement. I had to be willing to advocate for what I needed, asking faculty to point me toward nonacademic opportunities and searching for support elsewhere for translating academic experiences into resumés for industry. This took extra mental energy when I was already running on fumes. During this time, I've served as a member of an antiracist working committee and an accessibility working group, a graduate student representative, co-chair of the Rhetoric Society of America, and program recruitment assistant. With less than a year to find a job, I thought, *will I even finish the diss??* As I worried about this one night, I remember my younger daughter wanting to play a board game. I didn't want to. I was tired. I had been up with her in the middle of the night. I had worked all day, moving from task to task to task. My to-do list was unfinished, but I played the game. I woke up early the next day to try again.

Gitte and Danielle: As working parents and PhD candidates, we found that we needed a feminist survival toolkit specific to graduate school. Following Sara Ahmed's method of gathering practical, material, and embodied tools to sustain oneself, we end by offering a worksheet to help you build

TABLE 23.1 Create a Toolkit Worksheet

Tool	What we found	What you need or want
Community	We learned early on that community wasn't just about attending socials. It was about finding someone we could share stories, failures, resources, and life with.	To feel like I have the support of a community, I need/want
Mentoring	We needed to seek out mentorship specific to our unique context. We had to ask our mentors for time, resources, and guidance through processes as first-gen students. And many times we had to seek answers on our own.	To feel like I have the support of mentors, I need/want
Self-Care	We needed to define what authentic self-care meant for us. As moms, we have a high capacity to continue taking charge, taking the lead, or taking the load. We learned to say no to extra projects or roles when we were already at capacity. We practiced taking time off or time away from graduate school to recharge or focus on family. We had to be kind to ourselves. Even at our most efficient, we could only do so much.	Self-care for me looks like
Lived Experiences	We pulled from our everyday "mom" experiences to be successful in our leadership roles. We noticed these skills: organization, scheduling, efficiency, and problem solving. We spoke up for ourselves and others. Most importantly, we saw that the big picture was essential to balancing our lives in and out of PhDing.	To keep track of all parts of my life, I need or want

your own feminist survival toolkit—because you will need it—and we invite you to consider what else might be added to your unique toolkit. Parenting while PhDing is extremely difficult. Write when you can, be present when you can, and trust your skills and experiences. You can survive parenting while PhDing, and you can even make something beautiful out of it.

WORKS CITED

Ahmed, Sara. 2017. *Living a Feminist Life*. Duke University Press, 2017.

Delpit, Lisa. 1995. *Other People's Children: Cultural Conflict in the Classroom*. New Press.

hooks, bell. 2020. *Feminism Is for Everybody: Passionate Politics*. 2nd ed. Routledge.

King, Thomas. 2003. *The Truth about Stories: A Native Narrative*. University of Minnesota Press.

Malatino, Hil. 2020. *Trans Care*. University of Minnesota Press.

Powell, Malea. 2014. "A Basket Is a Basket Because . . . : Telling a Native Rhetorics Story." In *The Oxford Handbook of Indigenous American Literature*, edited by James H. Cox and Daniel Heath Justice, 471–488. Oxford University Press.

Puig de la Bellacasa, María. 2017. *Matters of Care: Speculative Ethics in More than Human Worlds*. University of Minnesota Press.

24 ▸ JUGGLE WHAT MATTERS

An Autoethnography of a Graduate School Mom, Educator, and Caretaker

CELESTE L. GRAHAM

After completing my master's degree, I decided that I needed a break away from academia and school. My time completing my master's degree was filled with pitfalls I couldn't have imagined. As a Black woman, I had often felt alienated, like my contributions to the classroom and academia as a whole didn't really matter. After my first semester, I nearly dropped out after suffering from exhaustion and a mental health breakdown. I finally completed my degree and graduated at the end of the fall semester in 2015. I was uncertain about whether I would continue my education and pursue a terminal degree in sociology or attend law school. I knew that I wanted to do one or the other, but I needed time to decide what would ultimately end up being my future destination. But first, I needed a break.

While completing my master's degree, I also completed an alternative teaching certification program and began my career as a history teacher at a public school in Dallas, Texas. After a year of teaching and doing research about law schools and doctoral programs around the nation, I found out I was expecting a little girl. Immediately, the stakes for my future and her future became incredibly high. I've always viewed education as a way to better my life. Now I had someone else's life in my hands. I was going to do whatever was in my power to provide for my daughter. I began applying for programs, and less than a month before I had my daughter, I received an acceptance letter to the program of my choice. Seven days after I celebrated my daughter's four-month birthday, I attended an orientation for new PhD students and began my journey as a mother in graduate school.

As mothers have ventured into the workforce and assumed roles within academia as scholars over the last sixty years, numerous academic works have been published that assess how these roles have either affirmed or negated their identity as women or mothers or both. In recent years, there has been a wave of literature that has addressed mothers in graduate school and academia specifically (Ellis 2020; Kulp 2020; Yeigh 2020). Historically, academia—with its strenuous demands and requirements—has been best suited for well-off men with the means to devote their entire lives to academic pursuits. Single and married men have often been had the luxury of pursing advanced educational goals because they are not expected to take on as many familial responsibilities and burdens. The exact opposite has often been true for women and mothers. Due to societal expectations, mothers have often been confined to domestic spaces and excluded from the workforce. In addition, when mothers have entered academic spaces or the workforce, they have faced extreme pushback, hostility, and a general lack of support for their roles as women and mothers (McWilliams 2018; Prikhidko and Haynes 2018; Lauer et al. 2019; Deng et al. 2022).

LIFE IS LIKE A CIRCUS

I'm used to getting things done no matter what, but I have mixed feelings about this. On the one hand, I know I can count on myself to manage my responsibilities and ensure that my family and I are taken care of. On the other hand, I understand that my status as a single Black mother, a graduate student, a caretaker, and an educator all coalesce to make my life chaotic, fast paced, overwhelming, and often exhausting for a variety of reasons. I come from a family of strong Black women, and although we are living through a resurgence of misogynoir in popular culture that decries strong Black women as being too strong, too masculine, and too aggressive, I do love my strength. Strength has not been a burden to my life. Rather, the circumstances that have forced me into having no other option than to be strong have been the real burden. More importantly, without strength, many Black women and mothers wouldn't be alive. That's certainly true for me.

I wear many hats all at once. I believe this to be true for most people, and this is why intersectionality is so important. Intersectionality is a term coined by legal scholar Kimberlé Crenshaw that means acknowledging that people often operate in and live within a variety of different identities that all culminate to make a person who they are (Crenshaw et al. 1995). These critical pieces of one's identity cannot be set aside at any given moment; rather, they coalesce to carve out individual identity. I am many things at once because that's who I am and that's who I have to be. I accept this as my reality, and I don't try too hard to fight who I am. I'm at peace with having a variety of roles and responsibilities, and I enjoy the diversity of who I am called to be at any given time. While I acknowledge strength and the role it has played in my life, I tend to see my life as a constant juggling act. I've been able to effectively discern which parts of my life need to take priority over others, but it took me years to reach that point.

Juggling various parts of my identity began early for me. I had a happy childhood, but it was marred by my mother's battles with chronic illness. When I was nine, my parents separated, and due to stress and preexisting medical conditions my mother lost the majority of her sight and was diagnosed as legally blind. My mother was a nurse by trade, but because of her disabilities she could no longer work in the same capacity. I remember our lives changing drastically within a matter of months. At nine and fourteen years old, respectively, my sister and I were now also caretakers to our middle-aged mother. I remember being told by extended family members that I needed to grow up and that I wasn't a child anymore, that my sister and I needed to help take care of our mother. I remember taking on this very grave personality and attitude about life and feeling like I needed to do everything I could to better my life and not be a burden to my mother. Even years later as an adult, I remember what I felt like in those moments and how I decided then that I must prioritize my responsibilities to my family above all else.

One of the most significant parts of my childhood was being continuously told that education would better my life, open doors, and generally ensure my success. School and how seriously I should take it have been an integral part of my identity for as long as I can remember. I excelled in my academic pursuits and they became a huge part of how I would measure my worth for years to come.

At times, my educational pursuits have affirmed who I am as a person. At other times, succeeding in my educational pursuits has felt like a burden that was unattainable and could be accomplished only through sacrifices that would ultimately be worthless and leave me unfulfilled.

By the time I was in high school, I understood clearly that academia and school were not spaces that were historically or traditionally designed for me. Although I have spent years being praised for academic gifts and acumen, I knew even as a child that I was considered an anomaly by my largely white educators. I was special. Other Black girls weren't like me. They weren't as smart. They weren't as capable. I also knew and felt that I had to be better than my white classmates to be considered even remotely as good as them. My mind and my body became attuned to the ways that my white classmates could use their privilege to make our educational systems work in their favor. After all, those systems were designed to affirm them. However, I had to extract whatever affirmations of my abilities I could gather while simultaneously accepting that many of the positive sentiments my teachers and classmates expressed were half-compliments rooted in classism and anti-Blackness that ultimately encouraged me to deny critical parts of who I am. This would be a pattern in my life until I wrapped up my K-12 education and began and finished both my undergraduate degree and my master's degree.

I KNOW WHO I AM

When I entered my PhD program, my experiences and my perspective on what it meant to be a graduate student had shifted from what I had experienced during my MA program. I was a mother now. School was not new to me, but experiencing school as a mother has been drastically new in both positive and negative ways. As a new mother, I was consciously aware of how academia, the doctoral program I was in, and my professors acknowledged or refused to acknowledge the various parts of my identity. On the one hand, I understood the vast undertaking I had before me as a doctoral student. I was aiming to complete a terminal degree in a highly competitive field that requires hundreds of hours of study, research, writing, and publication. As a career student, I understood from my previous experiences that academia would not bow to me. No matter what. On the other hand, I was also older during this round of graduate school. I did not feel the need to prove myself in the same ways that I had before. I was a mom now. My daughter and her well-being meant and still mean everything to me. Although I understood the huge task that lay ahead of me and the innumerable sacrifices that I would have to make in order to successfully complete this program, I would not sacrifice motherhood or my well-being. I began to list and prioritize my chief responsibilities. First, I had to be a mother to my daughter. Secondly, I had to be a dedicated student and do my absolute best to excel in and eventually complete my doctoral program. Third, I could not let my responsibilities as a teacher fall apart because that was my livelihood and I depended on my job to provide for my daughter and myself.

The first two years in my PhD program were the hardest logistically because I was doing coursework. The constant struggle of having in-depth assignments due every week, planning out and completing projects in advance, and writing and submitting papers for presentation and publication constituted the most stressful period of my life to date. During my 27th and 28th years, there were nights when I literally did not sleep. The university I attend is forty-five minutes away from my house, and for two years straight, I would commute there at least twice a week after work. There were nights when I would stay up until 2 or 3 A.M. writing and then get up at 6 A.M. to get my daughter ready for daycare and myself ready for another day teaching middle school history. I was barely making it, but somehow I pushed myself to keep going and to juggle everything.

After I had completed the first two years and all the required coursework in my PhD program, my mother became too ill to live alone, so she came to live with me during the COVID-19 pandemic. Although my mother had been chronically ill since I was a child and I was used to taking care of her in many ways, the pandemic exposed cracks in my life that nothing else probably could have. After two long, hard, and grueling years of juggling all of my responsibilities, I was beyond exhausted. I would wake up tired in the morning, already anticipating everything that had to be done. By this point, the relationship I had with my daughter's father had broken down beyond repair, and what little support I had from him was now so inconsistent that it didn't even feel like it was there at all. I no longer got along with the principals at the school I taught at, and on more than one occasion I was accused of and penalized for prioritizing my graduate program above my teaching responsibilities. I was now the primary caregiver for my mother, who was now much older and much sicker and required much more of my time and attention than at any other time in my life. Academically, I was excelling, as always, but it didn't feel as good this time. I was happy that something in my life was going right, but it didn't feel right that my personal life, which mattered most, was falling apart all around me. I knew adjustments needed to be made and my priorities needed to change.

THE RINGMASTER

I once heard a saying: when juggling, you need to know which balls are rubber and which balls are glass. Or in essence, in life you have to know which responsibilities and obligations you can sometimes set aside and which ones must constantly be tended to. School, and more specifically graduate school, has provided me with opportunities I could not have gotten elsewhere. I understand that and I'm eternally grateful. When I'm finally finished, I think I will fully feel that I will have accomplished my original goal, one that will put me in a position to permanently better my life and that of my daughter. However, school and this graduate program and its numerous responsibilities aren't all of who I am. I am so much more than that, and to be the best version of myself, I need to feel fulfilled in all areas of my life, not just some. School has been great. What my education has and is doing for me is incomparable, but I reached a point where I refused to wake up and go to sleep everyday exhausted and empty. Once I had completed my coursework, it was time to focus on juggling the things that served me the most. I couldn't make academia bow to me, but I could pick it up and set it to the side while I worked through my life and reprioritized what really matters. And I did.

I ended up leaving my job and pursuing employment elsewhere. At the new school where I teach, I feel seen, cared for, and supported in my goals outside the workplace. I joined a gym. I began cooking again. I prioritized spending time with my daughter and really began to enjoy motherhood. I have come to terms with the fact that my daughter's father is content with not being around, and I'm now in a financial and personal position where I can fully provide for my daughter. My mother became increasingly ill during her time with us and had to be admitted into a long-term care hospital. Although we miss her, love her, and wish that she could have lived with us longer, she is now in a place where she can get the type of care that she needs to be able to live out the rest of her life healthily and with dignity. Life is a constant juggling act, but for now, I am satisfied with protecting the glass balls and letting the rubber ones fall; I know I'll pick them up on the rebound on my terms..

WORKS CITED

Crenshaw, Kimberlé, Neil Gotanda, Gary Peller, and Kendall Thomas, eds. 1995. *Critical Race Theory : The Key Writings that Formed the Movement.* The New Press

Deng, Yuwei, Jacob Cherian, Kalpina Kumari, Sarminah Samad, Jawad Abbas, Muhammad Safdar Sial, József Popp, and Judit Oláh. 2022. "Impact of Sleep Deprivation on Job Performance of Working Mothers: Mediating Effect of Workplace Deviance." *International Journal of Environmental Research and Public Health* 19 (7): 3799. https://doi.org/10.3390/ijerph19073799.

Ellis, Erin Graybill. 2020. "Giving Birth in the Ivory Tower : a Closer Look at the Unique Needs of Pregnant and Mothering Graduate Students." PhD diss., Texas Woman's University.

Kulp, Amanda M. 2020. "Parenting on the Path to the Professoriate: A Focus on Graduate Student Mothers." *Research in Higher Education* 61 (3): 408–429. https://doi.org/10.1007/s11162-019-09561-z.

Lauer, Eric A., Karla Armenti, Margaret Henning, and Lissa Sirois. 2019. "Identifying Barriers and Supports to Breastfeeding in the Workplace Experienced by Mothers in the New Hampshire Special Supplemental Nutrition Program for Women, Infants, and Children Utilizing the Total Worker Health Framework." *International Journal of Environmental Research and Public Health* 16 (4): 529. https://doi.org/10.3390/ijerph16040529.

McWilliams, Wendy. 2018. "Supporting Mothers in the Workplace: Breaking Down Isolation of the Working Mother through Workplace Interventions." Masters thesis. Saint Mary's College of California.

Prikhidko, Alena, and Cliff Haynes. 2018. "Balancing Graduate School and Mothering: Is There a Choice?" *International Journal of Doctoral Studies,* no. 13, 313–326. https://doi.org/10.28945/4109.

Yeigh, Maika J. 2020. "Motherhood's Complicated Roles in a Graduate Teacher Licensure Program." *Teacher Development* 24 (3): 333–347. https://doi.org/10.1080/13664530.2020.1765008.

PART 4 PUSH BACK

25 ▸ YOU CAN BE BOTH

Navigating Complementary, Not Contradictory Roles as a Conservative Muslim Mother and Academic

NABILA HIJAZI

STUFFED GRAPE LEAVES for Monday, bulgur mujadara[1] and cucumber yogurt sauce for Tuesday, riz wa bazella[2] and fattoush[3] for Wednesday, and the list goes on. Deciding on the meals I have to cook for my family on a daily basis is always on my mind as I plan for the upcoming week. Raised in a conservative Muslim household in Syria until high school, I was always taught that my family and my children should be my priority. However, I always dreamt of attaining a PhD, becoming a college professor, and challenging the narrative that a Middle Eastern wife and mother does not need higher education. With twin sons in middle school and a daughter in high school, I sought graduate studies in English, specializing in rhetoric and composition, at the University of Maryland, College Park.

MY DILEMMA: CHALLENGED BY ACADEMIA AND CULTURAL NORMS

My story reflects the challenges of navigating familial expectations, as I faced criticism from family members for stepping beyond traditional roles—balancing my responsibilities as a Muslim Syrian wife, daughter, and daughter-in-law while pursuing a PhD and succeeding in academia instead of focusing solely on my family and my children. To prove to them and everyone else who has challenged my conservative upbringing and my ability to succeed in domestic and graduate spaces, I knew I needed to put in extra effort to balance my life, fully commit to my family, and raise my children in the best possible way. I had to organize my life in a way where I was able to maintain a healthy environment for my family and still complete my graduate coursework, my research, and my dissertation. My definition of balance may seem radical to Western feminists and even to contemporary Islamic feminists, who might call me too willful for being an obedient wife who makes sacrifices for her family, especially her children, instead of quickly chasing her academic dreams.

To move away from the reductive, limiting image that academia, my culture, and my family have attached to my persona, I've paved my own way—my way of excellence and balance—between my domestic responsibilities and my graduate work responsibilities. For me, achieving balance has taken many forms that stem not only from my academic success, research papers, conference presentations, or even glowing course evaluations but also through the fulfillment of my duties toward my family and through my children's success: winning a science fair competition and advancing to the state level, securing a position on the soccer team, completing Girls Scouts events, or even doing simple tasks of cleaning the house and sorting clothes. Balance and contentment even came in the form of caring for my elderly parents, especially my mother, who I was blessed to have around, showering me with her *duaa* (Islamic supplications)—a source of blessing and unwavering love that brought harmony into my life.

Maintaining all the moving parts and keeping my composure required taking on extra responsibilities and more discipline. I had to do house chores, cook healthy fresh meals on a daily basis; drop my children at school; pick them up; help with their homework; read them bedtime stories; and, along with my husband, take them to soccer and swimming practices, which we both enjoyed; coach them in academic competitions; and take care of my elderly parents, especially my mother, who I went to see at least four times a week to spend time with her and bathe her. I told her about my day and my career plans and I filled her day with activities, such as stuffing grape leaves or squash, chopping parsley for tabbouleh,[4] rolling dough for sambousek[5] or shish barak,[6] making ma'amoul,[7] folding clothes, connecting her with friends and family members she left behind in Syria, and taking her for walks around the neighborhood in her wheelchair. Being around her provided me with nourishing self-love and energy to continue doing my best, especially since she taught me everything I know and shaped me into the person I am today.

Living with extended family as a support system, the norm of many Syrian immigrant families, meant cooking and caring for not just my children but also for my nephews and friends who came over for dinner on weekends by cooking lavish meals, a sign of hospitality in Syrian culture. While all of this took a toll on my body and sometimes even my mental health, I've always found ways to enjoy what I was doing regardless of the amount of physical work or the pressure I had to endure. Having a set and sometimes rigid schedule made family and graduate work manageable for me.

Because my schedule was packed, I knew my only way to success was structure. I devoted two hours of my day in the early morning to completing my readings and writing my dissertation and I participated in biweekly writing groups that helped me maintain a steady pace and provided me with constructive feedback. I also organized my life around my family and involved them every step of the way. For example, my children would suggest a different dish for every day of the week. We went grocery shopping with my husband and completed house chores together: we did laundry, folded the clothes, and put everything back in the drawers together as one team. This team practice was done in every part of our life. While I was tasked with cooking, I had my children help me clean the kitchen afterward. Each one knew what task to do: one twin son washed the dishes, the other son cleaned the countertop and made tea for the family, and my daughter sorted the dishwasher while I fixed lunch boxes. As we were completing the chores, we laughed, argued, and even yelled at each other. It was a time for us to vent and sort out our problems. Kitchen time or laundry time was game time or even singing time, even when my children sometimes resented these tasks.

In her essay "Narrating Our Lives: Retelling Mothering and Professional Work in Composition Studies," Loren Marquez argues that "our lives cannot be so neatly divided into separate spheres" (2011, 74), and I see my academic space and graduate work as an extension of my intimate space of motherhood. I embody Eileen Schell's view that "motherhood always struck me not as a war or as wonderful but as a lot of hard and unremitting labor—labor with its rewards and joys" (2002, 409). My role as a mother extends beyond my kitchen or my children's study sessions. When I left home each morning to go to campus and drop off my kids at school, I did not leave my nurturing role behind; it accompanied me to my classes, to mentoring meetings, and even to research sessions. I see these spaces as complementary, informing and infusing each other, allowing me to move beyond static experiences. I see the classroom as a space where I fuse these experiences and disrupt dominant views that see the hijab as a symbol of backwardness and oppression in academia and assume that a conservative, orthodox Muslim woman cannot have authority in the classroom and be a committed wife and mother.

MY DEFINITION OF SUCCESS

My children have recently become college students, and I have kept the same bond with them by driving them to campus, taking walks with them, buying them coffee, helping them select classes, and discussing their research papers. Marquez describes how other scholars in her field "find and build mentor/mentee relationships, to publish, be collegial, to stay true to and be good to yourself" (2011, 44). I find myself in the same spot: I run my lesson plans, PowerPoints, and discussion questions for my classes by my daughter, and she did the same with me when she was a senior in college and when she was teaching a psychology lab at her institution to first-year students. She continues to have this collegial relationship with me as a mental health provider and PhD student herself. Because my daughter was born and raised in the United States, she understands the nuances of American culture more than I do, so I ask her for feedback and run my discussion questions by her. Even though I encourage my students to question their own categories of analysis, challenge their beliefs, and recognize their biases and assumptions, I make sure the questions I raise are not offensive. She acts as my advisor, and I do the same for her. I share with her my struggles in academia in terms of my accent and conservative hijab, and she shares her professional struggles with me. We get spiritual energy and professional advice from one another.

Before going to conferences, I would read my presentations to my children—a practice I started when they were in middle school—seeking constructive feedback from an audience outside my field. My husband, who used to attend these conferences with me, would also listen in. My children have continued this tradition. Now they read their work for their classes to me and we work together on their college and graduate school application essays. I also ask them to read my essays, seeking both affirmation and even refutation. Outside my academic work, I engage in some of the traditional gender roles. I teach my children—especially my daughter—how to cook, keeping the same tradition: the idea that a conservative Syrian Muslim woman can be a successful academic, housewife, and mother. I keep emphasizing the view that as women, we can shift back and forth between private and public spaces and still maintain success.

Because my definition of success and "making it" is different or nonnormative, I am calling for the widening of the spectrum and further breaking down of binary understandings. I call for studies of women who do traditional rhetorical work and to reconsider work that has not previously been valued as rhetorical. I evoke Charlotte Hogg's remapping of the terrain within women's rhetorical studies, which calls for deviation from "the binary constructions of women as either feminist or not," for "expansiveness of feminist research," and to "engage conservative women who fall outside our feminist frameworks" (2015, 393). My definition of conservative is different, however, since it refers to Muslim women who uphold Islamic beliefs with their traditional gender roles and family structure. I hope that our academic community will acknowledge and celebrate multiple definitions of academic success and balance even if they seem at odds with each other and to accept conservative religious views that present the mother as the nourisher, nurturer, and savior who helps her family through numerous sacrifices. I am calling for the honoring of women's ability to choose to adhere to the ascribed, traditional gender roles presented by their religion and for support for those who do so. A standard that demands that women choose between domestic and wage-earning labor fails women, particularly women who are intersectionally marginalized by virtue of their race, class, religion, nationality, and other key factors. I hope to move beyond dichotomous terms and to recognize and celebrate all women and their achievements—to broaden the scope of the field by redefining the standards of rhetorical effectiveness (Mattingly 2002). Ultimately, I hope to celebrate the successes I am having on both levels, and I am continually eager to celebrate my academic self in conjunction with my orthodox Islamic beliefs—not declaring a state of *death* on either of them.

In their 2011 article on motherhood and academia, Christine Peters Cucciarre, Deborah Morris, Lee Nickoson, Kim Hensley Owens, and Mary Sheridan expanded the definition of success and "making it" in academia as rhetoricians with children and families. They suggest that we move beyond the binary that sees women academics either as successful because they do not bear the burden of family responsibility or as lagging behind because of they started a family at a younger age. As an orthodox Sunni Muslim, a Syrian rhetorician, an academic, and a female junior scholar who believes in traditional Islamic gender roles in which each gender provides equally significant contributions to the family realm and in which the woman, the mother is the nourisher, I posit that motherhood can be the impetus for success, not just in domestic spaces but also in public domains, more specifically the academic domain. I argue against the reductive, stereotypical view that Muslim mothers are subjugated and cannot balance graduate work and succeed in academia. I invoke Lindal Buchanan's argument that the "Woman-Mother" dynamic is less binary and that the discussion of "intersectional difference" (2013, 19) is essential for recovering other voices and ways that do not necessarily conform to the mold of white, middle-class American motherhood. I echo the argument of Cucciarre and colleagues that we need to move beyond "the individualistic idea of choice" (2011, 58) toward family-friendly academic structures, in which both academic and familial roles are nurtured and celebrated, not as contradictory but rather as complementary, and in which storytelling and lived experience are sites of inquiry and the rhetorics of motherhood in life and work are sites for research and advancement. I call for a wider representation of multiple views of "making it" in which not just one single idea of success in the academy flourishes, but rather, we include multiple visions of success, even if these visions are contradictory to each other.

Women have been facing a tough choice, a choice of family or career, and bringing these worlds together is and can be difficult. In *Women's Ways of Making It in Rhetoric and Composition*, Michelle Ballif, Diane Davis, and Roxanne Mountford (2008) demonstrate that women's success generally happens more easily when she doesn't have children, when she doesn't have to make a hard choice between public and private success. Many female academics have to choose between staying and flourishing in graduate school or giving up academia to start a family, a situation in which academic success is halted. Arguing against the limiting view that the ideal academic is always available, is always working, and is childless or has a spouse at home to take care of family obligations, Cucciarre and colleagues describe the experiences of several rhetoricians with children "making it": "As a group, we are able-bodied, white, straight academic women with children whose experiences have varied considerably. Our range is not exhaustive, but includes being a single, adoptive parent on the tenure track, being a returning graduate student with nearly-grown children, and being securely tenured with school-age children" (2011, 41).

They acknowledge that their argument, while not exhaustive, celebrates the success of many women in academia. However, to paint a more inclusive picture, I argue for minority women "making it." These women aim for academic balance and success but constantly face not only the obstacles of the field but also the scrutiny of their families and relatives in the name of religion. The notion that working Muslim mothers cannot be good wives and caretakers is a conundrum, my conundrum, which Senegalese and feminist author Mariama Bâ succinctly describes in her semi-autobiographical epistolary novel, *So Long a Letter*:

> Try explaining to them that a working woman is no less responsible for her home. Try explaining to them that nothing is done if you do not step in, that you have to see to everything, all over again: cleaning up, cooking, ironing. There are the children to be washed, the husband to be looked after. The working woman has a dual task, of which both halves, equally arduous, must be reconciled. How does one go about this? Therein lies the skill that makes all the difference to a home. (1989, 20)

I challenge two polarizing forces: the dominant view that conservative, orthodox Muslim women academics are deficiently unfeminist and do not fit the mold of the white successful female feminist academic and the cultural view of Muslim working women as inept, non-nurturing wives and mothers. Female Muslim academics can thrive in both private and public paradigms and successfully go about PhDing while honoring their gender roles and varying responsibilities by knowing their priorities, organizing their lives around and with their family and children, and surrounding themselves with sources of unwavering love: motherly love, self-love, and soul-nourishing love.

NOTES

1. Mujaddara is a vegetarian Syrian dish that consists of lentils cooked with groats, generally bulgur (cracked wheat), and garnished with sautéed onion.
2. Riz wa bazella is a rice and peas dish that is topped with sautéed ground meat and nuts.
3. Fattoush is a fried bread salad that typically includes lettuce, tomatoes, cucumbers, radishes, and fried or baked pieces of pita bread.
4. Tabbouleh is a Syrian salad made mostly of finely chopped parsley with tomatoes, mint, onion, and bulgur that is seasoned with olive oil, lemon juice, salt, and sweet pepper.

5. Sambousek is a mini savory pastry that has either spiced meat or cheese filling.
6. Shish barak is pillowy dumplings filled with seasoned meat and served in a silky warm yogurt sauce.
7. Ma'amoul is baked shortbread pastries filled with pistachios, dates, or walnuts.

WORKS CITED

Bâ, Mariama. 1989. *So Long a Letter*. Heinemann.

Ballif, Michelle, Diane Davis, and Roxanne Mountford. 2008. *Women's Ways of Making It in Rhetoric and Composition*. Routledge.

Buchanan, Lindal. 2013. *Rhetorics of Motherhood*. Southern Illinois University Press.

Cucciarre, Christine Peters, Deborah Morris, Lee Nickoson, Kim Hensley Owens, and Mary Sheridan. 2011. "Mothers' Ways of Making It—Or Making Do? Making (over) Academic Lives in Rhetoric and Composition with Children." *Composition Studies* 39 (1): 41–61.

Hogg, Charlotte. 2015. "Including Conservative Women's Rhetorics in an 'Ethics of Hope and Care.'" *Rhetoric Review* 34 (4): 391–408. https://doi.org/10.1080/07350198.2015.1073558.

Marquez, Loren. 2011. "Narrating Our Lives: Retelling Mothering and Professional Work in Composition Studies." *Composition Studies* 39 (1): 73–85.

Mattingly, Carol. 2002. "Telling Evidence: Rethinking What Counts in Rhetoric." *Rhetoric Society Quarterly* 32 (1): 99–108.

Schell, Eileen E. 2002. "Feminist (Un)Motherhood: Reigning Rhetorics of Mothering Inside and Outside of Academe." *JAC* 22 (2): 404–413.

26 ▸ YOU DON'T HAVE TO KEEP GOING

Reflections on Navigating Crises and Precarity as an Excluded Scholar

AMIE MCLEAN

PERSONAL CRISES ARE NOT—or are not only—a simple matter of the cruel winds of fate. The likelihood of students experiencing personal crises is shaped by a complex matrix of influences, and systemic social injustice plays a major role. In this chapter, I reflect on my experiences of parenting and PhDing through a series of crises. I attempt to account for the complex, nonstatic experiences of privilege and oppression that have been at work in my journey in and out of academia and to link those experiences to broader social contexts and power dynamics. Overall, I argue that the program and career exclusions that I and other PhD students who have parented through crises have experienced are neither inevitable nor the tragic result of cruel happenstance. Rather, they are the result of systemically extractive and oppressive models, processes, and practices of doctorate programs, graduate student career education, and academic labor.

The calls to action here are twofold. First, at the institutional and departmental levels, we need to develop equity supports for PhD students experiencing crises. This will require nurturing solidarities between established academics, excluded scholars, and graduate students. Second, I want to inspire critical reflection among faculty supervisors, mentors, and colleagues who might be advising graduate student parents and early career academics experiencing crises. I encourage such folks to carefully attend to the lived realities of the students and their families. In particular, I urge advisors to consider the realistic, long-term implications of that person's specific experience of crisis (or crises) in the context of an academic labor market structured by exploitation, precarity, and oppression.

THE SETUP

I grew up in a rural community in British Columbia, Canada. The town was predominantly White, segregated culturally and physically from surrounding St'át'imc Indigenous Nations. Most of the White population consisted of relatively wealthy farming, logging, and public service workers. There was also a sizable underclass of poor White families to which I belonged. When I was a child, my single-mother family was brought into some St'át'imc friendships and survival networks in ways that sustained us and fundamentally shaped my worldviews.

For me, those relationships fostered a deep and early awareness of differentially classed, gendered, and racist violences. Although we all lived in fear of social workers, it was disproportionately Indigenous children who were taken into foster care (see Blackstock et al. 2020). My brother having his hands ruler-whipped by an elementary school teacher was remarkable only because he was the only non-Indigenous kid it happened to (see Cote-Meek 2014; Milne and Wotherspoon 2020). Very early on, I learned the wisdom of holding a determined, quiet terror of educators and the educated, even as I knew that my brother and I were safer than many others. Our privileges within and sometimes violent exclusions from educational systems were apparent long before high school.

Like many folks of my class background, I was actively discouraged from seeking higher education (see Bettie 2014; Hardy and Marcotte 2022; Westover 2018). The journey to grad school was long and fraught in ways that are beyond the scope of this paper to address. Suffice to say that throughout my postsecondary education, I weathered an array of crises related to my impoverished background. In particular, my mother's poverty and worsening health presented a constant stream of small and not-so-small family crises as she struggled with divorce, housing insecurity, labor precarity, mental illness, and substance abuse and developed life-threatening diseases and life-altering disabilities. These pressures were especially acute in grad school. However, except for occasional medical emergencies that could be decontextualized from the stigmas of poverty, they were something I never mentioned to program faculty. As a first-generation scholar, I had no interest in drawing attention to the gulfs I perceived between myself and those around me.

Scholars have recognized that the structures of graduate programs, academic careers, and parental leave policies often encourage women to delay pregnancy (Crawford and Windsor 2021). Among other things, this can increase health risks for themselves and their children. While I was writing my dissertation, I secured a one-year lecturer contract. I knew this might be my only chance to have a child while I was in still in my thirties and was eligible for parental benefits. I had a planned pregnancy, gave birth, and went on maternity leave from the program. I was two weeks away from returning when doctors found a mass inside my baby's spinal cord, just below the brain stem. The prognosis was terrifying and life altering.

As the fraught process of securing treatment for my child began, my experience of parenting and PhDing through crises entered a new, far more intense phase. I entered a cycle of compassionate leaves and attempts to return to the program. I began regularly traveling across the country so my child could access experimental treatments and clinical trials.[1] I soon stopped telling people when I made attempts to return to my PhD. Many working-class folks had already accused me of having forgotten where I came from, of betraying my roots. I knew that the fact that I would take time away from my seriously ill, disabled child to pursue a degree that many members of my community believed I could not benefit from would be seen as a profound failure of motherhood and good sense.

The two faculty members I partially confided in had their own lived experiences of personal crises as academic parents. They were unwavering in their support, they listened, they provided advice, and they were willing to follow my lead. I will be forever grateful to them. My capacity to progress under these circumstances must be taken as a testament to the depths of their support and the quality of their mentorship. At the core of our interactions, though, was the abiding sense that if I possibly *could* complete my PhD, I definitely *should*, because it would surely be worth it in the end. And of course, the implied "end" was a tenured faculty position, which would also mean secure wages and medical benefits that I desperately needed.

I realize now what I should have realized then: I and (I suspect) the faculty members advising me were being guided by the same meritocratic ideals we sought to challenge in our teaching and research. We never made the connection that my situation, the oversaturation of the academic labor market, and the exploitative conditions of academic labor meant that I might well have been better off to quit (Caterine 2020; Cassuto 2015; Tennant 2020). Moving my child to multiple different health jurisdictions in pursuit of academic postings, postdocs, or tenure-track jobs would have endangered his life and well-being. The intensity of my caregiving labor meant there that would be no opportunity to engage in the normative, exploitative expectations that early-career scholars will write for free, edit for free, engage in service for free, and teach for obscenely low wages without benefits (Caterine 2020; Home 2018; Rose 2020; Tennant 2020).

From the moment my child was diagnosed, I never had a chance. Every truck driver I ever met was ahead of the academics in terms of recognizing the differential value of postsecondary degrees for working-class folks. I reflect now and wonder: What would things have looked like if instead of receiving advice from tenured faculty, I had spent time with members of the entrenched academic precariat?[2] Folks who are disproportionately women, people who are racialized, people with disabilities, parents of kids with disabilities, people from working-class backgrounds, and so on (Arday 2022; Gagnon 2022; Home 2018; Ivancheva et al. 2019; Villar-Aguilés and Obiol-Francés 2022; Warnock 2016)? I look back at the long nights of PhDing by my son's hospital bed and have to wonder if we all would have been better off if I had closed my laptop, picked up my son's hand, and walked away.

But I did not. I kept going. I kept going through my child's spinal cord surgery, through his temporary paralysis, through rehabilitation, through Ronald McDonald House, through new disabilities, through endless cross-country trips for treatment, through drug trials, through years and years and years of chemotherapy. At the same time, the "regular" crises associated with my impoverished background continued apace as those closest to me wrestled with housing and food insecurity, exploitative and degrading work, health challenges, mental illness, substance abuse, and violence (including the yet-unsolved murder of my stepfather). I wanted the life of a professor, longed desperately to give my children the life I saw the children of professors having.

When I was eight months pregnant with my second child and my son was still in treatment, I successfully defended my dissertation. But this is not a story of triumph. As I said before, our vulnerabilities to personal crises and our capacities to weather those storms are intertwined with our experiences of power, privilege, and oppression. Despite the systemic disadvantages I faced, my capacity to get my PhD within these contexts was critically entwined with my experiences of privilege, in particular White able-bodied cisgender privilege.

And this is also not a story of triumph because the story does not end there.

THE TAKEDOWN

One month after my second child was born and two months after I defended my dissertation, my partner was diagnosed with stage three cancer. Clutching my newborn in my arms, I stared blankly as he told me. Immediately I recognized that we needed help and that his geographically distant family were the only ones who could offer it. I consulted my vanishingly small group of academic colleagues and mentors and they agreed that the move was the only thing that made sense. As I contemplated life in a relatively rural city with one small university, I could see the door for an academic career closing on me. But there were no good choices left.

So while members of my cohort were publishing and writing applications for postdocs, I was breastfeeding a newborn, taking my eldest child to endless doctor and therapy appointments, flying across the country to pick up experimental medications, researching accessibility supports, administering my child's twice-daily chemotherapy, nursing a dying dog, taking my partner to oncology, to radiation, to surgery . . . the list goes on. Much of that time is blurry. I vividly remember the first time I changed an ostomy bag and the long nights of rocking my daughter to sleep, wishing I had more to give her.

I remember convocation in pieces. My partner was barely walking after surgery but insisted on coming. My family arrived late, my partner was in great pain, and my family was too far back to even see me. I remember, for some reason, how the university program failed to acknowledge my prestigious doctoral funding while others had been clearly listed. And worrying my child might need to breastfeed while I sat on stage. I should not have gone. It was never meant for people like us. People like me.

The depth of our precarity only became clearer when we arrived in our new city and moved into my partner's parents' basement. He was still in treatment, adjusting to emergent disabilities, and unable to work. I was ineligible for maternity benefits or other social supports due to the gendered structure of those social programs and having been in the PhD program. Suddenly the sole potential provider for a family in dire need of benefits, I desperately needed to find work to support us all.

I set about applying to every job with benefits that I could find, whether in or out of academia. I eventually secured a temporary part-time sessional position in intercultural learning. My daughter was still breastfeeding, and as I moved into a full-time temporary role, my partner would drive her to the university a few times a day so I could feed her. My heart and my body ached as I left her, but that was just one of the everyday betrayals I needed to commit to keep everyone alive. I would wake every morning and have to decide: do I tend to my partner's ostomy bag and open wounds first or administer my disabled son's chemotherapy or breastfeed my hungry daughter?

At great expense to me and my family, I excelled at my job. I worked long hours. I worried about the long-term implications of working outside of my discipline in an instructional support role, but I was assured by faculty and administrators that this was my best opportunity to eventually secure a tenured position: I just needed to keep going. But as my second yearlong contract was ending, COVID-19 was setting in. My child was still on chemotherapy. Our family entered cycles of often-intense isolation that continued for years. Fears about the financial implications of the epidemic gripped the university. Despite a performance review that indicated that I had exceeded the terms of my appointment, my contract was not renewed. My partner, now permanently suffering from at-times debilitating episodic disabilities, had only temporary contract work. By then, there was no one around to tell me to keep going, to suggest what to do. Road maps and encouraging words had fallen away.

Although I applied for a wide range of positions, my academic credentials left me both overqualified and underqualified for local industry, government, and NGO positions. Through intense networking, I secured a temporary remote staff position at the university I had graduated from. It was outside my field and it offered no opportunity for building toward a faculty career, but it was employment. Over the next two years, I interviewed six times for versions of the same job as I cycled from contract to contract. Each time, health benefits for myself and my family would be suspended for the mandatory probationary period, even as my own health eroded. I applied extensively for other positions and repeatedly was the unsuccessful of two finalist candidates. The combination of unending engagement in the ever-expanding unpaid labor associated with university application processes and my intense caregiving demands eroded possibilities for writing or publishing.

ON THE ROPES

Back home, mine is a cautionary tale about to how academia is not for the rural poor. More difficult for me, though, has been my inability to meaningfully engage with the social issues that were the basis of my PhD. My dissertation examined links between deregulation, neoliberalization, and the bolstering of patriarchal White supremacy in the long-haul trucking industry. An entire chapter examined how these dynamics contribute to differential risks associated with collisions and carnage involving trucks. Just months after I defended, I watched in horror as a truck-involved collision in Humboldt, Saskatchewan, took sixteen lives and injured many others. The racialized, classed, and gender dynamics associated with the collision exemplified many of the issues I had outlined in my dissertation (see Kennedy et al. 2019; McLean 2017). In 2022, as I sat with my family in extreme isolation, I witnessed as the truckers' convoy and attendant glorification of patriarchal White supremacy shut down Canada's capital and many other areas in the country.

But I am nowhere in these conversations. I have to find adaptive footwear for my child, to measure and administer chemotherapy, to secure doctors' referrals, and to figure out how we will pay for the next hospital trip. I cannot do all that and be competitive for a secure faculty position; I cannot be part of the conversation if I am not in a faculty position that makes space for that work.

Constantly working late nights and largely uncompensated overtime, I eventually was hired remotely into a continuing but undervalued staff position in the field of equity, diversity, and inclusion. As I was still living in a distant city, the university returned to in-person work and my position was put at risk in a different way. I went through the brutal process of applying for a human rights exemption to continue to work remotely, which I received. However, I remained precarious in that twice a year I had reapply for the exemption. For three years, I would go downstairs and work alone in my basement every day, trying to imagine some way out or forward.

Instability is the hallmark of precarity, and my employment situation continues to fluctuate even as I write this chapter. Eventually I took a leave from my remote position and returned to the same precarious, local role in intercultural learning that I was in before the pandemic. Moving all of my child's extensive health networks to a distant, expensive city where my partner has no work and we have no support is not an option. I have no choice but to keep going, but by now it is very clear that I am going nowhere.

CONCLUSION AND RECOMMENDATIONS

Transformative changes are needed in academia in order to create truly just, inclusive, and empowering experiences for graduate student parents navigating crises. The constant perpetuation of, participation in, and even valorization of exploitative working conditions serves to magnify the privileges of some scholars at the expense of others. Responding to these injustices requires developing equitable practices and response mechanisms for PhD students and early career academics who are experiencing personal crises.

I urge those working at the departmental and institutional levels to consider the following as you revisit workplace culture, policies, and practices:

- Create opportunities for graduate students to receive advice from students who have left your programs without completing or who completed and garnered disproportionately lower benefits as well as from members of the academic precariat.
- Consider how "stop the clock" policies and other equity measures might inform inclusive hiring processes that refuse to punish people for becoming pregnant, for becoming parents, and for having children who are medically vulnerable and/or disabled.
- Study the intersections between graduate students' work structures and social programs (such as parental leave, employment insurance, disability benefits, and so on). Identify opportunities to restructure to maximize access.
- Organize, support, and advocate for equitable treatment of the precariat even if that is not part of your lived experience.

This story is my own and I do not presume to speak for others. However, as I write it, I am holding close the stories of other graduate students and academic parents I know who have navigated a wide spectrum of crises that threatened their academic future. In my experience, such people are almost always encouraged to keep going. I hope that this chapter will inspire some critical reflection about whether encouraging students to continue is always a reflection of the actual best interests of the student and their families. If we know that academia is unsafe, exclusive, and exploitative, then why are we still encouraging vulnerable folks to chase these careers? What are the consequences for them, their children, and their families?

I count the few academic folks who have stood by me as friends. I admire them, I am grateful to them, and my life is richer because of them. However, I think that there needs to be an intentional effort to cultivate more space for people who need to walk away from academia to be able to do so with dignity and with their sense of self fully intact. I often reflect on what it would have been like to hear that I did not have to keep going, that it probably would not be worth it in the end. The following are my recommendations for folks who support graduate students navigating personal crises:

- Attend carefully to the systemic oppression and power dynamics that negatively impact members of equity-denied and deserving groups. Members of these groups continue to face unjust pressure not to enter academia in the first place and/or to leave without reason. Here I want to differentiate such oppressive pressures from supportive encouragement to continue in the context of personal crises. More than that, I invite folks to reflect on the ways social injustice may factor into the experiences of graduate students and the advice they are given. Does encouragement place an undue burden of resisting social injustice onto that person or does it offer much-needed solidarity and support?
- Reflect on how your biases and lived experiences inform your advice. Are you telling students to keep going because you were able to benefit from a PhD? Is it as likely that they will benefit at this time and under their specific circumstances? How has the job market changed in the last several years? What challenges have other students from your institution had in securing permanent employment?
- Reflect on systemic and unconscious influences. Might you experience benefits from their continuation? What pressure is the department under to accept and support students to continue?
- Think expansively about supporting nontraditional career paths. Create space for graduate students to meaningfully consider *not* continuing and normalize exploring and pursuing alternate career paths.

There is an obvious gap in my lists. There are no strategies I can offer folks parenting and PhDing through crises. We keep ourselves afloat in whatever ways we can. But for all the individually unique ways graduate student parents' experiences of personal crises manifest, the relative impacts of those experiences are structured by social injustice and the exploitative conditions of academic labor. And it is not just us excluded scholars who are diminished as a result: postsecondary institutions, academic scholarship, and public dialogue all suffer for it.

It should not be this way.

It does not have to be this way.

It is time to acknowledge that the risks and impacts of experiencing personal crises while in grad school are borne unequally. With this acknowledgment comes a responsibility to identify mechanisms of collective action and solidarity so that experiences of personal crises while parenting and PhDing are not antithetical to academic flourishing.

NOTES

1. Many treatments and their associated costs were not covered by the Canadian health system. They were accessible through fundraising and extended benefits. Nonetheless, the health system has protected us financially and in terms of treatment access. In contrast, many international students in Canada are not included in the nationalized health system; members of equity-denied groups receive differential access and care (McGibbon 2016), and folks in countries without a nationalized health system would have considerably different experiences.
2. The academic precariat comprises non-tenured, contract faculty who are generally subject to exploitative working conditions, few benefits, low compensation, and little or no employment security (Burton and Bowman 2022; Standing 2011). The rise in unstable employment arrangements, the erosion of workplace rights and the increasing casualization of academic labor are strongly associated with neoliberalization (Rogler 2019; Rose 2020). Evidence suggests that women, racialized folks, people with disabilities, and folks from working class backgrounds are much more likely to be relegated to the academic precariat (Arday 2022; Gagnon 2022; Ivancheva et al. 2019; Villar-Aguilés and Obiol-Francés 2022; Warnock 2016).

WORKS CITED

Arday, Jason. 2022. "'More to Prove and More to Lose': Race, Racism and Precarious Employment in Higher Education." *British Journal of Sociology of Education* 43 (4): 513–533.

Bettie, Julie. 2014. *Women without Class: Girls, Race, and Identity*. University of California Press.

Blackstock, Cindy, Muriel Bamblett, and Carlina Black. 2020. "Indigenous Ontology, International Law and the Application of the Convention to the Over-Representation of Indigenous Children in Out of Home Care in Canada and Australia." *Child Abuse & Neglect* 110, part 1: 104587.

Burton, Sarah, and Benjamin Bowman. 2022. "The Academic Precariat: Understanding Life and Labour in the Neoliberal Academy." *British Journal of Sociology of Education* 43 (4).

Cassuto, Leonard. 2015. *The Graduate School Mess: What Caused It and How We Can Fix It.* Harvard University Press.

Caterine, Christopher. 2020. *Leaving Academia: A Practical Guide.* Princeton University Press.

Cote-Meek, Sheila. 2014. *Colonized Classrooms: Racism, Trauma, and Resistance in Post-Secondary Education*. Fernwood Publishing.

Crawford, Kerry, and Leah Windsor. 2021. *The PhD Parenthood Trap: Caught between Work and Family in Academia.* Georgetown University Press.

Gagnon, Jennifer. 2022. "The Inaccessible Tower: Disability, Gender, and Contract Faculty." In *Disability and the Academic Job Market*, edited by Christopher McGunnigle, 139–160. Vernon Press.

Hamilton, Patricia. 2021. *Black Mothers and Attachment Parenting: A Black Feminist Analysis of Mothering in Britain and Canada.* Bristol University Press.

Hardy, Bradley, and Dave Marcotte. 2022. "Ties that Bind? Family Income Dynamics and Children's Post-Secondary Enrollment and Persistence." *Review of Economics of the Household* 20, 279–303.

Home, Alice. 2018. "Challenging Hidden Oppression: Mothers Caring for Children with Disabilities." *Critical Social Work* 3 (1).

Ivancheva, Mariya, Kathleen Lynch, and Kathryn Keating. 2019. "Precarity, Gender and Care in the Neoliberal Academy." *Gender, Work, & Organization* 26 (4): 448–462.

Kennedy, Liam, Derek Silva, Madeleine Coelho, and William Cipolli III. 2019. "'We Are All Broncos': Hockey, Tragedy, and the Formation of Canadian Identity." *Sociology of Sport* 36 (3): 189–202.

McGibbon, Elizabeth. 2016. "Oppressions and Access to Health Care: Deepening the Conversation." In *Social Determinants of Health: Canadian Perspectives*, 3rd ed., edited by Dennis Raphael, 491–520. Canadian Scholars' Press.

McLean, Amie. 2017. "We Used to Be Kings of the Road: Negotiations of Ethics, Embodiment, and Subjectivity in the BC-Based Long Haul Trucking Industry." PhD diss., Simon Fraser University. https://summit.sfu.ca/item/17764.

Milne, Emily, and Terry Wotherspoon. 2020. "Schools as 'Really Dangerous Places' for Indigenous Children and Youth: Schools, Child Welfare, and Contemporary Challenges at Reconciliation." *Canadian Review of Sociology* 57 (1): 34–52.

Rogler, Christian. 2019. "Insatiable Greed: Performance Pressure and Precarity in the Neoliberalised University." *Social Anthropology* 27 (52): 63–77.

Rose, Deidre. 2020. "A Snapshot of Precarious Academic Work in Canada." *New Proposals* 11 (1): 7–17.

Standing, G. 2011. *The Precariate: The New Dangerous Class.* Bloomsbury Academic.

Tennant, Jon. 2020. "Time to Stop the Exploitation of Free Academic Labour." *European Science Editing* 46: e51839. https://ese.arphahub.com/article/51839/.

Villar-Aguilés, Alicia, and Sandra Obiol-Francés. 2022. "Academic Career, Gender and Neoliberal University in Spain: The Silent Precariousness Between Publishing and Care-Giving." *British Journal of Sociology of Education* 43 (4): 623–638.

Warnock, Deborah. 2016. "Paradise Lost? Patterns of Precarity in Working-Class Academic Narratives." *Journal of Working-Class Studies* 1 (1): 28–44.

Westover, Tara. 2018. *Educated*. Random House.

27 ▸ KNOW THE PROBLEM ISN'T YOU

Addressing Systemic Barriers for Parents in PhD Programs

LOURDES FERNANDEZ, JESSICA MCCAUGHEY, AND RACHAEL GRAHAM TIN

THE CHALLENGES OF being a PhD parent can be as varied and demanding as those of parenting itself, but as Springer, Parker, and Leviten-Reid write, "being both an academic and parent is quite incompatible in practice" (2009, 436). This was certainly the case for us, three recent PhD graduates who were also parents while in our program. As we each separately encountered these incompatibilities, we initially assumed that the problem was unique to us and stemmed from poor decision-making: starting a PhD while pregnant, as a single mother with an infant, and as a military spouse raising two children in elementary school with no community support. However, over time we realized that we were not the problem. The problem was that our program knowingly and actively recruited students like us without adapting or updating a system that is designed for young childless students who can prioritize the PhD above all else.

In this chapter, we recount our varied experiences in our writing and rhetoric PhD program at a large research institution. Although we came to the PhD program with different backgrounds regarding ages (our own and our children's), employment, goals, challenges, and privileges, we encountered very similar systemic problems in pursuing a PhD as a parent. We document here three of those systemic issues: 1) course scheduling that does not consider parents, 2) additional resource expenditures required of parents in order to meet expectations designed for childless students, and 3) limited and inaccessible university resources for parenting students. At the end of the chapter, we suggest potential paths forward.

First, however, we provide context for our individual experiences in order to fully situate our challenges, our impact, and our desire for change.

JESSICA'S CONTEXT

I entered the PhD program at age thirty eight when I was four months pregnant. I am a first-generation college graduate and I was lucky to have already secured a full-time faculty position at a nearby university. In many ways I was pursuing the degree as a credential to help me be taken more seriously. I also felt I lacked the research chops I needed to complete the scholarship I was interested in pursuing. During the first years of my coursework the main challenges were straightforward. Between my full-time job and my newborn, I simply never felt I had enough time for anything. Then, during my final semester of coursework, the pandemic hit, so my exams and my dissertation process were completed entirely online (often with a toddler in my lap).

And yet, in many ways, I was still set up for success beyond what most PhD students could imagine. First, I had a co-parent at home who was entirely supportive of my work and I had additional family nearby who loved caring for my daughter. Financial support from my home university helped me persist in my coursework. Finally, as a white, straight, cis woman, I enjoyed privileges attached to those identities.

RACHAEL'S CONTEXT

I entered the PhD program at twenty-six years old with a twenty-two-month-old daughter and a three-month-old son just nine months after my late husband's sudden death. Before entering the program, I had a decent income from a proposal-writing job that I loved, but the job demanded more than fifty hours away from my children each week. I found a rare opportunity to switch to a career with fewer and more flexible hours: delivering writing training through my parents' small consulting business. A PhD was a job requirement, but I was lucky to live within a thirty-minute commute of a university with a new writing and rhetoric PhD program. To ensure a future in which my children could spend the majority of their nonschool hours with their one remaining parent, I spent the next five years balancing enough paid work to not go into debt and enough schoolwork to graduate before my son entered kindergarten.

As a grieving single parent, I faced some unique challenges as a PhD student, but as a straight, white, cis, second-generation PhD from an upper-middle-class family, I also enjoyed some unique privileges. My late husband's parents paid my mortgage for three years and local family members offset much of my childcare costs. I had a good job waiting for me after I graduated, and even though I had an undiagnosed learning disability, my parents had positioned me for academia since before I could read.

LOURDES'S CONTEXT

I began the program at thirty-eight years old after being a successful program manager and instructor at several military bases in the United States and Europe. At the time I had two boys, aged eight and eleven, and I was in a stable marriage. I had been an army wife for seventeen years. I was used to moving and creating community, and I understood how to find resources. I wanted the PhD because I wanted to practice research methods and earn a credential. Even though I had the preparation and maturity to do the work, the lack of a local network and childcare created persistent challenges that shaped the trajectory of the work. While my husband was incredibly supportive and was an amazing partner, he was not with us when we moved and was absent for long periods of time during the PhD. Despite these challenges, I had financial stability, access to great health care, and supportive family and friends scattered around the world.

LESSONS LEARNED

In the next three sections, we tell our stories partly as lessons learned for incoming PhD student parents but mostly to provide institution-level recommendations as graduate programs continue to actively recruit nontraditional students. Therefore, we speak to our individual experiences encountering what we identify as three major systemic barriers for PhD parents.

Barrier 1. Courses are scheduled with the traditional, childless student in mind, overlapping with elementary school schedules or bedtimes.

JESSICA: When I began the PhD program, I was prepared for it to be challenging, but I knew I could draw on my existing impressive support network: a husband who was an equal partner in parenting as well as in-laws living twenty minutes away who were excited about my academic endeavors and excellent babysitters. I tried my best to contort myself into the kind of student the program seemed to be designed for. Still, I struggled; my attention was split unevenly and inadequately between my studies and my daughter (not to mention my job, my husband, and countless additional obligations). I missed bedtimes, meals, and several "firsts." I also chose to prioritize my course *content*, rather than course schedule, as I was unwilling to miss two nights in a row of playing, reading, feeding, and snuggling during bedtime with my child.

Then, when my daughter had just turned two, COVID-19 hit. While I was no longer missing time with her, it's fair to say that my attention simply deteriorated completely. We feared so much in those early days for the health of our elderly parents that we didn't see them at all, let alone ask them to babysit. My daughter was shuffled each hour of the workday between my husband and me as we both tried to maintain our full-time jobs from home. In the evenings, I found myself longing to be in a classroom rather than at my kitchen table, taking research methods on Zoom while listening to my daughter sob for me from upstairs. More than once I claimed connection issues and switched to audio only—sometimes so I could pull her, screaming, into my lap and sometimes so I could cry myself. And yet the expectations from faculty were clear: *our standards for students have not changed.* I felt that my roles outside of my PhD program were viewed as less important than my role as a student. And yet as the pandemic upended our lives, I, like most parents, found myself much more intent on keeping my family safe and healthy than I was on anything else. More than ever, my priorities were very different from the expectation I felt from my program faculty.

RACHAEL: All graduate courses were offered in one of two time slots set by the university: 4:30 P.M. to 7:10 P.M. and 7:20 P.M. to 10:00 P.M. Neither program faculty nor students wanted courses in either time frame, but none of us had the power to change them. So my evenings with classes went one of two ways, especially in the beginning of my PhD, when I still had a salaried job, a toddler, and a breastfed infant.

To attend a 4:30 P.M. class, I left work early, which meant staying past dinner time another evening that week to compensate for the lost time. I drove straight to class, apologizing profusely if I hit traffic and arrived late. I hadn't pumped breastmilk since my lunch break at work, so my breasts were painfully engorged by the time class ended. Having gone twelve hours without seeing her only parent, my toddler was too excited for bedtime, which came less than an hour after class ended. So I breastfed my son with one arm and wrapped the other arm around my daughter, trying to turn the pages of a storybook without moving either arm. I might have a late dinner after the children fell asleep and freed my arms, but often I went to sleep hungry instead.

To attend a 7:20 P.M. class, if I was lucky enough to finish work in time, I rushed to my late husband's parents' home to eat something while breastfeeding my son and giving my toddler enough attention that she'd later be willing to sleep without me. As I ran out the door, leaving my children in the care of my in-laws for a second time that day, I said good-bye when I really meant good night. Because I couldn't afford a sitter to watch the children in our home and I didn't want to wake them when I returned hours after they'd fallen asleep, after class I returned to my-laws' home, dressed in pajamas that I had left behind the previous week, and crawled into the guest bed I shared with my children. Less than six hours later, I woke as quietly as possible to avoid waking the children or the grandparents and started a new workday, knowing that by the time I returned, the Earth would have completed another full rotation since I last saw my children.

A simple change to a 5:30 P.M. to 8:10 P.M. class time would have made all the difference.

LOURDES: In July 2014, a month before the beginning of the PhD, we moved back to the United States after being stationed in overseas military bases for six years. My husband had to stay in Germany until late August, then from September through December he was temporarily stationed three hours away. He spent the following fall semester once again stationed three hours away before spending nine months doing rotational shift work. The kids were not toddlers but were unable to stay home alone or drive themselves to after-school activities.

Because classes are in the afternoon, they cut right into my driving time for after-school activities. The 4:30 P.M. timeslot proved difficult. Finding babysitters was my priority, but I had not yet built the usual network of moms and friends. I ended up finding a church, asking parents in the Sunday school for recommendations, and making it work from week to week as I figured out who would have the kids while I was in class. I could tolerate the logistics and precarity of babysitters. But while the program communicated the expectation that I be in class on time and ready, that expectation did not apply to faculty. After rushing to class, hoping the sitter would make it to multiple pick-up points and then waiting for a faculty member who arrived forty minutes late and unprepared, I got the message that the system built in flexibility for faculty and none for students. The lack of flexibility in course times and attendance policies shaped the trajectory of my coursework, which then shaped the trajectory of my research, which should have been shaped by my goals, interests, and skills instead.

Barrier 2. Many professors base their expectations on past experiences as traditional students, thereby forcing students with children to expend additional financial and social resources to appear competent.

JESSICA: Although I believe that my graduate program tried to be welcoming and accommodating to parent graduate students, as far as I know, none of my professors had children when they were graduate students themselves (and many remained childless). They had been "traditional" graduate students, and they told tales of stern, demanding, and at times demoralizing graduate professors and advisors. Sometimes they seemed to me to embody such characters. One professor opened our first night of the semester by informing us that graduate students *do not* miss class, even once, and if that was going to be a problem we should reconsider our commitment to the program.

Exactly one week later, my cell phone rang as we were settling in for our second class meeting, and when I picked up, my husband frantically told me that our infant daughter could not stop vomiting and that her fever had spiked to 104.5 degrees. I loaded my laptop back into my bag and offered a brief apology to my professor, whose eyebrows raised in what I interpreted to be disapproval as I rushed out the door. I spent the rest of the semester staying late to chat and being the first to speak up during discussions—all with the memory of my unacceptable missed class on my mind.

RACHAEL: PhD students are supposed to attend and present at conferences—our professors made it clear that conference participation was essential for academic success. But for the first three years of my PhD, traveling to conferences was not an option. I could not bring my children with me and I could not find anyone willing to take them overnight. Because I had zero access to these "essential" opportunities for professionalization, I created new opportunities.

I compensated for my lack of conference participation in those three years by organizing guest lectures on my university campus. Instead of writing proposals and traveling for presentations, I was running a student club, hosting club meetings, inviting guest speakers, partnering with an on-campus nonprofit, applying for funding for the honoraria and catering, reserving campus space, creating promotional material, reapplying for funding when my applications were rejected on illogical technicalities, ordering catering that I put on my credit card, coordinating with the speaker, begging students and faculty to attend the event, driving the speaker, meeting the caterer, and crossing my fingers that my $500 to $1,500 worth of reimbursement requests would be accepted before my next round of utility bills. I was doing five times the labor for less of a CV line and fewer networking opportunities than conference participation provided, but I was using the only option available to me.

Even then, this option was available to me only because of the charity and compassion of my late husband's mother, who provided the majority of my childcare and was flexible and generous with her own time. Eventually, when my children reached three and four years old, she would watch them overnight so I could travel to present at conferences in my last two years of the program, masquerading as the dependent-free student that my program was designed to support.

LOURDES: We don't know what we don't know. Well-meaning mentors, advisors, and colleagues will give advice that centers the experience of the person giving the advice instead of the experience of the person receiving the advice. I learned that I needed to be cautious when I listened.

Our doctoral program recruits nontraditional students like me who may not want a tenure-line job. Yet the advice I received consistently centered a national job search and assumed boundless time, regardless of what I said I wanted. As I explored areas in workplace studies, I thought about taking a course in nonprofit management that could help me learn the structures of the sector in preparation for a potential project. The suggestion I received was to "volunteer at a nonprofit five to ten hours a week rather than take a class. Why waste a course?" The advice repeatedly failed to consider parenting.

I came into the program with previous mentoring and coaching experience. I knew that flexible, diverse professional and personal networks are better for seeking advice that fits the actual context rather than the ideal context. So ultimately I ignored most of the advice I received, from how to structure my CV or how to spend time and resources. Instead, I developed the strategic relationships (mostly in nonacademic spaces) that helped me successfully navigate the program and professionalize within the constraints of my life at the time.

Faculty and administrators often create expectations that do not serve a strategic purpose but simply reinforce the idea that time is endless and must be wholly devoted to academic networking and professionalizing. That is not true. There are multiple avenues to meeting and exceeding expectations, but faculty need to be open to the possibility that they are not equipped to have those conversations and programs need to imagine that students know their own constraints and can figure it out with targeted support and advice.

Barrier 3. University resources are designed for traditional students and are largely inaccessible to parents.

JESSICA: As a first-generation student, I've always felt the sense that I might not belong at a university and that I just don't get how things *work* in a university. I felt it at eighteen and I still feel it now sometimes, even as an associate professor with a PhD.

What would have helped me tremendously as a graduate student to feel that sense of belonging—and to squash my imposter syndrome—would have been to develop stronger relationships in my program. But this rarely happened, either in the form of attending office hours or even grabbing coffee before class with my peers. As it was, I rushed from my teaching job in the city, which was an hour or more away during rush hour, straight to class, which left barely enough time to scarf down a granola bar while I sprinted from the parking garage to my classroom, my phone jiggling with each step as I FaceTimed my husband and daughter to say good night. The same goes for other campus resources—everything from the gym (ha!) to special speaker events.

And I'm far from the only parent who had this experience. In a recent study I conducted, nonparent graduate students accessed campus resources notably more than graduate students with children (McCaughey 2022). Although I never heard about it when I was a student, my institution does, apparently, have a University Parents Student Group. I also recall a colleague in my PhD program sending out an email to gauge interest in setting up an informal group for parents in the program. It is utterly unsurprising that in the end, despite the need, not one of us had the bandwidth to get it off the ground.

RACHAEL: During the time when I was the president of my program's only professional association student chapter, I learned that the university resources dedicated to supporting student clubs—like mine—could not function without a level of face-to-face interaction that is untenable for students with children, careers, and homes off campus—like me.

When funding requests were denied for self-contradictory reasons (e.g., the instructions are to submit applications six to eight weeks in advance, but six weeks is not eight weeks and therefore the form is late if it is submitted six weeks in advance), an explanatory email or phone call to the student chapter office was useless. Instead, if I wanted access to my own funds, I needed to visit the student chapter office in person and smile and chat with the office manager until she clicked the button to approve the request. Or when my board members—fellow graduate students—were denied reimbursement for expenses they put on their credit cards, expenses that had already been approved for funding, I needed to visit the accounts payable office in person to settle the dispute.

I know other student clubs shared my frustration with the lack of communication and competence from these university offices, but for full-time working parents, the solution was costly. Every campus visit lengthened my daily commute by forty-five to ninety minutes and required me to pay for campus parking. Depending on my childcare situation that day, the time lost settling these issues in person cost an additional \$30 to \$45 in childcare costs and an additional \$50 to \$100 in hourly wages for work I should have been doing in that time. I justified these costs because the work of the student chapter provided resources that were otherwise inaccessible to students like me, but the inconsiderate, inefficient, poorly managed processes of university resources were an entirely unnecessary and avoidable additional cost to my time, money, and energy.

LOURDES: Accessing university resources often requires being physically present, including at times when parents may be picking up or dropping off children. I do think my university tried to create a community and provide opportunities to create professional and personal networks for graduate students, including game nights and professional development events. Many events did not include children or happened at times of the day when I was driving children around, so I did not engage with the broader university community. I did take advantage of library and writing center write-ins, which gave me time to focus on my writing for a variety of projects. Write-ins worked only because they were scheduled during the school day, but they did not expand my local network.

RECOMMENDATIONS FOR SYSTEM-LEVEL CHANGES

We want to note that although these issues presented considerable stress and other costs, a common theme in our stories is that we were able to overcome these barriers because of our respective privileges. We all count ourselves lucky to have entered a program that was geographically convenient and seemingly welcomed us as nontraditional applicants with children. But as our stories show, we struggled more than we needed to for an already-challenging level of study. So we wonder: How are students with less privilege supposed to overcome these barriers? Can PhD programs ethically recruit and admit students like us if they rely on the students to bring the kinds of privileges that only just made our success possible? Given that the three main barriers we encountered were systemic, we argue that programs must pursue system-level changes to undo these barriers.

To that end, we offer recommendations for system-level changes for programs. These changes benefit not only parents but every person who interacts with the PhD program, including other students, faculty, and university staff.

1. Empower programs to schedule class times outside the standard registrar options.
2. Provide faculty training in how to mentor nontraditional students with nontraditional PhD goals. You don't know what you don't know, and many program faculty only know the academic career path they took. Help them broaden their conceptions of the PhD student experience.
3. Facilitate administrative staff training in mentoring nontraditional students with nontraditional academic goals. Especially if administrative staff are trained to work with undergraduate students, help them understand how they can meet a broader range of student needs.
4. Ensure that the program's expectations for students align with your admissions process. Do your faculty share the expectations that you communicate to prospective students, including nontraditional students, during recruitment? If not, either your faculty expectations must change or your approach to recruitment and admissions must.
5. Deliberately build a culture in which students have lives outside the program. Whether in orientation, in the classroom, during faculty meetings, or while having coffee with a student, build in reminders for faculty, staff, and the students that a PhD program is one facet of their human experience and not the whole of their existence.

RECOMMENDATIONS FOR STUDENTS

These changes, if they come at all, will be slow and imperfect. Both programs and higher education at large need to make a shift in how they think about who is welcomed in and how they are supported. Yet in the meantime, of course, we still want parents to succeed if they choose this path. Here we offer small ways to operate within such systems that are not designed with you in mind:

1. Be creative with how you approach networking. Do not limit yourself to the opportunities your university or program provides. Chatting with a parent at the playground can reveal an opportunity if you're open to it, especially since people always ask what you're studying. Tell them!
2. Don't be afraid to ignore advice that does not apply to you. Remember that your program was likely not designed with you in mind, so the advice you receive might be inappropriate for a student like you and for what you need.
3. Go to the occasional social event in your program so you can get the information that the program does not communicate in official channels. It is worth the time and cost of extra babysitting to learn which faculty to approach or avoid before you assemble your committee, for example.
4. Do reach out into other networks for people who succeeded without necessarily following traditional, child-free, boundless-time type of advice. There are multiple paths to success and at least one other person has figured it out before you. Find that person.
5. Urge your program to develop and facilitate a parent support group, not as a social obligation but to provide access to resources, such as shortcuts to babysitters or quick answers about the elementary school calendar.

The barriers we encountered as PhD parents are systemic in graduate programs that can seem to be designed to monopolize students' time and attention for years. Programs must do better. Students can call them out, deal with it, and make alternate plans, but ultimately, it's the programs that need to change.

WORKS CITED

McCaughey, Jessica. 2022. "'This Seismic Life Change': Graduate Students Parenting and Writing During a Pandemic." *Peitho* 24 (2). https://cfshrc.org/article/this-seismic-life-change-graduate-students-parenting-and-writing-during-a-pandemic/.

Springer, Kristen W., Brenda K. Parker, and Catherine Leviten-Reid. 2009. "Making Space for Graduate Student Parents: Practice and Politics." *Journal of Family Issues* 30 (4): 435–457.

28 ▸ QUESTION NORMATIVE TROPES

Possibilities for Queer Parenting in Graduate Programs

BETH BUYSERIE

I WAS A PARENT before I ever had children. As the oldest of seven kids, I cared for my siblings in a more-than-sister role as my mother battled cancer, and with my father, I was a primary caretaker for them during my years as a community college student. As a result, I have never believed that parenting is limited to biological birth. Now that I have my own two biological children, I consider them my "second wave" of childrearing (although I should clearly have learned more from my first wave). Yet despite the fact that my world has often revolved around children, I have also often felt discomfort when entering conversations on parenting in academia.

One reason for this wariness is because conversations on parenting often privilege those who either want or already have biological children. At various points in my life, I have adamantly not wanted children (I eventually changed my mind, but that took a while: #oldest-of-7), raised my sister during her tenth-grade year, experienced difficulty conceiving, grieved after a miscarriage, and supported my friend as she navigated the adoption process for my two godchildren. Despite the fact that I now have my own two biological children, I also have experienced frustration and pain when conversations on parenting are less than nuanced and overlook or exclude the multiple ways people may engage in, long for, and intentionally refrain from parenting.

But another reason for my unease is that conversations on parenting, both in and outside of academia, have often felt oppressively gendered. As Ellie D. Berger writes in her coedited collection *The Parent Track: Timing, Balance, and Choice in Academia*, women in academia often experience stigma and discrimination, both implicit and explicit, when discussing their choices to parent, a frustrating reality that unfortunately is commonplace. Berger explores the tensions many academic women face, noting how "identity negotiation continues to be a constant struggle, reflecting [a] desire to be both a productive academic and a good mother" (2017, 24). As both an affirmation of these challenges and a counternarrative to the presumption that academic life and parenting are incompatible for women, there have been important longitudinal studies, such as Kelly Ward and Lisa Wolf-Wendel's *Academic Motherhood*, that highlight how academic women also have multiple strategies for productively negotiating these gendered expectations. "Academic women with children," Ward and Wolf-Wendel stress, "can do more than simply survive the rigors of the tenure track [or PhD school]—they can find satisfaction and success in all of their many roles" (2012, 2). Simply reading Kelly Ward[1] and Wolf-Wendel's gentle reminder that we can "make an academic career and motherhood a viable combination" (2012, 12), especially when intentionally supported by the institution, provides me with deep comfort and guides my work as a parent and a writing program administrator despite the legitimate challenges.

However, as a person who strives to question gender binaries (Halberstam 2012), engaging in discussions on academic parenting—a term often coded as motherhood for white, cisgender, straight women—is challenging. Despite the fact that these conversations are vitally important, I feel as though in order to enter this conversation I am expected to reinforce the trope of the gender binary as well as my place in that binary in ways that I am not entirely comfortable with. I struggle with the tension inherent in my discomfort: I often avoid gendered conversations that privilege me and might provide me, as a white cisgender woman, with identity-based support, yet I recognize that I am possibly shirking such conversations due to internalized gender bias. I also ruffle at the expectation that I am expected to struggle simply because of my gender . . . and openly acknowledge that, despite my aversion to this expectation, I have wrestled with the conflict between academia and parenting based on my gender. As we discuss the truly important role of PhD students caring for other human beings in their lives, I hope that we might more intentionally challenge discourse that reinforces a gender binary and instead make space for multiple lived experiences.

Yet while I seek to engage in a more gender-inclusive conversation on academic parenting, that is not my singular goal in this chapter. I also question the norms that conversations on academic parenting often seem to replicate—norms about whether particular bodies are expected to have children and which bodies we expect not to have children—and how we reinforce those norms in the language we use when communicating with PhD students. I join the conversation on academic parenting now because I am interested in how these norms affect the well-being of PhD students, particularly graduate students who identify broadly as queer. Therefore, in this chapter I seek to challenge the normative narratives that often frame such discussions of parenting while pursuing a PhD. To do so, I weave insights from my own experiences of coming out as a queer parent while working full time as a contingent writing program administrator and simultaneously earning a PhD. I end with suggested guidance for how program administrators might better support graduate student parents in ways that are more inclusive of gender, sexuality, and life experiences.

A QUEER PARENTING JOURNEY

I began questioning my sexuality in my mid-thirties, while I was in my PhD program in cultural studies. While I struggled for multiple reasons with this unexpected—yet not unwelcome—transition in my sexuality, my children were a very visible reminder that I was supposedly not queer. My shifting identity was further complicated by the fact that there was a notable lack of discussion in my academic coursework for parenting as a queer scholar or as a PhD student. With the exception of J. Jack Halberstam, all our queer theory texts focused on the more "academic" aspects of queer survival. Yet each day after our queer theory class, I would go immediately to our campus childcare center to pick up my children. Although the daycare center was inclusive, the juxtaposition between worlds was palpable. Reading texts on bisexual erasure (e.g., Yoshino 2000) further compounded my yearning to embrace my new sexuality while navigating how to do so in a relationship that outwardly appeared to be heteronormative, a relationship that I could ultimately not sustain in its original form. And my well-being as a PhD student, a mother, and a queer person coming into her identity suffered.

As an administrator who works closely with graduate students, I now wonder how the lack of queer parenting models affects our support of PhD students, particularly students who identify as queer. As Sarah R. Pickett writes in "Legacy and Vulnerability: Queer Parenting in the Academy," "there is a paucity in the literature around women becoming pregnant, lesbian women parents, and the fictions surrounding these in the academy. . . . Historically, the literature has been heteronormative, often rendering same-sex/queer couples and/or same-sex/queer couples who are also parents invisible" (2017, 154). As a bisexual-identified woman who had for many years been in a cross-sex marriage, I add that bisexual erasure (Yoshino 2000) is also part of this story. While I cannot speak for all queer or bisexual individuals, my experience of being invisibly bisexual meant that I also had to negotiate coming out as a queer parent without the support of a queer community.

My kids were, not surprisingly, key to my survival during this unforeseen time of identity shifts: from straight to queer parent, from marriage and a caring husband to co-parent with a supportive former spouse, from contingent faculty and PhD student to a tenure-track writing program administrator. My children were a constant reminder that I could not work all the time, that I needed to make time for play and exercise, that definitions of children and parenting were fluid, that I was unequivocally loved. When I neglected these lessons and these responsibilities to them and myself, my mental health suffered drastically and in ways that are still healing. But they taught me that parenting as queer is not only possible but delightful. We read picture books on the history of the pride flag, wore matching rainbow socks, and together navigated how to attend pride events not as allies but as a rainbow family still largely perceived as heteronormative. I still smile when I remember how my six-year-old announced that he was going to add pink to the pride flag for boys who like pink. And I experienced both apprehension and joy when my middle schooler quietly, yet firmly, informed his friends that they were not to make any homophobic comments in his presence.

While I am no longer a PhD student, queer parenting still affects my daily interactions with academic life. Last semester, when we attended an open house for my son's new elementary school, I was relieved to find that "safe space" signs were posted on many of the classroom doors. While I do not pretend that a safe space sign automatically guarantees that a classroom *is* safe, the sign on the door was a relief to me and my children: a visual proclamation that at least some of the teachers and administrators would actively support our family. However, that year, one kindergarten mother complained about the signs: her daughter was now drawing rainbows in the shape of a pride flag instead of in the arc her mother desired. The mother claimed that she did not have any way of talking to her daughter about what the safe signs meant and she urged the school board to ban teachers from posting such affirming signage—not because she was prejudiced, she emphasized, but because her daughter was supposedly too young for such conversations (Marchant 2022). Although I experienced many emotions at this homophobic incident, I also tried to interpret the event through an educational lens. What are the ways that our programs are essentially posting "*not* a safe space" signs, both for queer parents and for those who want to challenge the idea that parenting should be the norm? And how can programs, regardless of the sexual identities of their students, apply a queer reading—a questioning of standardizing norms—to interrogate potentially harmful normative tropes of parenthood?

QUESTIONING TWO NORMS IN PHD PROGRAMS: PRODUCTIVITY AND PLANNING

Productivity

Parents, many of whom identified as women, dropped out of the workplace at an alarming rate during the pandemic. Parents in academia, a job with the potential flexibility to teach online or grade after children fell asleep, experienced severe pressure at simultaneously having to parent and work in shared spaces and at all hours. The closure of schools due to COVID-19 illustrated how dependent all of us are on reliable and affordable childcare, regardless of whether we are parents or not. Considering the needs of parents, therefore, is crucial if colleges want to support graduate students and faculty in their productivity as scholars and teachers.

Yet productivity is one norm we might question as we consider parenting and the resources of academics. Ward and Wolf-Wendel expose how the norms of the ideal productive worker can be harmful for academic parenting, particularly women. Pickett, too, describes how she felt compelled to keep working on research even while on leave, afraid that her university would not renew her contract if they perceived her to be unproductive. During my two pregnancies, I taught course overloads so that I would not be perceived as "slacking" in my role as a contingent writing program administrator and so the department wouldn't be as negatively affected during the semester I would be on family leave. However, as Ward and Wolf-Wendel remind us, "There is more to an academic career than just the pretenure period [or the dissertation] and more to parenthood than just taking care of an infant—careers and parenthood are lifelong propositions. Attending to the needs of faculty members at early, mid, and even later career is essential" (2012, 12).

Planning

As I read Pickett's chapter on the joys and challenges of being a lesbian mother in academia, I noticed for the first time how the concept of *planning* affects our discourse on graduate student expectations for productivity. Pickett, who actively sought to become pregnant at a time that coincided with the start of her academic career, points out that as a lesbian woman, she did not have rhetorical access to the narrative that her pregnancy was unplanned and hence could not pretend that her commitment to academia and her work were paramount in her life.

While I now identify as a queer parent, I have not always identified as such, and Pickett's point about the affordances of heteronormative tropes forces me to consider the ways that even our most well-meaning supportive measures still privilege particular identities, values, and norms. In considering planning, I reflect on the extenuating circumstances I have encountered in my twenty-year career as a writing program administrator, circumstances that required graduate students to pause their academic pursuits: the death or illness of a family member, a mental health crisis, and personal illness. Nearly always, these situations were unexpected or unplanned. While I am proud that our department was often able to support the graduate students (who did not have official sick leave), I now recognize how much our efforts—and our feelings of empathy—were based on the fact that many of the life-changing situations were unplanned. In contrast, other events, such as pregnancies, were at times subtly critiqued for *not* being better planned–that is, not occurring at a time that would minimize the impact to the department's teaching schedule.

CONCLUSION: SUGGESTIONS FOR GRADUATE PROGRAMS

I realize now as an academic and a writing program administrator that I am guilty of promoting similar heteronormative moves. I make baby blankets as gifts to new parents—but this last time I recognized and openly discussed how problematic that practice might be. How can I balance the perhaps-conflicting emotions of those who have lost children, cannot have children, or are struggling to care for children at the expense of their own mental health or those who feel cultural pressure to have children but who may not want them? And how can I support and encourage graduate student parents without implicitly promoting heteronormativity? How might I instead communicate that I understand this support to be a queer or caring practice? In my PhD queer theory class, we briefly discussed the image of a woman pushing a stroller—a typical heteronormative image until we consider it through a queer lens. How might we reconsider what the stroller signifies when we imagine the parent as lesbian, queer, bisexual, or trans? What might that metaphor of queering the stroller teach us? How might we restructure our graduate programs differently to imagine who might be pushing this stroller, who might not, and why?

Now, five years after earning my PhD, I am a writing program administrator working closely with graduate students. If graduate programs cannot prioritize the caretaking of self and others, then we are harming the students who constitute the heart of our programs. In my case, openly identifying as a queer woman and a parent and talking about how these identities intersect not only destabilizes heteronormative perceptions of who can be a parent but also opens up discussions and makes visible the significant time constraints of PhD students who have children. In this sense, while not all students may be parents or caregivers, the idea of children, of elderly parents, or of caregiving for others in any capacity helps prioritize well-being in graduate programs, regardless of whether any current student actually has such caretaking responsibilities. Possible suggestions graduate programs might employ include the following:

- Acknowledging that the program should *not* always be a student's priority, and/or making space to discuss strategies for negotiating multiple, sometimes conflicting priorities.
- Explicitly discussing with PhD students the importance of prioritizing something *other* than teaching, research, and coursework.

- Creating program structures that support PhD students in caretaking responsibilities (flexible schedules for teaching and grading; advocating for paid leave; being knowledgeable about breastfeeding resources and childcare options, etc.).
- Incorporating readings by queer and BIPOC scholars who are also parents or caregivers and discussing how this aspect of their identity might (or might not) influence their scholarship.
- Reframing parenting while PhDing as an already queer practice, particularly for women, queer parents, and trans folk, one that potentially challenges the normative expectations of who might be considered "scholarly."
- Seek and read the literature on queer parenting, and reflect on how to apply concepts from that literature to disrupt normative tropes.
- Discuss the joys of caregiving, for children, elders, friends, family, community, and self.

Although a focus on parenting—or rather, on caregiving—is not without problems, it allows programs to communicate the possibility that academia cannot be our sole priority, regardless of whether all want to or will become parents. Considering and caring for others in this way can help us question the normative tropes inherent in our PhD programs. We are intersectional beings, so a queer approach to parenting—one that recognizes the multiple and complex identities that a person carries—can benefit all graduate students and teachers in our programs.

NOTE

1. Kelly Ward was a brilliant academic mother and scholar in my former hometown. I could not have finished my PhD in a timely manner without her support. She died unexpectedly in 2018 and our community deeply mourned her passing. I intentionally cite her work as an honor to her memory.

WORKS CITED

Berger, Ellie D. 2017. "Work-Family Balance? A Challenging Yet Rewarding Journey through Gendered Academia." In *The Parent Track: Timing, Balance, and Choice in Academia*, edited by Christina DeRouche and Ellie D. Berger, 23–27. Wilfrid Laurier University Press.

Halberstam, J. Jack. 2012. *Gaga Feminism: Sex, Gender, and the End of Normal*. Beacon Press.

Marchant, Brock. 2022. "'A Rainbow Flag Is Not a Political Statement': Pride Flags Debated at Logan School Board Meeting." *The Herald Journal* [Logan, UT], September 14. www.hjnews.com/news/local/a-rainbow-flag-is-not-a-political-statement-pride-flags-debated-at-logan-school-board/article_b081ef88-3491-11ed-9b73-9b0258cfb6cb.html. Accessed May 19, 2023.

Pickett, Sarah R. 2017. "Legacy and Vulnerability: Queer Parenting in the Academy." In *The Parent Track: Timing, Balance, and Choice in Academia*, edited by Christina DeRouche and Ellie D. Berger, 149–161. Wilfrid Laurier University Press.

Ward, Kelly, and Lisa Wolf-Wendel. 2012. *Academic Motherhood: How Faculty Manage Work and Family*. Rutgers University Press.

Yoshino, Kenji. 2000. "The Epistemic Contract of Bisexual Erasure." *Stanford Law Review* 52 (2): 253–461.

29 ▸ GET RID OF THE GAUNTLET

Redefining a Scientist's Parenting Experience in Academia

KRISTIN L. OSBORNE

IT WAS A perfect maritime day in September: the sun was shining, the breeze was blowing, and waves were tumbling over the breakers as we drove our car onto campus. Water churned against ships' hulls as they charged their way through the massive canal system bordering the road, inching toward its end against a strong current. This campus is a special place. Set on the shores of the Cape Cod canal, it is a site that tourists and weekend captains flock to during the New England summers for the famous striper fishing and iconic views and one that prospective students visit with awe on campus tours year-round. It is also a special place where I have always felt at home.

My passion for ascidians, commonly referred to as sea squirts, was born from an undergraduate course I had taken at this very campus many years before as an undergraduate. I immediately found their propensity to survive intense environmental change and flourish in new, polluted ecosystems inspiring, even though it is a brainless and spineless (although not heartless or gutless!) life form. I returned years later to complete my PhD dissertation research on the impacts of marine pollution and invasive species in benthic ecosystems and then discovered a passion for teaching through a chance adjunct vacancy and the encouragement of my peers in the department. I temporarily set aside my aspiration to pursue marine research, but it did not take long for the siren song of graduate school to lure me into the tedious application process in the hope of a permanent faculty position. I envisioned studying at a seaside campus with easy ocean access to explore nooks and crannies of the craggy Massachusetts coastline. I eventually accepted an offer in the PhD program at a university in the heart of Boston, Massachusetts. Although the school was in close proximity to the Boston seaside, that campus shoreline was far from accessible; the campus was pockmarked with an endless slew of construction projects and barriers typical of metropolitan institutions with an ocean view.

As we drove onto my favorite campus for class and lab work, my mind wandered to the metaphorical foundation I was laying for my career, with each course I taught here as another brick and social connection, the mortar firming the foundation of my tie to this location. This place became an escape from the city. I could study the ocean *in* the ocean without the metropolitan obstacles. But as I approached campus that day, I did not feel the healing calm of the sun and waves. Instead I felt physical pain along with mental terror as I imagined the terrible illness that must be inside of me. I was struggling with mysterious symptoms, forcing myself to operate in a thick cloud of exhaustion for weeks while searching for tests or treatments that might identify my condition.

My fear, though, was also tied up with the disappointment of what this might mean for our desire to have children. With cyst-riddled ovaries and a drugstore-receipt-length history of autoimmune disease, I had carefully guarded my secret wishes for a family from everyone except my husband during our seven years of marriage. Although the plan was to wait until after graduate school and a career was secured, I compartmentalized my desires and visited them. I responded to insensitive inquiries of "when will you finally have kids?" with noncommittal and often comedic responses in an effort to suppress my fears. After all, the probability that I could have a successful pregnancy was already likely low, and I feared that this sudden illness meant that things were getting worse, dropping our chances from slim to zero.

THE CALL

The phone rang as we neared the campus parking lot. I had been waiting for my doctor to call but I still answered it with dread. After scans, tests, pokes, and prods, there was finally an answer for the extreme malaise I had been battling for weeks. Ulcer? Tumor? Cancer? I mentally braced myself for the assault. But as my doctor explained my condition, my physical reaction was more akin to what I experienced when I was in first grade and slipped on the balance beam, falling forward with split legs directly onto my breastbone—a dense, suffocating haze. I hung up, unable to explain anything to my concerned husband and mother for what felt like several full, heavy minutes.

"She said. . . . I'm pregnant."

The words pummeled me, like what I imagine hermit crabs feel when they crawl along the beach only to be knocked about by the surf with each crashing swell. Did she say "pregnant"? Almost eight weeks? But the CAT scan I had just had . . . the medication I had taken . . . the vitamins I had not taken. What horrible mistakes had I already made?

I closed my eyes and tried to refocus my thoughts. Through the panic and uncertainty, I could just make out the faint inner voice reminding me of how happy I should be. And I realized that I was. New plans needed to be made, new efforts undertaken. I would forge my way through the fear about this new title of "mom" I could now call my own.

COUNTDOWN

A week later, I was sitting in my PhD advisor's office with my heart pounding and the words of my carefully practiced speech jumbling around in my head. I had felt this dread many times before; the four-year gauntlet of grad school thus far had left me riddled with anxiety and self-doubt. I was devoid of the confidence to advocate for my own needs, let alone for the person growing inside of me. I had entered as a confident, motivated young woman and was presently drowning in a sea of funding failures, botched exams, and imposter syndrome. The words tumbled out messily and bounced off the office walls, and the clumsy monologue finally ended in a flood of awkward tears.

I mourned the person I once was, one who believed she was more than capable and refused to accept no as an answer. I grappled with the enormity of tasks piling up as my anxiety grew exponentially. I made my advisor promises to work harder, faster, and more than ever—all this despite the rising panic and terror I felt about exposure to chemicals in the lab, long hours, and the monumental academic tasks ahead. This surprise pregnancy had accelerated my personal need to graduate. I felt like an infant who was forced to take steps before I was ready; this was not in my well-laid plan. I had to make it closer to the finish line before the most important deadline of my life, which was approaching in only seven short months.

It often felt like I was running one-legged races toward two finish lines at two dramatically different speeds: the speedy rabbit's PhD deadline and the plodding tortoise's second trimester safe zone. I worried endlessly about all the ways I might have already impacted my unborn child and if they were healthy. During my twelve-week ultrasound, fear and excitement bubbled inside me as the black-and-white blobs came into focus and a tiny hand waved at me on the screen. The technician was kind and reassuring, printing out a few extra shots of the teeny nose and feet. It was the most peaceful moment I had felt in a very long time.

When I was finally able to use the bathroom after fifteen minutes of measuring, probing, and listening, I stood to leave the room. Light-headed from lying down, I walked across the hall and took a few deep breaths, trying to ignore the sensation and instead appreciate the good (unremarkable) results I had just received. But I knew something was wrong as I closed the door and felt darkness creeping in from the corner of my eyes. All went black, and when I came to, I felt searing pain on my side and hobbled out of the bathroom. I made it to a chair, just in time to be swallowed into darkness again.

An ambulance ride and one probable fractured rib later, I was sent home to rest. The fear of endangering my baby surged back in with a vengeance. Gone was the momentary tranquility and confidence in myself that I felt. This episode planted a permanent seed of doubt in my brain about whether I could maintain a healthy pregnancy for the next twenty weeks.

Despite this worry, I was still faced with many tasks ahead. I was in a tug-of-war between academic duty and self-care. My insecurities prevailed, and I showed up to teach the next class with a heavy feeling of guilt in tow. I feared my own choices, yet I felt powerless to change them. My experiences had led me to observe unspoken rules that prescribe that grad students must work harder, faster, and longer than their colleagues to earn their place in the academic food chain. I *needed* to earn my place and live up to that reputation of a model grad student because that is what is expected—required—for success. At the time, I believed that asking for accommodations would mean using my pregnancy as a crutch or an excuse. In hindsight, I recognize that this was sadly inaccurate.

A HEAVY LOAD

Days turned into weeks and I could not avoid a conversation with my TA supervisor any longer. I was assigned to an environmental science course designed for non-science majors, which meant that there were hundreds of students enrolled at once. I had already begun the pregnancy in less than ideal health, and now supporting this course was consistently physically demanding. I silently carried on with the grueling ninety-minute commutes at 10 P.M. after grading 300 exams and transporting boxes full of handouts across an entire campus myself. I strove to exceed expectations and never asked for official accommodations.

That choice, sadly, felt especially safe after one request for help on a particularly snowy and frigid early morning as I arrived for another long day of lab work. In my desperation to maintain balance on the icy satellite parking lot with a belly the size of a beach ball, I sheepishly knocked on the window of a campus police cruiser and asked the officer for a ride to the bus stop. This attempt to overcome my fear was squashed, as he smirked, dismissed me, and rolled up the window—an unkind act that pushed me farther away from that goal and left me reeling over the interaction many times since. I considered reporting the officer, but I never did.

With spring fast approaching, my grad school pals planned science cafes and after-lab happy hours while I split all of my time between churning out statistical analyses, revising dissertation chapters, and turning my drum room into a baby nursery. Preexisting feelings of isolation and loneliness grew exponentially; it was rare to meet another pregnant STEM grad student at my university. Although I found solidarity with my close peers and labmates, I often felt alienated from my larger cohort. None of my close friends had yet become parents and my extended family did not include others who went to graduate school. They did not understand that it was more than an interest to fill my days, more than a full-time job, and so much more than just being a student. I felt adrift in an unfamiliar ocean, struggling to find shore alone.

As my due date neared and the dizzy spells I had been experiencing increased in frequency, I was advised to stop driving. But how would I get to class? I could not take the train and still make it to the endless doctor's appointments every week. I could have asked to teach remotely. I could have asked to call in for lab meetings. In retrospect, I wish I had, but instead I was shuttled around by my spouse or my parents because I was too afraid to ask for such reasonable accommodations.

I worked during the hours leading up to the birth. A wave of temporary relief washed over me as labor began and I was able to clock out. I have never been able to fully dismiss the guilt of being absent from the lab and the classroom, even though I wasn't entitled to any paid time off from my TA or adjunct faculty positions. Neither my advisor nor my department chair applied any pressure; instead, they actually encouraged me to take some time for my growing family. I managed to take a week off before grading final projects and exams for my courses. The work did not suffer because of this choice, but I did. I was constantly anxious. I put enormous pressure on myself to complete tasks that should never have taken such priority during the overwhelming first-time postpartum days.

The summer went by in a blur as I prepared to defend my dissertation in the fall. I never imagined that I would have the indescribable privilege of dedicating that document to my first-born child. Her presence reinvigorated me to push forward and succeed when I wanted to quit. She relied on me for basic human needs that no one else could provide her. That reliance gave me a renewed sense of purpose and defined me in a new, profound way. Being a mother has taught me countless lessons over the years, but perhaps the most important is to recognize my worth and the importance of advocating for myself, because I am advocating for my kid by extension.

A MINDSET SHIFT

I had a very different mindset going into my second pregnancy as junior tenure-track faculty member years later at my cherished alma mater. I knew from the earliest days that I needed to prioritize my mental and physical well-being. I reminded myself many, many times that my academic world would continue turning if the well-laid plans had to change. It was okay if assignments were graded a week later. I offered this grace to students by extending their deadlines too. This mindset allowed me to pivot when an obstacle presented itself (e.g., all-day nausea in the first trimester) and helped me maintain control of my courses. I also found that being open with my students (e.g., telling them when I needed extra, unplanned ultrasounds that overlapped with project presentations) improved the transparency of my decision-making to them and humanized me, giving us the opportunity to better connect.

I was determined to advocate for more flexible working conditions postpartum, especially as I was also preparing to send my first-born to kindergarten in the fall. I asked administrators uncomfortable questions and put my health concerns first. I devised a proposal with the enthusiastic support of my department chair to complete alternative responsibilities in lieu of a traditional teaching load that would still benefit our department. I was able to produce quality work with a more reasonable balance between work and family time. I am sincerely grateful for the support and encouragement I received from all of my colleagues to contribute in a unique way and still enjoy time with my newborn and my older child as she transitioned into the big-kid school system.

Although I cannot change my graduate school motherhood experience, I encourage others to focus on offering creative solutions to challenges instead of trying to maintain the perfect graduate student image. I realize now that I simply assumed that others shared my unrealistic expectations and was afraid of voicing my concerns when it was later apparent that they did not. For example, I made this mistake when jumping into lab work with potentially dangerous chemicals early in my pregnancy. I was nervous about using them, but asking for an accommodation (such as additional protective equipment) felt embarrassing. The supervisor simply did not think of this issue when they made it clear that they expected the lab work to be done. With my second pregnancy, I felt empowered to ask for what my family needed and to advocate for us even when it became difficult or uncomfortable.

If I could speak to my younger self today, I would make sure she hears me when I repeat this over and over again: You are your own and your baby's strongest advocate. You are a person who deserves to be heard and supported, and you are no less valuable than any faculty or administrator at your institution. It may cause waves, but you are strong enough to withstand them and to chart your own course ahead.

30 ▸ PUSH BACK

Identifying and Handling Retaliation in Order to Stop a Leaky Pipeline

SIHAM LEKCHIRI AND
BARBARA A. W. EVERSOLE

SIHAM'S EXPERIENCE

I began my PhD in human resource development as a single person and later got married. I became pregnant with my first child in the same year I was expected to take preliminary examinations. While my committee members had been fully supportive of my academic plans up to that point, the sentiment soon changed after I announced my pregnancy. Two male members were serving on my committee, and to my surprise, their perception of my academic abilities swiftly changed. Apparently, having a child while pursuing my PhD suggested that my academic priorities had shifted and were no longer important. At least that was their own perception. This was manifested through constant questioning about my future academic plans, through casting doubt about my ability to finish the program with a baby, through talking about how challenging it can be to find that balance, and through telling me that my academic endeavors could be compromised.

My doctoral chair and mentor Barbara, however, had been through similar struggles as an academic mother and did not want me to go through the same experience. Barbara is currently married, a full professor, and the mother of two young men in their twenties. As an international student, I was still learning about and adjusting to the culture. Because I was not sure if voicing my concerns would be perceived as a lack of respect for my committee members, I was reluctant to voice my concerns because I feared backlash. My male committee members became different and questioned all my decisions and commitments. My pregnancy was not planned—it just happened—but I wasn't sure how to handle the doubt that was cast on me. I was told that discussions about my commitment began to occur behind closed doors, but Barbara knew what was happening and began to document everything. I was advised to do the same.

I was in labor when I received an email confirming that my preliminary written exams had been scheduled for 4 weeks later. I was happy about this progress, but I was also extremely nervous. My delivery was complicated and I ended up staying in the hospital for six days after the delivery. I had to remain on bed rest and Barbara was able to request the proper accommodations for me to take my exams, given my condition. I spent several weeks preparing for this, even with an infant and an exhausted, sleep-deprived body. It is also important to note that I was on an aggressive schedule to finish because of my immigration status. I had to take the exams in the summer and my committee had a quick turnaround time for deciding if I had passed my exams so that I could register for dissertation hours to maintain my status. Despite the intense schedule, on the day of my written exams, I felt confident that my answers had been comprehensive and would satisfy my committee.

Initially, my committee members' review of my answers rated them as comprehensive and I moved to the next phase, the oral exam. However, after deliberating on the orals, one committee member, whom I'm calling John, decided to retract his initial rating of my written exams. Barbara was able to forestall this outcome given that all committee members had already approved my written exams before I was able to move to the orals. His rationale for this sudden change was that he felt that I was distracted with my newborn and that my priorities had shifted. The second male committee member agreed with him even though he also had initially rated my written exams as comprehensive. As a result, I felt compelled (and was advised by Barbara and other scholars) to replace both committee members for my dissertation work. Unfortunately, John, a full professor, was also the PhD program coordinator for the college and he still had to approve the newly appointed committee members and approve my final dissertation committee.

Barbara had been through a similar experience, so I leaned on her for advice. I considered myself a novice in the politics of academia. *How do I navigate this? How do I communicate with a coordinator who didn't believe I was cut out for this program because I decided to have a child? Really! How dare I?* The stories I heard about John's behavior with other academic mothers did not make it easier for me to deal with his constant challenging of my work. Barbara and I had to be strategic and careful because we feared retaliation. Although we were successful in changing my committee members, John found other ways to make matters difficult for me. While I was working on my dissertation proposal, John often suggested that he might challenge my qualitative methodology (he was more of a quantitative scholar), and he also suggested that he would challenge the other committee members who were supportive of my methodology. I dreaded meetings with John; they felt confrontational, and he often challenged decisions I made.

As a new mom, I was already on a continuous learning journey into motherhood. I was often overwhelmed, stressed, and sleep deprived. I started my tenure-track position while I was ABD, so I was juggling finishing the dissertation, a new job, and an infant all in the same year. The support and trust I got from Barbara helped me get through the roadblocks I was facing. Her trust and reassurance were significant in getting me through my doctoral journey. I often tell her that I don't know how I would have done it without her support and encouragement and that I was very lucky to have her as my chair and my friend.

BARBARA'S EXPERIENCE

Going through this experience with Siham, I was reminded of my own struggles when I was in graduate school. It was like déjà vu. When I was earning my master's degree, I was a first-generation student struggling with infertility. When I finally became pregnant, I was accepted into a doctoral program. I started my doctoral program when I was six months pregnant with my first child. I experienced a toxic relationship with my male advisor, who was also my supervisor (because I was his graduate teaching assistant), my instructor, and the head of my program. For example, finding childcare when my son was born was very difficult, even though I took only one course after he was born. My advisor insisted that I take an experiential outdoor adventure river-rafting team-building course after my baby was born, but I refused this demand because I was nursing. We had one course where we were allowed to grade ourselves. I justified a grade of A, but my instructor said he thought it should be an A-. When I asked why he thought I deserved a lower grade, he said it was because I was distracted by my child—reminiscent of what Siham had been told.

A year and a half later, I suffered a miscarriage but I never took any time off. As far as I knew, there were no services available to me as a new graduate student mother. There were only a few other women in the program and some had only grown children, so I had few other students with whom to empathize. A year later, I had another child. Fearing retaliation from my advisor, I felt that I needed to replace him with another faculty member. It took me nine years to finish my doctorate.

When Siham became pregnant, I did not expect any problems with her committee. I knew that one of her committee members, John, had an issue with faculty mothers (e.g., he was discriminatory in hiring and in issues mothers faced in teaching hours), but I did not think that John would extend such hostility toward his students. In retrospect, especially given my own previous experiences, I was being naïve. When John started to give Siham a tough time about her written exam responses, I fought back. I pointed out that her responses were on par with other student responses that I had read. However, I was stunned to learn that John was able to persuade the other male faculty member on the committee to retract his approval as well. What was even more stunning was that they both wanted her to rewrite her exam answers because they felt Siham was not scholarly enough in her answers. This opinion was expressed at the oral exams even though they had already signed the paperwork approving her candidacy. They both let me know that they were of this opinion because they felt that Siham was not devoting the required amount of time or attention to her studies because she had given birth to a child right before the exam. Equally stunning was that they verbally mentioned this to me, knowing that I had children as well.

These faculty members were initially quite supportive of Siham and her progression in the program. The only characteristic about her that had changed was her pregnancy. This was very familiar to me since I had experienced the same discrimination when I was a graduate student mother. I was determined that Siham would not have the same experience as me. I let Siham know that she did not have to continue working with these two recalcitrant faculty members on her committee, and she was able to replace them with committee members who did not see her motherhood as a detriment to her scholarship.

Our university did not have any programs in place to help Siham. If I had not been her advisor, it is likely that her PhD would have been derailed. It is important to note that several scholars have advised that the typical graduate school timeline is often the optimal time for women to have children (Johnsrud 1993) since it is difficult to have them on the tenure track even if the clock is stopped and after tenure can be too late (Eversole et al. 2015; Powell 2021). However, if women scholars have their children in graduate school, institutions need to be more supportive of their graduate student mothers. Programs should be supportive of graduate student fathers as well.

REFLECTIONS ON OUR EXPERIENCES

Graduate school is an enormous undertaking, and women graduate students cannot pause their biological clock until they're done with school. Pregnancy will happen, whether it is planned or not. Siham and Barbara's experiences were mirrored in findings from a study led by Mirick and Wladkowski (2018) on graduate student mothers. They stated that "there is a perception that doctoral student mothers are less committed to their work, progress more slowly, drop out at greater rates, and perform less well than academic fathers and childless women" (256). These perceptions pose significant barriers for graduate student mothers whose academic paths could be derailed because of perceptions of their abilities and the stigma that their capabilities and their commitment to academia are somehow less once they become pregnant or have children (Mirick and Wladkowski 2018). Other studies suggest that women have long managed to maintain their dual identities in an environment that perceives motherhood and academic studies as not the norm, pushing student mothers to have to work harder to prove that motherhood will not obstruct their educational endeavors (Moyer et al. 1999). Mirick and Wladkowski (2018) also reported that pregnancy was often described as the elephant in the room, a topic that was often avoided. This leads to an environment that is deaf when it comes to the expectations of student mothers.

If the topic of pregnancy is avoided, then the related topics of infertility and miscarriage are even more taboo, although they too are likely to be common experiences for graduate student mothers (Mirick and Wladkowski 2022). Barbara experienced both and suffered in silence through both experiences. As Mirick and Wladkowski noted, there is considerable pressure for women who have experienced pregnancy loss or fertility treatments to continue as if nothing had happened, hampering their ability to take the time needed to heal. There were no supports available for Barbara at her institution.

Finally, Armenti (2004) reported that there is a lack of role models for graduate student mothers in academia that can impact their educational timeline, as was the case for Barbara. Siham was lucky enough to have Barbara as her mentor, role model, and supporter who made sure that Siham did not go through the same challenges.

STRATEGIES OF INSTITUTIONAL CHANGE

A central purpose of this chapter is to identify the ways graduate programs should support graduate student mothers. Previous research has shed light on the ongoing challenges graduate student mothers face, and it was also clear that the support student mothers received was informal through other faculty mothers or direct family. Thus, graduate programs and schools should implement the proper strategies to support student mothers. Supervisors and graduate program directors need to be trained to support these parents through their challenges and to train faculty members who serve on committees, particularly on what to do about and how to protect graduate student mothers who face retaliation for having the temerity to become pregnant during their graduate program. Institutions need to adopt and enact policies that support graduate student mothers during pregnancy and motherhood, normalizing these two states in graduate education. Kulp (2019) stated that several of the policies identified in the American Association of University Professors' 2001 Statement of Principles on Family Responsibilities and Academic Work also apply to graduate students and should be adjusted to meet the needs of graduate student mothers. Strategies are needed both at the institutional and department levels (Eversole et al. 2015).

Three Specific Recommendations:

First, the environment in graduate programs should become more welcoming to and inclusive of women doctoral students. In other words, graduate student mothers should be valued for their unique identities, not penalized for them. Women faculty mothers should also serve as role models and mentors for graduate student mothers and should help them identify institutional programs that could benefit them (Mirick and Wladkowski 2018, 2022) and protect them from retaliation from other faculty members, especially committee members. Department chairs are particularly important as role models and mentors (Eversole et al. 2015).

Graduate school supported high-quality and affordable childcare would also create an inclusive and welcoming culture (Eversole et al. 2015; Mirick and Wladkowski 2020). This includes providing financial support so that graduate student mothers can afford childcare while attending conferences (Mirick and Wladkowski 2020). Financial aid and other forms of financial support are also needed (Eversole et al. 2015; Powell 2021). In addition to that, it's important to recognize academic motherhood by openly considering the various aspects of mothering/parenting in academia without any pressure (Mirick and Wladkowski 2018). This would be the first step academic programs could take to create a supportive environment for academic mothers/parents.

Second, individual departments and colleges should provide emotional support programs to their graduate student mothers, including for women who have experienced pregnancy loss or fertility treatments (Mirick and Wladkowski 2022). Parenting has been and continues to be a challenging task, especially for first-time mothers. Prikhidko and Haynes (2018) revealed that student mothers often struggle with cognitive dissonance and experience greater levels of guilt when it comes to balancing their academic and mothering roles. Thus, programs should provide appropriate counseling services to help student mothers adjust to the reality of balancing both identities and roles. Prikhidko and Haynes suggested the use of cognitive behavioral therapy (CBT) "as a resource for the counseling support. CBT theory embraces the rationality and irrationality of particular beliefs along with finding emotions that affect irrational ideas about life" (324). Prikhidko and Haynes add that using cognitive behavioral therapy can help academic mothers understand and reconcile the emotional challenges that come with parenting.

Emotional support services should extend beyond parenthood and beyond only the graduate student who is affected. As part of this emotional support, institutions should enact a policy for graduate students that allows them to take time off for their grief. Scholars have suggested a grief absence policy for students that would allow students to take leaves of absences and make up work after they have experienced a loss (Servaty-Seib and Chye 2019). Department chairs can also offer emotional support (Eversole et al. 2015). Emotional support can also be offered to faculty members who experience difficulty in supporting graduate student mothers or who have a difficult time believing that parents belong in graduate school at all. By helping these faculty members deal with these feelings, retaliation can be stopped before it begins.

Third, flexibility is extremely important for graduate student mothers. Universities should give graduate student mothers the same flexibility that they offer faculty mothers or should even go farther to formalize policies to offer greater protection (Mirick and Wladkowski 2022). Policies such as paid leave, reduced workload, and extending the limits to the time to earn degrees are all important for graduate student mothers (Eversole et al. 2015; Mirick and Wladkowski 2020). Department chairs can help by providing flexible scheduling and allowing virtual office hours (Eversole et al. 2015). Flexibility can be encouraged at the institutional level through training for program directors and chairs and through a menu of alternate pathways regarding potential research, coursework, and/or graduate assistantships. These can be encouraged at the faculty level through professional development and at the chair level through clear and accessible policies and templates.

THE PLACE, NOT THE PERSON

We have focused in this chapter on institutional rather than individual strategies for change. That is because we feel that the key to retaining and promoting mothers in the faculty pipeline is to change the culture of academia to be more friendly to families and that this must start in graduate school. Individual strategies can only take students so far. The culture must change if the academic motherhood pipeline is to stop leaking graduate student mothers. We as individuals had to find our own ways through toxic and obstructive circumstances, and we advocate here for systemic change so that aggressive defensive strategies will no longer be required for those already doing the important work of both parenting and PhDing.

WORKS CITED

Eversole, Barbara A. W., Cindy L. Crowder, Siham Lekchiri, Amber Clark, and Toni S. Zimmerman. 2015. "Mothering and Professing in the Ivory Tower: Supporting Graduate Student Mothers." *Journal of the Motherhood Initiative* 6 (2): 65–80.

Johnsrud, Linda K. 1993. "Women and Minority Faculty Experiences: Defining and Responding to Diverse Realities." *New Directions for Teaching and Learning* 1993 (53): 3–16. https://doi.org/10.1002/tl.37219935303.

Kulp, Amanda M. 2019. "Parenting on the Path to the Professoriate: A Focus on Graduate Student Mothers." *Research in Higher Education* 61 (3): 408–429. https://doi.org/10.1007/s11162-019-09561-z.

Mirick, Rebecca G., and Stephanie P. Wladkowski. 2018. "Pregnancy, Motherhood, and Academic Career Goals." *Affilia* 33 (2): 253–269. https://doi.org/10.1177/0886109917753835.

Mirick, Rebecca G., and Stephanie P. Wladkowski. 2020. "Women's Experiences with Parenting during Doctoral Education: Impact on Career Trajectory." *International Journal of Doctoral Studies* 15, 89–110. https://doi.org/10.28945/4484.

Mirick, Rebecca G., and Stephanie P. Wladkowski. 2022. "Infertility and Pregnancy Loss in Doctoral Education: Understanding Students' Experiences." *Affilia* 0, 1–22. https://doi.org/10.1177/08861099221084974.

Moyer, Anne, Peter Salovey, and Shannon Casey-Cannon. 1999. "Challenges Facing Female Doctoral Students and Recent Graduates." *Psychology of Women Quarterly* 23 (3): 607–630. https://doi.org/10.1111/j.1471-6402.1999.tb00384.x.

Powell, Kendall. 2021. "How Mothers Get Penalized in the Scientific Race." *Nature* 595, 611–613. https://www.nature.com/articles/d41586-021-01993-x.

Prikhidko, Alena, and Cliff Haynes. 2018. "Balancing Graduate School and Mothering: Is There a Choice?" *International Journal of Doctoral Studies* 13, 313–326. https://doi.org/10.28945/4109.

Servaty-Seib, Heather L., and Chye Hong Liew. 2019. "Advocating for Bereavement Leave Policies for College Students." *Journal of College Student Development* 60 (2): 240–244. https://doi.org/10.1353/csd.2019.0021.

PART 5 LEAVE A NOTE

31 ▸ THERE'S NEVER A GOOD TIME

Navigating Graduate Medical Education While Pregnant

STEPHANIE L. GRAFF

THIRTY-EIGHT HAD ALWAYS been my scary age—the age my mother had me, and thus the age I felt was a reasonable time to have a baby. As I moved through medical school, I gathered anecdotes about residents, fellows, and early-career physicians who were on bed rest with difficult pregnancies, going through infertility treatments, grieving miscarriages, or who were childless and were surrounded by whispered innuendo. These examples in my day-to-day life did little to shake my confidence that I was fine as long as I had not reached my thirty-eighth birthday. So when I married my thirty-four-year-old physician husband when I was twenty-eight, perhaps I should not have been surprised that it was his biological clock that was ticking more loudly than mine. We both wanted more than one child, and as we talked about our peers and colleagues having difficulties getting pregnant and the natural space we would want between children, he would nervously quip about being retired by the time the youngest graduated high school.

As I thought more realistically about having children, friends started sharing stories with me about how long after stopping birth control it took them to achieve pregnancy. Countless friends, most of whom were medical residents or fellows like me, had tried for months or a year or longer before those two blue lines appeared on a pregnancy test. Many had to wait a full year before they could be referred for infertility treatments that then took many more months to coordinate and ultimately result in a successful pregnancy. My loose awareness of the struggle of those around me started to develop into something more tangible. Long, irregular hours in the high-stress position of medical trainee, when the trainee is constantly on their feet with limitations on their ability to control for even simple variables like when they might drink water meant that medical school, postgraduate medical education, and early-career physicians were experiencing complications in everything from fertility to pregnancy to breastfeeding. The scientific literature gradually exposed the full spectrum of difficulties residents faced around parenting and pregnancy (Gabbe et al. 2003; Lee et al. Lee; Rangel et al. 2018; Sandler et al. 2016). So three months after our wedding, I stopped my birth control pills, expecting to follow the long wait of those before me.

Fourteen days later I was pregnant.

That sounds dramatic, but it was as exacting as clockwork. I stopped my birth control pills, which I had been taking uninterrupted to avoid having periods, and with the first dropped pill, I started my period. Being a physician, I had great insight into ovulation, so fourteen days later, I thought "Hey, I'm probably ovulating." Even though I was exhausted, I lured Jason into the bedroom without mentioning my careful math. Two weeks later, when I should have been starting my period again, we had a weekend trip to Vegas booked. I remember stepping off the plane into the Las Vegas airport, which is always a shock to the system—the constant clattering and ringing of slot machines, the flashing neon in every direction, and the dense cloud of smoke—and instantly feeling nauseated. I have never liked the smell of cigarette smoke, but this was wretched. I hurried through the airport, collected our bags, and got in a cab. The cab ride made me car sick, also not entirely unheard of for me. When I walked into the lobby of The Venetian Resort, I again experienced the crushing sensory overload I had felt at the airport. When we finally entered our hotel room and closed the door I went over to our bed and collapsed in exhaustion, exhaled deeply, and then bolted upright, looked at Jason, and said, "Does our room smell like cigarette smoke to you?" He laughed and told me I was probably just smelling it on my hair or clothes from the lobby or the airport.

No, this was different. I could smell *everything.*

Later that day, we walked through the hotel, and every person's perfume, body odor, and cocktail grabbed my attention in a way I had never experienced. Each fresh smell buried me under a fresh wave of nausea, and I knew. I took a pregnancy test when we got home three days later, four days late for my period, and my suspicions were confirmed. Already fearing miscarriage, I waited another two weeks before I told my husband.

Initially I had planned on not disclosing my pregnancy at work—my hematology and medical oncology fellowship graduate medical education training program—until I was three months pregnant. However, in January, when I was only about eight weeks pregnant, I was rotating on the bone marrow transplant service, and that created numerous obstacles. The first obstacle was the risk of infection. Given the very nature of bone marrow transplants, patients are profoundly immunosuppressed, and as such, they develop illnesses that are not encountered in the normal world. Diseases like disseminated shingles, cytomegalovirus (CMV) pneumonia, and toxoplasmosis are all possibilities—and all are potentially transmissible to pregnant women with dire consequences to mama or baby. Naturally, it was just a matter of time until one of the patients I was caring for was diagnosed with something that made it hard for me to safely provide care for them and my unborn child simultaneously.

When the first scenario arose, a patient with CMV pneumonia, I pulled the female nurse practitioner aside and stammered, "I'm pregnant. It is early so . . . well . . . I am not really talking about it yet, but should I really be going in room 12? What do I do?" She simply traded patients with me without missing a beat, and the attending male physicians, those responsible for my performance reviews and education, never noticed the shift. Unfortunately, the second obstacle was harder to disguise than the first. Another complexity of caring for bone marrow transplant patients is that we wear layers of protective equipment—face masks, shields, gloves, and gowns—to protect the patients from us when we enter the room. All the extra gear added to the fact that the patients are chronically cold and their rooms are kept at 80 degrees Fahrenheit meant that I often went into a patient's room and quickly felt overheated. When coupled with the horrible hospital smells hanging in these rooms, which include the smell of body fluids, hospital-grade disinfectants, hospital food, and the chemical stench of the medicines we use, this culminated in my intense morning sickness being hard to manage. About ten days into the rotation, I found myself dashing from a patient room, tearing off layers of face masks and eye shields and just barely making it to the hallway, where I threw up in the trash can outside the patient's room. The attending bone marrow transplant oncologist sauntered out a moment later, held my hair back and offered me a wet paper towel, smiled knowingly, and said, "I love babies."

I have now been a mother for thirteen years, and with each new stage I am surprised that I have totally failed to anticipate obvious next events and prepare accordingly. I had not realized until I sat counting out the math of when the baby would be born that I would need to figure out how to take time off my fellowship training, which the Accreditation Council for Graduate Medical Education (ACGME) regulates tightly. Sure, I had vacation days, but that is all. The baby was due September 9, 2009 (09/09/09—I liked that). Given that our year was calculated from July 1 to June 30 each year, if I took all my vacation/sick time in September for "maternity leave," a phrase I use loosely since using your vacation and sick time is not exactly the same as true leave for welcoming a human into your family, it would result in me having no days off for the next nine months.

Working in healthcare opens your eyes to the terrifying reality of what can go wrong. I needed to find a way to work flexibly because at any time in those nine long months the baby could get sick, I could have postpregnancy complications, I could get sick, my elderly parents could have issues, and on and on. If I used time beyond my allotted sick or vacation time, my fellowship program and the ACGME rules meant that they could give me a zero credit for that month's rotation, and there is no guarantee that if a trainee fails to complete the required thirty-six months of rotations in three years that a trainee will get to stick around for an extra month for a do-over, as each program is also only allowed so many trainees at any given time. My program had a track record of being phenomenally collaborative, forgiving, and creative in order to help trainees complete their requirements and graduate, even if it meant a little extra time, but the gamble with my career felt terrifying. Even asking for this type of help felt dangerous, like admitting a weakness that I did not want to expose.

My mentor was one of the few female faculty at my institution. She was childless, although I did not know if that was a choice, a consequence of infertility, or any other potential scenario. This unknowing was a weight of awareness I carried when I went to speak with her about my pregnancy. Would she be supportive or would she perceive my pregnancy as a lack of commitment to academic career development?

Luckily for me, she was brilliant. She quickly told me that she would request to have me on a research month with her for the month of September and that we could count the book chapter we were already well on our way to completing as part of that time. That would give me, assuming I delivered at the appointed hour, about three-and-half weeks of maternity leave without using any vacation or sick leave.

Thirteen years later, I realize the absurdity of this luck. Maternity leave should not require a due date to align with an academic calendar or a female mentor who can cleverly manipulate research months into productive time by weighting previously completed work. Those in graduate school should not have academically fruitful research time taken from them and used as unacknowledged maternity leave because it is scenarios like this that start to lay the groundwork for the gender gap—a handful of fewer publications, a seemingly insignificant number of missed connections, a slightly shorter list of specialized skills, and I'm suddenly in a different category of applicants. With no changes to my skills, potential, or expertise, I'm automatically relegated to less competitive positions, lower pay, and less prestigious job placements that limit my income and my progression for the rest of my career.

But in that moment, in 2009, pregnant with my first child and just wanting to graduate on time without getting myself into trouble for deigning to have a family during training, I was overjoyed.

Our academic calendar for September was set to rotate on September 8. September 7 was Labor Day, an observed holiday, so the rotations would change for all the fellows that Tuesday after the holiday. I needed to carry the pregnancy until Friday, September 4. I found myself nervously counting days to the rotation change more than the delivery date. By that Friday, my gynecologist was advising me that I was nowhere near going into labor based on my exam and cervix position and that the baby was estimated to be nine to ten pounds. She was worried that as a first-time mom I might go two weeks past my due date, and given how large the baby already was, that could be a big problem. Turning on a dime, I started to worry about what would happen if I went weeks beyond September 9. We would rotate again October 5, so if I did not deliver until September 16 or 23, my maternity leave could in fact end up being quite short. And if my huge baby was born via Caesarean section or a traumatic birth, that might not even leave me time to adequately physically recover.

These were the thoughts circulating in my head as I went to sleep on September 4, having cleared that first hurdle. As I woke to the familiarity of heartburn and a full bladder in the darkness and stumbling back to bed with the unbalanced gait of a woman at forty weeks gestation, I had an accident. Had I really urinated on myself? I grabbed a clean set of pajamas and left our master bedroom to change clothes, humiliated that despite having just gone to the bathroom, I had somehow still managed to leak urine. Then it occurred to me that perhaps it was not urine but my water breaking. However, it wasn't the rush of fluid that soaks the sidewalk in rom-coms, and I certainly was not in actual labor. No. I debated with myself for the better part of an hour using techniques that ranged from failed attempts at self-exam to internet searches ("how do you know if your water broke?"), to prayer when I decided that, yes, I was definitely in labor. I woke my husband, and he drove us faster than I have ever known him to drive to the hospital as my contractions grew steadily more painful. I gripped the car door with a white-knuckle grip, partly in pain, partly in fear of my husband's driving. A few hours later, my beautiful Gabriel entered the world.

Family leave was a blur. Gabriel screamed the first nine months he was alive. At first, I just thought newborns were hard. Then I thought babies were hard. Then I thought maybe I did not have enough breast milk. Then I thought he had gastroesophageal reflux disease (GERD). At the end of my four weeks of family leave, Gabriel had not slept for more than two hours consecutively, and that was normally only achieved if he was sleeping upright against my chest. This means that I had essentially not slept at all. We had arranged for Jason to take two weeks of paternity leave at the end of my four weeks of maternity leave, so Jason tried as hard as the dad of a breastfed baby could to help me get some sleep. At the end of Jason's two-week leave, we agreed we would just tag-team the screaming. Then Jason fell asleep driving to work one day and crashed his jeep into a concrete retaining wall. While he was unscathed, it was a wake-up call. The only thing worse than being sleep deprived while your infant screams and you try to manage your graduate education would be losing your husband in a car accident. We agreed that he would need more sleep and I started carrying more of the burden.

Honestly, it was horrid.

Again, in what I know to be tremendous luck and privilege, despite my postgraduate life, I was married to a full-time attending physician earning attending physician pay, so we were able to hire a nanny to stay home with the baby. Our nanny was a hero. She made Mary Poppins look like an amateur. Just her simple acknowledgment that this crying was not normal was a tremendous relief. We took Gabriel to the pediatrician and had him treated for GERD, which did not help, and ultimately just came to accept that he had colic and someday would outgrow it. We tried "cry it out" and it nearly killed us. But magically, at nine months, Gabriel finally slept. It was only years later when I would stand and watch his little sister sleep peacefully in her crib for hours a mere week after being brought home from the hospital that I fully understood how terrible those days were. I look back at that time and wonder how I should have asked for help or what help I should have asked for. I have wondered if I needed treatment for postpartum depression or better lactation support or what? I don't know. I know how powerful it was for me to have our nanny acknowledge what a hard baby Gabriel was, and I wonder if simply having a stronger support network would have made a world of difference. But you don't know what you don't know.

While Gabriel stayed home with our nanny, I pumped breastmilk at work. As an oncology fellow, I had a variety of work environments: the outpatient clinic, the university hospital, and the Veteran's Affairs (VA) hospital. Each had its own unique challenges and barriers. In the clinic, I could use a patient exam room to pump, but the doors do not lock for reasons of patient safety. I would go inside and draw the patient privacy curtain around the door, set up a laptop so I could continue to do charting and orders, and hope I could stop any wayward guest between the time they opened the door and drew back the curtain. In the hospital, I had options, but all of them were bad. I could pump in the workroom I shared with the nurse practitioners. They were all women and mothers, all incredibly supportive, but it wasn't the pinnacle of privacy. I could walk across the hospital with all my stuff to the lactation suite if it were not being used by someone else, but the time commitment and chances of finding it occupied by others made this a frustrating endeavor.

My best strategy was to try any number of random lockable doors and hope that no one tried to come and kick me out—small conference rooms, single bathrooms, the offices of other people who were kind enough to let me borrow them. The latter was my preferred approach. The VA had different discomforts. I could pump in my shared office with other fellows in the oncology program, but they were men and it felt uncomfortable. I could ask them to stay out, but that felt selfish or rude in a way I was not sure how to navigate. Not to mention that the fellows' office door had a window to the main hospital hallway. Or I could pump in the Pyxis room on the oncology nursing floor. A Pyxis is a locked, computerized medicine station—a nurse comes in, selects a patient and a medication order, and a drawer or cabinet with that medication for that patient magically opens. They are huge and are often kept in rooms that are further protected by a badge or a key-code-enabled door for security. At our VA, the Pyxis room also had a private desk and a computer, which meant that if I pumped there I could continue working, with interruptions only when a nurse needed to get a patient medication. Guess what? The nurses always need to get the patients' medication. While I wore a nursing cover, the sight of me pumping and working on the computer in the Pyxis room was commonplace for the oncology nurses. In this way, the months slipped past, marked by hundreds of disposable freezer bags of expressed breast milk and dozens of colleagues seeing or hearing my breast pump. I was able to nurse Gabriel for a year, although with supplemental formula and meager supply by the end.

I have three children now, I have felt the unimaginable grief of miscarriage between the second and third, and I remain constantly unprepared for the surprises around the corner that motherhood brings. I look back and feel that I had such a wonderful, lucky experience—faculty who embraced my morning sickness on rounds, mentors who accommodated maternity leave, delivery at the exact right window, coworkers who did not bat an eye at an oncology fellow pumping breast milk in the Pyxis room or who did not complain about bags of breast milk in the freezer, the social support to afford a nanny. And yet these examples, both subtle and obvious, of pregnancy, lactation, and motherhood discrimination are outrageous. Even with all of my privileges, I still had to navigate exposure to teratogenic infections during graduate education, there was no clear policy or accommodation for family leave or lactation support that make them universally understood, and there was no easy-to-access support for childcare.

Ultimately, I think we each must do what makes sense for our own situation. In the meantime, I do not wish you luck—I wish for you policy change and elimination of bias in the intersection of parenting and career. And maybe a little bit of luck. When mentees ask me questions about the "best time" to have children, I always offer a knowing laugh and say that it is never a good time and it is always the best time.

WORKS CITED

Gabbe, Steven G., Maria A. Morgan, Michael L. Power, Jay Schulkin, and Sterling B. Williams. 2003. "Duty Hours and Pregnancy Outcome among Residents in Obstetrics and Gynecology." *Obstetrics and Gynecology* 102 (5 Part 1): 948–951. doi:10.1016/s0029-7844(03)00856-1.

Lee, Anna, Aleksandra Kuczmarska-Haas, Shraddha M. Dalwadi, Erin F. Gillespie, Michelle S. Ludwig, Emma B. Holliday, and Fumiko Chino. 2022. "Family Planning, Fertility, and Career Decisions among Female Oncologists." *JAMA Network Open* 5 (10): e2237558–e2237558.

Rangel, Erika L., Douglas S. Smink, Manuel Castillo-Angeles, Gifty Kwakye, Marguerite Changala, Adil H. Haider, and Gerard M. Doherty. 2018. "Pregnancy and Motherhood during Surgical Training." *JAMA Surgery* 153 (7): 644–652.

Sandler, Britt J., John J. Tackett, Walter E. Longo, Peter S. Yoo. 2016. "Pregnancy and Parenthood among Surgery Residents: Results of the First Nationwide Survey of General Surgery Residency Program Directors." *Journal of the American College of Surgeons* 222 (6): 1090–1096. doi:10.1016/j.jamcollsurg.2015.12.004.

32 ▸ THINGS DON'T ALWAYS GO ACCORDING TO PLAN

Navigating Pregnancy Loss and Challenging the Culture of Silence as a PhD Candidate

MARIYA TSEPTSURA

Disclaimer: This chapter discusses pregnancy loss.

When we start our graduate programs, we embark on a demanding journey of planning: we plan which courses to take, which research projects to work on, when and how to pass our examinations, how to write a successful dissertation, and much more. There is abundant advice—both public and private—on how to plan our graduate student trajectory. For those of us who also want to start a family, some common advice is to start planning early: "You need to think about having children as a goal, in the same way that you think about finishing that dissertation or landing that tenure-track job as a goal" (Connelly and Ghodsee 2011, 55). And while women in academia who have children early are statistically less likely to achieve tenure (e.g., Mason et al. 2013), that fact might not outweigh the pressure of biological clock and the risk of reduced fertility while waiting for a more stable tenured position. That consideration might persuade many to start planning early.

Such advice commonly views pregnancy and the path to parenthood as a plannable, controllable series of events. You might even hear advice or stories about "timing" the birth of the baby to coincide with the beginning of winter or summer break. This mindset is not unique to academia. As Lara Freidenfelds points out, the technological advances in birth control and the reproductive freedoms of the late twentieth century made it possible for women to have much greater control over not only their life trajectories but also their pregnancy experiences: "This new intention to control fertility, realized with ever-greater precision using sophisticated new modes of contraception, eventually resulted in an unrealistic expectation of near-perfect control of conception and pregnancy outcomes" (2020, 31).

While for some the path to parenthood can resemble a direct line where they achieve their "goal" within the established time frame, many others face challenges that are outside of their control or powers of prediction, as I did. There is ample advice about parenthood but far less guidance that addresses common and unpredictable roadblocks to parenthood such as infertility and miscarriage. Moreover, there is a culture of silence around miscarriage and pregnancy loss that helps maintain unfair working conditions and prevents people from seeking support and healing after they have experienced miscarriage. In this chapter, I present a personal account of my experience with miscarriage to illustrate some of these issues, offer advice, and try to break the silence around this topic.

MISCARRIAGE AND THE ACADEMIC JOB MARKET

I became pregnant with my first child in the third year of my PhD program in English. I was lucky enough to be at a post-coursework stage in my program, which meant I did not have a strict course schedule to follow. I was also a teaching assistant in the writing program, teaching two courses per semester. I was lucky enough to have supportive mentors and colleagues who not only helped with advice and baby hand-me-downs but also allowed me to teach online for a year when my newborn daughter needed a lot of attention. I passed my comprehensive exams when I was six months pregnant and completed my dissertation proposal during my daughter's first couple of months of life. With the flexibility my position allowed, I had found a way to make it work with the support of my mentors, friends, family, and, when I had to go back to teaching on campus, our nanny.

However, I knew I wanted to have a bigger family, and as I was already over thirty, I did not want to wait much longer before trying for another child. I hoped that I would be able to have another baby before graduating from the program. Based on my experience with my first child, I did not expect that this goal would be difficult to achieve. However, it took over a year before I saw my first positive pregnancy test in January of my last year in the PhD program. I was getting ready to defend my dissertation, and I was on the job market looking for a suitable academic position. Getting pregnant at that time was definitely a complicating factor, but after struggling with trying to conceive for over a year, I was relieved more than I was worried about having a brand-new baby and a new job at the same time. My first campus visit was scheduled for the second week of February. My graduate program provided extensive support and mentoring for students navigating the academic job market, which included mock job talks and teaching presentations. I was eight weeks pregnant, but I felt good as my mock job talk was scheduled for two days before my first campus visit.

Forty-eight hours before the mock talk and four days before my first campus visit, my miscarriage started.

When I first noticed light bleeding, I called my OBGYN's office. A nurse recommended that I "take it easy" and watch for any worsening signs. A day later, I was experiencing heavy bleeding and severe abdominal pain. I went through my mock job talk in a state of acute pain and distress. I remember one of my mentors, unaware of my situation, kindly pointing out that my facial expression was too tense and that I should try to smile. The next day, my doctor recommended that I go to the ER to check for an ectopic pregnancy. I spent five hours in the ER waiting to see a doctor, get an ultrasound exam, and confirm that there were no signs of ectopic pregnancy. Both doctors recommended that I stay at home for at least a week in case my symptoms worsened. Instead, I packed my suitcase and was on a plane to go to my first campus visit the following morning. The heavy bleeding and pain only intensified. I took large doses of Ibuprofen and purchased every sanitary product I could find at the drugstore. The visit went well despite my overwhelming distress and frequent bathroom visits. I received a job offer (which I ultimately accepted) a week later. It took two weeks for the bleeding to stop and it took me much longer to recover from the emotional fallout of that experience.

BREAKING THE SILENCE AND PLANNING FOR THE UNPREDICTABLE

On the surface, my narrative might seem like another success story of beating the odds and overcoming challenges. Some of the most popular books on surviving the academic job market contain similar stories. For example, in *The Professor Is In*, Karen Kelsky cheerfully points out that "more than one of my readers has shared a story of conducting a full day of faculty interviews and job talk from her hospital bed, and still getting the job" (2015, 298).

However, the physical and emotional pain I had to go through makes me question if this grueling process is the only way the academic job market can exist. Some might suggest that I could have asked to reschedule my campus visit or requested an online visit instead. I also could have disclosed my condition during the visit. In fact, at one point I almost confessed the fact that I was actively having a miscarriage when, during a one-on-one informal chat, the head of the search committee mentioned they were hoping to have a child in the near future. Ultimately, however, I did neither of those things because I was concerned that I would be perceived as a lesser candidate. My concerns were not unjustified: research confirms that pregnant women are seen as less reliable and less committed, and the pregnancy status itself calls attention to their bodies, which are perceived as delicate and unhealthy (Porschitz and Siler 2017, 567). Not surprisingly, women commonly avoid disclosing their pregnancy in the workplace for as long as possible. Disclosing a miscarriage puts a woman in an even more precarious position because it also "reveals the secret of her pregnancy and the 'compromised' position of her body" (571). I did not want to draw attention either to my body and its (mal)functioning or to the fact that I was hoping to have another child in the near future,—which can also affect a woman's chances of being hired despite the fact that such discrimination was prohibited first by the Pregnancy Discrimination Act of 1978 and more recently by the Pregnant Workers Fairness Act, which went into effect in June 2023. In the end, I said nothing during and after my campus visit, and I am not sure I would have mentioned anything if I had had to go through the same process again. In hindsight, I know that this search committee would have been accommodating had I requested a change of date or mode for the visit, but that knowledge came only from getting to know the committee members on a personal level later on. For PhD candidates entering the job market, I can only recommend using their best judgment as to whether they should disclose pregnancy or miscarriage-related conditions and how much it would be prudent to disclose.

I hope that as more miscarriage and pregnancy loss narratives enter the public conversation, these conditions will become less of a taboo topic in academic workplaces, especially considering that my experience with miscarriage is far from unique. Statistically, 10 to 20 percent of all known pregnancies end in miscarriage (Porschitz and Siler 2017), although the number is commonly assumed to be much higher when unknown pregnancies are included in calculations. Infertility, defined as the inability to conceive within a year of trying, is also experienced by 19 percent of couples trying to conceive, according to the Centers for Disease Control (CDC 2022). Yet despite how common both experiences might be, they are often omitted from discussions about family planning and handling the responsibilities of graduate school and parenting. Instead, we are encouraged to plan our pregnancy, birth, and parenting as if it were another job. It is not. After having had four pregnancies and two living children, I have come to accept that when you decide to become a parent, you have to let go of trying to control how this journey is going to unfold, from conception and pregnancy to birth and beyond. But if we cannot control our path to parenthood, what can we do?

ACCEPTANCE, COMMUNITY, AND ADVOCACY

First, although it can be hard to accept that we cannot always predict or plan our future, accepting the limits of our control will help reduce stress and anxiety if such events do take place. Miscarriage might be fairly common, but the way people experience it and react to it can vary drastically. Some miscarriages might take a few hours and some can last for days (Porschitz and Siler 2017) or, as in my case, weeks. The way people react to miscarriage also varies greatly, and factors such as gestational age, parents' age, prior losses, living children, and social support all play a role in shaping the emotional and psychological aftermath of a miscarriage (Brier 2008). For many people, a miscarriage can lead to anxiety, depression, or a sense of grief similar to that following the death of a family member. Accepting your reaction, whatever it might be, as normal and valid can be the first step. Seeking out resources and help to cope with a depression or grief can be another, whether it is through family and friends, therapy, or published resources (e.g., Osborn's *The Miscarriage Map Workbook* [2021] helps dispel some common myths about pregnancy loss and offers some helpful strategies for dealing with grief). Most important, we need to allow ourselves the time, space, and grace to process the emotional fallout of miscarriage or infertility.

Second, recognize that the emotional toll of miscarriage can be exacerbated by the cultural silence around it and the lack of an "existing societal framework or narrative" for it (Porschitz and Siler 2017, 568). Many parents choose not to disclose a pregnancy until the second trimester (or until it becomes too visible to conceal), and since most miscarriages take place in the first trimester, they often remain undisclosed. At the same time, sharing their experiences and communicating their needs help women cope with the negative feelings and emotional distress following a miscarriage (Kroth et al. 2004). Jansen and colleagues point out that people who experience miscarriage "want open communication about their losses" and "expect a sensitive and empathetic attitude from others" (2022, 1). While not disclosing miscarriage can have some benefits such as not having to deal with insensitive or intrusive comments or attitudes that are less than empathetic, working through miscarriage grief in silence can be isolating and can potentially worsen the negative psychological effects it might have. Talking—and writing—about this traumatic experience is what ultimately helped me heal. When I started my new job, I learned that one of my colleagues had experienced miscarriage as well, and together with two other coauthors who had struggled with infertility, we wrote a chapter on infertility and miscarriage in academic workplaces (Clinnin et al. 2023).

While I was still in my PhD program, I disclosed my miscarriage to a few of my mentors and colleagues, but not many. In hindsight, I wish I had been more open about my experience with my friends and mentors in the program, not only because I was not able to find sufficient support in my family but also because discussing it more openly would have opened the conversation about pregnancy complications, miscarriage, and loss to other graduate students who might find themselves in a similar situation. Ideally, finding a supportive community in the workplace would not be too difficult. However, reality is often less than ideal, and in such cases I recommend reaching out to friends outside the workplace as well as community-based or online support groups.

Third, in addition to seeking a supportive community within or outside the academic program, I recommend being a more active advocate for your own needs and rights. Some researchers suggest that organizations can provide critical support services that "help women process the emotional trauma of miscarriage," such as explicitly including miscarriage in the sick leave and family leave policies (Porschitz and Siler 2017). However, such organizational change at the graduate school level is unlikely to be swift or common, and in its absence, we have to be our own advocates. In many cases, being a PhD student or candidate allows certain flexibilities in scheduling that might provide time for recovery and healing. If that is not the case, it is worth exploring other options for taking time off and seeking out ways to adjust your schedule based on your own needs.

My experience was abnormal in the sense that job interviews and campus visits are generally more high-stakes and less flexible events, but in the current post-COVID-19 climate, flexibility has become more normalized even in the academic job market. Remote or hybrid interviews and campus visits have become a lot more common, and there have been arguments for a combination of virtual and in-person interviews where the in-person visits are reserved as an opportunity for the candidates to learn about the institution after the job offer has been made (Termini et al. 2021). My campus interviews took place before the pandemic, when the online format was a lot less common, and I did not want to appear less interested in the position or put myself at a disadvantage compared to the candidates who were able to be physically present during their visits. If I had to go through the same experience now, I would request a virtual campus visit and a change of schedule.

MAKING SPACE FOR UNEXPECTED PATHS

For graduate students, planning their academic career is a crucially important skill, so naturally, we try to apply the same planning techniques to starting a family. However, as paths to parenthood can take unexpected turns, we need to be prepared for the unexpected and seek ways to keep those plans flexible and adaptable. As we might have to advocate for increased flexibility and accommodations during especially challenging moments, being able to openly discuss topics like pregnancy complications or miscarriage will help alleviate some of the emotional and mental burden. Although we might still need to exercise good judgment when deciding on when to tell someone and how much information we want to disclose, breaking the silence around pregnancy and miscarriage will help us build more supportive communities within academic spaces.

WORKS CITED

Brier, Norman. 2008. "Grief Following Miscarriage: A Comprehensive Review of the Literature." *Journal of Women's Health* 17 (3): 451–464.

CDC. 2022, March 1. "Infertility FAQs." CDC Reproductive Health. https://www.cdc.gov/reproductive-health/infertility-faq/?CDC_AAref_Val=https://www.cdc.gov/reproductivehealth/infertility/index.htm.

Clinnin, Kaitlin, Jennifer Eidum, Morgan Hanson, and Mariya Tseptsura. 2023. "Ready for a Career and a Family: Experiencing (In)fertility as an Early Career WPA." In *Understanding WPA Readiness and Renewal,* edited by Joseph Janangelo and Mark Blaauw-Hara, 61–71. Peter Lang Verlag.

Connelly, Rachel, and Kristen Ghodsee. 2011. *Professor Mommy: Finding Work-Family Balance in Academia.* Rowman & Littlefield Publishers.

Freidenfelds, Lara. 2020. *The Myth of the Perfect Pregnancy*. Oxford University Press.

Jansen, C., E. Kuhlmann, P. Scharli, M. Schick, B. Ditzen, L. Langer, T. Strowitzki, R.-J. Kuon, and T. Wischmann. 2022. "'A sorrow shared . . .': A Qualitative Content Analysis of What Couples with Recurrent Miscarriages Expect from One Another and Their Families and Friends." *Human Reproduction Open* 2022 (3): 1–11.

Kelsky, Karen. 2015. *The Professor Is In: The Essential Guide to Turning Your Ph.D. Into a Job*. Crown.

Kroth, Jerry, Marylynne Garcia, Michelle Hallgren, Emilyann LeGrue, Maureen Ross, and Juliana Scalise. 2004. "Perinatal Loss, Trauma, and Dream Reports." *Psychological Reports* 94 (3): 877–882.

Mason, Mary Ann, Nicholas H. Wolfinger, and Marc Goulden. 2013. *Do Babies Matter? Gender and Family in the Ivory Tower*. Rutgers University Press.

Osborn, Sunita. 2021. *The Miscarriage Map Workbook: An Honest Guide to Navigating Pregnancy Loss, Working through the Pain, and Moving Forward*. PESI Publishing & Media.

Porschitz, Emily T., and Elizabeth A. Siler. 2017. "Miscarriage in the Workplace: An Autoethnography." *Gender, Work and Organization* 24 (6): 565–578.

Termini, Christina M., Florentine U.N. Rutaganira, Caroline B. Palavicino-Maggio, Chelsey C. Spriggs, Chantell S. Evans, and Melanie R. McReynolds. 2021. "Using Virtual Interviewing to Create a More Accessible Hybrid Academic Job Market." *Cell* 184 (26): 6217–6221.

33 ▸ INVESTIGATE AND INVEST IN SUPPORTIVE SPACES

Doctoral Programs That Accept and Enhance the Experiences of Graduate Student Parents

MORGAN BUCHS, RACHEL FLYNN, LAURA LEIGH MENARD, AND BRANDIE BOHNEY

THE AUTHORS of this chapter are four mothers who met at Bowling Green State University (BGSU) in the Rhetoric & Writing Studies PhD program. BGSU is a public postsecondary institution in northwest Ohio. Since 1980, over 160 students have gone through and graduated from the program. Many of these students were parents who completed coursework, taught undergraduate classes, served in administrative roles, and went through the dissertation process in the hope of getting to their final destination: graduation. This chapter highlights our stories as current students and recent graduates of this program. Through the form of a group conversation, we share how we navigated the dual identities of parent and student. Each of us represents a different stage of parenthood, ranging from dissertating during the early months with a newborn to researching with a child after completing the degree.

Based on our experiences, we argue that the Rhetoric & Writing Studies program at BGSU provided a space that not only accepted our identity as mothers but also actively worked to support us and ensure our success in coursework, teaching, and scholarship. We found support as graduate student parents within the structure of the program from our faculty advisors and from assistantship opportunities that contributed to a culture that embraced and encouraged us.

At the time of drafting this chapter:

- Morgan was the mother to an eight-month-old son. After becoming pregnant and giving birth during her fourth and final year of the program, she drafted, revised, and defended her dissertation and went onto the academic job market with the support of her advisor.
- Rachel began her graduate school journey as the mother to a toddler and preschooler. Throughout her time in the program, she balanced coursework, full-time work, and navigating the scheduling associated with being a parent to young children.
- Laura, who came to the program from a background in law, was the mother to a middle school student and a recently graduated college student. She balanced parenthood and graduate school by leaning into the flexibility faculty provided: she brought her daughter to class, attended class virtually, and completed her assistantship remotely.
- Brandie joined the program as a mother of two high school students. Like Laura, she utilized the flexibility of the program courses and assistantship structures. This enabled her to consistently put her family first.

WHAT WE KNOW ABOUT RESEARCH ON GRADUATE STUDENT PARENTS

According to Yoo and Marshall, "The recent data on profiles of graduate students shows that 35.5% of all students enrolled in master's programs and 28.4% of students enrolled in doctoral programs have dependent children. . . .

They constitute a unique subpopulation in higher education that accounts for a large proportion of graduate students" (2022, 260), On top of a demanding graduate school program, graduate student parents have responsibilities such as childcare, food preparation, and domestic labor, often during nonnegotiable time frames. These critical and labor-intensive tasks are often incompatible with the demanding nature of graduate studies. Adding to the grading, reading, and writing associated with graduate studies, graduate student parents are responsible for arranging childcare, transportation, and various other tasks needed in the daily care of children. Springer and colleagues explain that "being both an academic and parent is quite incompatible in practice. Women, in particular, who find themselves precariously trying to balance these two roles often struggle and sometimes fail. . . . These tensions and contradictions can be particularly explicit during graduate school, when aspiring academics are being 'socialized' into their new vocations, and when many women are experiencing motherhood for the first time" (2009, 436).

As we, the authors, know all too well, it is incredibly difficult to balance parenthood and graduate studies, especially when the two begin in the same period of time. As a result, graduate student parents often develop individualized strategies to help them navigate their graduate programs. Sallee noted the development of these strategies in the findings of an exploratory qualitative study that interviewed eighteen graduate student parents: "Participants identified many ways in which they attempted to meet the responsibilities required of them as students. Nearly all of the participants discussed how they adopted strict schedules and became conscientious [about] time management in order to complete homework. Other participants noted they occasionally made choices about their assignments, particularly when contending with work and family demands" (2015, 406). While individual strategies put into place by graduate student parents themselves are important, more pressing factors are sometimes overlooked. We argue that considering programmatic factors and influences is also crucial in creating successful graduate program experiences.

Although we have experienced such challenges, our specific context as mothers within a supportive graduate program enabled us to beat the odds and pursue and find success in our studies. The conversation depicted in the following section between Morgan, Rachel, Laura, and Brandie highlights factors that made this possible and points to how other graduate student parents can seek out such supportive programs.

A CONVERSATION ON "FINDING A PLACE" IN GRADUATE SCHOOL WITH FOUR MOTHER-STUDENTS

What specifically about this program community and environment created a space that supported parents?

RACHEL: When I first visited campus (before accepting my offer), I was torn between whether or not to reveal that I was a parent. I was worried that faculty might have concerns about my parental responsibilities. After hearing another graduate student talk about their children, I talked to a faculty member about my children and family responsibilities and he didn't show the slightest hint of concern. He directed me to a list of childcare providers maintained by the university and suggested a faculty member to speak to about additional childcare options. That's when I finally felt confident that this program would support me and my family.

LAURA: And that support continues into the program. When my ten-year-old child didn't have school, she was allowed to come with me. When she was diagnosed with epilepsy, my professors were incredibly supportive. One professor even offered to turn off the lights in the classroom (knowing that fluorescent lighting can trigger seizures) on a day my daughter would be with me in class.

BRANDIE: My kids were also welcomed to class with me, and in every case, my professors encouraged them to participate by fully folding them into class activities. No one—faculty or fellow students—ever questioned that parenting was my primary focus and grad school was never more important than my family. I included my experiences as a parent in my coursework, and they were always considered valuable contributions: no faculty ever questioned familial experiences as tangential.

MORGAN: I agree. After completing my master's program at BGSU, I felt comfortable committing to a program that would be there to help me grow academically while recognizing that scholarship is not the most important aspect of my life.

What about your graduate appointment made parenting possible during your PhD program?[1]

MORGAN: The assistantships in our program are manageable, many opportunities for remote work exist, and fourth-year fellowships are available. I appreciated that I never had to teach more than one course at a time and that I spent the bulk of my time in coursework completing flexible assistantships, such as being the doctoral program assistant and a new graduate teaching assistant (GTA) mentor. These opportunities were possible largely due to the awareness and advocacy of the program faculty: they recognized that not only would various types of assistantships provide more breadth of experience for GTAs but also that a lower teaching cap invited more engaged teaching and program involvement. This came in especially helpful during my fourth-year fellowship when I was busy with doctor appointments and all of the other tasks that come with being pregnant and taking care of a newborn.

BRANDIE: Yes! The fact that the program updated the requirements for GTAs in the past five years to require us to manage only one course (instead of the standard two or even three for GTAs in other programs) was terrific. Even though I had to prepare for a new course nearly every semester–which was unique to my situation—my background in teaching made handling a single, relatively small class manageable for me to balance with my coursework and family demands. Many GTAs without the same background taught first-year composition for their first two years in so they could gain experience with teaching the same course prior to designing and teaching a new one. Our program also requires every incoming graduate student to take a Composition Instructors' Workshop course their first semester, which is helpful for students coming in with no experience. At first, I was deeply irritated to have to take such a course when I had fifteen years of classroom experience, but I found the experience valuable in both sharing my own teaching expertise and learning from others.

LAURA: Initially, I started the program with a teaching appointment that required a lot of time on campus. In my second and third years, though, I applied and was selected by the program director to manage the English department's website and social media pages and was an assistant to the program's director. These appointments allowed me to work remotely and choose my hours so that I could work around my younger daughter's school day and doctor's appointments.

MORGAN: I really appreciated the flexible nature of many of the assistantships, and I definitely spent around half of my time in the program doing remote work. The existence of these opportunities not only demonstrated the faculty's trust in our ability to work well in administrative and research capacities; it also enabled us to develop skills and gain experience in multiple areas within the university setting beyond teaching. For many in the program, simply asking for alternate assistantship arrangements was something that faculty were willing—and happy—to accommodate.

What can faculty do at other institutions to support graduate students who are parents?

MORGAN: Encourage flexibility for work-life balance. I told my dissertation advisor that my dissertation timeline was based on my desire to have a child before graduating, and he responded, "Great! I did the same!" Deadlines and meetings were scheduled around doctor's appointments, I was given as much time as I needed after giving birth—without pressure to "take a break" from the program or rush back before I was ready—before continuing dissertation work, and my newborn often joined virtual meetings once I came back.

LAURA: And not just in meetings; welcoming students' children into the classroom, too, makes a huge impact on parents. My daughter not only attended classes, she was also able to raise her hand, answer questions, and truly feel involved and welcomed.

MORGAN: Yes! I remember when your daughter came to class and how excited she was to be there and participate. While I never brought my son to class, he joined me for a lot of meetings and committee work. Now I specifically note in my syllabus that students are welcome to bring their children to class. This is something that faculty members should be encouraging other faculty to do as well, instead of leaving such requests to graduate student parents themselves. I think it is important that we take on that responsibility, especially within our perceived positions of power, to ensure that welcoming and supportive environments are created for all students who have varying needs.

BRANDIE: From those up all night with infants to others juggling school pick-up schedules, parents need to be able to choose an assistantship that meets their needs. For me, it was continuing to teach rather than pushing me toward more administrative positions. For others, it's precisely having those administrative sorts of positions available that makes parenting while PhDing possible. The structure of the program allowed us to apply for the positions that interested us, and we were almost always given an opportunity to try out what interested us at least once in the program. Beyond the application process, the faculty definitely considered our personal circumstances and worked with us to find alternative assignments when necessary.

RACHEL: And really, faculty should keep in mind the strengths parents bring with them to graduate school. There are a lot of skills–time management, setting boundaries, creating effective routines—that parents can leverage as graduate students and that aren't always recognized.

RECOMMENDATIONS AND KEY TAKEAWAYS FROM OUR EXPERIENCES AS GRADUATE STUDENT PARENTS

Through our stories of mothering across all stages of childhood and adolescence, we have come together to provide recommendations and considerations for prospective PhD student parents and faculty who lead graduate programs. Specifically, we first provide recommendations for student-parents before they join a program and after they are enrolled in a program. Second, we provide recommendations for faculty and administrators who hold positions of power and are capable of influencing the design of such programs to better support student-parents.

Graduate Student Parents

1. Prior to accepting a program offer
   Before applying, look for programs that support a work-life balance through the assistantships they offer and the opportunities available for funding. Talk to faculty about the opportunities available but also seek out the perspectives of current graduate student parents in the program. Ask questions and demand answers before committing to a program:
   - What assistantship opportunities are available to parents that allow for flexibility?
   - What extracurricular commitments are expected from students?
   - How do faculty accommodate students who might have last-minute schedule changes due to childcare or illness?
   - How have previous graduate student parents involved their children in their studies and assistantships?
2. Research the childcare and schools in the area.
   Figure out how transportation, cost, and commute time will impact your work in the graduate program. While these considerations may not seem directly related to your success in the program, finding out that childcare in the area could cost as much as your stipend checks provide would be a shock. Looking into this before committing to a program is essential.
3. Be transparent.
   Explicitly talk about the role of parenting and family in your life before joining a program. Seeing the reactions of faculty and current students can provide a good sense of how parents are treated once they are accepted into the program. Will faculty understand if you need to bring a child to class every once in a while? Will they be prepared to arrange a substitute for your classes if childcare arrangements fall through due to illness?
4. After accepting an offer
   Once you are in a program, choose an advisor who fully supports the role of parenting in your life and will not hold you back when family needs to come first. While we are graduate students, we are also individuals with lives outside of academia. Finding this balance is essential, and a program that is not supportive of parents is likely also not sup-

portive of efforts to create positive learning environments that consider the whole individual.

Faculty and Administrators of Graduate Student Parents

We believe that graduate program faculty and administrators can make specific moves to better support graduate student parents:

- Our first recommendation is that faculty be flexible regarding attendance (allowing for virtual attendance), due dates, and projects.
- Additionally, we recommend that faculty allow students to bring their children to class when necessary. Many of us benefited from the opportunity to bring our children along. This enabled us to remain engaged with the class content and not have to worry about what we were missing.
- Finally, we recommend that the structures of programs themselves be supportive of graduate student parents, as shown through their course offerings, assistantship opportunities, and community gatherings.

CONCLUSION

While supportive faculty can go a long way in helping graduate student parents find success, without a supportive program in place, graduate student parents will continue to face barriers to success. These obstacles also threaten the success of individuals who serve as caretakers, must work full-time jobs, have disabilities or chronic illness, or grapple with other extracurricular demands. Removing the rigidity of traditional programs removes another barrier that is unnecessarily burdensome to so many students.

Our doctoral program not only accepted our lives as parents but provided a space where being a parent was actively supported through faculty involvement, coursework, and assistantship offerings. Graduate student parents bring unique skills into the academy. Our faculty (who are parents themselves) recognized and supported this. We hope that our stories will provide valuable insight for prospective graduate student parents as they enter graduate programs and the faculty who work with such students as shape the future of graduate programming.

NOTE

1. Faculty advocacy for graduate students has led to multiple changes in the program over the past few years, such as decreased assistantship responsibilities, increased stipends,

and more flexibility in coursework offerings. Because of these changes, Morgan, Brandie, Laura, and Rachel were all able to participate fully in the program while still dedicating the necessary time and energy to their families. Importantly, the roles they took on did not exclude or alienate them from the program community; if anything, the program structure and policies for GTAs discussed below strengthened the program community by helping students (especially student-parents) feel welcomed and supported.

WORKS CITED

Sallee, M. W. 2015. "Adding Academics to the Work/Family Puzzle: Graduate Student Parents in Higher Education and Student Affairs." *Journal of Student Affairs Research and Practice* 52 (4): 401–413. https://doi-org.uc.idm.oclc.org/10.1080/19496591.2015.1083438.

Springer, K. W., B. K. Parker, and C, Leviten-Reid. 2009. "Making Space for Graduate Student Parents: Practice and Politics." *Journal of Family Issues* 30 (4): 435–457. https://doi.org/10.1177/0192513X08329293.

Yoo, H. J., and D. T. Marshall. 2022. "Understanding Graduate Student Parents: Influence of Parental Status, Gender, and Major on Graduate Students' Motivation, Stress, and Satisfaction." *Journal of College Student Retention: Research, Theory & Practice* 26 (1): 259–282. https://doi.org/10.1177/15210251211072241.

34 ▸ IT'S NOT ALL SUNSHINE AND RAINBOWS

Mentoring Graduate Student Parents in the Writing Center

JENNIFER PHILLIPS-DENNY

I BEGAN MANAGING A campus writing center in 2011 during what I consider the sunshine and rainbows years of parenting. My son was eight, the age when parents start to regain some of the freedom that a child's developing independence brings. Nine-year-olds embody wonderment, what Piaget defined as the concrete operational stage (Piaget and Barbel 1972). Gone were the days of diapers and tantrums; instead, our days were filled with adventure as my son was creating a decentered worldview. My son grew up for most of his life with the writing center at the center of my professional life. These sunshine years of motherhood nicely coincided with my move into managing the labor and logistics of the writing center and was a time when I had ample reserves of emotional labor to dedicate to student clients and tutors.

While I have been parenting, I have also been mentoring and supervising undergraduate and graduate student writing tutors. Although some of these graduate students have been tutoring while completing coursework, they have also been or are themselves currently parenting. In the early days of managing a writing center, I never thought much about the emotional labor that goes into tutoring writing, or the emotional labor of being a parent, even though I had done and was doing both. Tutoring and parenting share that ultimate test of one's own emotional regulation: deliberate patience. A contemplation of why some of us are patient and some of us aren't, what specific firing of neurons keeps some people feeling like they're always in a hurry, is beyond our scope here. Suffice it to say that writing center work demands a great deal of emotional labor. Nelson and colleagues (2020) point out that this emotional labor takes place at many levels.

In the administrative realm, writing center administrators are faced with funding challenges that often require us to advocate for our services by soliciting money from other campus entities. At the center level, our days are full of emotional work, mentoring tutors, collaborating with campus partners, and promoting our center. I always understood that the production and management of emotions, emotional labor, is a component of my job and my role as a parent, just as it is for graduate student tutors. I have long tried to implement clear boundaries to reduce emotional labor for everyone in the long term, and in this piece, I reflect on my experiences managing and mentoring the graduate student parents under me and how I might recommend that others move differently. Particularly through the lens of the gender-based systematic inequities, we as writing center administrators might more carefully consider the specifics of boundaries, policies, and outreach on a case-by-case basis.

THE (PARENTAL) GENDER GAP

Since I work at a university that primarily serves women, it's no surprise that I've had more mothers than fathers tutor in the writing center while pursuing graduate degrees. The demographics of my writing center staff and clients represent my university's overall demographic of 13 percent men to 87 percent women (Texas Woman's University 2023). But over time I have come to see how the toll the emotional labor of tutoring, just like parenting, takes is based on a variety of external factors.

The first writing tutor I had who became an expectant parent was a male undergraduate early in the first years of my position. He was the only man then working in the writing center, and we joyfully planned a baby shower for him and then enjoyed baby visits once the baby was born. Aside from perhaps the first week after his baby was born and perhaps some sleepless nights here and there, parenting didn't outwardly affect his attendance or performance in the writing center. I didn't think much of it at the time, but later, another expectant father was again lavished with baby gifts, and like the fathers before him, he shared baby pictures between tutoring sessions on his first day back but generally returned to the writing center with minimal discussion about how he was juggling his graduate work, his other job as a paramedic, his work as a graduate assistant in the writing center, and a new baby.

Another father who worked as a tutor while pursuing his graduate degree seemed to have a much more complicated family dynamic. The emotional labor of parenting seemed to take more of a toll on him, but since he never offered many details, I didn't ask, although I supported him on a few occasions when he asked if he could bring his nine-year-old child to work. When I reflect on the experiences of these fathers compared to the connections I share below with women graduate student parents, I realize that I failed to build connection and mentorship in those moments. By failing to engage graduate student fathers in talk about the emotional labor involved in both tutoring and parenting, I missed the opportunity to mentor them about balancing graduate school, tutoring, and parenting. This mentorship is particularly important for writing center directors to reflect on now more than ever before. Millennial graduate students expect mentorship and encouragement from their supervisors. That mentorship involves talking about and modeling the juggling act of our various identities and the emotional labor associated with them, regardless of gender.

In retrospect, I suspect I attended more to the emotional labor of women parents in the writing center because I was trying to offset the fact that women writers are already performing within a patriarchal system that has systematically attempted to silence women's voices (Cixous 1976, 875). Moreover, feminists have extensively explored how women perform the disproportionate amount of emotional labor in both the workplace and the household since Arlie Hochschild coined the term "emotional labor" in her work *The Managed Heart*. Emotional labor, as defined by Hochschild, is "labor that requires one to induce or suppress feeling in order to sustain the outward countenance that produces the proper state of mind in others"

(1972, 20). Since women write and mother within the patriarchy, it goes without saying that the patriarchy has expectations that women will induce or suppress their feelings (the process) in order to write in a way that supports the patriarchy (the product). But all things considered, perhaps I have been remiss in discerning that graduate student fathers may also fall victim to gender roles.

BUILDING BRIDGES BETWEEN RAINBOWS AND STORMCLOUDS

That acknowledged, I have easily connected with many of the graduate student mothers who have tutored in the writing center over our shared mothering experiences. In some cases discourse about parenting was the only water-cooler talk I ever engaged in with these tutors. Several of the mothers I have supervised have set firm boundaries separating work and parenting that I admire, not only as a feminist and mother but also as a supervisor. Stephanie, a mother of two school-aged children, and I built an immediate rapport. As a mother with an adult son, I loved hearing stories about her kids, and we commiserated over the challenges of parenting in today's world. She was very clear in her work boundaries and had limited availability, but she was also incredibly present, all vibrant energy, during her working time. Welcoming our students back to campus after the pandemic, she promoted the writing center at our new student orientations and resource fairs with her effervescent personality. While many of us in the writing center were still trying to reacclimate to being around people after working remotely for over a year, she managed the transition to postpandemic public speaking seamlessly. Paying forward the flexibility my previous chairs and managers had given me as a mother, I worked to be flexible with Stephanie and our other parents who needed to schedule their academic work during school hours. I certainly can't begrudge Stephanie the inflexibility of her schedule, especially when her performance, just as this season of her parenting, was sunshine and rainbows.

But storms can penetrate those boundaries, so when things aren't sunshine and roses, writing center administrators are uniquely situated to hand a parenting graduate tutor that metaphorical umbrella. That umbrella should be a mentoring approach that acknowledges the complex web that is the emotional labor of parent, scholar, writer, and tutor. One strategy that I found successful as a first line of support for any overwhelmed tutor is offering them a schedule change, empowering such graduate students to rearrange blocks of time. Although a schedule change was ineffective for one graduate assistant tutor, I have seen graduate student parents turn their semester around simply by changing their writing center schedule.

One mother, for example, was consistently running late for her shifts. She is a person with a vibrant presence who whizzed into the writing center about three minutes late most days—often while a student writer was waiting for her. In all other ways, this graduate student fit the academy's definitions of professionalism, so as three minutes late turned to seven minutes late and then ten minutes late over several shifts, I called her into my office. She stormed into my office and folded herself into the office chair across from my desk and unloaded.

"I know I'm late everyday" she said defensively. "I'm sorry, but there isn't anything I can do about it."

Her anger broke, and on the verge of tears, she continued, "I can't get through the fucking car line at the elementary school, and no one will help me get my daughter to kindergarten. I'm so frustrated. She takes the bus to my mom's house every day after school, but I have to take her. I'm always running late everyday, and then I'm all stressed out the whole rest of the day. And I can't even focus. This is too hard, and I should probably just quit."

"Would it be helpful if we changed your writing center schedule?" I asked.

She questioned, "Is that even possible at this point? You said that the schedule was set."

I explained, "What I mean by a set schedule is that our work schedule is the same each week. That doesn't mean that we can't change it."

She started crying, "I thought that I wasn't allowed to change it, but I didn't know how long the car line was going to take. Oh my god, if I could change my schedule by one hour that would literally change my life."

While handing her a tissue, I laughed and said, "Well, I don't know about that. But we can definitely start your day out a little bit less rushed."

She left my office smiling when she had thought she would be in trouble. After a simple schedule change, this graduate student mother seemed much less stressed and even brought her daughter to the writing center for Bring your Daughter to Work Day. This is just one example of a kind of metaphorical umbrella writing center administrators can hold over graduate student parents when the sunshine and rainbows become a storm of emotional labor.

The other umbrellas we can offer our graduate assistant parents are more obvious after the past few years, primarily the flexibility to work from home on online writing consultations, but also scheduling more breaks throughout the workday. Some days, I offer lower-level emotional labor tasks when a graduate student parent is overwhelmed (Nelson et al. 2020, 171). Tasks, such as creating handouts, developing workshops/presentations, organizing supplies, running campus errands, or reading and annotating an article that could benefit the center can give tutors a break from the deliberate patience that the best writing tutors bring to every session. We also learned in the pandemic that doing something different, even for a day, stimulates different parts of the brain and can increase energy and decrease boredom. Although writing center budgets are pervasively underfunded and understaffed, low emotional labor days with different tasks would benefit all writing center tutors, but especially graduate student parents who are already carrying a heavy emotional load. A compromise I've adopted is that some days tutors have only asynchronous online appointments, which require significantly less emotional labor than live tutorial sessions.

ENCOUNTERING THE STORM

But when things aren't sunshine and rainbows, navigating the emotional labor of writing center work and parenting may be more than our graduate students can or should have to bear. As my family, especially my father, and friends will attest, I am rarely in a hurry and generally operate on the assumption that nothing is particularly urgent. I'm just wired with deliberate patience that has suited me well, I think, to both parenting and writing center work. But in a few instances, that deliberate patience has been tested when efforts to create flexibility have been pushed too far.

In one instance, a mother who was a graduate assistant in the writing center seemed highly involved in the drama of her three teenaged children, but she enthusiastically accepted a position in the writing center. This graduate assistant tutor frequently needed to request time off during her regularly scheduled shifts for shifts for her children's multiple appointments and events, but she was communicative about her requests and during shifts was a highly effective and rhetorically sophisticated tutor. Unfortunately, over time I observed that the emotional labor of parenting three teens while pursuing a master's degree and tutoring writing started to chip away at the deliberate patience on which writing center work is predicated. The feedback she gave students became more terse and less substantive. She started calling in sick for "emergencies" quite often. I changed her work schedule to help her chunk her time and create better flow in her work week, but she wanted the freedom to tweak her schedule on a weekly basis, vexing the other tutors and creating tension in the writing center. My patience began to run out when another graduate student tutor and I were forced to complete her missed online appointments until late into the evening on a Friday night.

Another mother was assigned to work in the writing center as a graduate student tutor through a cross-training program. Influenced by her faculty who looked down on writing center directors as administrators rather than teacher-scholars, this tutor seemed distant and reluctant about her assignment in the writing center. Her attitude seemed to change abruptly, however, when it was time for her to attend a series of her daughter's elite sporting events, and it felt like she suddenly tried to bond with me about mothering and youth sports since I was a city youth soccer coach that year. I felt an element of manipulation, although I acknowledge that it could have been unintentional on her part. She needed something from me, but she performed the emotional labor of letting me know how important it was to her. I obviously was happy to give her the days off for her daughter's soccer games. Why wouldn't I? But I soon realized that she wasn't really asking me if she could miss those shifts; she was telling me she wouldn't be at work. She was asserting her boundary that for that week, she would be putting all her physical and emotional labor into motherhood.

BALANCING THE LOADS

Much has been written and discussed about the extra emotional load women carry, and conversations about emotional labor have made their way into writing center discourse (Nelson et al. 2020). Because our writing tutors are students, many of them graduate students, they know, and I understand, that their parenting is takes precedence over their schooling and their schooling takes precedence over their tutoring work. Given the emotional labor required for effective tutoring, it's especially important for writing center directors to encourage graduate student parents to confidently set boundaries around their parenting, schooling, and tutoring work. As Dr. Allessandria Polizzi, an occupational health and safety liaison, explains, "Societal norms and expectations of being on display deeply influence how women feel empowered to establish boundaries. When you live in a world where strangers think it is appropriate to stop you and tell you to smile, boundaries aren't something you are expected to have." Mothers especially should be encouraged to state clear boundaries around their labor, which is often more difficult for women, especially women of color, and especially in the workplace. Dr. Polizzi further explains how those in helping jobs have a high risk of compassion fatigue that can result in serious mental and physical health issues (Verdant Consulting 2022). This dynamic makes it even more important for them to set boundaries. While conversations about boundaries are potentially awkward and uncomfortable for both parties, if writing center administrators can move through them with a collaborative mindset, we can better serve our goals of mentorship for our student employees and support for our student writers.

This feels especially critical since our newest parents who will be coming up, our Gen Z graduate students, have lived through a variety of catastrophes, such as the pandemic, climate crises, and civil unrest escalating to the insurrection, to name a few. Managing and training this next generation with what I perceive as a strong survivalist mindset means that we will need to engage with their assumption of flexibility that seems greater than for any previous generation of graduate students who have entered the halls of academia, not to mention the American workforce. I would describe their hallmarks as evolved expectations of mental health wellness, inclusivity, and acceptance from those who came before them, change that seemingly demands more emotional labor from administrators.

We might do well to remember that these hallmarks also reflect values that can only enrich the writing center environment. Expectations of wellness inclusivity, and acceptance challenge us to embody an ethos of dialogic learning, where respect and shared-knowledge building are lived out in the writing center. At its core, the writing center has always been meant to be a space of intentional flexibility.

So while the expectations of Gen Z graduate student parents who are writing center tutors might bring complex administrative challenges, the hallmarks of this generation are reinvigorating our spaces with the sunshine and rainbows of writing center work.

WORKS CITED

Cixous, Helene. 1976. "The Laugh of the Medusa." Translated by Keith and Paula Cohen. *Signs* 1 (4):. 41–50.

Hochschild, Arlie Russell. 2012. *The Managed Heart*. 3rd ed. University of California Press, 2012.

Nelson, Matthew T., Sam Deges, and Kathleen F. Weaver. 2020. "Making Visible the Emotional Labor of Writing Center Work." In *The Things We Carry: Strategies for Recognizing and Negotiating Emotional Labor in Writing Program Administration*. edited by Courtney Adams Wooten, Jacob Babb, Kristi Murray Costello, and Kate Navickas, 161–175. Utah State University Press.

Piaget, Jean, and Barbel Inhelder. 1972. *The Psychology of the Child*. Basic Books.

Texas Woman's University. 2023, May 23. "Fact Book." *Texas Woman's University*. twu.edu/institutional-research/fact-book/. Accessed May 25, 2023.

Verdant Consulting. 2022, September 10. Interview with Allessandria Polizzi. Transcript in author's possession.

35 ▸ MY PLACE IN THE WOLFPACK

The Importance of Cultivating MyPacks and Providing Student Parents with Opportunities to Belong

JACQUELINE CERDA-SMITH

For the strength of the Pack is the Wolf, and the strength of the Wolf is the Pack. —RUDYARD KIPLING, *The Jungle Book*

MY DECISION TO APPLY for graduate school in 2019 after teaching public school for seven years was not an easy one because I thought that being a good mom was incompatible with being a good doctoral student. With my husband as an MD/PhD student, I worried that we wouldn't have enough time, money, and energy to parent effectively and earn our respective degrees, but his encouragement gave me the push I needed to apply. I was six months pregnant when I started a doctoral program in developmental psychology at North Carolina State University (NC State) amid the COVID pandemic. Now I am a doctoral candidate, our daughter is a toddler, and we have another baby on the way. Overall, I am proud about how we balanced our roles as parents and doctoral students. That said, my journey was difficult and has highlighted several areas in which students, faculty members, and institutions can do much more to support student-parent belonging.

The entire grad and undergrad student body at NC State is referred to as "the Wolfpack," suggesting an inherent sense of belonging, psychological membership, and connection within the institution. However, the institution currently offers few policies that support pregnant and parenting students despite its strategic plan to champion a culture of equity, inclusion, well-being, and belonging (North Carolina State University 2022, 10–11). NC State is not an anomaly. Institutions of higher education were designed for childless students and therefore pose obstacles for student-parent success and belonging (Lewis 2021). Thus, in order to truly create a Wolfpack[1] for all, institutions and faculty members have a responsibility to purposefully provide interpersonal, instructional, and institutional opportunities that foster belonging for marginalized individuals (Gray et al. 2018). More specifically, interpersonal opportunities build peer and student-teacher connections, instructional opportunities bridge students' lived experiences to course content, and institutional opportunities change structural practices and policies to address the needs of marginalized groups (Gray et al. 2018).

The personal experiences I describe below demonstrate how these three opportunity structures can support student-parents and reaffirm their belonging in higher education. Given those experiences, however, I also wanted to highlight the importance of student-parents cultivating their own packs (MyPacks) composed of similarly situated individuals that make them feel acknowledged, valued, and welcome, in order to combat and overcome barriers in graduate school.

STARTING MYPACK: CHOOSING AN ADVISOR

When I was applying and interviewing for graduate school, I knew I needed to find an advisor who would support my professional and personal goals, but I felt uncertain about when and how I should ask prospective mentors about navigating parenting during graduate school. Would it be considered inappropriate to do so in the interview? Would it reflect poorly on me as an applicant? Could it inhibit my chances of being accepted? I saved this conversation until I was deciding which program to accept. Dr. Kelly Lynn Mulvey, who would become my mentor, solidified my choice to go to NC State when she responded, "Graduate school is a great time to have kids. I had all my kids in grad school!" Since then, Dr. Mulvey has shared her experiences as a doctoral student-parent, helped me access resources (e.g., lactation rooms, funding opportunities), and advocated for my childcare needs at NC State and with our funding agency. Dr. Mulvey's support has been unwavering, which is why she is a primary (alpha, if you will) member of MyPack.

INITIAL BARRIERS TO CULTIVATING MYPACK

My first year of graduate school was during the height of the COVID-19 pandemic (2020–2021), which posed unique challenges to building meaningful relationships with peers. Despite the best intentions of instructors, organic, relationship-building conversations did not happen in virtual classes. I also felt out of place compared to other doctoral students, which exacerbated the difficulties posed by online learning. I had recently turned thirty, whereas my classmates were in their early twenties. While I was researching baby gear or waking up five times a night to pee or nurse, I enviously imagined that my peers were drinking rosé, eating soft cheeses, and sleeping soundly. Everyone was friendly, but I felt so different, a lone wolf.

A lack of supportive policies and networks at NC State also limited my ability to cultivate MyPack and discouraged any sense of belonging to the Wolfpack during my first two years of graduate school. Research indicates most student-parents have children who are preschool aged or younger (Hensly et al. 2021), so having access to affordable and convenient childcare is an important factor in student- parent well-being and retention (Wladis et al. 2018). Unfortunately, the number of colleges and universities that offer on-campus care has decreased steadily in the last fifteen years, especially since the onset of COVID-19 (Field 2021). With both my husband and I in graduate school, finding affordable childcare was tricky. We make enough money to not qualify for welfare programs, but not enough to comfortably afford the cost of quality, full-time care, which is necessary to complete our degrees. Given the high demand for childcare in our area, we secured a spot for our daughter at a reasonably priced center (about $1,100 per month, approximately 55 percent of my income) well before she was born. We planned to enroll her at three months old, but when the time came, no spots were available due to staffing issues related to the pandemic.

After spending an entire semester as a full-time doctoral student and full-time parent, I couldn't persist without childcare. We frantically searched for other options but every place was full and waitlists were over a year long. I thought I found hope in NC State's webpage for graduate student parents, which directed me to another university webpage listing partnerships with local childcare centers offering subsidized rates. I was relieved when a center director informed me of an immediate opening. After enrolling my daughter, NC State denied the subsidized rate, saying that it was offered only to staff, faculty, and postdocs. We couldn't afford the regular rate (about $1,800 per month, approximately 90 percent of my income), and that put my family in a very precarious position. Eventually, friends who weren't graduate students connected us to an opening at their center.

I sent a letter to several university administrators describing my experiences and concerns about the lack of childcare support for student-parents. In response, the graduate school initiated a task force that explored ways to support the childcare needs of student-parents. This group met several times in 2021–2022 but disbanded at the end of the academic year. Although individual group members sympathized with my situation and recognized it as a larger issue, their work was slow due to the bureaucratic system and a dearth of knowledge about the student-parent population at NC State. As far I am aware, no changes were made despite their efforts.

The institution had shown me again there was no place for me in their Wolfpack.

After this experience, I realized that I needed other student-parents in MyPack, as those connections would have enabled us all to build a support network, pool our resources, and collectively advocate for our needs. I was the only parenting doctoral student in my program. In the absence of interdisciplinary formal or informal student-parent networks (like a student-parent association or social media groups), I found it difficult to connect with other student-parents. I tried to initiate these networks one summer by creating a Facebook group and a brief survey for student-parents, but I didn't have the time needed to bring those efforts to fruition. After all, I was barely able to keep up with my parenting and graduate school responsibilities while showering on a semi-regular basis. Taking hours of unpaid time to cultivate MyPack by seeking out and organizing parents across the university would have been detrimental to my well-being and scholarly productivity.

NONPARENTING STUDENTS JOIN MYPACK

I began to feel a greater sense of interpersonal belonging in my second year with the return of in-person classes because I got to know my peers. Our relationships bloomed in little moments that are often overlooked, like asking how someone's weekend was before class or complaining in solidarity about upcoming assignments. Graduate school is hard for everyone. Generally, I've found that nonparenting doctoral students have considerable respect for parenting students because they recognize the additional cognitive, emotional, and practical demands that come with raising kids.

I felt especially seen when my nonparenting peers listened to and empathized with me as I shared some of the frustrations I faced as a doctoral student-parent. They went above and beyond to support me during a final class project. We proposed a new model of on-campus childcare that leveraged older adult volunteers as teaching assistants in the childcare center in order to minimize childcare costs for student-parents, offer high-quality care, and promote well-being for all. After the class finished, my classmates put in hours of work to prepare and present our model to NC State's Graduate School Childcare Task Force. This made me feel seen and valued.

MyPack was growing.

In my third year, I received valuable support and encouragement from a nonparenting student, Deveshwar Hariharan, the president of the Graduate Student Association (GSA). After sharing my concerns about lack of institutional support for student-parents with the Graduate School Childcare Task Force that he served on, Devesh helped me navigate the process of founding the Student Parent Association and adopting it as a GSA special interest group to elevate student-parents' voice and power within the graduate school. He simultaneously pushed to amend the GSA constitution to provide for special-interest-group funding. He also connected me with others at the university interested in supporting student-parents. These experiences exemplify the support that nonparenting doctoral students gave me and highlight the importance of including nonparenting allies in MyPack.

EXPANDING MYPACK: FACULTY SUPPORT

The biggest ways my professors supported me is by being flexible and by accommodating my parenting needs when they clashed with course expectations. In addition to allowing me to join class via Zoom when my daughter was sick, a few examples from the 2021 spring semester stand out. That semester was very rough because for the entire fifteen weeks, I was a full-time doctoral student and a full-time parent to a newborn. My daughter was just five weeks old when classes started. Per NC State's policy, I could not take maternity leave because I had been at the university for less than a year. Thankfully, all of my classes were online. Before the semester, I communicated my needs and childcare situation to my professors. They allowed me to mute my camera and microphone when I needed to, understanding that I was simply unable to participate at times. During that hellish semester, instructors also recorded their lectures and posted them online for all students. Postpandemic, all classes are automatically recorded using Panopto and can be shared with student-parents and others with extenuating circumstances. I frequently missed parts of class to feed, change, and soothe my daughter (and myself). I was so sleep deprived that even when ~~she wasn't~~ we weren't crying, I struggled to concentrate and follow along. Being able to save and access instructional materials later was the only way that I kept up with my courses. I still review those materials to this day because the newborn phase is essentially a black hole in my memory.

My instructors in the developmental psychology program also provided opportunities to connect and share my parenting experiences in class. This gave me the time and space to explore research that was personally relevant, and that informed my parenting practices and advocacy work. I recognize that my department's accommodating and supportive culture is likely shaped by the intrinsic value members assign to parenting. Although other program areas might not be able to provide opportunities for student-parents to connect their parenting roles to class content, all faculty members should be capable of offering student-parents grace and flexibility. Having faculty members in MyPack makes me feel like my identity as a parent is valued in academia.

CULTIVATING MYPACK WITH INSTITUTIONAL SUPPORT

In 2022, I applied for and received a small diversity grant ($1,000) offered by NC State's College of Humanities and Social Sciences that funded my previously attempted but failed efforts to understand student-parent experiences and needs and build both informal and formal networks of student-parents on campus. This funding enabled me to give back to the university by founding the Student Parent Association and providing some much-needed information about NC State's student-parent population, while furthering my personal research agenda, getting additional compensation, and cultivating MyPack. As a result, I began to see myself as part of the larger Wolfpack and understood the strength that student-parents can provide their Wolfpacks when given the support to do so.

MY LESSONS LEARNED

In reflecting on my graduate school experiences, I've realized how interpersonal, instructional, and institutional opportunities have supported my sense of belonging as a parent. Given the limited support of the Wolfpack, my experiences highlight the importance of cultivating MyPacks that empower student-parents to break through barriers to belonging and succeeding in higher education (Lewis 2021). I end this chapter by summarizing the key lessons I learned throughout my journey that might inform ways that future student-parents, nonparenting students, faculty members, and institutions can foster a welcoming place for student-parents within their respective Wolfpacks.

1. *Advocating for myself:* Initiating conversations about my parenting needs with my advisor, faculty members, and peers helped me receive accommodations necessary for my success, persistence, and belonging in graduate school. Although initiating these conversations felt awkward at times, making my priorities and expectations clear was crucial to selecting the right mentor and members of MyPack who value my family, respect my boundaries, and are willing to advocate on my behalf.
2. *Advocating for other student parents*: After facing institutional barriers, I thought that there was not a place for student-parents in the Wolfpack. I saw this as inequitable and decided to initiate conversations about policies and programs that limited my ability to succeed as a student-parent with classmates, faculty members, advisors, and university administrators. My ability as an individual to affect change was limited, so I had to cultivate and lean on MyPack for support.
3. *The importance of nonparenting student allies*: The support I received from nonparenting peers helped me feel a sense of belonging at the interpersonal and institutional levels. My nonparenting peers have offered interpersonal support by validating my frustrations about balancing school and family responsibilities, accommodating my schedule by meeting at a time that might not be ideal for them, and introducing me to other student-

parents. They even babysit for free! Nonparenting peers have also offered institutional support by advocating for student-parent access to childcare benefits, connecting me to campus groups and resources that can support student-parents, and helping me navigate the system to found the Student Parent Association and gain political power for student-parents in the GSA.

4. *The importance of faculty allies*: Faculty members have been flexible and accommodating while maintaining high expectations for me. When I ask, they allow me to join classes or meetings online, work during nontraditional hours or in unexpected locations, and reschedule meetings. Most instructors post their instructional materials online, which helps me if I need to leave or skip a class or have trouble concentrating. Some faculty members also share their own parenting experiences and attempts (successful and unsuccessful) to manage work and family responsibilities. At times, faculty members have connected me to resources at the university and in the field and have advocated for these resources on my behalf if they do not exist. Faculty members might also consider including a statement in their syllabus that acknowledges student-parents and invites them to share their parenting-related needs as well as educating themselves about policies and resources available to student-parents at their institution.
5. *Recognizing and removing institutional barriers*: Student-parents strengthen their Wolfpacks when institutions acknowledge and support their needs. NC State did not have any data about its student-parent population. It was unwilling to change inequitable policies or practices without this information but took minimal effort to gather it. With NC State's funding support, I collected this data, but it was difficult without established informal or formal student-parent networks on campus. Institutions of higher education should leverage their resources to collect data on student-parents' needs and policy recommendations. Institutions might also (a) consider student-parents as a minoritized group that is at risk for dropping out (U.S. Government Accountability Office 2019); (b) include student-parents in policies that support diversity, equity, and inclusion; (c) actively seek out student-parents to serve on committees or policy boards and pay them for these positions; (d) establish or maintain childcare benefits for student-parents; (e) host a special event for student-parents and their children to help them connect; and (f) coordinate with mental health counselors to form support groups for parenting students.
6. *The need for support from funding agencies and foundations*: Receiving financial support to conduct research on and initiate networks of student-parents

was vital to finding my place in the Wolfpack and contributed to the institution's strategic mission to support diversity, equity, and inclusion. To my knowledge, *no* funding sources specifically target or mention student-parents. Many grants or fellowships target traditionally underserved populations but refer specifically to racial/ethnic identity, gender identity, disability status, and so forth. Student-parents should also be considered as an underserved and vulnerable population. However, institutions have yet to recognize their status and offer support. Funding agencies and foundations might consider offering childcare grants or fellowships specifically for doctoral student-parents.

NOTE

1. Throughout this chapter "MyPack" is used to represent individuals that support my sense of interpersonal connection whereas "Wolfpack" is used to represent a broader sense of connection to the institution.

WORKS CITED

Field, Kelly. 2021. "The Pandemic Accelerates a Decline in Campus-Based Child Care." *Chronicle of Higher Education,* December 15. https://www.chronicle.com/article/the-pandemic-accelerates-a-decline-in-campus-based-child-care

Gray, DeLeon L., Elan C. Hope, and Jamaal S. Matthews. 2018. "Black and Belonging at School: A Case for Interpersonal, Instructional, and Institutional Opportunity Structures." *Educational Psychologist* 53 (2): 97–113.

Hensly, Catherine, Chaunté White, and Lindsey Reichlin Cruse. 2021. *Re-Engaging Student Parents to Achieve Attainment and Equity Goals: A Case for Investment in More Accessible Postsecondary Pathways.* Institute for Women's Policy Research. https://iwpr.org/wp-content/uploads/2021/07/Re-Engaging-Student-Parents-to-Achieve-Attainment-Goals_FINAL.pdf.

Lewis, Nicole Lynn. 2021. "How Colleges Tell Student-Parents They Don't Belong." *The Atlantic,* May 26.

North Carolina State University. 2022. *Wolfpack 2030: Powering the Extraordinary.* https://strategicplan.ncsu.edu/wp-content/uploads/2023/03/21-PROV-1088-strategic-plan-layout-2021-2030-3.pdf.

U.S. Government Accountability Office. 2019, August 20. "Higher Education: More Information Could Help Student Parents Access Additional Federal Student Aid." https://www.gao.gov/products/gao-19-522.

Wladis, Claire, Alyse C. Hachey, and Katherine Conway. 2018. "No Time for College? An Investigation of Time Poverty and Parenthood." *Journal of Higher Education* 89 (6): 807–831.

36 ▸ RACE AT YOUR OWN PACE

A Story of How Caregiving Sometimes Means Changing Lanes or Start Times in Graduate School

JOAN JIYOUNG HWANG

GOOD GRIEF! TOMORROW *the property tax is due! Thank God. I didn't miss it, at least.* My planner is buried under a pile of journal article printouts, bills, and scattered Post-its. Luckily, I have marked the due date on my calendar with a bright highlighter, so this time, I won't miss it.

Missing due dates is not uncommon anymore, but the feeling of failure or inadequacy when I do miss them persists. As I look for the tax invoice, my younger son bangs open the door: "Mom, I am not feeling well. My head hurts."

Yes, here it goes.

The second draft of my prospectus is due in two weeks and meetings are lined up for the coming weeks: department meetings, workshops, and program meetings where I will contribute readings or presentations. As if these hectic days are not enough, my kitchen sink has been leaking since yesterday. I do a quick emergency fix, but the leaking is getting worse and it doesn't look like my repair will last through the next few weeks until I get through the urgent deadlines. I text my handyman, but he replies that he is out of town and won't be back until a week later. Gee. It's Saturday. Tomorrow I am supposed to drive my older son back to his college at the end of his fall break. The prospectus is far from being in good enough shape to be sent to my chair. The younger one's fever is now approaching 99 degrees.

Does all this sound like a theatrical script? This is not a dramatization. Being unable to prioritize chaos happens whether your children are infants or in elementary school or even in high school and college. These events unfolded at a time when I had only one week to submit a manuscript for my chapter proposal. As the saying goes, when it rains, it pours. Unexpected accidents hit at the busiest point in the semester or near the end of the term when something is due every other day: returning feedback to students, completing grading, attending conferences, finishing term papers, or presenting a final project in my doctoral courses. The accidents happen in various ways: visits to a pediatrics office during the flu season, coping with a flat tire while picking up my child from his tennis practice, encountering a dead car battery in the morning, finding that a garage door won't open even in manual mode, or getting locked out of the house with my cell phone and my wallet inside.

I have run into all types of emergencies and I don't have any extra hands to borrow: I have neither a spouse nor parents. I am a single parent on an international student visa in a PhD program.

I sometimes feel eerily uncomfortable when things don't go wrong, like on Sunday mornings in July. I am more uneasy when I am less busy. My seasons are divided into three periods: pre-storm, storm, and post-storm. So I learned to draft rescue plans and practice drills during the period of pre-storm with my children. When the storm hits, I stay calm and tackle one at a time. Post-storm, I gather myself and give myself some breaks. I am alone throughout these seasons. My children grew up hearing me say, "Forewarned is forearmed."

Despite my preparation, something always falls out of the range of my control. Then I have to go with my gut. I am afforded no time or luxury to weep or lament because I don't have parents who can pick up my children from their sports practices to take them to the emergency room when they are severely injured or drive them to the bus stop in the morning when their schools open two hours late due to inclement weather but my class begins at 9 A.M. *Get up and move,* even when you have no plan. *Ideas will follow.*

Meanwhile, I am becoming less shocked, less frightened, and I criticize myself less often. I have grown more immune to, I have adapted to, and I have become confident about dealing with unexpectedness and disappointment. My perspective has changed since I accepted that life is not supposed to unfold as planned and that that's okay. *No plan is perfect, and any plan can go wrong.* So then what can I do? Is there anything I can do better? Yes and no. Sometimes there are lessons to be learned. But sometimes there is nothing else you can do but stand mindlessly and wait for the storm to clear. Still, in those moments, I learned that hardships strengthen not fail me even when I have had to take a detour down a long and winding road, especially for someone like me who carries multiple identities: a single parent, a teacher, a student, a researcher, a colleague, and a firstborn child in an Asian family.

In 2012, I was working as a research assistant after completing a master's degree in English at George Mason University when my department announced that it would launch a doctoral program in writing and rhetoric the following year. My advisor, who had hired me as a research intern, strongly recommended I apply to the PhD program and continue to work on my research project. I was a single mother without local family or support and my mother had come for a long-term visit to help me with my children, who were aged eight and seven. In that same year, however, she fainted, was transported to the emergency room, and was diagnosed with a rare case of malignant bone marrow cancer. She returned to Korea for treatment immediately. A year before that, my brother, who had obtained a doctoral degree in genetic science in the United States, was hired in a tenure-track position in one of the prestigious medical schools in my home country. I naturally thought that he could nurse our sick mother because he had finally secured his position in academia. I felt that it was now my turn to plan for graduate study in a doctoral program. At the same time, however, I felt tremendous guilt about passing the role of caretaker to my younger sibling and the fact that I would be 7,000 miles away from my cancer-fighting mother.

My guilt became compounded when my siblings and other relatives voiced their concerns that my mother would need me most since I was the eldest and she felt most comfortable with me around. I was also the most attached to her of her children, especially since my father passed away in 1993 and she had gone through many legal proceedings that had resulted in the bankruptcy of his business. She'd gradually become fragile, more vulnerable, and more dependent on me. I had given up the plan of applying to a graduate program when my father died and had immediately gotten a job in a financial institution to become the breadwinner for my family until my brother received his tenure-track position.

When I told my mother in 2008 that I was considering applying to a master's program, she was more supportive of my decision than anyone else and came to the United States to look after my children, who were four and three years old at the time. She stayed as long as her traveler's visa permitted, giving me her full support before returning to Korea after several months. She repeated those stays a few times throughout the year until I completed my master's degree. Without the support and care she gave my children and me, I would not have been able to finish the master's degree in time. When I learned about her cancer, I felt guilty. I worried that maybe she had become ill from supporting my children and me across continents. However, although I was disheartened and desperately wanted to be with her, I thought my brother was in a much better position to take on the role of a caregiver than I was. But instead, this time again, it was on me; I was recalled to return. Amid mounting guilt from within myself and outright demands from without, I could not speak up for myself.

However, the situation was not as simple as the issue of whether or not to go back to Korea; it meant a permanent departure from the United States. I would need to reapply for a student visa to return to study in the United States because I had an international student visa. The student visa in the United States strictly requires that international students be enrolled in coursework during the semester and travel overseas only during summer and winter breaks. I was not free to travel to Korea to see my mother except during those academic vacations. Returning to Korea implied that I no longer intended to study in the United States in the program. If I were to return as a student, the likelihood that I would be issued a new student visa was very low and was contingent on policy changes in the United States or between the United States and Korea. As huge and risky as my decision was, my siblings and relatives expected me to return immediately. Their discussion developed into a consensus that I should be the caregiver. The more I delayed my decision, the faster their consensus escalated to collective blame for my hesitation about coming back. I was devastated by their unchanged perspective that it was still my duty because I was a woman, a first-born child in my family, financially more stable than my siblings, and most of all, because they believed that caring for my mother had been my role and responsibility since my father had died in 1993.

What remained unchanged, too, was my lack of courage to speak up for my desire to continue my graduate work. I guess the power of social and cultural expectations outweighed my own desire because I was raised to live up to the expectation that I be a compliant, responsible, exemplary first girl child and to bring honor to my family. Even though I knew that I should be more outspoken about my legitimate desire for independence, I gave in to my feelings of guilt and to the pressure to please others.

I went back to Korea. My beloved mother, who remained quiet at the center of this heated debate, passed away a year later, in 2014. I am grateful that I could be with her in the last year of her life, although that meant a dramatic change in the course of my life. I watched her strong body, which had suffered her father's death during the Korean War and her husband's ten-year battle with cancer, slowly wane and diminish. Yet, as always, she remained calm, positive, graceful, and grateful throughout the year, which included several ambulance trips to the emergency room and multiple hospitalizations, chemotherapies, and radiation therapies. As she had been throughout her life, my mother was very receptive to her situation even when she had every reason to be angry and frustrated about her abrupt illness. She didn't seem desperate to fight cancer. Instead, she was submissive even though her condition was deteriorating. I also sensed that she tried not to elongate her life because she didn't want to be a burden to her children. Until the last moment, she cared more for her daughter more than she did about her own life.

After my mother's death, I applied for a teaching position in Korea. However, even part-time jobs were not readily available to women over forty without any connections in local universities. I submitted dozens of CVs but was never offered a single interview. Positions for writing instructors in colleges in Korea were filled by young graduate students in their late twenties to early thirties or those who had obtained doctoral degrees prior to reaching their mid-thirties. Age and gender matter a lot in my home country. Only after working as a substitute teacher in an international elementary school for a few years was I able to get a job as a full-time assistant teacher. However, to be a full-time classroom teacher in an international school, I needed a US-certified teaching license or the equivalent of a license issued in an English-speaking country. The teaching job in an international school overseas did offer a range of excellent benefits compared to the local schools, which hire only college graduates from domestic undergraduate education programs. So I decided to venture out one more time to make a living for my children as a single parent and applied to a program in the education department at my university that offered a teaching license. In 2017, I returned to Virginia for my second master's degree in education.

When I returned, I dared not consider entering the rigorous academic life of a doctoral student because it was more important for me to secure a stable teaching position in my home country as soon as possible to raise my children. At the same time, I was mindful of my age and my lost confidence. When I returned, I got back in touch with Anna, who was the associate director of the writing center where I had worked as a tutor during my master's program. Sophia, who is an associate director in the composition program now, offered me a position teaching writing courses designed for international undergraduate students. Thanks to Sophia's open-mindedness and trust in someone's potential rather than their proficiency, I began a teaching career, to my great surprise.

Never had I imagined having this kind of opportunity when I returned to the United States. Frankly, I was devastated and exhausted by a series of difficult life events. At the age when my mother lost her husband, I had become a single parent. I had even forgotten that I once desired to study in a doctoral program. Anna's willingness to give an opportunity to someone like me who had minimal teaching experience and was on an international visa opened many more doors that led me to what I am now. One of the professors who observed my teaching suggested that I apply to a doctoral program in writing and rhetoric if I was interested in teaching college writing. Although I still lacked confidence, I gave it a shot and was admitted to the program. A desire I once hoped to pursue that had vanished into a tornado-like life event came back to me six years later in 2019. I became a doctoral student in the writing and rhetoric program on a full-time teaching assistantship.

That experience brought many unexpected and exciting things that I had not known previously. The tuition waiver and the stipends are amazing equal opportunities for international graduate students. More significant than financial gain was finding a sense of belonging in the doctoral program that instantly empowered me with a new layer of identity as an academic professional. This new identity became more influential than my gender, my age, or my marital status. The opportunities that could be taken for granted in US higher education, such as granting full-time assistantships in teaching or research positions with a tuition waiver regardless of a graduate student's immigration status, are more powerful than I had previously thought because they offered me a sense of belonging to a community.

This inclusivity helped change my self-identity to that of a prospective academic who was not just an international student. Being a member of an underrepresented group in a globalized society goes beyond carrying an identity marker; it is emotional baggage that feels like carrying the extra weight of sandbags attached to the ankles or wrists when jogging or running. This new community membership also empowered me to embrace my other identities: an Asian female international graduate student who is a single parent. These are the markers of the marginalized identities I wanted to erase. Once I became more willing to embrace these aspects of my identity, I could confidently embody them. So yes, it is true that being a non-mainstream member of academia comes with additional hurdles to tackle. But they became assets when I persevered and worked with inclusive, supportive faculty and colleagues in a program like mine. I became committed to representing and advocating for multilingual and multicultural faculty and students like myself in other academic communities.

My story is not a story of success or survival that leads to a tenure-track position. Instead, it is an ongoing story of a race that I have been running at my pace. Although my clock was set back by six years, the journey has been full of learning, unlearning, and relearning about life, and my children have observed and shared the lessons I have learned along the way. As I reflect on my journey, I realize that the journey would have never been possible had I not been a mother. As I juggled between the two equally significant roles in my life, I learned to stay focused, positive, hopeful, humble, and patient. Strengths I gained as a mother fed into a source of my power to be a reliable and empathetic colleague. In turn, my passion for teaching and research in my field translated into modeling to my children what it meant to be a member of high integrity in a professional community.

This is also a story of the women in my life and in the program, without whom I would not be what I am today: my mother, a source of my love for my children and work; Anna, my mentor and friend who opened so many doors along my professional path; Courtney, the chair of my dissertation committee, who constantly encouraged me whenever I doubted myself; Sarah, Emily and Esther, the three women I call sister-friends; and all the other women I have met in various academic or professional occasions. Regardless of their marital or parenting status, they have been sources of empowerment that motivated me to stay in my race at my pace.

In April 2024, I successfully defended my dissertation, and I finally graduated with a PhD in writing and rhetoric in May. In the fall semester of 2024, I began working as an assistant professor in the same institution. After almost sixteen years of being a graduate student and a mother of two beautiful children who will soon be young men, I call myself a PhDing mom or a parenting PhD. Either way, the two identities are not in conflict anymore; they are infused into each other.

37 ▸ LEAN ON

Planning For, Insisting On, and Accepting Support

SARA BARTLETT LARGE

Disclaimer: This chapter discusses pregnancy loss

I HAVE A DISTINCT MEMORY of my husband arriving home from work one evening, exhausted, to find both children screaming, the house a mess, dinner half-prepped, and me unshowered, half-dressed, and all but falling apart. I was somewhere in the fifth year of my PhD, on a leave of absence with a two-year-old and a newborn, struggling to finish my dissertation while teaching online. He had started a new job in academic administration at a university in Boston, commuting up to three hours a day on two trains and a bus, working to support us financially in a state with a high cost of living. We both looked at each other, accusingly, thinking, *Why can't you do more*?

In this moment, my husband said, "You're giving 100 percent, I'm giving 100 percent, and somehow we both need to give another 50 percent."

We didn't know where we would find it. This picture of doing it all is precisely what being a parent, especially a mother, in academia looks like, because we were never supposed to do it all.

When women enter traditionally male-dominated fields, including those in academia, we often hear that we need to "lean in," that we need to assert ourselves in a broken structure, navigate it deftly, and do what it takes to "have it all." Yet this neoliberal view ignores the fact that systems and institutions, for the most part, have not changed to support professional mothers in the same way that women at home have always supported professional fathers. As Sallee and colleagues point out, "historically, the ideal professor was not expected to be bothered by family or domestic demands; those were presumably handled by a support system at home, including a wife, domestic help, or some combination thereof" (2016, 191). The model professor in this system is male, and if a woman wants to compete in this system, then she must adhere to these same work-focused values regardless of her roles outside the university.

Academia, a system built on hegemonic masculinity, neoliberalism, and ideal-worker norms, emphasizes competition; performance on research, scholarship, and publication metrics; and dedication to work above all else (Van Engen et al. 2021, 1494). Across disciplines, the academic metrics used to determine success call for uninterrupted attention and commitment to one's academic pursuits and identity, and academia rewards those who are present, visible, and self-sacrificing in this pursuit (Allen et al. 2021; Sallee et al. 2016; Van Engen et al. 2021). This does not leave much space for academic mothers, who face gender norms that also expect them to perform with the same level of dedication and single focus as mothers (Hermann and Neale-McFall 2018; Sallee et al. 2016) while negotiating constant feelings of guilt and shame when they cannot meet the high expectations of both roles (Sutherland 2008). When we fail to do it all, which we inevitably do, we blame ourselves instead of the system.

While on the surface most institutions have implemented family leave policies designed to support employees who give birth or adopt (including in many cases doctoral students with assistantships), these policies vary wildly across institutions, often provide only minimal assistance, and tend to be vague regarding certain aspects of the leave (Zahneis 2023). In many cases, these policies are unpaid solutions that may also negatively impact a student's path to degree. Further, such accommodations are not always enthusiastically supported across campus, and those who do take time may be made to feel that they are showing weakness, missing opportunities, failing to compete, and/or falling behind their peers (Cummins 2017; Sallee et al. 2016; Van Engen et al. 2021). Moreover, such policies do not provide ongoing flexibility and support throughout the PhD and parenthood journey, leaving parents to employ specific discursive strategies to negotiate careers and family within the larger system of academia, strategies that are often constrained by material structures and fail to disrupt the status quo (Van Engen et al. 2021, 1500).

This is why women pursuing an academic life are often told to wait to earn tenure before starting a family, advice that is not given to their male peers. Of course, such advice ignores the realities of the biological clock and the fact that many women struggle with fertility. According to the most recent census data, the average age of first birth for American mothers is thirty years (Morse 2022). Yet the median age a person earns their doctorate degree is thirty-five years old (Kulp 2020, 415), and "the average age when tenure is granted is at 39" (European University Institute n.d.). Thus, the years spent pursuing a PhD and the tenure track tend to coincide with the time frame when many American women start families. Academic women who want to become mothers might delay family planning while also fearing that later might just mean never.

MY STORY PART 1: THE FIRST FOUR YEARS

While I was aware that pursuing an academic life meant choosing a path that does not traditionally value work-life balance, I figured that if I planned carefully enough, I could become a mother while earning my PhD, that I could "do it all." While I could never have imagined trying to write a dissertation between cluster feedings with Daniel Tiger singing in the background, I did understand what it took to make things work—logistically, financially, emotionally—and this was just one more time I was going to do it. I made sure I had a good support system in place. I was married with a husband who was providing part of our income and taking on a fair share of the household responsibilities, and I had chosen a doctoral program that was within driving distance of my husband's parents. At thirty-two years old, I started my PhD in rhetoric and writing studies and we started trying for a baby. If we conceived in September, I would deliver in June and have a pre-made maternity leave in the summer. I got pregnant on our first try, setting my plan in motion. I was a strong woman, ready to face any challenges ahead.

I miscarried at six weeks. I didn't tell anyone in my program and I didn't skip a beat. I went to class the next day, worked my tutoring shift in the Writing

Center, and wrote a paper about peer review. I filled my days and my mind with coursework and teaching to distract me from the loss, and at night, I grieved between pages of journal articles on my reading couch in a room I hoped to one day turn into a nursery. As I healed, I realized that having a child was not something that I could fit neatly into a plan and that if it was something I wanted badly enough, I'd have to figure out a way to make my life accommodate my dream instead, even if it meant giving birth in the middle of a semester. So that January, after my body had fully healed, we tried again. Again I got pregnant almost immediately.

When I began bleeding just before my six-week appointment, the one where I was supposed to hear the heartbeat, my own heart sank. The ultrasound showed that the embryo had implanted in my fallopian tube. If allowed to grow, the little ball of cells would eventually cause my tube to rupture, likely killing me in the process. I went to the hospital, to the cancer ward, where patients sat with IVs receiving chemo, while the nurse injected me with methotrexate and sent me home. I remember curling up in a ball on my reading couch in the most severe pain of my life as the drug removed what I wanted most in the world from my body. This time, I emailed my professor to let her know that I wouldn't be in class the next day, trusting her with the reason for my absence. She offered support and understanding, but despite this, it was still challenging for me to admit that I couldn't do it all in that moment. Taking time to mourn a pregnancy loss (or two) doesn't fit neatly into the narrative of doing it all in academia.

The next fall, I started my second year in the doctoral program with a new role as assistant director of the rhetoric and writing studies program, a collaborative research study underway, and a conference presentation acceptance. I felt like I was accomplishing my goals as a PhD student, but I wasn't ready to give up on my dream of becoming a mother. Maybe my original plan would work out after all, just a year later. We tried again, and again I lost the pregnancy at six weeks. I underwent a lot of tests and we made an appointment with the only fertility specialist in the area, an appointment we had to wait months for. And we mourned, not only the loss of three pregnancies but also the loss of a future family. That January, a year after the ectopic pregnancy, we decided to give it one last-ditch effort. If I miscarried again, my body would be healed for the specialist appointment and series of tests that would follow. This would be our last attempt.

We conceived for a fourth time. We held our breath and kept the news to ourselves for weeks while my daughter held on. Seeing that little smudge grow bigger on the ultrasound and hearing her heartbeat week after week was magical. When I told my professors, all of whom were women, about the pregnancy, they were ecstatic and supportive, even when they learned that my daughter was due in early October, smack dab in the middle of the fall semester of my third year in the program. They were determined to help me figure it out and support me through the next steps. While I would finish coursework in the spring and take comprehensive exams in summer, we depended on the small stipend associated with my teaching assistantship. As in many PhD programs, there was no paid maternity leave for graduate teaching assistants and, at least at the time, no option for teaching remotely for part of the semester.

Luckily, a competitive administrative assistantship for a new certificate program opened up in my department. I applied, knowing that it would provide a flexible work schedule and help me maintain my income while negotiating my various responsibilities effectively. I was offered the position and took it, although I worried that some might view it as special treatment. I wanted those around me to know that I was selected based solely on my academic and professional merits and that I could handle this responsibility despite having a newborn. While these were reasonable fears, I was a bit surprised to find that no one ever questioned whether I was deserving of or capable in my new role. In fact, those in leadership made me feel like having a child was part of, not a barrier to, my academic and professional journey.

As a testament to this, the project lead, who also served as the chair of the department, came to my house for meetings on the certificate program. For the first of these meetings, she arrived with a big stuffed toy for my daughter and rocked her while we discussed course design. Over the first two years of my program, she had served as a mentor to me, someone I could confide in who supported my goals, encouraged me, and offered me opportunities to grow in my career, like serving as assistant director of the program and working on the certificate program. The way she embraced my working from home while caring for my daughter contributed to a culture of acceptance for such accommodations at the departmental level. Because of this support, as I juggled a newborn, an assistantship, and a dissertation prospectus, I felt empowered. I felt like I could (and was) doing it all, not only because of my planning but also because of the support I was lucky to have from my department and the individuals in it.

The following spring, I returned to campus to write my dissertation prospectus. My university had onsite daycare reserved for faculty, staff, and students, offering childcare on a weekly, daily, or hourly basis from early morning until later in the evening. It was partially subsidized by the university and partially by the YWCA, and the full-time weekly rate for students was $100. When my daughter turned four months old, I started bringing her in three days a week around 10:00 A.M., and then I would work on my prospectus in the library before returning to pick her up after lunch. I was usually able to pump enough breastmilk for her, but if I was unable to do that or even if I just wanted to visit, I'd pop in and nurse her in one of the rocking chairs. In my fourth year, I brought her in five days a week from about 9 A.M. to 5 P.M. During that time, I'd work on my dissertation, teach my class, and even work out at the gym. Meanwhile, my daughter was busy and engaged with other kids, safe, and well taken care of. Importantly, my day was balanced.

This access to flexible, reliable, and quality childcare was central to my success as a PhD candidate and to my mental health. It was something I recognized as a real privilege, a support that was not available at most institutions, although it should be.

The support I received on an institutional, departmental, and individual level was no accident; it was built into the mission of the university I attended. Looking back, I see strong women in positions of power at my institution and in my department, women who promoted feminist perspectives and policies in their areas of influence and encouraged me to strike an effective work-life balance. On an institutional level, access to affordable, flexible, reliable, and quality daycare allowed me to spend time focused on my dissertation while feeling comforted by the fact that my daughter was cared for. On a departmental level, having the opportunity to pursue an alternative assistantship allowed me to spend those first crucial months focused on my daughter without suffering financially. And on an individual level, my professors' and advisor's care, support, and accommodation allowed me to suffer my losses and celebrate my joys without sacrificing my career or academic goals. Taking advantage of the opportunities offered and accepting help was the hard part. I had to quiet the voice in my head telling me that asking for or accepting help was—or at least looked like—weakness.

MY STORY PART 2: IN ABSENTIA

While I reaped the benefits of this culture in my first four years, I also got a taste of the other side, of what many other PhD student parents experience, when my family moved across the country for my husband's job in my fifth year. While I had hoped to graduate in four years, my dissertation research proved more time consuming than originally planned, a realization that came a bit late, after my husband had already applied for jobs in academic administration in New England, where I was from and where we had decided to settle after graduation. This move was a decision I had discussed with my advisor during one of our regular meetings. I remember the stricken look on her face when I told her I was planning to limit myself geographically on the job market. Of course, being open geographically means higher odds of securing a tenure-track position and advancing one's career. But for me, as had been the case when searching for PhD programs, location mattered. Her face relaxed (slightly) when I said that I was limiting myself to New England, a region with a large number and wide variety of institutions of higher learning. I wanted to have it all again: an academic career and the opportunity to raise my family near my parents and extended family. This was especially important because I was pregnant with my second child.

That summer, with my dissertation half-written, we moved to Massachusetts. I was not allowed to maintain my teaching assistantship by teaching online because it was seen as setting an undesirable precedent, a step too far. Instead, I took a leave of absence, a compromise designed to save me from having to pay full out-of-state tuition, and taught online as an adjunct faculty member. Unfortunately, moving away from campus meant I no longer had access to affordable childcare. I was floored by the cost and inflexibility of daycare in the Boston area. There were only full-time, full-day slots; a waiting list at all locations within a five-mile radius; and costs in the thousands, not hundreds, of dollars per month. So mostly I worked while the kids napped (if they napped and if they napped at the same time), on the weekends when I would lock myself in the bedroom office with white noise blaring through my headphones, or when I could get my mom or friend to watch the kids for a few hours. At least I was close to family and friends who could help and I had a husband who took over at home when he wasn't at work so I could write.

That fall, as I clawed my way through day-to-day life as a work-from-home mom caring for a toddler and newborn, writing a dissertation, and teaching courses online, I had very little energy left over for the job market and couldn't do it alongside everything else. Moreover, I had started to question whether I wanted to pursue the tenure track. I worried that it would lead to even more burnout as I struggled to keep up with demanding requirements for scholarship, service, and teaching while being a mother. I worried that I would never see my kids, that I would be too buried in work to be there for them in the way I wanted to be. I thought maybe I'd teach part-time for a couple of years and then figure out what to do next. Then I saw a job announcement for a full-time multi-year contract, teaching-track position at a nearby institution and thought it looked like a good fit. I put together my materials and submitted an application, my only application that fall. I did my phone interview at my husband's office while he took the kids to a faculty meeting, and I went to my campus interview on two hours of sleep.

I got the job.

With plenty of individual and family support but without institutional support, I secured a job, successfully taught my classes, and finished my dissertation while nursing a newborn through the night, changing a billion diapers, and entertaining a very active two-year-old. That summer, I flew back to Texas with my nursing son to defend my dissertation and earn my doctorate. I defended successfully, but the stress of the year caught up to me, and upon returning home, I came down with shingles. My mental and physical health had both suffered as a result of the ordeal of the past year. When I look back at the difference between my first four years and my fifth year, I see the role that institutional support played in my ability to "do it all." While on campus I had access to quality, affordable childcare; an assistantship that provided flexibility and financial security; and present, supportive mentors, but when I was on a leave of absence, I felt the full absence of this support. I carried everything, and it wore me down to the bone.

CONCLUSION

The role of support for parents who are PhDing cannot be overstated, and it needs to be in place at not only the individual level but also at the institutional level if we are serious about systemic change in the area of diversity, equity, and inclusion. For too long, women, especially those who are also mothers, have been asked to bear the full burden for their participation in academic life. They are expected to plan, to cope, and to negotiate as they pull themselves up and through. As they do it all, they burn themselves out, suffering mentally, physically, and in their personal lives. For example, Tedra Osell writes, "After five years of overcoming the odds, surrounded by caring friends and colleagues but without real institutional backing, the anxiety I'd coped with in grad school had deepened into a heavily medicated depression, complete with suicidal thoughts, a marriage in crisis, and the conviction that for the time being *I could no longer do it all*" (my emphasis; 2008, 235).

This burnout has real consequences for women's, especially mothers', participation and advancement in academic life. Many mothers who choose to forgo the tenure track or leave academia cite the lack of work-life balance as a motivating factor in their decision, as the culture can be especially challenging for mothers on the tenure track (Sallee et al. 2016; Van Engen et al. 2021; Low and Martin 2019). While having policies in place to support parents such as family leave and tenure-clock adjustments are a step in the right direction, they do not serve to change the culture. Mason and Goulden (2004) found that married women with children are significantly underrepresented in the tenured professoriate, suggesting that somewhere along the professorial path, they are achieving this goal at levels lower than their married father counterparts. The so-called motherhood penalty, the "barriers academic mothers face within the academy that cause their careers to lag behind those of academic fathers and non-academic women" (Allen et al. 2021, 2), contributes to this trend (see Kulp 2020). My own experience serves as an example of this. Without institutional support, my energy was so sapped that I did not have time to adequately prepare for the job market and felt incapable of pursuing a tenure-track position.

In their aptly titled article "Surviving, but Not Thriving: The Politics of Care and the Experience of Motherhood in Academia," Low and Martin share their experience as new mothers in academia who faced a real "fear of being viewed as not coping, or not doing [their] job 'well enough'" (2019, 427). However, this fear, which is not unfounded, can lead to a kind of internalized pressure to not ask for or accept departmental or institutional support. Instead, mothers negotiate or suffer through the system, leaving "the status quo intact" (Van Engen et al. 2021, 1502). Even when parents resist the dominant discourse in these spaces, they often suffer as a result, so they work instead to negotiate within the existing system to achieve their own work-life balance (Gatta and Roos 2004; Allen et. al 2021; Van Engen et al. 2021). In some cases, like mine, there are women in positions of power who serve as allies, but institutions should not rely solely on the generosity of individuals, who are often women burdened with their own professional barriers, to support graduate student parents.

As long as parents continue to conform to the dominant discourse, negotiate on an individual basis, suffer silently, or leave academia altogether, the same problematic narratives and structures remain. Van Engen and colleagues argue that "agency can only lead to transformation when transcending individual awareness by moving toward collective action" (2021, 1493). We need to unapologetically seek out those institutions that are providing supports, ask for accommodations when we need them, and accept help. Since the implicit biases of those who make up an institution allow structures of inequality to continue, it is only by drawing attention to them, over and over, that we can change the discourse around academic parenthood to provide stronger support for us and for those who follow us. While this does come with risks, so does the alternative. It's time for all of us to start collectively *leaning on* institutions to do better.

WORKS CITED

Allen, Kelly-Ann, Kerryn Butler-Henderson, Andrea Reupert, Fiona Longmuir, and Ilana Finefter-Rosenbluh. 2021. "Work Like a Girl: Redressing Gender Inequity in Academia through Systemic Solutions." *Journal of University Teaching & Learning Practice* 18 (3):, 1–15. https://files.eric.ed.gov/fulltext/EJ1304423.pdf.

Cummins, Helene. 2017. "Literature Review of the University Teaching Trap of Academic Women." *Advancing Women in Leadership* 37, 13–19. https://awl-ojs-tamu.tdl.org/awl/article/view/9.

European University Institute. N.d. "USA, Academic Career Structure." https://www.eui.eu/programmesandfellowships/academiccareersobservatory/academiccareersbycountry/usa#:~:text=Typically%2C%20the%20research%20expectations%20for,is%20granted%20is%20at%2039.

Gatta, Mary L., and Patricia A. Roos. 2004. "Balancing without a Net in Academia: Integrating Family and Work Lives." *Equal Opportunities Journal* 23, 124–142. https://doi.org/10.1108/02610150410787765.

Hermann, Mary, and Cheryl Neale-McFall. 2018. "Experiences of Pretenure Counseling Professor Mothers." *NASPA Journal about Women in Higher Education* 11 (3): 265–283. https://doi.org/10.1080/19407882.2018.1477682.

Kulp, Amanda M. 2020. "Parenting on the Path to the Professoriate: A Focus on Graduate Student Mothers." *Research in Higher Education* 61 (3): 408–429. https://doi.org/10.1007/s11162-019-09561-z.

Low, Katharine, and Diana Damian Martin. 2019. "Surviving, but Not Thriving: The Politics of Care and the Experience of Motherhood in Academia." *Research in Drama Education: The Journal of Applied Theatre and Performance* 24 (3): 426–432. https://doi.org/10.1080/13569783.2019.1619450.

Mason, Mary Ann, and Marc Goulden. 2004. "Marriage and Baby Blues: Redefining Gender Equity in the Academy." *Annals of the American Academy of Political and Social Science* 596 (1): 86–103. https://doi.org/10.1177/0002716204268744.

Morse, Anne. 2022, April 6. "Fertility Rates: Declined for Younger Women, Increased for Older Women." *United States Census Bureau*. https://www.census.gov/library/stories/2022/04/fertility-rates-declined-for-younger-women-increased-for-older-women.html?utm_campaign=20220406msacos1ccstors&utm_medium=email&utm_source=govdelivery.

Osell, Tedra. 2008. "Motherhood Is Easy; Graduate School Is Hard." In *Mama, PhD,* edited by Elrena Evans and Caroline Grant, 231–236. Rutgers University Press.

Sallee, Margaret, Kelly Ward, and Lisa Wolf-Wendel. 2016. "Can Anyone Have it All? Gendered Views on Parenting and Academic Careers." *Innovations in Higher Education* 41 (3): 187–202. https://doi.org/10.1007/s10755-015-9345-4.

Sutherland, Jean-Anne. 2008. "Ideal Mama, Ideal Worker: Negotiating Guilt and Shame in Academe." In *Mama, PhD,* edited by Elrena Evans and Caroline Grant, 213–221. Rutgers University Press.

Van Engen, Marloes L., Inge L. Bleijenbergh, and Susanne E. Beijer. "Conforming, Accommodating, or Resisting? How Parents in Academia Negotiate Their Professional Identity." 2021. *Studies in Higher Education* 46 (8): 1493–1505. https://doi.org/10.1080/03075079.2019.1691161.

Zahneis, Megan. 2023. "What Higher Ed's Paid Parental-Leave Policies Look Like." *Chronicle of Higher Education*, March 28. https://chronicle.com/article/what-higher-eds-paid-parental-leave-policies-look-like.

38 ▸ LEAVE A NOTE

Powering through an Academic Job Market as a Breastfeeding Mom

DANIELLE DEVASTO

In the first year (2017–2018) that I was seriously negotiating the job market as a graduate student, I was pregnant. It was hard (and weird). In the second year (2018–2019), I was breastfeeding. Negotiating the job market got harder (and weirder). Instead of trying to dress (read: hide) my pregnant body, I was trying to advocate for and juggle the logistics of transporting, pumping, and storing breastmilk while interviewing for tenure-track faculty positions. Intermingled with books on rhetorical theory and technical communication, Heidi Murkoff's *What to Expect* books sat on my bedside table, offering a detailed account of what my body and my baby might or might not experience. However, the texts provided no advice on the experiences I was having in graduate school.

Being a breastfeeding mother forced me to make visible parts of my personal life that are generally not rewarded in academia, let alone disclosed upfront in a high-stakes, competitive job market context. As a graduate student parent, I felt particularly vulnerable as I had to do things like ask search committee chairs for accommodations, carry a large soft cooler around campus, or protect my already scant pumping breaks. My identities as a graduate student and a parent were colliding in ways they usually didn't.

Traversing one US airport late at night in 2019 with my work and pumping bags slung over my shoulder, I found the lone lactation pod in the terminal. To my surprise, the sterile, white interior was covered with handwritten notes. Far from home, weary from the emotional, social, and intellectual gauntlet that is a campus interview, I found myself surrounded and uplifted by the words of other traveling moms who had previously used the pod to nurse or pump.

Like the notes in the lactation pod, this short piece aims to uplift and support graduate student mothers in similar situations by sharing my lived experiences of being a breastfeeding mom while job marketing. This piece also aims to build awareness in faculty and administrators, particularly those who are on search committees or hosting job candidates.

ARRANGING

Landing an in-person campus interview is a glorious and terrifying experience. After months of applications and phone interviews, it was relieving and exciting to receive a phone call or email from the search committee chair inviting me to campus. It was also the moment that I, as a mother, had to finally face the enormity of the task before me. I couldn't afford (and more importantly didn't want) to stop breastfeeding while traveling, but it also wasn't something I could avoid or hide while completing a thirty-six-hour academic marathon. I could no longer only lead with my professional identity, which flew directly in the face of much of the general advice I had been given. Instead of feeling things out and divulging aspects of my personal life on my terms, I had to show my cards and draw attention to my identity as a mother immediately.

Sometimes in my communication over travel arrangements, I was asked directly if I had any special needs; other times, I had to ask for them. In either case, I definitely did not relish the idea of talking to an older (typically male) authority figure I had just met about breastmilk. As a Midwesterner, making a request that would likely inconvenience someone made me want to crawl out of my skin. As a graduate student, advocating for the accommodations I needed often felt like a painful extra reach given where I sat on the academic ladder. But I learned to ask tactfully and specifically for what I needed: a private space with an outlet and a twenty-minute break every three to four hours to pump and clean up.

TRANSPORTING

I put a lot of mental and emotional energy into figuring out how to transport multiple days' worth of breastmilk. After many hours of research, I settled on the following plan. I couldn't afford a courier service (e.g., Milk Stork, FedEx), and the thought of being separated from my breastmilk amid the uncertainties of air travel was stressful. So I carried the milk with me in a soft-sided cooler that had a leakproof zipper and closed-cell rubber foam lining to ensure that it would stay cold. The cooler was large enough to hold all my pumping equipment, two reusable ice blocks, and a large stainless steel water bottle, but small enough that I could fit it under my seat or in an overhead bin (even on the tiny regional puddle-jumpers, if I put it in just right).

Armed with my cooler, the next hurdle was getting on the airplane, which meant navigating Transportation Security Administration (TSA) officials and airline employees. Security will inspect any breastmilk at the airport. They will open the cooler and take out each container of milk. I minimized the handling of the milk by storing it in one large stainless steel water bottle. (Unlike other liquids, breastmilk is exempt from the 3.4-ounce rule whether baby is present or not.) If milk is frozen solid, TSA just looks. If it's in liquid form, as mine was, they test. After pulling out all the contents of my carefully packed cooler, they rarely put it back in for me. It's difficult to unravel all the reasons why this bothered me so much. But I suspect it had something to do with what felt like a disregard for the labor that had gone into packing the cooler with Tetris-like precision and a disregard for my dignity as something very personal was being laid bare alongside strangers' cell phones and shoes in the screening area.

Already feeling a bit raw and exposed from a multi-day interview, I tried to plan extra time to handle all of this but not so much that my ice packs would start to melt (because then TSA might confiscate them). This juggling act was the trickiest when my return flight from my campus interview was scheduled such that I had to spend part of the day on campus while already checked out of the hotel before being deposited at the airport.

Recombobulated and past security, I made my way to the gate to find out on more than one occasion that the gate agents were checking passengers' bags due to lack of overhead bin space on busy flights or on regional planes with smaller bins. I never had to part with my cooler of milk and pumping equipment, but that sometimes came at the price of losing access to my other carry-on luggage. Unfortunately, there's a lot of confusion about whether or not breast pumps are considered medical devices (which would not count as a carry-on bag). According to the FDA, a breast pump *is* a medical device. But each airline has different policies, so it was another detail to confirm and keep straight—and then mentally prepare for any potential conflict or sparring at the gate.

PUMPING

As a doctoral student working long days on campus without my own office, I knew that finding a spot to pump was not always easy. So I tried to prepare for all possible scenarios. I packed both my electric and manual pumps. I downloaded an app to help me find places to pump while I was traveling. I searched airport websites and terminal maps for information about lactation spaces and cross-referenced that with my itinerary. When would I need to pump? Which terminal was I likely to be flying into? Would I have enough time during my layover to get from terminal A to terminal C to use the lactation pod or would I need to use a delightful airport restroom? Would the lone pod be available or occupied when I got there? I entered the airports with Plans A–E in mind, knowing that the exact plan would come together in the moment due to many factors outside my control (e.g., delays, gate changes, renovations, whether or not a pod was vacant). More often than not, I ended up in a bathroom stall using my manual pump while traveling, praying I would not drop anything and wishing I had an extra hand so I could use the time to review my research presentation notes. Hopefully this scenario will be less common for future graduate student moms thanks to the Friendly Airports for Mothers (FAM) Act and the FAM Improvement Act, which required every small, medium, and large hub airport in the United States to have a dedicated lactation space in every terminal by October 2022.

Throughout my time interviewing on campus, my soft-sided cooler filled with pumping paraphernalia was my constant companion. While I had arranged for scheduled breaks, I didn't always know where those breaks would be or how I'd be getting to them. And I rarely pumped in the same place twice. I pumped in empty offices, borrowed offices, campus lactation rooms, and staff break rooms. Well-meaning faculty from the hosting university repeatedly assumed that the breaks in my itinerary could be overrun. Schedules often run late, especially in a jam-packed campus visit. My pumping breaks regularly took the hit, leaving me scrambling to pump whatever I could in five or ten minutes—much less than the recommended twenty to thirty minutes necessary for maintaining a healthy milk supply. Even if everything was running on schedule, the time it took to get to the empty office across campus hadn't been factored in or someone wanted to follow up on a question from my research talk or wouldn't I like to see the library? At one interview, a senior faculty member spontaneously reviewed my itinerary and told me that I didn't "really need that break" and proceeded to fill my time as he saw fit. As a job candidate and graduate student, I never felt like I could say no. I regularly felt the pressure to make the break as short as possible. I pumped where and when I could, often trying to make up for it later, hoping I would not end up with clogged ducts, mastitis, or a dip in my supply.

STORING

I assumed that storing breastmilk at the hotel would be relatively straightforward, that if I could only get it there, I would be able to tuck the milk safely into a mini-fridge in my room. But I quickly learned otherwise after spending the better part of my evenings troubleshooting milk storage instead of practicing my research talk or tailoring my list of questions. As it turns out, many hotel mini-fridges are really glorified coolers. They are often set or capped at a temperature that keeps drinks cool but isn't cold enough to keep food or medications out of the danger zone. So I desperately Googled for hacks to make the fridge colder. I scoured the units for make and model numbers so I could track down fridge manuals online and determine if 1 or 6 was the coldest setting.

This was, of course, *if* I was able to secure a mini-fridge. Some places charged. Some places were first come, first served. Some places (like the fancy nonbox hotels that schools sometimes like to put candidates up in to impress them) just didn't have any. At one hotel, I was told that fridges were given out to people for whom they were medically necessary. My logic—breastmilk is the only thing my baby eats, therefore it is medically necessary for her—was ignored. Never mind that breastmilk is the clinical gold standard for infant nutrition, that it is uniquely tailored to meet the needs of a growing baby, that it is a live substance with unparalleled immunological and anti-inflammatory properties. Instead I was invited to bring my milk down to the front desk, where they would store it for me in an actual fridge in an employee area (not the most convenient, but good to know in a pinch). I learned to get the hotel's information (even though I often was not the one making the arrangements), call ahead, claim medical necessity, and, upon arrival, look for functioning ice machines like Jason Bourne looks for exits.

NOTING

Through most of the two years I was on the job market, I kept my personal life quiet and powered through my searches, balancing the weight of family, teaching, research, and future planning. On the surface, this practice of "powering through" could be equated to the positively perceived concept of "grit." Except that privately powering through does not prove grit so much as it contributes to a toxic and antiquated situation not only for ourselves but also for those who come alongside and after us in these transitional periods of lactating and job marketing. The silence of powering through steals opportunities to uplift each other. Drafting job talks while breastfeeding, reviewing notes for the next campus meeting as the pump drones on, filling hotel sinks with ice to keep the milk cold—these beautiful experiences, intense but fleeting, are meant to be shared. Even if it's just small, anonymous notes scribbled between flights and stuck to the wall of an airport lactation pod.

For me, it was not even so much *what* was written but that a note was left written at all, leaving behind traces of those experiences, providing a moment to slow down, and lifting me up in community with others who were once also there in transit.

CLOSING THOUGHTS

From Survival to Self-Preservation

JENNA MORTON-AIKEN

I CONCURRENTLY CRIED AND laughed when my advisor hugged me and told me I had passed my dissertation defense. I kept laughing and crying all night, knowing that I had done the thing. I felt free, unleashed, and utterly grateful that it was over after five years of so much work.

I still think the three best things I have done in my life so far are to marry my husband, complete my PhD, and have my children. These choices and all the steps that led up to them have helped me become the person I wanted to be. But at the same time, somewhere around reading *Burnout* (2020) by sisters Dr. Emily Nagoski and Dr. Amelia Nagoski, I realized I couldn't see *me* anymore. I wondered if this was just what happened to smart and amazing women like me as we got older and became parents. I might be able to recover from burnout, but essence—the spark, the light, the feeling of power and possibility—would never shine as brightly again.

And then I decided that was bullshit.

In the ten years since I started my PhD and became a mother, I've finally realized that self-care and aiming for daily survival isn't enough. Through multiple, painful, raw moments, I've decided that I don't want to triage my existence for the rest of my life. Not as a parent and not as an academic.

In an early draft of this piece, a reader asked me what the difference was between survival and self-preservation. I had to think about it, finally parsing out in conversation that survival is keeping my children alive and healthy, attending to relationships, pushing forward to meet my professional goals even as they have changed, and now even keeping a cat alive.

But self-preservation is the defending, maintaining, and nourishing of the things that have made me **me** when I was eight and twelve and sixteen and at every other point in my life, the things that exist without my titles of mom, wife, professor, or academic, and they are the things that were starved of oxygen when I was literally and metaphorically giving that oxygen to others.

I am now trying to prioritize my self-preservation, spending time figuring out what revitalizes me and anchors me and finding ways to actually do those things on a daily basis so that I can be the parent, spouse, teacher, facilitator, and human I want to be in the world. (I wish I had known about Eve Rodsky's *Find Your Unicorn Space: Reclaim Your Creative Life in a Too-Busy World* [2022] a long time ago).

We—parents and arguably especially mothers—should all be able to choose when and how to nourish our sense of self, but when the demands of parentings, PhDing, and meeting the needs of others forces us into survival mode, we can begin to believe that we can't put ourselves first. We can start to risk starving our sense of self, ignoring creativity, rest, and self-centric joy because we focus on simply surviving day-to-day life. We might tire of enforcing boundaries, give up balancing too many balls, and become caregivers and/or academics in the ways others want us to be, not the ways we might imagine for ourselves. We might give up our unicorn space, the "active and open pursuit of creative self-expression in any form that makes you uniquely YOU" (Rodsky 2022) because it's just easier to give in than stand tall against buffeting winds day after day.

I've written about my experiences with clothing as multimodal rhetoric in my life before and after graduate school, examining how I've used blazers and other specific clothing choices to try to carve out a sense of myself (Morton-Aiken 2019). Looking back at that piece, I realize it was an external attempt to address an internal problem, an effort to combat the survival mode I'd been living in to get through the PhD and the job market while navigating pregnancy, parenting, and relationships.

This book is something of a love letter to my past self, recognizing that while I pride myself on facilitating the growth of the humans around me, the human I have historically neglected most often is myself. I wish I could go back and tell her she's amazing and she is not alone. I wish I could help her understand that she needs to be healthy in all the ways to do her work in the world.

I can do all the things, but I need to define those things, draw a boundary around them, and protect my ability to do them. Now, ten years after the beginning of my motherhood and PhD journey, I am in a job I love, with elementary school-aged children, and still with my supportive partner. In some ways, I feel like I've done it—we're all still here and we still like each other.

But I need to keep my *self* alive too. And just as I parent my children to facilitate their growth as humans who will thrive in the world, I need to be a better facilitator of myself.

THE COST OF SURVIVAL

In retrospect, I'm grateful that I didn't know the hardships to come over the five years of my PhDing while parenting.

I didn't know that I would increasingly dislike being pregnant, the second one feeling like an uninterrupted continuation of the first. That I would go in planning for a "natural birth" with my first child, laboring first without medication, then with an epidural, and ultimately end up with an emergency C-section. That my milk wouldn't fully come in, resulting in involuntarily supplementing with formula, and that I would have postpartum life-threatening high blood pressure that went undiagnosed for nearly too long.

I didn't know I would resent my body for what I perceived as its failure to deliver children "naturally" (as if there's any good way to get a baby out of a woman's body) or its failure to provide enough milk. I didn't know that I would struggle as my usually turbocharged brain now had to negotiate the physical limitations of nourishing life within and from my body. I didn't know I would need to rest, to sleep, and to acknowledge I must do less than I was intellectually capable of doing.

I didn't know I would feel rage when my child needed to breastfeed when I was in the middle of any activity or when my body wouldn't move the way it did before pregnancy. I didn't know that pregnancy and parenting would be conditions I could not simply grit my way through, so I would never be able to give graduate school my full attention and effort.

I didn't know I would feel disillusionment and disappointment when well-intentioned faculty, advisors, and others gave me incorrect, inapplicable, or inappropriate advice—like to reject a TA position—that would prove costly later on.

I didn't know I would feel deep shame as I was dependent on my spouse to pay all our expenses, including childcare, since the $13,000 I made a year as a TA hardly covered a single child's tuition. That my shame would encompass my C-sections, painful recoveries, formula use, and time spent away from my babies (even though I certainly did not want to be a stay-at-home parent).

I didn't know I would feel terrified when I eventually fully comprehended the reality of a job market that is untenably uncertain, insanely competitive, and completely divorced from the health of our family. I didn't know I would feel heartbreak and despair as I thought about leaving academia so that we could intentionally remain in the life that we had built as a family, especially given the low financial returns on an academic salary.

But despite everything I endured, I would do it all again.

FROM SURVIVAL TO SELF-PRESERVATION

At the time of drafting, I'm forty-one years old, happily employed, and six years out of graduate school. My kids are awesome, my marriage is healthy, and I feel like I'm in a good place. That last one in particular has not always been the case.

While most of this book has focused on experiences while in graduate school, I want to close with what I wish I had known when I was finishing my PhD that could have helped facilitate my *self* sooner:

- Benefits and salaries matter to me more than I want them to, especially as I age. I'm still wrestling with my ego, reminding myself that academic prestige will not pay for anything we need. I also can't stand thinking about the lost payments toward retirement or the starting salary well below what I could have had in industry.
- I didn't find this to be true for myself, but I have observed the pressure faculty and advisors put on graduate students to get the "best" job. Much as the best dissertation is a done dissertation, the best job is the one you actually have, not the promise of what might come. Everything is different than when previous generations (or even cohorts) went on the market. I try to encourage others to have grace for their blinkers while giving space

and permission to explore what success looks like for individuals and their families, including outside academia.

- So far, I've found that academia is the same as grad school—it's hard, unrelenting, underpaid, undervalued, and will take everything you give it. The specifics may change, but the battles never end. I do find it rewarding, but I try to consistently revisit the cost of my professional accomplishments against the needs of myself and my family.
- I will never get missed sleep back. I need to guard sleep and genuine rest with my life because sleep is, quite literally, what will keep me alive and keep me strong for the work ahead of me.
- If I drop dead tomorrow, work won't really miss a beat and academia won't really care. But my children would lose their mother and my husband would lose his wife. If I am so central to them and not to the work, then I need to make them central to me over the work.
- Getting therapy and medication make me stronger than trying to muscle through. In fact, much to my surprise, therapy, meditation, and medication have given me the tools to be myself more authentically and more consistently. I need, want, and deserve to do more than just survive every day. I hadn't realized how much I missed myself until I saw **me** in the mirror again just a few months ago.

IN CLOSING

I feel very vulnerable sharing so much about these struggles, wondering often if it's self-indulgent or unnecessarily private or raw to speak my truths in writing. Even in what is now my third piece (and entire book!) dedicated to the personal-professional experiences of parenting while PhDing, I steel myself with Asao Inoue's call to be vulnerable and reassure myself that, as Kidder and Todd wrote, "how the writer conveys present knowledge of past experience is a delicate problem for a[ny] memoirist" (2013, 53). Their book on creative fiction, *Good Prose: The Art of Nonfiction*, reassures me that "the good and honest memoir is neither revenge nor self-justification, neither self-celebration nor self-abnegation. *It is a record of learning*" (53, my emphasis).

We close this book with three appendices meant to model that record for learning: my "self-preservation toolkit" that describes all the hacks and helps I discovered along the way; two of contributor Stefanie Graff's memorable out-of-office example emails; and contributor Keith Jackson's Labor Log Template. We also encourage you to use the hashtag #GradSchoolParentsSurvival to share all of the things like books, blogs, food, and technology that helped you shift from survival to self-preservation.

Before you go, though, I would like to ask you: What do *you* need? What will change and save your life? Because we need you. Your work matters, inside and/or outside of academics. We need your strength, your vulnerability, your voice, and *your self* in the world.

On the days that are hard, lonely, and overwhelming, know that everyone in this book and so many others are with you.

Remember: You are amazing, and you are not alone.

WORKS CITED

Inoue, Asao B. 2019. "How Do We Languaging So People Stop Killing Each Other, Or What Do We Do About White Language Supremacy?" Keynote address, Annual Meeting of Conference on College Composition and Communication, Pittsburgh, Pennsylvania, March 14. https://docs.google.com/document/d/11ACklcUmqGvTz CMPlETChBwS-Ic3t2BOLi13u8IUEp4/edit?tab=t.0.

Kidder, Tracy, and Richard Todd. 2013. *Good Prose: The Art of Nonfiction*. Random House Trade Paperbacks.

Morton-Aiken, Jenna. 2019. "Dressing for Childbearing, the Patriarchy, and Me: Auto-Ethnography in Three Parts." *Journal of Multimodal Rhetorics* 4 (1): 196–211. https://doi.org/10.23860/diss-morton-aiken-jenna-2017.

Nagoski, Emily, and Amelia Nagoski. 2020. *Burnout: The Secret to Unlocking the Stress Cycle*. Ballantine Books.

Rodsky, Eve. 2022. *Find Your Unicorn Space: Reclaim Your Creative Life in a Too-Busy World*. Penguin.

APPENDIX A

Jenna's Self-Preservation Toolkit

THIS IS A LIST of things that have helped me find myself over the last two or so years. Nothing here is meant to be an endorsement (although I would accept endorsement income; I am an underpaid academic, after all), and they are certainly not meant to be prescriptive for you. I'm sharing what works for me so that you can use it as something of a heuristic to consider intentionally how to make your own decisions about what you need and how to preserve your *self* as you continue through life.

Here are the women, resources, technology, and other hacks that I genuinely believe helped save my life during and since the pandemic.

BOOKS/SPEAKERS

- *Period Repair Manual* by Dr. Lara Briden
- *Burnout* by Drs. Emily and Amelia Nagoski
- *Untamed* by Glennon Doyle

- *Find Your Unicorn Space: Reclaim Your Creative Life in a Too-busy World* by Eve Rodsky
- *Rising Strong, Dare to Lead* and probably anything by Dr. Brené Brown
- *Playing Big* by Tara Mohr
- *This is Your Brain on Food* by Dr. Uma Naidoo

FOOD, MIND, AND BODY RESOURCES

- Food
  - *The Anti-Inflammation Diet and Recipe Book* by Dr. Jessica Black
  - *Dinner Made Simple* cookbook by the editors of *Real Simple*
  - Glutenfreedrugs.com
- Mind
  - Coaching (Some employers offer coaching as a benefit, often through platforms like SpringHealth.)
  - Therapy (Zencare.co is a great platform for searching.)
  - Medication (This is not intended as medical advice. Always consult with your doctor or healthcare provider.)
  - Morning affirmations (I came to this very reluctantly, but I think it's making a difference for me.)
- Body
  - Chiropractor who specializes in whole-body strength such as Synergy Chiropractic & Sports Rehab in North Kingstown, Rhode Island
  - Pelvic health floor specialists
  - Bodyworkers like Caitie Kelly (@releasebodywork on Instagram)
  - (Peri)menopause specialists like those on the North American Menopause Society website

FOOD, MIND, AND BODY APPS AND TECH

- Food
  - Grocery delivery services like Rosie
  - Fig (Food Is Good) app to easily monitor allergies
  - Thrive Market and Grove for helpful subscriptions
- Mind
  - Headspace app
  - Chani astrology app (I was skeptical but it really works for me.)

- reMarkable2 (expensive but amazing digital tablet for handwriting, typing, and electronic markup)
- Monday.com or the Notion app
- NCFDD (National Center for Faculty Development and Diversity) writing challenges[1]

- Body
  - Happy light on a timer
  - Lumie alarm clock
  - Lily Watch (which I truly believe saved me from having a heart attack)
  - The Underbelly Yoga (Yoga with Adrienne is also a highly regarded YouTube resource that is free)
  - MommaStrong online workouts
  - Environmental Working Group's Healthy Living App
  - Vionics shoes
  - M.M.LaFleur clothing (so expensive but elegant and easy to wear and care for) and ShortStoryBox.com subscription for petite women
  - Betabrand yoga-work pants

MY SPECIFIC LIFE HACKS

- Hair Prep:
  - The Dyson Airwrap: It's expensive, but it gives me tools for blowing my hair out twice a week to set the foundation for the styling to come. (I've also heard about Shark FlexStyle as a cheaper option.)
  - Dove dry shampoo: For the five days a week I don't blow my hair out. Not sure it's the best and I don't like that it's an aerosol, but it lifts, gives structure, and cleans enough and it's not super expensive. (SGX NYC's Do-It-All 3-in-1 Dry Texture Spray is also great.)
  - The Small Things blog for training and resources on techniques, tools, and products for haircare, makeup, and more.
- Music Playlists
  - I use music playlists to activate different states of mind for different tasks, such as academic writing, getting through tasks I hate, and activating good vibes when I'm feeling down. Every activity or mindset has its own playlist and they make life easier for me every day.
  - I'd also like to thank Gloria Estefan for saving my life during the pandemic. I titled my primary playlist *Feel Better with Gloria Estefan,* opening with "Get On Your Feet," "Turn the Beat Around," and "1, 2, 3," and it never fails to make me feel better every time I listen to it.

- Gluten-Free and Dairy-Free Hacks
    - Zojirushi rice cooker that has two pre-programming options so I can enjoy fresh oatmeal in the morning and then fresh white or brown rice with dinner. It's magic.
    - Bob's Red Mill gluten-free oats, chia seeds, and flax seeds for the oatmeal
    - King Arthur gluten-free options
    - Nutpods for coffee/tea
    - Genexa over-the-counter options
    - Unreal and Enjoy Life chocolate options
- Life-Balancing Routines
    - Getting up early (ugh) to go for a mindfulness walk if it's light out or The Underbelly morning yoga if it's dark out.
    - Morning affirmations while doing neck stretches. I was skeptical, but they work for me.
    - Painting our rooms in colors that bring us joy, regardless of what's on trend or will add to resale value.
    - Investing in fake plants. All the joy and health benefits, none of the work!
    - Setting up Alexa routines and reminders to help all of us do the things we're supposed to do.
    - Programming sleep mode on my phone to shut me out of all phone activity before it's time for bed.
    - Scheduling meals a week at a time and just cycling back through the same plans to make life easier and so we can use the same online grocery order.
- Parenting Help
    - Primary.com for high-quality clothing in all the colors for all the kids.
    - *It's NOT the Stork* book series. It will give you all the words to talk about puberty, sex, and the other tough topics.
    - Daycare: Daycare isn't a good (or available) choice for everyone, but it was for us. Goddard School, thank you for all that you do!
    - Trixie Tracker: While I am a humanities scholar, I love data, and this app saved my sanity when I needed to find patterns and set habits for myself as a grad student with infants. Sadly, it looks like this app has been retired at the time of publishing.

NOTE

1. The actual NCFDD monthly writing challenges are wonderful but they are behind a paywall. If you can't afford that, you can replicate their program directly in Google docs. Everyone's is different, but I've provided both the images and the HTML code for mine below. Update for yourself!

Goal: Write 30 minutes every workday
Projects: Book, article R&R (woohoo!)
Celebrations: Book proposal met with great interest!

Tracking Key:
= 30 minutes
= didn't hit 30 minutes but wrote something
= didn't write at all
= work travel/all day demands
= out of the office
= family has to come first today
= stage complete!

Oct 02–06:
Oct 09–13:
Oct 16–20: ()
Oct 25–29:
Oct 30–31:

```
HTML:
**Goal:** Write 30 minutes every workday
**Projects:** Book, article R&R (woohoo!)
**Celebrations:** Book proposal met with great interest! :champagne:
**Tracking key:**
:smiling_face_with_three_hearts: = 30 minutes
:melting_face: = didn't hit 30 minutes but wrote something
:dotted_line_face: = didn't write at all
:briefcase: = work travel/all day demands
:hibiscus: = out of the office
:fog: = family has to come first today
:fireworks: = stage complete!

**Oct** 02–06:: smiling_face_with_three_hearts:: dotted_line_face:: dotted_line_face:: dotted_line_face:: dotted_line_face:
Oct 09–13:: dotted_line_face:: dotted_line_face:: dotted_line_face:: dotted_line_face:: briefcase:
Oct 16–20:: dotted_line_face:: dotted_line_face:: briefcase:: briefcase:: briefcase: (:sob:)
Oct 25–29:: smiling_face_with_three_hearts:: dotted_line_face:: smiling_face_with_three_hearts:: dotted_line_face:: smiling_face_with_three_hearts:
Oct 30–31:: smiling_face_with_three_hearts:: dotted_line_face:: dotted_line_face:: dotted_line_face:: smiling_face_with_three_hearts:
```

APPENDIX B

Out-of-Office Replies from Stephanie Graff, MD

REPLY 1—THE SWEET SPOT

My children are in that sweet spot. You know the one—where they are old enough to go to museums and read things, still think being with mom and dad is tolerable, and don't require naps, pureed food, or diapers. *And it is phenomenally short.* One of the weird blessings of being an oncologist is the regular reminders of exactly what matters in life. So we are off on a two-week bucket-list vacation!

Immediately upon return, I leave again for professional travel, so I am not fully operational until August 21. My inbox will likely be unmanageable at that point. You may want to send a new message! In the interim, my admin can help direct you to the best contact for most issues (contact below). For clinical concerns, call the cancer center main line and the APP or covering physician of the day will assist you.

Growing up, my family did not travel much. Instead, I dreamed of the destinations in the handful of full-color coffee table books my mom and dad kept including: *Wonders of the World, Excursion to Enchantment,* and a peculiar assortment of [insert random country]". Decades later, those destinations still are at the top of my "must see" list.

So, while I'm out of office—tell me what are your bucket-list vacation destinations? What coffee-table books shaped your childhood or do you have now that may be influencing those around you? What has been your most memorable family vacation? *Go ahead—fill my inbox with stuff that will be a joy to read.*

Stephanie L. Graff, MD, FACP

Director of Breast Oncology, Lifespan Cancer Institute

Co-Chair, Breast Cancer Translational Disease Research Group, Legorreta Cancer Center at Brown University

Associate Professor of Medicine, Warren Alpert Medical School of Brown University

Medical Advisor, Dr. Susan Love Foundation for Breast Cancer Research

pronouns: she/her/hers

Mailing: Rhode Island Hospital, 593 Eddy Street, George 304, Providence RI 02903

Find me at Brown University | Lifespan | LinkedIn | Twitter & Instagram @DrSGraff

Read my work at: ASCO Connection | Dr Susan Love Research

REPLY 2—YOUR FAVORITE NATIONAL PARK

"Everybody needs beauty as well as bread, places to play in and pray in, where nature may heal and give strength to body and soul alike."—John Muir

I am enjoying a family vacation through some of America's western national parks. **During my absence, for any clinical concerns that arise, please contact the Lifespan Cancer Institute and you will be connected to the physician or APP of the day for coverage.**

One of the highlights of coming back to an overflowing post-vacation inbox is the sprinkling of messages I have from my colleagues, collaborators, and external partners sharing responses. I would love to hear about **your favorite national park.** What makes it your favorite? Why did you fall in love? If you have never visited, is there one you would really like to see?

Also, did you know about **Every Kid Outdoors**? Fourth graders all have access to the national park system for free, courtesy of a cool program designed to inspire them to explore the world around them, to connect with nature and history, and to ask questions. So, my fourth grader is the unofficial trip sponsor of my travels. Learn more or tell a fourth grader all about it: https://everykidoutdoors.gov/index.htm

I look forward to coming back renewed, ready to tackle unanswered questions, the wonderful work of patient care, and of course, ***your email.***

"The wilderness holds answers to questions man has not yet learned to ask."—Nancy Newhall

Stephanie L. Graff, MD, FACP, FASCO,

Director of Breast Oncology, Lifespan Cancer Institute

Co-Chair, Breast Cancer Translational Disease Research Group, Legorreta Cancer Center at Brown University

Associate Professor of Medicine, Warren Alpert Medical School of Brown University

pronouns: she/her/hers

Mailing: Rhode Island Hospital, 593 Eddy Street, George 304, Providence RI 02903

Find me at Brown University | Lifespan | LinkedIn | Twitter & Instagram @DrSGraff

APPENDIX C

Labor Log Template from Keith Jackson

TABLE C.1 Labor Log Template

Location	Start Time	Goal	Goal met?	Duration	Engagement	Mood	Interruptions
ex. couch	ex. 3 P.M.	ex. "revise introduction"	y/n/partly	mins/hrs	1–5 (4 & 5 = flow)	ex. energized, bored, etc.	# or type

ACKNOWLEDGMENTS

We owe a debt of gratitude to Juliette Holder, who was instrumental in helping this book move from passion project to publication. As our fabulous research assistant for three semesters, Juliette helped us communicate with authors, accommodate dozens of different rolling deadlines for author revisions, identify key themes across sections, and organize chapters into sections. In addition, she provided an invaluable graduate student perspective. We are also grateful to the Department of Language, Culture & Gender Studies and College of Arts & Sciences at Texas Woman's University for funding Juliette's support of the project.

We will never be able to adequately thank senior editor Peggy Solic, whose limitless enthusiasm and guidance confirmed that Rutgers University Press was the perfect home for our project. Peggy saw the significance of this collection from the beginning and advocated for the literal and metaphorical space we needed to share the words and wisdom of our contributors.

Jackie: Thank you to Buck for striving to be an equal partner, to my children for the laughter, and to my graduate students for every ounce of inspiration. Special thanks to my parents, my mother-in-law and sister-in-law, and the many childcare providers and teachers whose invisible labor made this book possible. Lastly, thank you to Jenna for your tenacious spirit, relentless support, and many good stories. I sensed early on that you'd be a brilliant scholarly partner and a fast friend, and both instincts have proven true. I wish every academic parent had a Jenna in their corner.

Jenna: I want to recognize my husband Anthony for being a rockstar in all things, especially his culinary masterpieces, and for still making me laugh twenty years later. Elizabeth and Katherine, you are amazing. I admire how strong, loving, and silly you are, and I am so grateful for the magic you bring to our family. Mom, Dad, and Kaitlin, I wouldn't be where I am without you. Thank you for "party" dinners, "ding!," and WYAAWYLT conversations. Caroline, Libby, Nedra, Ingrid, and Dani, thank you for being co-conspirators on my PhDing journey. Last but not least, Jackie—you have been a truly amazing partner on this project. Thank you for your patience, passion, good humor, and grit; this book would not exist without you.

Finally, to our contributors: Where do we even begin? You have made us cry, laugh, rage, and wish we could talk face to face over a beverage of choice. You are understanding, determined, thoughtful, vulnerable, and fierce. We are so proud to bring your stories to these pages and so grateful that you were willing to share your much-needed narratives with the world. We continually learn from you and are better parents, scholars, and people for working with you. Thank you.

NOTES ON CONTRIBUTORS

JUDITH CHRIQUI BENCHIMOL holds a doctorate in English education from Teachers College, Columbia University, where she teaches nonfiction writing to preservice English teachers. She has three young children, two of whom were born during her time as a PhD student. Her most recent publications include an edited collection of essays called *Challenging Antisemitism: Lessons from Literacy Classrooms*, which aims to equip secondary and postsecondary English teachers with practical strategies for addressing anti-Semitism and amplifying Jewish voices in their curricula.

ALICIA CHRISTINE BERETTA is a PhD candidate in rhetoric at Texas Woman's University (TWU). She has taught first-year writing for the past six years and technical communication for the past four years. She aims to direct a first-year writing program with emphasis on enhancing student engagement and transfer of knowledge and skills. With her wonderful husband of seven years, Beretta had her daughter, who is now two, in the middle of the pandemic and the second semester of her PhD program. Her research centers on archives in the undergraduate classroom and student transfer of knowledge and skills and includes subdisciplinary studies, such as multimodal and feminist pedagogies. She currently teaches first-year writing at TWU and technical communication at the University of North Texas. Student engagement is one of the driving factors behind her pedagogy, and she loves to create fun and effective activities and assignments for her students.

BRANDIE BOHNEY received her PhD in rhetoric and writing studies from Bowling Green State University in 2021 while her children were both in high school. She now serves as a literacy consultant and dyslexia specialist for North Central Ohio Educational Service Center, where she provides support in evidence-based practices for improved literacy experiences and outcomes to teachers and administrators in primarily small, rural K–12 school districts. Her research focuses on how educators best learn to teach literacy, professional learning communities, and non-mainstream dialects in ELA and phonics instruction.

MORGAN BUCHS is an assistant professor-educator at the University of Cincinnati. Prior to that, she graduated with her PhD from Bowling Green State University in 2022 when her son was four months old. Her research interests include dual enrollment, dispositions, and writing transfer. Her work is published in the *Virginia English Journal* and in various edited collections.

BETH BUYSERIE is director of composition and associate professor of English at Utah State University. Her work focuses on writing program administration, the teaching of composition, critical pedagogies, professional learning, and the intersections of language, knowledge, and power through the lenses of queer theory and antiracist pedagogies. Outside of academia, she is often known as Benjamin and Samuel's mom—and she is grateful that each day they continue to teach her about the joys of (queer) parenting.

JACQUELINE CERDA-SMITH earned a PhD in Psychology from North Carolina State University in 2024. She is currently an assistant professor at Illinois State University. Her research focuses on school belonging and critical consciousness socialization. Outside her teaching and research, Cerda-Smith tries to advocate for student-parents. After having two daughters during graduate school, she founded the Student Parent Association at North Carolina State to build a support network and collectively advocate for student-parent needs within the institution.

APRIL COBOS is lecturer in the English department at Christopher Newport University in Newport News, Virginia. She received her PhD from Old Dominion University in 2019 when her children were thirteen and eleven years old. She has taught traditional, online, hybrid, and live-streaming composition, rhetoric, technical and professional writing courses, as well as grant writing for civic engagement and nonprofits at various universities and community colleges over the past twenty years. She is currently in the process of publishing her dissertation as a book manuscript. Her recent publications include book chapters and articles on online learning considerations for military-affiliated learners, teaching international and nonnative English speakers, graduate student labor in a hybrid doctoral program, and the rhetorical considerations of teaching grant writing to undergraduate students.

DANIELLE DEVASTO is assistant professor in the Department of Writing at Grand Valley State University. Her research has appeared in *Technical Communication Quarterly, Communication Design Quarterly, Journal of Multimodal Rhetorics,* and other publications. She is the mother of four children under the age of seven and thus a reluctant fan of Daniel Tiger.

BARBARA A. W. EVERSOLE, PhD, is a professor of human resource development at Indiana State University, Indiana. She teaches courses in work-life integration, human resource development strategy, organization development, and managerial coaching. Eversole's primary research interest is studying how to make workplaces more accommodating to the nonwork lives of employees, both in the for-profit sector and in the academy. She also studies managerial effectiveness, women leaders, and the careers of mother-scholars in academia. Eversole has published in a variety of scholarly journals and has presented at national and international conferences. She also serves on a number of editorial boards and is coeditor in chief of *The International Journal of HRD Practice, Policy and Research.*

LOURDES FERNANDEZ is a researcher at Mathematica, a policy research company. Her boys are eighteen and twenty-one years old and her husband is now retired from the military. Fernandez and her family live in Virginia.

RACHEL FLYNN is a PhD candidate in rhetoric and writing studies at Bowling Green State University. Her research focuses on race and transfer in writing assessment. Her two boys were toddlers and preschoolers during her PhD studies. Flynn currently teaches dual-enrollment first-year composition and senior language arts at Riverside High School in Boardman, Oregon.

GITTE FRANDSEN is a teaching assistant professor at Marquette University in Wisconsin. Her research interests include transnational literacy studies, linguistic justice, and cultural rhetorics. Her work has been published in *Composition Studies* and *College Composition and Communication.* At the time she wrote her chapter, she was a graduate student at the University of Wisconsin-Milwaukee. She graduated in May 2023.

STEPHANIE L. GRAFF received her MD in May 2004 and went on to complete postgraduate training in internal medicine (2007), hematology (2011), and medical oncology (2011). She is now an associate professor of medicine at the Legorreta Cancer Center at Brown University, where she leads the division breast oncology program and is mother to three children born in the period 2009 to 2015. In addition to numerous scientific publications, Dr. Graff is member of the *Journal of Clinical Oncology* and the *Art of Oncology* editorial board, and examples of her medical humanities writing are published there. She is a contributing author to the 7th edition of the *Dr. Susan Love Breast Book.*

CELESTE L. GRAHAM is a special education teacher with nearly twelve years of experience working in the education field. She has taught at every level, including K–12 public education and college-level courses. She is currently a doctoral candidate and graduate teaching assistant at Texas Woman's University in the department of social sciences and historical studies, where she is completing her dissertation on formerly incarcerated mothers. She is a single mother of a five-year-old girl also named Celeste.

CAROLINE M. GRANT earned a PhD in comparative literature from UC Berkeley and taught writing at UC Berkeley, Stanford, and the San Francisco Art Institute before becoming a parent and shifting to writing and editing outside the academy. She served on the editorial board of LiteraryMama.com for ten years, including five as editor-in-chief, and has coedited two anthologies: *Mama, PhD: Women Write about Motherhood and Academic Life* and *The Cassoulet Saved Our Marriage: True Tales of Food, Family, and How We Learn to Eat.* Caroline has published personal essays in the *New York Times,* the *Washington Post, Salon,* and a number of other journals and anthologies, both in print and online. She is also cofounder and director, with her husband, of the Sustainable Arts Foundation, which worked for nearly fifteen years to support writers and artists with children. They recently sunsetted the foundation and returned its funds to Indigenous communities. She lives in San Francisco with her husband and their two young adult children.

ELISE A. GREEN is an assistant professor of English and writing at Longwood University. In addition to teaching rhetoric and composition, she coordinates writing-infused courses across the core curriculum and serves as the faculty consultant for teaching writing.

EMILY GRESBRINK is an assistant professor at Minnesota State University, Mankato in the Integrated Engineering Program. Her ongoing research focuses on technical communication and digital risk and crisis communication. Gresbrink is a co-parent and "guardian of the galaxy" to two kids and three dogs. On any day that is not booked with taking a kid to D&D campaigns, baseball, or violin lessons, you can catch them camping, road-tripping, gardening, announcing local roller-derby bouts, or binge-watching old seasons of SVU.

LAURA FITZWATER GONZALES is resident assistant professor in the Department of Sociology and Criminal Justice at Pacific Lutheran University. She received her PhD in May 2017 from North Carolina State University, when her children were two and four years old. Her research focuses on family and gender inequality, particularly the mental work that women do in families.

JAMES B. HARR III received his PhD in communication, rhetoric, and digital media from North Carolina State University in the fall of 2021, around the time that his beautiful children, James IV and Bridget, turned five and his brilliant spouse, Melissa, graduated magna cum laude with her BSBA in business and law and began her career in accountancy. (He's obviously really proud of his family.) After a one-year postdoc with North Carolina State's Data Science Academy, he joined Christian Brothers University in Memphis, Tennessee, as assistant professor of literature and languages, where he specializes in medieval studies and digital humanities. When he isn't teaching for Christian Brothers University, he is a visiting lecturer for the digital humanities summer minor at the University of California, Berkeley, a book review editor for *Speculum: A Journal of Medieval Studies*, and a regular contributor to both *Studies in the Age of Chaucer* and *Digital Philology*.

DANIEL HENKE is director of writing programs and associate director of the writing center at Lake Forest College, where they teach college writing, writing center theory and practice, and narrative and knowledge production. Their research interests include first-year composition, narrative, queer theory, writing center theory and practice, and qualitative research methodologies.

ERIN HENKE is a board-certified behavior analyst working outside academia, where she helps children with autism and their families thrive. Her passions include early intervention, one-on-one teaching, facilitating communication, and trauma-informed care.

NABILA HIJAZI is a teaching assistant professor of writing at the George Washington University. Her research interests include Muslim and refugee women's rhetoric(s) and literacy practices, writing center theory and practice, and multilingual writing. She graduated with a PhD from the University of Maryland College Park in 2020, as her eldest daughter graduated with a bachelor's degree and her twin sons began college. Her dissertation, "Syrian Refugee Women in the Diaspora: Sustaining Families through Literacies," received an honorable mention for the 2020 President's Dissertation Award presented by The Coalition of Feminist Scholars in the History of Rhetoric and Composition.

DANIEL L. HOCUTT received his PhD in 2019, when his daughters were aged seventeen and fifteen. He earned his doctorate in English from Old Dominion University, specializing in technical communication. He co-parents both daughters, now college students themselves, with his supportive spouse. He has published in *Technical Communication*, *Computers & Composition*, and *Communication Design Quarterly*, among other journals and edited collections.

He serves as web manager on a marketing team at the University of Richmond, where he also teaches as adjunct professor.

JACKIE HOERMANN-ELLIOTT is an associate professor of English and director of Texas Woman's University's First-Year Composition Program, where she teaches first-year writing, professional writing, and graduate-level pedagogy courses. She has published in several journals, including *College English, Writing Program Administration Journal,* and the *ADVANCE Journal.* Her first book, *Running, Thinking, Writing: Embodied Cognition in Composition,* was published in 2021 and explores the creative effects of running for writers. She enjoys playing outside with her four kids, trying new recipes, and the collective effervescence of a weekend 5k race or community festival.

KEITH JACKSON is a PhD candidate in Ball State University's Rhetoric and Composition Program. He works as an instructor of first-year writing and digital literacies. His work as an assistant director led him to his interests in labor and labor exploitation. He also specializes in digital literacies and digital writing. He is pursuing his PhD, held together by the love from his two-year-old daughter, eight-year-old daughter, and ten-year-old son, but it is his wife's support that keeps him grounded.

JOAN JIYOUNG HWANG started her journey as a graduate student when her children were four and three years old and had been on that journey until very recently, when she earned her PhD in writing and rhetoric. Her two sons, who have grown into beautiful young men, are both in college. Her research centers on promoting translingual students' rhetorical agency, responding to students' writing, and the intersection of multimodality and writing transfer. She spends her nonwriting or nonteaching time in nature, hiking or exploring ideas of her painting of nature.

RACHAEL JORDAN is a PhD candidate at Texas Tech University and has been a full-time lecturer in the English Program at California State University Channel Islands since 2012. She has an eight-year-old child with her incredible spouse and a fourteen-year-old child with a wonderful co-parent. She is a queer, cisgender white woman interested in queer theory's application to technical communication. You can find her Pushcart Prize–nominated work in *Emrys Journal* and an array of other creative publications. Her scholarly work appears in *Composition Forum, Open Words,* and the *SAGE Handbook for Online Learning.*

JENNIFER C. JUDD is a PhD candidate studying rhetoric at Texas Woman's University (TWU), where she researches theories of belonging, disability and feminist rhetorics, and embodied and contemplative writing pedagogies. She is also a wife and a mother to five inspiring children, some of whom are pursuing their degrees alongside her. She is a graduate research assistant for the TWU First-Year Experience Program and the English Bachelor of Arts Program advisor in the TWU Department of Language, Culture, and Gender Studies. She has taught themed first-year composition courses on belonging and wellness and currently teaches technical communication at the University of North Texas. Judd is a passionate advocate for disability justice, and her writing on disability rights has appeared in the *Dallas Morning News*. Her creative writing for children has appeared in various children's magazines, poetry anthologies, and picture books.

DANIELLE M. KOEPKE completed her PhD in public rhetorics and community engagement at University of Wisconsin–Milwaukee in 2023, when her kids were fourteen and nine years old. She is currently a teaching assistant professor at Marquette University, where her research interests include cultural and digital rhetorics, reproductive justice, and feminist and queer theories. These areas of study have been foundational to her teaching praxis in courses such as business writing, health science writing, and writing for social action. You can find her work in *Composition Studies, The Digital Rhetoric Collaborative,* and *ACLS*.

KATE LAFFERTY-DANNER is assistant professor of medical humanities and community engagement at Geisinger Commonwealth School of Medicine. She holds a PhD in humanities and an MA in bioethics and medical humanities from the University of Louisville and completed her BA and MA in English at Rutgers University–Camden. She lives with her spouse Patrick, her seven-month-old daughter Sally, and three cats in Scranton, Pennsylvania.

SARA BARTLETT LARGE is an associate professor of writing and coordinator for writing across the curriculum at Lasell University in Massachusetts, where she has spent the last eight years of her career. She earned a PhD in rhetoric and writing studies from the University of Texas at El Paso in 2016 and an MFA in creative writing from Georgia State University in 2008. She lives in the Boston metro area with her spouse and two children.

SIHAM LEKCHIRI received her PhD in May 2017, when her child was two years old. She received her PhD in technology management with a specialization in human resource development and industrial training from the Indiana State University Consortium. Her research interest is on the challenges that women face in the workforce in male-dominated environments and cultures.

She is currently an associate professor and program director in the MS in Human Resources Program at Western Carolina University. Her teaching background includes courses in strategic HRD, organizational development, consulting, research in HR, and talent acquisition and retention, among others. She is also coeditor-in-chief of the *Industrial and Commercial Training Journal*. Before joining academia, she was a human resources consultant in Morocco.

JESSICA MCCAUGHEY is an associate professor of writing at George Washington University, co-owner of Golden Line Writing Academy, and mother to a six-year-old daughter.

MEGAN L. MCKITTRICK received her PhD in 2020, when her son was four years old and her daughter was one. While working as a full-time lecturer, she earned her doctorate in English from Old Dominion University, where she researched the crossroads between technical communication and game studies. She has published pieces in *Technical Communication Quarterly*, *Computers & Composition*, and *The Journal of Teaching and Learning*, among others. She now teaches English in the Upper School at Norfolk Academy, the eighth oldest school in the country, where her son attends, as will her daughter when she's old enough.

AMIE MCLEAN, PhD, is a sociologist, writer, educator, and parent whose academic interests focus on equity and social justice issues in Canadian postsecondary education and work with an expanding focus on disability justice. She has published on postsecondary funding policies for Indigenous students, neoliberalization and trucking-industry regulation, and the racialized politics of mobility among long-haul truckers. She previously served as co-chair of the Learning at Intercultural Intersections: Towards Equity, Inclusion, and Reconciliation International Conference and coedited a special issue in the *Journal of Intercultural Studies*. She is currently faculty in intercultural learning at Thompson Rivers University.

LAURA LEIGH MENARD received her PhD in English (rhetoric and writing studies) in August 2023 from Bowling Green State University. Her work includes being cohost of the limited-run podcast Digital Rhetoric, Digital Methods and editor of the Digital Rhetoric Collaborative 2023 blog carnival titled Digital Rhetoric in the Age of Misinformation and AI Advancements. She is currently adapting her dissertation to become a book and creating a corresponding podcast.

JENNA MORTON-AIKEN is a senior associate director for writing and English language support and a lecturer in English at Brown University. She started her PhD in English (rhetoric and composition) very pregnant with her first daughter and passed comprehensive exams even more pregnant with her second. Before attending Brown, she was an assistant professor at Massachusetts Maritime Academy, where she taught academic, professional, and creative writing. Her research has appeared in publications such as *Technical Communication Quarterly, WPA Writing Program Administration,* the award-winning *Routledge Handbook of Scientific Communication,* and the award-winning *Journal of Multimodal Rhetorics Special Issue on Carework and Writing during COVID: Part I.* She loves hearing her children laugh, coaching their (separate!) robotics teams, waltzing with her husband, and watching romantic K-dramas with her lovely cat.

CALVIN OLSEN is a senior lecturer in the English department at Ohio State University. He holds a PhD in communication, rhetoric, and digital media from North Carolina State University and an MFA in creative writing from Boston University. His research interests lie at the intersections of electronic literature, digital humanities, critical making, and monster theory. In addition to his academic work, Olsen's poetry and translations from Portuguese have appeared in *The Adroit Journal, AGNI, Asymptote, The London Magazine,* and many others. More can be found at calvin-olsen.com.

COURTNEY LUND O'NEIL received her PhD in May 2022, when her second child was ten months old and her first child was five years old. Her PhD is in English with a specialization in both creative nonfiction and rhetoric and writing studies from Oklahoma State University. Her first book, *Postmortem: What Survives the John Wayne Gacy Murders,* debuts in 2025. Her writing has appeared in the *New York Times,* the *Washington Post,* the *Columbia Journal,* and elsewhere. She currently teaches writing at the University of California San Diego.

KRISTIN L. OSBORNE earned her PhD in marine science and technology from the University of Massachusetts Boston on her oldest child's first birthday. She is an associate professor at Massachusetts Maritime Academy and is interested in expanding scientific research opportunities for the regiment of cadets. Her scholarly work has been published in *Marine Ecology Progress Series, PLOS Climate, Management of Biological Invasions, BioInvasions Records,* and *Northeastern Naturalist.*

JENNIFER PHILLIPS-DENNY received her BA in sociology from Texas Tech University and has an MA and PhD in English from the University of North Texas. She is a senior education specialist for the Research Foundation for the State University of New York. Previously, she managed the writing center at Texas Woman's University. She has been married to David for fifteen years, and her son, Devin, is a college student.

JENNIFER BURKE REIFMAN is director of lower-division writing and assistant professor of rhetoric and writing studies at San Diego State University. She earned her PhD in education and writing, rhetoric and composition studies from UC Davis and an MA in English composition from San Francisco State University. Reifman has been teaching postsecondary writing courses for over twelve years. Her research is deeply concerned with participant-centered methodologies to better understand the impact writing program policies and writing pedagogies have on undergraduate learning and experience. Her work on writing placement and student agency has appeared in the journal *Assessing Writing*, and her work with undergraduate researchers has been featured in several collections and journals, including *Peitho*, *The Learning Assistance Review*, and *Intersection: A Journal at the Intersection of Assessment and Learning*.

WHITNEY ZAHAR RICH is a PhD candidate in University of Texas at San Antonio's Counselor Education and Supervision Program. She, along with her spouse of twenty-five years, is a biological and foster parent. Her research centers around trauma, marginalized populations, cultural humility, sex trafficking, neurofeedback, law enforcement, and resilience. A deep belief in the healing power of connection drives her work. Her writing has appeared in the *Journal of Mental Health Counseling*.

CAMILA (CAMMY) RING is a PhD candidate in English at Case Western Reserve University, where her research focuses on poetry as a form of theological innovation. She has both critical and creative work published or forthcoming in various venues, including *English Literary History* and the *Colorado Review*. She and her family live in Cleveland, Ohio.

NATASHA TRACE ROBINSON, PhD, is an associate dean of academic affairs and workforce at Collin College in Plano, Texas. Previously, she was a full-time faculty member at Collin College. Robinson and her husband Craig are parents of two clever children, Orion and Celeste, whom she gave birth to during graduate coursework and exams. She finished her dissertation despite COVID-19 and daytime solo parenting.

DALEL SERDA is a PhD candidate at the University of Houston (UH) and a Texas-Mexico borderland native. At UH, her emphasis is on rhetoric, composition, and pedagogy. She is a tenured instructor of English at the College of the Mainland, a Hispanic-serving community college in Texas City, Texas. She is also the proud mother of two Chicanitas and the spouse of an incredible co-parent who is her personal cheerleader. Her creative and academic work always centers on marginalized folks worldwide. Her creative work can be found in *The King's English*, *Amarillo Bay*, *New Border Voices*, and the *Literary Bohemian*. Her academic writing appears in *CCTE Studies Journal*.

KAREN TELLEZ-TRUJILLO is an assistant professor at California State Polytechnic University, Pomona, in the Department of English and Modern Languages. Her educational background and research interests include border, feminist, and cultural rhetorics. She is the writing in the disciplines coordinator and graduate assistant advisor for rhetoric and composition. Karen enjoys working with undergraduate students as a mentor for the Research through Inclusive Opportunities Program and as the writing studies coordinator. Her work has appeared in the interdisciplinary journal *Writers, Craft, and Context* and the edited collection *Revising Moves*. Tellez-Trujillo also received NCTE's Early Career Educator of Color Leadership Award for 2022–2023.

BRITA M. THIELEN earned her PhD in English from Case Western Reserve University in 2022, when her son was fifteen months old. Her scholarship on food writing, rhetoric, and composition pedagogy has been published in *Rhetoric Review*, *Composition Studies*, and *Pedagogy* and in the edited collection *Consumption and the Literary Cookbook*. She and her family live in the Twin Cities metro area, where Thielen now works as a development researcher at the University of Minnesota Foundation.

TIFFANI K. TIJERINA is a PhD candidate in the Technical Communication and Rhetoric Program at Texas Tech University (TTU) and an online instructor of technical writing for TTU and Kennesaw State University. Her research focuses on open educational resources in technical communication and instructional design, and her work includes the internationally award-winning *Open Technical Communication* textbook and an edited collection, *Pedagogy Opened: Innovative Theory and Practice*. In addition, her scholarship has appeared in *Programmatic Perspectives*, *Communication Design Quarterly*, and *Journal of Open Educational Resources in Higher Education*. Tijerina and her husband live in Athens, Georgia, with their toddler daughter, one dog, and two cats.

RACHAEL GRAHAM TIN is writing instructor and writing consultant with Graham Associates and adjunct faculty teaching the requisite writing course for American University's key executive MPA. She is a mother and stepmother to three preteen children and one infant.

MARIYA TSEPTSURA directs the Online Writing Program at the University of Arizona. Her research focuses on online writing instruction, second-language writing, and writing program administration. She earned her PhD in rhetoric and writing from the University of New Mexico when her daughter was two years old, and she had her rainbow baby during her first year as full-time faculty and writing program administrator.

ALEASHIA WALTON VALENTIN is a PhD candidate in rhetoric and composition at the University of Cincinnati. She has a master's degree in composition and rhetoric and a bachelor's degree in journalism from Northern Kentucky University. She is a series coeditor for the WAC Clearinghouse's Practices & Possibilities series and a member of the Accessibility Committee of Writing Program Administrators–Graduate Organization. When she's not working on her dissertation or teaching, Walton Valentin enjoys traveling, gardening, and playing Barbies with her daughter Lizzie.

HAYLEY E. VERDI is a PhD candidate in English at Case Western Reserve University. Her work sits at the crossroads of medical humanities and literary studies and focuses on illness narratives, specifically those from a nineteenth-century British context. She has taught numerous classes in the English department at Case Western Reserve University and is currently a graduate assistant at the Baker Nord Center for the Humanities. She gave birth to her first child four months before entering the PhD program and now, in her sixth year, has three children. She and her family live in Cleveland, Ohio.

ELIZABETH M. WILLIAMS is an instructor in the Department of Writing & Rhetoric at the University of Mississippi. She recently earned her PhD in English from Middle Tennessee State University, where she also worked for the General Education English Program. While completing her degree, she gave birth to her first child, Gwen. Williams's work has been featured in *Peitho*, the *Journal of Multimodal Rhetorics*, and *Rhetoric Society Quarterly*. Her daughter and her husband are her greatest joys in life.

LISA E. WRIGHT is lecturer in the University Writing Program and affiliate faculty with the Medicine, Science, and Humanities Program at Johns Hopkins University. Her writing courses center on Black maternal health, reproductive justice, and Black midwives. She is a faculty fellow with the Center for Social Concern at Johns Hopkins. She received the 2022 Women's Faculty Council Student Research Award at Oklahoma State University, and the 2022 Geneva Smitherman Award for Research in Black Language, Literacies, Cultures, and Rhetorics. Wright is currently working on a manuscript "The Ring of Fire: A Memoir," which chronicles her homebirths with her mid-husband. It further examines Black women's birthing choices with a particular focus on the delegitimization of Black midwives and on creating safe birthing spaces inside and outside medical institutions. Her writing has appeared or will appear in *Meridians Journal, College English, The Writing Center Journal, Praxis, Axis,* and *Hippocampus Magazine.*

INDEX